The Purpose of Forests

JACK WESTOBY

The Purpose of Forests

Follies of Development

With a Foreword by
A. J. Leslie

Basil Blackwell

First published 1987

Basil Blackwell Ltd
108 Cowley Road, Oxford, OX4 1JF, UK

Basil Blackwell Inc.
432 Park Avenue South, Suite 1503
New York, NY 10016, USA

British Library Cataloguing in Publication Data

Westoby, Jack
 The Purpose of Forests
 Follies of Development.
 1. Forests and forestry — Developing
 countries
 I. Title
 338. 1' 749'091724   SD247.5

    ISBN 0-631-15657-7

Library of Congress Cataloging in Publication Data

Westoby, J. C. (Jack C.)
 The Purpose of Forests
 Follies of Development

 Includes index.
 1. Forests and forestry — Economic aspects.
 2. Forest products industry.   3. Economic development.
 I. Title.
 SD431.W47   1987   333.75   B7–861
 ISBN 0-631-15657-7

Typeset in 10 on 12pt Baskerville
by System 4 Associates, Gerrards Cross, Bucks
Printed in Great Britain by
T. J. Press Ltd., Padstow

Contents

I

Foreword

The writings and speeches in this volume have been selected to illustrate Jack Westoby's contributions to international forestry over the last two decades and more, and to show something of the evolution of his thinking. The problems he addresses are ones central to international forest policy and to the proper social responsibilities of foresters. This collection thus offers a welcome opportunity to bring within one cover papers which, together, form a significant part of the arguments within the field.

They have been selected with Westoby's advice, but to avoid the complications of hindsight none of them has been revised, beyond the editorial standardization necessary to bring them within one volume. I have arranged them into three Parts, whose approximately chronological sequence reflects – with some unavoidable arbitrariness – the recent history of arguments about forestry's contribution to economic and social well-being. Part I is a selection of papers which Westoby wrote during the 1960s, as an officer of the Forestry Department of the United Nations' Food and Agriculture Organization, on forest industries and their part in propelling economic development. The papers of Part II (also mainly written while he was with FAO) explore the responsibilities and dilemmas of the forestry profession in deciding which, among conflicting interests, to serve, and criticize its frequent subservience to economic and political power. Those of Part III (written since Westoby's retirement in 1974) carry further the work of developing and enlarging his ideas of what forestry should be about – which he earlier defined as 'making trees serve people'.

Forestry has now come into unprecedented, international public prominence – principally through the widespread concern and publicity about the fate of the tropical forests. But the problem of the tropical forests is by no means the only issue involved. Nor is it independent of the others. In fact the crisis of the tropical forests can be seen as an inevitable consequence of the failure to recognize the implications of an objective process of internationalization of forest usage and dependency upon forests. Westoby was among the first to describe this and urge that it be recognized. He once outlined the problem as follows:

The world's forest resources have a global aspect in the sense that the amount, quality and functions of forests in any one country inevitably affect the interests of many people in many other countries, and this for a very wide variety of reasons. Ergo, each individual country ought, in deciding what to do about its forests, to make its decisions after having taken into account their role as part of a global resource. Since, however, few countries are willing to accept many limitations on their national sovereignty, the problem is how far can they be led (or coerced) into harmonising their national forest policies – or, taking it further, participating in a world plan for forest resources.

Apart from being an architect of international forestry in this sense, and one of its most convincing advocates, Westoby became, above all, its conscience. Had more notice been taken of the conditions which he saw were the prerequisites for forestry to develop for the betterment of all mankind; had more attention been given to his warnings as those conditions were breached and ignored, fewer of the present day problems of the tropical forests would have arisen.

These papers illustrate this at various points. But they do so almost incidentally. They have been chosen to illustrate the evolution of that aspect of international forestry concerned with using forestry to fight poverty and social injustice in the developing world. With the world's tropical forests concentrated in developing countries it was natural for a forest-based assault on underdevelopment to look to the industrial exploitation of tropical forests. Tracing the evolution of the concepts and methods of forest-based economic and social development, we also witness the evolution of the tropical forests issue. Both are facets of the internationalization of forestry and both arise from international action in forestry.

Westoby's world view of forestry and the applications he has made of it grew out of more than two decades of service with FAO, and more than another decade of working and writing in retirement. A colleague of his in FAO once said to me 'He may not know a felling cycle from a rotation, but he is the best forester of the lot of us'. The exaggeration contains a truth. Almost any of the standard forestry journals nowadays carry articles which show that many foresters share the inability to distinguish a felling cycle from a rotation. But there are two aspects to forestry – the how and the why. Most of forestry and most foresters are concerned with the first aspect, and most forestry writing concentrates upon how. Relatively few, however, concern themselves with why. Westoby made this his field, and it is in this sense that his colleague's comment holds true. Long before modern conservationists questioned what was being done in the name of forestry, Westoby was asking such questions from the inside. And unlike the few others who were also posing questions of why from the inside, Westoby was posing them on a world scale. In such questioning lay the germs of a consciously international forestry.

One of the first things he questioned was the conservatism which stood in the way of a revitalized forestry helping in the reconstruction of Europe after the Second World War. From there he turned to the conservatism which he saw stifling the forestry sector's potential for economic development in what is now called the Third World. Then later, as he saw the way that potential was being abused and misused to enrich a few, to tighten the grip of poverty over the majority and to destroy rather than to manage the forests, he questioned the alliance of foresters with interests which served neither their country nor their people. More importantly, however, be began to question his own concept of forestry in economic and social development; thence he was led to criticize the myopia of both forestry and modern conservation, unable to see the people for the trees. Thus, in 'Problemas Actuais da Economia Florestal' (Lisbon. Feb. 1967) – not included in this selection – he wrote:

In the early days of my exposure to forestry, I had occasion to discuss forestry problems with very many foresters, foresters of every conceivable specialization. Had I believed implicitly everything they told me, I would have been driven inexorably to the conclusion that forestry is about trees. But, of course, this is quite wrong. Forestry is not about trees, it is about people. And it is about trees only insofar as trees can serve the needs of people.

Westoby's urging of a forestry about people should not be confused with the current fashion for 'social forestry'. This expression, indeed, stands in acute need of definition. Forestry, after all, originated centuries ago, in the needs of specific services which forests, properly managed, can provide for as long as those needs persist. In that sense all forestry is social. It is a little confusing therefore to coin the term social forestry as a special new form of forestry. Yet, forestry which is about people is broader than forestry simply as a supplier of commercial, or even public, goods and services. In the latter – the conventional view of the social role of forestry – the objective is to meet expected, effective demand, whether that is expressed through economic or political power. On the other hand what I would prefer to call 'social forestry' – Westoby's people-centred forestry – is also, and primarily, concerned with people whose needs are not able to express themselves as effective economic or political demands. In fact, history is replete with examples of conventional forestry extinguishing whatever rights such people might have had or subordinating them to the welfare of the forest. Forestry which is aimed at reversing these priorities is clearly different and certainly new, and to call *it* social forestry is not a bad way of making the distinction. The danger, of course, is that quite other practices can masquerade under the same slogan.

Westoby's distinctive notion of forestry being about people, not trees, came to him neither suddenly, nor fully-grown. Over time his views as to how forestry should serve people, and which people it should serve, have evolved in a number of ways. One of my aims in organizing this volume (and in reprinting its papers without revision) is to show this. Signs emerge in his speeches and writings in the early 1960s. His work with FAO on the First European Timber Trends

Study (published in 1953) began to reveal the inconsistencies between traditional forestry and the actual social needs of post-war Europe. Whenever conventional forestry places the well-being of the forest above the welfare of people generally, it has an inherently anti-social tendency. Moreover, it is easy to fall into the trap of allowing hypothetical interests of future generations to rule present policies.

This conservatism could have become a serious obstacle when the FAO expanded its work in the developing countries. That it did not was largely due to the potential which Westoby saw for forest resources to give an impetus to economic development. The European study was followed, from the mid-fifties, by a cycle of studies of timber trends and prospects in Asia, Latin America and Africa. These Westoby directed, enlisting the cooperation of, and himself working with, the Regional Economic Commissions for these areas. This work led him to prepare 'The Role of Forest Industries in the Attack on Economic Underdevelopment' (1962), the key paper of Part I, which sets out how the potential of the forests can be transformed into kinetic energy for development. Since his proposals showed how important forestry and its associated forest industries could be in the national economy, they had an obvious appeal to all interests in the sector. Mobilizing the forest resource for development now became more attractive than hoarding for the future, and not only in the developing countries. The paper was, moreover, presented in the language of the development economics of the day. Not only did this strengthen the hand of those in the forestry sector who had to deal with the economic planners; it also introduced the planners and decision-makers to the realities of forestry, but in the terms which were then conventional in discussion of economic development.

The paper proved seminal. Its initial impact on thinking was felt mainly in FAO (where it also helped to consolidate the position of forestry in the organization). Then its ideas gradually spread throughout the international forestry sector and eventually into the development establishment itself. It even provided foresters in developed countries with much stronger arguments for forestry than had previously been available to them. Before long it released a flood of writing, studies and discussion about the impact of forestry on economic development. With it, in Part I, I have included an illustrative group of Westoby's own shorter papers, in which he explores the implications over a range of issues such as trade, forestry education, and the internationalization of forestry. Part I is thus, from one point of view, a display-case of some of the promising prospects for economic improvement which the industrial utilization of forest resources to take advantage of international trade appeared to offer in the 1960s.

It is surprising that, even twenty-five years after its publication, 'The Role of Forest Industries in the Attack on Economic Underdevelopment' remains a basic blueprint for forest sector planning in many developing countries and some developed ones as well. After all, economic development theory has been through many changes since the early 1960s. What is even more surprising is that the paper endures even though those intervening twenty-five years have produced little evidence that things actually work out as it said they would, at least in developing countries.

Most surprising is that it does so despite the fact that Westoby himself has long since rejected it. The 1962 paper ended as follows:

It is an illusion to suppose that there exists a choice between mobilizing the forests now, and leaving them intact until forest services have been built up to the point where it is safe to open the forest gate. The technical and economic conditions for establishing new forest industries in the developing countries are maturing fast. In the course of the coming years many new areas of forest are inevitably going to be brought into use. The choice is between mobilization in the public interest based on sound planning and with adequate safeguards and with the forest services taking an active part and being built up in the process, and mobilization taking place in an uncontrolled and haphazard way, while weak forest services stand by helpless. This is the real choice.

But, as Westoby put it in a recent commentary on the paper:

It is impossible to read the last paragraph of this article today without a wry and bitter reflection on what has happend since. The forest gate has been opened. Many new areas have been brought into use. There has not been sound planning. There have NOT been adequate safeguards. The weak forest services have stood by helpless – when they have not been accessories to the fact.

Why, he asked, has this been so? The papers in Part II, written a decade or so later, contain his responses to the disappointing performance of the original industrialization model. During the 1970s the realization was growing that things were not working out as they should have. Without doubt the forests of the developing countries were being used on a much larger scale than ever before, but the expected benefits were not following. These papers, however, go beyond pointing that out and explaining why; they also undertake a search for something better. His critique and his search began before he retired from FAO in 1974. I have included in Part II a previously unpublished paper from 1973 to which I have given the title 'Quo Vadis?' This was a note for discussion, raising the question of how forestry could act so as truly to serve people, which he circulated amongst the staff of the Forestry Department of the FAO. Another example is the paper entitled 'Responsibility', in which he discusses the dilemma which confronts foresters in weighing their responsibilities to society and the future against the demands of their paymasters. In answering the question he leaves no room for doubt about where he stands.

I also happen to know that it was Westoby's prompting, from retirement, that led to the adoption of 'Forestry for People' as the theme for the Eighth World Forestry Congress in Jakarta in 1978. It was the slowness of foresters, development agencies and governments to recognize the need for a change of direction which, as much as anything, eventually produced the reverberating forthrightness of the paper (Chapter 11) which forms the natural culmination of Part II. This guest speaker address to the Congress in Jakarta denounced the shameful part played by forest industries and sections of the forestry profession in the onslaught on the tropical forests. In so doing, it should be added, he affronted some amongst his hearers.

Westoby's Jakarta speech also sets the scene for the papers of Part III, written since 1974, in which he calls for a broader definition of forestry and makes it clear what he thinks foresters should be doing. Forestry and a forest policy, he recently wrote, 'should concern itself with all places where, and every conceivable way in which, forests, woodlands and trees can contribute to human welfare'. ('Yet more on forest policy,' *Commonwealth Forestry Review*, 1984). Forestry is not limited to a form of land management practised by foresters on land entrusted to them and earmarked for forestry purposes. He also makes it clear that the adoption of 'social forestry' is not a sufficient response to his plea for a people-centred forestry. In the rush of governments and international agencies to jump on the social forestry bandwagon, few of the projects to which the tag of social forestry has been affixed serve the interests of those who most need the goods and services trees can provide.

An important feature of Part III is the shift in audience. Addressing himself less to the policy advisers, the decision-makers, the planners, or the foresters and industrialists in control (if it can be called that) today, he now turns to their successors – the students – who given time, luck and fortitude, will some day hold those positions. It is almost as though he has given the present establishment away as a bad job – too intractable, too enchanted by the myths of 'reality', too daunted by the spurious appeal of what is practical, and too persuaded of the infallibility of the institutions which they helped to build and of which they are part.

He could well be right. The sad thing, of course, is that these very people were once the young generation, and they in their time were no less idealistic, no less enthusiastic and no less impatient with bureaucracy and the status quo. Does their fate await their successors? The possibility is not taken up here. But I suspect that Westoby, in urging them to a drastic breakaway from the traditional focus of forestry, to take seriously the ways in which the fate of the forests is bound up with human needs and human history, would give them a better chance of escaping. Whether they do and whether they can then change the history of forestry remains to be seen. It will not be Westoby's fault if they fail.

By and large the history of forestry is known only to foresters, and then imperfectly. This is a pity, on both scores. Foresters ought to know better how their predecessors dealt with the problems and adversaries of their day. They would find that things have not changed much, but they would also be heartened to find that there are solutions, and not unsatisfactory ones, for those who know what they are talking about. They would also see how deeply the origins of some of their present problems lie in those that their predecessors faced and the solutions they arrived at. Altogether they would be better equipped to deal with their future if they had a better understanding of their past.

Others, too, could learn from the history of forestry, and save a lot of misguided effort in face of today's environmental and social problems. The results of unbridled de-forestation form a classic example, well known to everyone. What more could a knowledge of forest history add to it? Well, for one thing, it would be seen that tropical de-forestation today has, like the great Mediterranean and European de-forestations of the past, deeper causes than simple cupidity and stupidity. Both, without question, play a part, but to arrive at a solution one must look deeper.

But there is more to the history than de-forestation. The 'discovery' of sustained yield by the modern conservationists, and the 'discovery' of discounted cash flow by the modern economists are examples of techniques which were developed long ago in forestry as standard working tools. Similarly, multiple-use management was the basic objective of most of the now denigrated classical, European silvicultural and management systems, because it had to be. Why was that knowledge not used or known outside forestry? Why did it have to be rediscovered?

To some extent the fault lies with the increasing specialization of modern society. Specialists are educated in and then confine their reading to ever narrower fields. Specialization allows little time for the luxury of keeping up with fields other than one's own. But that is the lesser part of the problem. Specialists rarely make it possible, let alone easy, for others to follow what they are doing, and foresters are no exception. On the whole they have kept forestry to themselves. One of Westoby's lasting contributions is to chivvy them out of their professional, national and social fox-holes. Since he is not a forester by formal training he has never learned how to write so as to keep the non-specialist baffled. Instead he writes in a style that is accessible and attractive to non-foresters. This collection makes it easy for them to take advantage of that.

They will be well rewarded. They will learn enough of forestry to apply a necessary scepticism to the simplistic solutions which are advanced on all sides to the increasingly controversial forestry issues of today and tomorrow. They will relish the prose of a craftsman in the use of English. And non-foresters and foresters alike will be brought to think more deeply about the future of the forests, and its relation with the future of human society.

A. J. Leslie

PART I
The Promise

1

The Role of Forest Industries in the Attack on Economic Underdevelopment

Forest industries present many special features. They furnish a very wide range of products, both consumption goods and intermediate goods flowing into many sectors of the economy; the demand for these rises sharply with economic growth. The industries vary considerably in their raw material and other factor requirements. In most of them alternative technologies can be successfully employed. They are based on a renewable resource. This resource is intimately linked with agriculture.

These features suggest that potentially forest industries can play a significant part in promoting economic growth in presently low-income countries. This chapter represents a preliminary attempt to assess their potential role. The analysis is far from complete, and many important aspects are treated cursorily or not at all. The purpose of the chapter will have been served, however, if it succeeds in drawing the attention of policy-makers to certain major considerations which are sometimes overlooked, and if it encourages economists and foresters to undertake a more profound and detailed study of some of the problems raised.

SOME ASPECTS OF DEVELOPMENT POLICY

The post-war period has seen a growing awareness of the need for economic development in those areas of the world which the industrial revolution had left untouched. Development problems have acquired first place not only in the attention of governments and international organizations but also in the

This paper was first published in *The State of food and agriculture 1962*, chapter III pp. 88–128, Rome, 1962. Reproduced with permission of the author and the Food and Agriculture Organization of the United Nations.

social sciences, where they have provided the common denominator for the integration of different branches of analysis and of different disciplines. This impact is also being felt in the specialized fields of study devoted to the economic and technical problems of single sectors or industries. Specialists and technicians can no longer disregard the wider context in which industries and sectors operate; that context is not a constant but a variable – perhaps the most important variable. Today sector problems and targets are at once subordinate to, and integral instruments of, general problems and aims of development.

In the following pages an attempt will be made to look at the forest industry sector in the light of the growth problems of economies at the beginning of their development processes. Forests are a most important asset of a country's wealth – an asset that even very poor countries possess or could possess – for they provide a renewable raw material for a whole range of industries which have acquired great importance in many industrially advanced countries. This asset is very often neglected in less developed economies, or exploited only as a raw material for export. This raises a number of obvious questions. What are the propulsive possibilities of the forest industries sector for the less developed areas? What can the role of this sector be in a development programme aimed at attaining self-sustained growth?

To answer these questions, vague and general considerations on what *prima facie* appear to be the merits of industries will not suffice. Economic theory and techniques of development programming have progressed considerably in the past few years. Although the field is certainly not clear of controversy and many unsolved points yet remain, substantial agreement has been reached as to the criteria which should orient choices and as to the data which are necessary to apply the criteria in practice. Thus sector analysis should follow the main lines set by general economic analysis, if the necessary integration between the two for the purposes of development is to be reached.

We shall therefore start by reviewing in general terms some of the considerations relevant in sector analysis, and by defining the data and the elements of knowledge needed to appraise the economic possibilities of the forest industries sector.

Development aims: a political choice

Underdevelopment is a relative and to some extent a subjective notion. Some economies are defined as underdeveloped insofar as there are others which are more developed; and the former 'are those which are dissatisfied with their present economic condition and want to develop'.[1] For such countries economic growth has become or is becoming a matter of ideology, since it is bound up

---

[1] J. Robinson, 'Notes on the theory of economic development', in *Collected Economic Papers*, vol. 2 (Oxford, 1960), pp. 96–7.

with the achievement of a truer independence – economic as well as political – and of higher standards of human dignity as well as of material well-being for the population. An understanding of the fact that development in its aims and motivations is not solely a matter of economics is essential in order to avoid false controversies on a number of points, and to apply economic tools with more accuracy and to better purpose.

First among these points is the need for public intervention. This follows almost by definition from the decision to change the existing situation of backwardness and from the fact that the existing situation is frequently the outcome of non-intervention or intervention of the wrong kind. If that decision is accepted, there can be no argument as to whether a power external to the market, for example, the state, should interfere with the 'free play of market forces'. In underdeveloped economies the object of intervention must be defined in very broad terms; since it is a question not of a single sector or of a single area but of the whole economy lagging behind, intervention should, directly or indirectly, in milder or more energetic form, embrace the whole system. This, of course, amounts to saying that planning is necessary, meaning by planning the overall coordination of public intervention in various fields, aimed at attaining clearly defined and mutually consistent targets of policy. Overall planning does not necessarily mean direct public intervention in all fields. It is compatible with the predominance of private enterprise (provided it is guided by an adequate system of incentives and sanctions). It means essentially awareness of the ends to be reached in the first place, and then systematic programming of the use of all the available policy instruments with these ends in view.

From this approach to development policy it follows that, once the plan frame is defined, a number of excessively debated issues, such as the demarcation of public and private sectors, or the contraposition of agricultural development to industrialization, take on a truer significance. The solution of these and other similar problems cannot be reached in the abstract, but must be instrumental to the final aims, and even more important, the actual administration of the plan. This also applies to a large extent to the controversy of light versus heavy industry or, more generally, of immediate welfare versus long-term growth. In all cases, while the solution will depend on the structural conditions and the physical endowments (that is, the data) of the economy concerned, the main element of choice is political, since the definition of the general ends of the plan is mostly the result of a political decision.

Financial appraisal and social evaluation

A second and equally important consequence following from the principles stated above concerns the evaluation of benefits and costs of investment policies and projects. Benefits and costs should be estimated with reference to the aims set in the plan, and policies and projects be classified accordingly. Since the aims of the plan or, more generally, of development policy concern the entire community and not single producing agencies, it is not surprising that this kind of evaluation may diverge, and indeed will often diverge, from the private criteria of evaluation.

The principle of distinguishing between private evaluation and social evaluation – between financial appraisal (in terms of monetary returns in the short run or to special groups) and economic appraisal (in terms of both short- and long-term returns to all people affected) – has already full acceptance in the advanced economies for all the so-called public utilities, that is, for sectors of general interest in which it is admitted that financial benefits and costs to particular firms may not coincide with the benefits and costs for the community. The good reason why the same principle has a much broader application in less developed economies is that in such conditions, at least for a time, nearly all economic activities must be considered as public utilities, since the historic trend has shown a general divergence between private and social interest.

Private and social evaluations may diverge for reasons which have their origin in micro- as well as macro-economic, in static as well dynamic, considerations. First of all the price system in an underdeveloped economy is often not 'significant', that is, is not such as to ensure either a technical or an economic optimum, since it does not reflect the relative scarcity of goods and factors; nor, *a fortiori*, does it reflect the scale of priority established in a development policy. Secondly, a given investment project may have a number of 'secondary' benefits which do not appear in the form of money returns to the firms most directly involved, but which should be included in an economic appraisal; these consist essentially in 'the increase in net incomes in activities stemming from, or induced by, the project'.[2] Finally, account should be taken of secondary effects from a dynamic point of view. These can be grouped under the heading of external economies of production and consumption: investment in a propulsive sector will on the one hand create favourable conditions on the supply side for investment in other sectors; on the other hand, through its demand for inputs and through the new demand arising from the higher incomes of the newly employed, it will enlarge the market for other industries, thus providing the incentives for new investment on the demand side. This last consideration reflects the fact that, with lack of capital, lack of demand is also a most important obstacle to development.

The data needed for investment decisions

Whichever investment criterion is adopted, certain types of data are needed to evaluate the economic impact of investment in a given sector. These can be grouped as follows.

[2] This is the definition given in United States Interagency Committee on Water Resources, Subcommittee on Evaluation Standards, *Report to Interagency Committee on Water Resources: Proposed Practices for Economic Analysis of River Basin Projects* (Washington, DC, 1958).

Technological data   Such data regard the shape and the range of the production function. Independently of whether the choice is oriented towards higher or lower capital intensity, it can be said that the wider the range of the production function (that is, the higher the number of techniques available), the more suitable, *ceteris paribus*, a sector is for investment in a less developed country, because the possibility of adaptation to the general aims of policy and to the structural conditions of the country is greater. The study of the production functions requires:

1   A knowledge of the internal structure of the sector (the wider and the more integrated this is, the greater the flexibility in decisions, owing to the possibility of combining different techniques at different levels of production);

2   A knowledge of labour productivity, value added, capital output ratio and surplus per unit of output and capital for each technique available; in this connection it should be noted that the production function relevant for an underdeveloped economy does not necessarily coincide with that of a more advanced country; technical progress has undoubtedly been biased by factor availability and prices of advanced countries, and there are possibilities, to which not enough thought has yet been devoted, of devising techniques more suitable to different conditions.

Investment and cost data   These data are needed not so much for estimating actual production costs, which vary with input prices, as for checking the consistency of projects against the availability of funds and the size of the market. Technological indivisibilities may prevent the adoption of a given technique at less than a certain minimum scale, which might turn out to be too large relatively to the size of the market and to the amount of funds available. This group of data can also include the physical characteristics of inputs and outputs, the relative weight of which plays an important role in deciding to what extent a sector has, in a given country, a relative advantage *vis-à-vis* the rest of the world, and where the industry should be located.

Demand data   These data, on the other hand, give an idea of the importance of the sector and condition the choice of techniques and sizes. Demand projections also make it possible to estimate the gross import-saving effect of investment in a given sector.

Secondary and indirect effects   Some of these effects belong to the general category of external economies. Others are more precisely connected with the creation of a new supply of some goods or services which will stimulate the development of other activities outside the sector. Still others stem from the creation of new demand which widens investment opportunities in other sectors: this happens through increased consumption expenditure by the newly employed, and through the input requirements of the new producing activity. The degree of backward and forward linkage of a sector with other sectors is considered a very important index of priority in sectoral allocation, since it measures the cumulative expansionary effect that a given investment may have on the whole economy.

In the following sections an attempt will be made to provide some of the data and elements of knowledge listed above for forest industries. We shall start with an assessment of present and future demand conditions for forest industries products, since these constitute an essential frame for the problems we are considering.

THE PRODUCTS OF FOREST INDUSTRIES IN THE ECONOMY:
PRESENT AND FUTURE

In this section we shall: (a) examine the structural characteristics of the demand for forest products, their role in the world economy, and the interdependence between forest industry and other sectors; (b) illustrate the present situation of production, consumption and trade of forest products in the two great blocks[3] into which the world can today be divided – the developed areas such as Western Europe, North America, the USSR, Oceania and Japan, and the less developed areas in Africa, Latin America and the rest of Asia; (c) analyse the dynamic characteristics of demand for forest products in order to estimate its prospects in the less developed areas; (d) draw some conclusions regarding the extent to which future requirements should be satisfied by local production in the less developed areas.

The structural characteristics of demand

Even if one decided to overlook the variety of products, techniques and economic organizations of the sector under examination, some major distinctions must nevertheless be traced inside it. Wood removed from forests can be used either as fuelwood or for industrial purposes; here we shall only be concerned with industrial wood, since it is evident that fuelwood is secondary[4] from the point

---

[3] The main justification for this crude dichotomy (with debatable components in either block) is statistical convenience.

[4] Secondary, but by no means negligible. Examples of a situation where fuelwood can contribute to economic growth are: (a) in heterogeneous hardwood forests, if alternative fuels are expensive or unavailable, species of negligible commercial value can be used to power wood transformation industries; (b) several successful iron-smelting operations make use of wood charcoal, thereby reducing the need for good coking coal; (c) in fuel-hungry South Asia, where most dung is burned instead of being returned to the soil, village fuelwood plantations may be the key to a rise in agricultural productivity.

of view of economic growth. Industrial wood can be employed either in uses where, though undergoing several transformations, it maintains intact its chemical and physical structure, or as a raw material in chemical processes where it loses, so to speak, its individuality. Thus we have on the one hand sawlogs transformed into sawnwood, which is in turn used for construction, shipping and manufactured products; veneer logs, transformed into veneers, plywood and blockboard, also used for construction and manufacture; logs transformed into sleepers; pitprops, piling and poles. And we have, on the other hand, pulpwood transformed into pulp by mechanical and/or chemical action, and then manufactured into paper and paperboard. An intermediate position between these two groups is occupied by two more recent products – fibreboard and particle board; from the manufacturing point of view they are nearer to the second group, but from the point of view of demand characteristics they should be considered in the first group, since they are employed in much the same uses as sawnwood and plywood.

In physical terms sawlogs account for a much greater volume than pulpwood. By far the most important use of sawnwood is construction, followed by packaging and manufacturing; the latter, however, covers an enormous number of products – from furniture to railway carriages, parts of motor vehicles, handles, toys, ladders and pencils. In residential building wood is essentially used for framing, sheathing, millwork and flooring. The major pulpwood product is paper, followed by paperboard; and the most important types of paper are newsprint, printing paper, paper for wrapping and bags.

It is unnecessary to give further details to show that wood products, directly or indirectly, must have a large share of final demand, and a share which is spread over a very large number of items.[5]

Both these facts are confirmed by quantitative observations. In 1953 the sector of forest and forest products (including both wood products and furniture and paper and paper products) accounted for 7.2 per cent of the total value added and for 9.25 per cent of total world employment of mining and manufacturing industries in the world, thus ranking fifth among industries in terms of value added and fourth in terms of employment.[6] The breakdown for the two main branches is the following: 4.2 and 3.1 per cent of value added and 7.9 and 2.2 per cent of employment respectively for wood products and furniture and for pulp, paper and paper products. This shows a remarkable difference between the two main branches in labour productivity, which is higher than the average in paper and paper products and much lower than the average in the other branch.

The spread of uses of forest products, or rather the extent to which they enter into other products (the degree of indirectness of the sector), is evidenced, with

[5] The major wood-transformation industries, and the uses to which their products are put, are shown graphically in figure 1.1 pp. 22–3.

[6] United Nations Statistical Office, *Patterns of Industrial Growth 1936–1958* (New York, 1960).

some limitations, in the available studies of inter-industry interdependence by means of input/output tables. Two coefficients are relevant in this connection: the ratio of the value of purchased inputs to that of total production of a sector, which indicates how far production in a sector 'involves the indirect use as compared to the direct use of capital and labor';[7] and the ratio of the value of intermediate demand to that of total demand for the products of a sector, which shows the extent to which the sector 'sells its output for further use in production'.[8] These ratios for a given sector should be compared with the average or mean values of the ratios for the whole economy. This comparison is provided in table 1.1 for four countries – Japan, Italy, the United States of America and Norway – which shows the average ratios for the economies as a whole and the ratios for wood and wood products and paper and paper products taken separately.

Table 1.1   Indices of interdependence of forest industries

	Ratio of value of purchased inputs to value of total production			Ratio of value of intermediate demand to value of total demand		
	Average all industries	Wood and wood products	Paper and paper products	Average all industries	Wood and wood products	Paper and paper products
Japan	48.7	68.2	62.8	46.1	29.6	80.2
Italy	43.8	71.6	53.8	41.1	43.1	75.3
USA	42.6	42.1	56.6	41.9	40.4	79.2
Norway	36.4	51.5	55.7	30.4	29.1	42.5

Source: Based on H. B. Chenery and P. G. Clark, *Interindustry Economics* (New York, 1959), p. 230.

It appears from these figures that in both subsectors and in all countries (with the exception of the United States for wood and wood products) the ratio of the value of purchased inputs to the value of total production is considerably higher than the average; it should be noted, however, that the purchase of inputs is concentrated, as is to be expected, in agriculture and forestry, from where the raw material is taken. More significant, as an indication of the linkages of the sectors considered with the rest of the economy, are the ratios of intermediate demand to total demand. Here there is a divergence between paper and paper products, where the value of the ratio is very much higher than the average, and wood and wood products, where it is lower (though not very much lower) than the average. This is essentially due to the fact that in

[7] H. B. Chenery and P. G. Clark, *Interindustry Economics* (New York, 1959), p. 205.
[8] Ibid., p. 201.

input/output tables, construction is included in final demand; as a consequence the share of wood and wood products used in construction, which would normally be considered as intermediate products (for example, wood for framing and sheathing or for concrete forms), appears only in final demand. Thus the values of the second set of ratios tend to be undervalued for wood and wood products relative to other sectors. When this is taken into account, and considering the high values of the ratio for paper and paper products, we reach the conclusion that the sector of forest products as a whole has a high degree of indirectness and of interdependence with other sectors.

Consumption, production and trade

Table 1.2 gives, for the two groups of areas, developed and less developed, the production, total consumption and consumption per head of the main categories of forest products. Several striking facts emerge from this table.

The production of forest products is very heavily concentrated in the developed world. Consumption is even more highly concentrated, the less developed areas relying on the advanced regions for a substantial proportion of their supplies of certain categories. At the same time the population of the less developed areas is over twice that of the developed areas. Thus consumption per head of forest products in the less developed areas is extremely low: one seventeenth of that in the developed areas for sawnwood; one twenty-third for paper and board.

The position of less developed areas *vis-à-vis* the rest of the world is further illustrated in table 1.2. Also, in the case of forest products the less developed countries are exporters of raw material and importers of manufactures; they export sawlogs; are more or less in balance, in quantities, for sawnwood (considering that their deficit is to a large extent due to the lack of coniferous forests, so that in aggregate they are exporters of broadleaved sawnwood but importers of coniferous sawnwood); and they are net importers of fibreboard and especially of pulp, paper and board. (The table does not include wood manufactures, such as furniture.) As a result, in spite of their very low level of consumption, the less developed countries show a net deficit in value terms. Not only is the unit value of products much higher than the unit value of materials (though not by so much as in the case of products of other industries, since raw material accounts for a very large part of inputs, especially in wood products), but also the value of imports is increased, relatively to the value of exports, by the whole amount of freight, which, for the largest part, accrues to developed regions who own the largest share of merchant fleets.

The final figures in table 1.3 show a net overall deficit in value terms (for SITC divisions 24, 25, 63 and 64) of US$467 million. Besides the items listed in the table, this figure includes certain manufactures of wood and paper. It excludes, however, many finished goods of wood and paper, such as furniture, prefabricated houses, books, newspapers and other printed matter, and so on.

Table 1.2 Production and consumption of forest products, 1957–9 average

	Unit	A Developed areas	B Less developed areas	Ratio A:B
Population (1958)	million	923	1,956	just under half
Production				
Industrial wood	million m³(r)	842.9	103.2	8
Sawnwood (including sleepers)	million m³(s)	288.3	33.7[a]	8
Wood-based panel products	million m³(r equiv.)	38.01	3.04[b]	13
Paper and board	million m.tons	60.0	3.4	18
Apparent consumption: total				
Sawnwood	million m³(s)	286.7	35.0[a]	8
Wood-based panel products	million m³(r equiv.)	38.3	3.0[b]	13
Paper and board	million m.tons	58.1	5.3	11
Apparent consumption: per 1,000 capita				
Sawnwood	m³	310.0	18.0	17
Wood-based panel products	m³ (r equiv.)	41.7	1.5	28
Paper and board	m.tons	63.0	2.7	23

[a] Including an estimate of 9.4 for unrecorded production.
[b] Including an estimate of 0.61 for unrecorded production.

(r) = roundwood; (s) = sawnwood.

Table 1.3 Trade of less developed areas, 1957–9 average

	Unit	Quantity million stated units			Value $ million		
		Exports	Imports	Net trade[a]	Exports	Imports	Net trade[a]
Sawlogs	m³ (r)	7.6	1.2	+ 6.4	152.3	40.0	+ 112.3
Sawnwood							
Coniferous	m³ (s)	1.5	3.6	− 2.1	68.8	155.3	− 86.5
Broadleaved	m³ (s)	1.6	0.8	+ 0.8	83.5	46.7	+ 36.8
Sleepers	m³ (s)	0.2	0.2	–	5.7	29.3	− 23.6
Veneers	m³ (s)	0.07	0.02	+ 0.05	4.6	3.9	+ 0.7
Plywood	m³ (s)	0.18	0.25	− 0.07	21.5	24.7	− 3.2
Fibreboard	m. tons	0.04	0.08	− 0.04	3.3	10.2	− 6.9
Particle board	m. tons	0.02	0.02	–	1.1	2.1	+ 1.1
Pulp	m. tons	0.06	0.57	− 0.51	9.9	83.4	− 73.5
Newsprint	m. tons	0.03	0.91	− 0.88	3.6	152.3	− 148.7
Other paper and board	m. tons	0.05	1.05	− 1.00	13.1	258.6	− 245.5
Total value[b]					406.0	873.0	− 467.0

[a] + = export surplus; − = import surplus.
[b] Including some manufactured products (SITC 24, 25, 63, 64).
(r) = roundwood; (s) = sawnwood.

Were these included the deficit would be considerably greater.

This situation is all the more striking considering that many of the less developed areas have their raw material ready at hand, and that not all the deficit sectors necessarily require, as will be seen later, exceptionally complex techniques.

The dynamic characteristics of demand

In estimating demand trends for forest products the main variable to be taken into account, as in the case of all other products, is income. However, a rather precise relationship between income and consumption holds only for pulp products. In the case of other forest products this relationship is complicated by the interaction of other factors, and especially by an interdependence, which becomes relevant particularly in low-income areas, between demand and supply.

Very high correlations have been obtained between consumption per head of paper and board and national income (normally gross national product) per head. These relationships hold both for paper and board in total, and for the several broad categories of paper and board. They hold whether the parameters are studied in space, through cross-sectional analysis, comparing many countries at a given time, or in time, comparing the evolution of consumption and income in a given country or region over a period of years.

The relationship is not a linear one; in fact income elasticity declines as income rises. Thus at income levels of around $100 per head, elasticity is as high as 2.5 to 3; at levels of around $200 to $400 per head, it ranges from about 1.5 to 2.5. At European income levels, roughly $500 to $1,000, it is well over unity. For the United States of America, with an income per head of well over $2,000, it is below unity for most categories.[9]

This decline in elasticity as income rises applies to each of the major categories of paper and board as well as to paper and board as a whole. But the decline is not uniform. Thus at low-income levels of $50 to $150 per head the elasticity for cultural papers (newsprint, printing and writing paper) is somewhat higher than that for industrial papers (other papers and paperboard). At $200 to $250 per head the elasticity is about the same – something under 2. At higher income levels, from $800 and up, the elasticity for industrial paper is much higher than that for cultural papers. These data lead to the conclusion that a remarkable expansion in the demand for paper and paper products is to be expected in the less developed countries – an expansion much more rapid, for equal rates of income growth, than in more advanced countries.

There has, in fact, been a marked increase in consumption per caput of paper and board in the less developed world over the last decade, as the figures in table 1.4 show.

In the light of the earlier quoted demand elasticities, it may seem surprising that relative progress in the less developed world has not been more marked.

[9] FAO, *World Demand for Paper to 1975* (Rome, 1960).

Table 1.4   Changes in per caput consumption of paper and board, 1946–8 to 1957–9

	1946–8	*1957–9*	*%* *increase*
	Kilograms per caput		
Developed areas	38.6	62.9	63
Less developed areas	1.49	2.85	91

It should be recalled, however, that during the 1950s the rate of per caput income growth in the less developed areas lagged considerably behind that in the more advanced areas.

When we turn to the other principal forest products, however, it is much more difficult to pronounce with certainty on demand trends. Factors other than income heavily influence the demand for sawnwood and for wood-based sheet materials. Demand for all these products consists overwhelmingly of derived demand. In many of the end-uses in which they are employed, these products can substitute each other to a high degree. Thus for many purposes plywood, fibreboard and particle board are all technically feasible solutions, and the material adopted will depend on relative prices. Moreover, all three can take – and have taken to a considerable extent over the last decade or two – the place of sawnwood over a broad range of end-uses. Finally, there is a high elasticity of substitution in many avenues of utilization between all the products of the forest industries sector and the products of other sectors of the economy such as bricks, cement, steel in construction, metals and plastics in furniture and packaging. These considerations tend to deprive the concept of income elasticity of demand of much of its empirical relevance, since the coefficients which can be estimated on the basis of time-series or of cross-sectional analysis conceal the effects on demand of the other factors which have been mentioned.

From what has been said it is clear that the trend in demand for these products will depend largely on their price relative to each other and to the products of other sectors. Simple price relatives furnish no clear guide, however, since technical progress – which always tends to be material-saving, both for wood and for its competitors – can considerably modify the impact of relative price movements.

An assessment of the available data[10] leads to the conclusion that, taking sawnwood and wood-based panel products together, demand does increase with income, and, at low levels of income, increases at a rate equal to or greater than the rate of increase in income.

Thus for sawnwood and wood-based sheet materials as well as for paper and board, economic growth will bring rapidly increasing requirements in countries at present with low incomes.

[10] Notably detailed surveys carried out recently in Uganda, Kenya, Tanganyika and Ghana by Pringle, Arnold, de Backer and von Maydell.

Future requirements and alternative supply possibilities

There have recently been prepared estimates of forest products requirements in the underdeveloped regions of the world by 1970. These estimates are based largely on regional studies of timber resources and requirements presently under way, or recently completed, by FAO in collaboration with the regional Economic Commissions of the United Nations.

A substantial rise in industrial wood requirements by 1970 is foreseen in all the less developed regions (table 1.5). This increase ranges from 56 per cent for Latin America to 83 per cent for Asia. For the less developed areas as a whole the increase is 72 per cent.

For these regions, the current decade will thus bring a need for an additional 32 million cubic metres (sawn) of sawnwood, 8.6 million tons of paper and board, and 8 million cubic metres (in roundwood equivalent) of plywood, fibreboard and particle board.

These estimates are relevant to the problem of investment in the sector of forestry and forest products, since they show the demand on which an expanded productive capacity could rely, or alternatively, the cost, in terms of foreign exchange, of not expanding productive capacity at a rate sufficient to meet additional demand.

Table 1.6 provides a tentative estimate of these costs, under various hypotheses. Hypotheses A and B represent two extremes; under A it is assumed that productive capacity will not be expanded at all so that all additional consumption will be satisfied by imports, and under B that production will be expanded so as to meet entirely the increase in consumption (that is, leaving net imports unchanged). Both hypotheses are rather unreal, but are interesting insofar as they show that the capital cost of expanding production capacity (hypothesis B) and hence of ensuring a constant flow of output, is not much greater than that of importing the required additional quantity of product in one year.

It is now possible to draw some conclusions regarding the demand side of forest products, with reference to less developed areas.

1   Forest products account, in the world total, for a substantial share of industrial production and industrial employment.
2   Consumption, however, is very unevenly distributed between the developed and the less developed regions – per caput consumption in the latter being extremely low.
3   The expansion of the forest products sector is strictly connected with general industrial expansion and with the growth of income both through technological inter-industry relations and through income/demand relations. The former are shown by input/output tables in the form

Table 1.5 Forest products: Recent consumption and estimated 1970 requirements in the less developed regions in roundwood equivalent

	Sawnwood		Wood-based sheet material		Paper and paperboard		Wood used in the round[a]		Total, industrial wood	
	1957–9	1970	1957–9	1970	1957–9	1970	1957–9	1970	1957–9	1970
					million m³ (r)					
Latin America	28.0	42.0	1.5	3.4	5.8	12.0	7.5	9.6	42.8	67.0
Asia (excluding Japan)	41.1	85.7	0.9	6.4	6.1	15.8	34.7	43.4	82.8	151.3
Africa	6.3	9.0	0.6	1.2	1.9	3.5	6.2	10.0	15.0	23.7
Total	75.4	136.7	3.0	11.0	13.8	31.3	48.4	63.0	140.6	242.0

[a] Includes in addition to wood used in the round some miscellaneous products not included under other categories (e.g., wood for turning, cooperage and shingle bolts etc.).

Table 1.6 Alternative supply prospects for additional forest products requirements

	Unit (millions)	1957/9 Average annual consumption	Estimated annual consumption by 1970	Additional annual consumption requirements	A Annual cost of additional imports by 1970 ($ million)	A Additional annual production needed by 1970 (stated unit)	B Additional annual wood requirements (million m³(r))	Cumulative capital requirements to 1970 ($ million)
Sawlogs and veneer logs	m³ (r)	51				70	70	
Sawnwood	m³ (s)	35	67	32	1,600	32	(64)	800
Wood-based sheet material	m³ (r equiv.)	3	11	8	314	8	(8)	277
Pulpwood	m³ (r)	–				18	18	
Pulp[a]	m. tons	1.7				5.7	(18)	1,710
Paper and board	m. tons	5.3	13.9	8.6	1,956	8.6	(18)	2,220
Total					3,870		88	5,007

[a] Does not include nonwood pulp.
A = If all additional requirements are imported; B = If volume of net trade remains constant – e.g., all additional requirements are produced at home.
(r) = roundwood; (s) = sawnwood.

of a high degree of indirectness of the sector; the latter find expression in high coefficients of income elasticities of demand. These relations show that, if the expansion of demand for forest products can be considered as an effect of income growth, the expansion of supply of forest products, on the other hand, owing to its forward linkages, can be a stimulus to the expansion of other sectors.

4   The share of less developed areas in total production is even lower than their share in total consumption. In other words, their productive capacity is not even up to their very modest requirements. As a consequence they are heavy importers of manufactured products, although net exporters of raw material (sawlogs and veneer logs).

5   The net trade situation in value terms is even more unfavourable. Transportation costs are very high for the exported raw material and are fairly high on the imported products, but transportation profits seldom accrue to the less developed areas, since they do not own important merchant fleets. On the other hand, the f.o.b. price of imported products is much higher than that of exported raw material, since the former embodies all the value added in manufacturing.

6   Future prospects for the less developed areas are no brighter as far as their net trade position is concerned. Income elasticity of demand is very high, not only for paper and paper products but also to a lesser extent for wood products. Even if the rate of expansion of productive capacity continued at the rate of recent years, the net deficit would increase substantially by 1970, with a considerable addition to the already heavy burden in terms of foreign exchange. Only if something more is done can this burden be reduced. The economic problem is to see which cost is higher relative to benefits – that of investing in the sector or that of paying for increasing imports.

This problem will be considered in subsequent sections, but two things should be said immediately. First, the problem of comparing costs and benefits is economic and not financial; all benefits, direct and indirect, short- as well as long-term, should be considered and weighed against costs for the community, that is, social costs.

Secondly, the problem cannot be given a ready-made solution on the basis of the traditional doctrine of international trade and specialization. A static theory cannot account for dynamic phenomena, nor can it justify the result of past trends, such as the concentration of forest industries (or of any other industries, for that matter) in more advanced areas. Traditional international trade theory takes for granted that industries are where they are, but cannot explain why they are there. Such a theory is founded on a given distribution of external economics and is valid within its limits, but it cannot be used to infer that such distribution is the optimal one or that it cannot or should not be altered. Very few advantages are really natural, in the sense that they cannot to some extent be created in the long run. In the case of forest products the natural element underlying the existing forest industry pattern might be the distribution of conifers. This in turn depends, however, on the favoured position of conifers, which technical progress, especially if consciously oriented, could undermine, not to speak of the fact that it might also be possible to alter the existing distribution of conifers. In any case, all arguments in favour of maintaining the status quo which are based on the theory of international specialization are only valid when long-term advantages in terms of accumulation and reinvestment, and social advantages in terms of external economics, are neglected – that is, only when applied to a static context – but cease to have any relevance when the question is exactly that of creating those advantages in order to change the status quo.

CHARACTERISTICS OF FOREST INDUSTRIES

The global pattern

The simplified forest products flow chart shown in figure 1.1 demonstrates schematically the place of primary forest industries in relation to the forest on the one hand and to other branches of the economy (including final consumption) on the other. It also brings out some important interrelations between the forest industries, whose demands on raw materials are largely complementary but in part competitive, and whose products, too, are to some extent substitutive and hence competitive, but also complement each other in many respects in satisfying the needs of other sectors and of final consumers.

A general idea of the relative importance of the major primary forest industries can be obtained from table 1.7.

The contrasts between the four main groups emerge clearly from a comparison of some of the ratios involved (table 1.8).

The pulp and paper industry, followed by board products, is a good deal more capital-intensive than either plywood manufacture or sawmilling. Moreover, it yields the highest gross product per unit of raw material. Since both pulp and paper and board products operate mainly on small-dimensioned woods, do not make use of high-value timbers and are in fact utilizing to an increasing extent wood residues, both from other forest industries and from forest operations, their lead over plywood manufacture and sawmilling in terms of value added per unit of raw material is even more pronounced than is shown in the table.

These aggregates and averages, however, conceal great differences in the scale of operations (and factor requirements) within each main group, as we shall see shortly when we discuss some of the principal features of each industry group in turn. First, however, we should note that there are a number of minor

Table 1.7 The world's primary forest industries compared (1960)

Forest industries	Roundwood equivalent of output		Gross value of output		Investments		Labour force	
	(million m³)	(%)	($ million)	(%)	($ million)	(%)	(millions)	(%)
Sawmilling	561	65.2	15,400	48.4	8,400	17.2	3.2	60.3
Pulp and paper	252	29.3	14,300	45.1	38,000	77.8	1.6	30.2
Plywood	38	4.4	1,500	4.7	1,700	3.5	0.4	7.6
Board products	10	1.1	573	1.8	740	1.5	0.08	1.9
Total	861	100.0	31,773	100.0	48,840	100.0	5.3	100.0

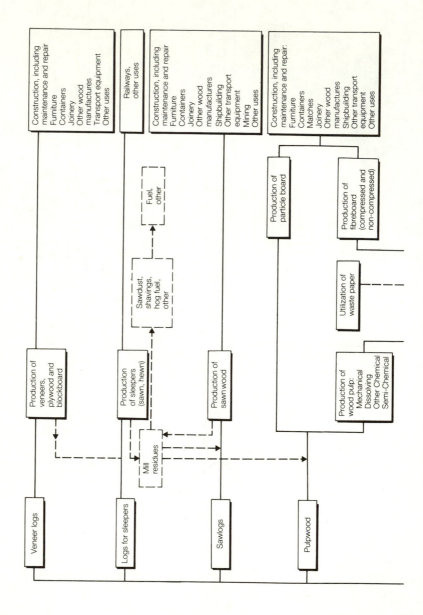

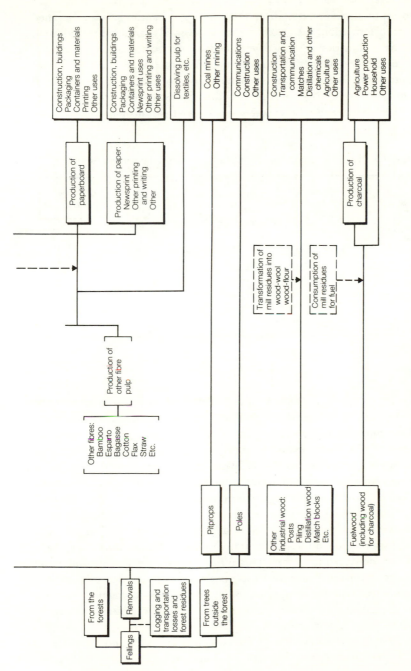

Figure 1.1 Forest products flow chart

primary forest industries omitted from these tables; other industries concerned with wood transformation, such as charcoal, wood-wool manufacture and wood distillation; and industries concerned with the extraction and refining of tanning materials, resins, lacs, oils and the like. Thus, total employment in the primary wood-transforming forest industries reaches close on 6 millions, while about the same number are engaged in the secondary forest industries – furniture, container, box, match and other wood-working, and various paper-converting industries.

Table 1.8   Selected ratios: The world's primary forest industries (1960)

Forest industry	Gross value of output per unit of raw material ($ per m³ (r))	Investment per person employed ($1,000)	Investment per unit of raw material ($ per m³ (r))	Employment per unit of raw material (no. per 1,000 m³ (r))
Sawmilling	27	2.6	15	5.7
Pulp and paper	57	23.8	151	6.4
Plywood	40	4.2	45	10.5
Board products	57	9.3	74	8.0

The sawmilling industry

In the sawmilling industry, the size of establishment varies from small mills (often mobile) in the forest, producing a few cubic metres a day for local needs, to highly mechanized mills with an annual capacity of several hundred thousand cubic metres, producing for export or serving large consumption centres. All have their place; optimum size and location can be determined only in the context of raw material supply, markets served, and communications between the two. Communications bulk largely in determining location, given the high incidence of transport costs on the raw material delivered mill and the finished product delivered to the market. Value added in processing is small, and economies of scale in the mill installation not of decisive importance. Typically the cost of logs delivered mill represents 50 to 70 per cent of mill production costs. Because of this, and because of the need to carry an adequate stock of logs to assure continuous operation and of processed sawnwood to meet customers' requirements, working capital needs are heavy, often amounting to as much as fixed investment.

Labour needs vary within very wide limits, depending on the type of material sawn, the degree of mechanization and, of course, on the efficiency of operations. To produce 1 cubic metre of sawn softwood in a mill of 10–15,000 cubic metres metres of annual capacity in a less developed European country requires

10 to 14 man-hours; in a larger mill of 20–35,000 cubic metres of annual capacity, only 7 to 10 man-hours are needed. The more homogeneous the log intake, the greater the possibilities of mechanization and labour-saving. Hence, labour productivity (as measured by output per man-hour or man-year) is normally much higher in sawn softwood mills than in mills sawing hardwood. In predominantly coniferous forest areas – North America, the USSR and northern Europe – softwoods comprise 85 to 95 per cent of the raw material for sawmilling as compared with 10 to 40 per cent in Asia, South America and Africa.

International trade in coniferous sawlogs is only about one third that in hardwood sawlogs; moreover, a much smaller proportion of the trade is inter-continental. The inter-regional hardwood sawlog trade consists mainly of tropical timbers. It is obvious that advantage would accrue to the developing countries if a greater proportion of their tropical timbers could be processed before export. Indeed, several countries have successfully adopted measures to favour exports of sawnwood instead of logs. There are limits, however, to what can be achieved in this direction since technical factors, perhaps no less than political factors, have determined the way in which this trade has developed historically.

International trade in tropical hardwoods includes a variety of stock, construc-tional timbers, but consists mainly of higher-value woods for use in furniture, and so on. In the past there have been many developing countries, for example in West Africa and Central America, which have achieved a considerable export of hardwood logs, and sometimes also of sawn hardwood, while the domestic market has absorbed little or no sawnwood. Today, domestic markets for sawnwood are beginning to grow. If efforts are made to find local markets for secondary species (perhaps after treatment) and sub-export grades of the better-known species, the cost of forest operations can be reduced, exporting power strengthened and perhaps, in some cases, the way opened for more processing before export. With greater emphasis in the developing countries on centrally inspired programmes for housing, school building and so on, there are new opportunities for positive action in this direction.

A large proportion of the raw material entering the sawmill, a proportion ranging from 25 to 50 per cent – perhaps averaging 40 per cent for the world as a whole – emerges from the process in the form of slabs, edgings and sawdust. This material, at one time wasted, today can be almost all turned to industrial account if there are appropriate forest industries in the vicinity to use it. The slabs and edgings can be chipped for pulp or board manufacture, and even the sawdust and shavings from planing mills can be utilized in other wood-processing industries. The possibility of utilizing sawmill residues has already considerably modified the economics of sawmilling in the developed areas of the world and has in many cases encouraged the integration of forest industries.

As yet, these potentialities have scarcely been realized in the developing countries. But if in most of these countries the time is not yet ripe for creating giant integrated forest industry complexes, there are few where it is not already possible to introduce successfully one or more small industries operating wholly or partly on mill residues, manufacturing particle board, or wood composition boards or blocks for constructional purposes. Alternatively, when a new sawmill is planned, the possibility of associating with it from the outset such a related enterprise may enhance both its prospective financial return and its social evaluation.

Sawmilling is usually the first forest industry to be established. It does not require a high degree of technical skill on the part of its labour force, but only on the part of a few key technicians. It is much more flexible in location, in size of plant, and in finished product than any of the other primary forest industries. If export demand is good, the industry can concentrate on high-quality production of lumber to dimensions required by the overseas market, using substandard production resawn for the local market. Should export demand cease or require different specifications, the industry can quickly adapt itself to the changed requirements.

The pulp and paper industry

Second of the primary industries in terms of raw material requirements and value of output, but far and away the largest in terms of capital invested, the pulp and paper industry has grown rapidly in recent years. During the decade 1950 to 1960 world production of pulp rose from 34 million tons to 59 million tons, and of paper from 43 million tons to 74 million tons.

This industry is much more heavily localized than the sawmilling industry, mainly because, although wood costs represent the main item in total production costs and a cheap wood supply is essential, other process materials and production factors assume considerable importance.[11] The pattern of production costs varies considerably with the process used, the size of plant, the location, and according to whether the process is integrated (pulp and paper) or not. Some of the main characteristics are deducible from table 1.9.

While wood costs still represent one third to one half of total production costs, it will be observed that, first, capital charges are high; secondly, process chemicals assume a considerable importance, especially for bleached grades; thirdly, power, steam and water represent a very important element; and fourthly, labour costs are relatively small.

Obviously wood costs have an important, though not, as in sawmilling, a dominant influence on total costs. The wood costs shown in table 1.9 are for wood delivered mill; labour represents the major element in this cost. Thus, while the mill operation itself is not labour-intensive, the associated forest

---

[11] Non-integrated paper production operating on purchased pulp, and production using a substantial furnish of waste paper or non-wood fibres, are not, of course, tied to the wood supply.

Table 1.9 Relative importance of various cost items in the production of pulp and paper

Cost item	Mechanical pulp integrated	Chemi-groundwood integrated	NSSC – pulp[a] (broadleaved wood) integrated		Sulphate pulp[a] non integrated				Newsprint, integrated mechanical pulp	NSSC[a] – corrugating board integrated
					Unbleached conifers	Bleached				
			Unbleached	Bleached		Conifers	Broadleaved wood	Straw		
					% of total production cost at mill					
Fibrous raw material	40	29	36	32	50	43	35	32	39	31
Chemicals	–	12	3	18	4	12	14	15	–	3
Other materials	3	3	4	3	3	3	3	3	4	5
Power, steam, water	21	18	12	10	2	4	5	5	15	13
Labour, incl. repairs	7	7	9	7	7	6	8	8	9	9
Supervision overhead	5	5	5	4	6	5	6	7	5	5
Capital costs	24	26	31	28	28	27	29	30	28	34

a With recovery of chemicals: NSSC – neutral sulphite semi-chemical process.
Production capacities: about 100 tons per day.

extraction operations are so. Investment needs for this industry are certainly heavy. Typical requirements (fixed investment in the mill only, excluding working capital and any necessary infrastructural investment) for medium-sized mills of 100 tons per day capacity (or 30,000 tons per year) in a less developed country range from $12 million to over $20 million, depending on location, process and production programme.

More than one half of this investment consists of equipment, engineering fees, and so forth, normally requiring foreign exchange outlay in a less developed country. On the other hand, pay-out time (total investment divided by annual gross output) is not high – ranging from eighteen months to three years.

However, there are a number of indivisibilities in the technological process which make for sizeable economies of scale. These are particularly pronounced for newsprint and for kraft pulp and paper. A general indication of the variation of capital costs with size of mill for some typical mills is afforded by table 1.10.

Table 1.10   Influence of type and size of pulp and paper mills on fixed investment

Mill type	Daily capacity (m. tons)			
	25	50	100	200
	Fixed investment in $1,000 per daily ton			
Non-integrated				
Unbleached chemical pulp	235	175	135	105
Bleached chemical pulp	325	240	190	150
Integrated				
Unbleached paper	300	230	180	140
Bleached paper	390	295	235	185

Source: Report of FAO/ECAFE Conference on pulp and paper development prospects in Asia and the Far East, Tokyo, 1960.

Clearly, given the high impact of capital charges on production costs, a small mill must enjoy compensating advantages to compete successfully with a larger rival.

Power requirements are also high, normally ranging from 350 to 550 kilowatt-hours per ton of bleached sulphate pulp to 1,700 to 2,000 kilowatt-hours per ton of newsprint. Hence the importance of cheap power supplies, especially for mechanical pulp and newsprint. Conversely, this industry, as a major industrial consumer, can assure power developments a needed outlet, thus influencing the feasibility of projected hydro works.

The fresh-water requirements in pulp and paper manufacture are quite high, especially for bleached grades of chemical pulp and certain special papers. Typical needs (in cubic metres of water per ton of pulp or paper) are:

groundwood, 50; unbleached sulphate pulp, 300; bleached sulphate pulp, 450; dissolving pulp, 600; newsprint (integrated with groundwood), 100; kraft paper (integrated with pulp), 400; paperboard (integrated with pulping of straw and waste paper), 400; and cigarette paper up to 1,000. An integrated paper mill with a daily output of 100 tons consumes about 40,000 cubic metres of water, which equals the needs of a city of some 150,000 inhabitants; in Finland forest products industries account for about 80 per cent of the entire water consumption.[12]

For the production of chemical pulp considerable quantities of chemicals are required, both for cooking and bleaching. Thus, for every 1,000 tons of bleached pulp produced, 200 to 500 tons of chemicals are consumed. This shows the importance, so far as chemical pulp operations are concerned, of convenient access to the basic materials, salt and limestone.

The bringing of large quantities of raw materials to the mill, and the shipping of the finished product, entails a considerable transport problem. Thus, for a 100-ton-per-day mill, daily transport tonnage may average 500 to 1,000 tons, and considerably exceed these figures at peak periods. Thus, not only is good transport organization necessary: heavy expenditure may be required on transport facilities, such as roads, railways, harbours, and lorries. This point also serves to underline the intimate relationship between pulp and paper development and general infrastructural development.

Space precludes a detailed discussion of available pulping processes, and of the fibrous materials to which each is specially adapted. It is sufficient to mention here that, even though the major part of the world's pulp and paper is still made from traditional coniferous species, there are very few timbers, coniferous or broadleaved, which cannot today be pulped by one or other of the available processes, and that there are processes suited to a wide variety of non-wood materials, including bamboo, esparto and other grasses, cereal straw and bagasse (sugar cane waste). It should be added, too, that one of the cheapest sources of fibre) for paper-making is waste paper, which can replace fresh fibre to a considerable extent in many grades, and wholly in some grades of paperboard. Thus, in Western Europe, no less than 25 per cent of paper consumed is recovered for re-manufacture, and waste paper accounts for 36 per cent of the fibre furnish of paper grades other than newsprint and kraft paper. The cost of waste paper is made up largely of collection and sorting costs; hence the higher and more concentrated the consumption of paper, the cheaper is waste paper as a raw material. With consumption rising rapidly in the developing countries the opportunities for utilizing waste paper are growing, and there are very many countries which could already support a small but economic paperboard production based on this material.

Though labour requirements for pulp and paper manufacture are modest

---

[12] Harald Tötterman, 'Die Wasserfragen der Finnischen Zellstoff- und Papierindustrie', *Paperi jàa Puu*, 43:4 (1961).

a fairly high proportion, ranging from 35 to 45 per cent, needs to be skilled. Hence the need for schemes of intensive mill training when starting new projects in the developing countries.

The characteristics of the pulp and paper industry already described may have given the impression that there is no scope for small-scale operations, for mills of 5 to 10 tons per day, for example. This is not so. Even in the industrialized countries, small mills often comprise 80 per cent of the total number, though accounting only for some 10 to 25 per cent of the total output of paper and board. These include mills making speciality papers,[13] such as cigarette, electrical and currency papers, which are almost universally produced in small units. But they include many more mills (usually non-integrated mills) making strawboards, tissues and other grades of paper and board for local consumption. Small-scale operations have the following favourable aspects: utilization of local fibrous raw materials and reduced transport charges; local sale with low distribution costs and ready adjustment to local market requirements; adaptation to limited water supply; fewer technical personnel and skilled labour needs; relatively small capital requirements (though this will not necessarily apply to certain, high-value, speciality papers); use of locally made machinery; geographical dispersal of employment opportunities. Quality need not necessarily suffer in small-scale operations.

Thus, while it would clearly be mistaken policy to plan the long-term development of the pulp and paper industry mainly on the basis of small-scale mills, such mills can sometimes play an important part in the early stages of the industry.

Plywood, fibreboard and particle board

Plywood   World plywood production, around 3 million cubic metres in 1938, today stands at well over 15 million cubic metres, having more than doubled during the last decade. There has been a great expansion both in the use of hardwood plywood for decorative purposes (panels, doors, table tops and the like) and of utility softwood plywood for constructional purposes. This expansion has been largely bound up with technical developments (improved glues, surface treatments, new products), with the favourable price trend of plywood as compared with sawnwood, and with labour-saving applications of plywood in the construction industry.

The most important factor in the location of plywood mills is the availability of large-diameter logs of good form, whether indigenous or imported, suitable for peeling or slicing. Much of the industry which has been built up in Europe and Japan has been based on imported tropical hardwoods. With veneer-size logs becoming progressively scarcer, technical progress in the industry has concentrated on making use of smaller-diameter logs and lower-quality material,

[13] For which demand is likely to be very small in countries in the early stages of industrialization.

for example, by cutting out defects, patching and reducing core size. The transformation coefficient in plywood manufacture is fairly low, losses on conversion amounting to 50 to 70 per cent (40 to 60 per cent on veneer manufacture). Frequently all or part of these residues will be used as fuel for steam and power needed in the plant for hot presses, driers, and so on. But if a commercial outlet is available for them, this can have a decisive influence on the economics of operation. Blockboard manufacture is largely a branch of the plywood industry. There is also a notable trend to integrate the plywood and particle board industries, not only because the latter uses the residues of the former, but also because much particle board is veneer-faced and because both industries serve the same consuming sectors, construction and furniture.

The cost of wood raw material represents 30 to 50 percent of total manufacturing costs, the other important process material being adhesives (resins, casein, blood albumen, soya bean, and so on), of which about 25 to 35 kilograms are required per cubic metre of plywood. With the growing importance of moisture-resistant and waterproof plywood, the consumption of urea and phenol resins has increased rapidly.

Investment costs, though higher than for sawmilling, are much lower than for pulp and paper manufacture – about $100–$200 per cubic metre of annual capacity. Scale economies are less pronounced than for pulp and paper; they relate mainly to power and presses. Only mills operating on large quantities of homogeneous material (for example, Douglas fir plywood) and manufacturing standard grades can fruitfully introduce much mechanical handling and some automation control.

Labour needs per cubic metre of output vary substantially, depending upon the degree of mechanization, log sizes, average thickness of veneer, need for patching, and so on. In less developed countries more than 100 man-hours per cubic metre may be used if circumstances favour heavy reliance on manual handling. The proportion of skilled labour needed may range from 20 to 35 per cent.

What has been said under sawmilling concerning the opportunities in developing countries for carrying out further processing before export applies also to plywood manufacture. Here it is perhaps useful to note a recent trend towards establishing non-integrated veneer plants, making green or drier veneer, to feed local or overseas plywood plants equipped simply with a press or drier and press. Such veneer mills require little investment, and can operate on a limited supply of veneer logs. Shipment of veneers saves weight and space compared with shipping logs.

Blockboard, laminated board and so on, are included in the broad category of plywood, and output of these products has increased parallel with the production of particle board. Blockboard can be manufactured almost manually, with but limited equipment. It is of considerable interest to many developing countries since it can not only replace imports, but also offers an outlet for thinnings and small-diameter logs from coniferous plantations as well as for sawmill residues.

Fibreboard The fibreboard industry, with a world output (1960) of well over 4 million tons, has many affinities with the pulp and paper industry. The problems of wood supply are similar, as is the stage of pulp preparation, if the traditional wet processes are employed. Process chemicals are not normally required, and the sizing materials and additives which impart particular qualities to the finished product do not represent an important element in total costs. Wood costs may account for 20 to 40 per cent of the total, depending on the size of mill (though they may fall to 10 per cent if cheap residues are available), while fixed charges (mainly depreciation and interest on working capital) may account for 20 to 30 per cent, again depending on size of mill. Thus, as with pulp and paper, scale economies are significant. Fixed investment per daily ton may range from $90,000 to $100,000 for a mill of 6,000 tons annual capacity, down to around $30,000 for a mill of 50,000 tons annual capacity. In fact, fibreboard production lends itself to small-scale operations less readily than several branches of the pulp and paper industry.

An adequate supply of fresh water is required; water needs are similar to those for newsprint production. Power requirements, at 300 to 800 kilowatt-hours per ton of product, are less than for newsprint but more than for chemical pulp. Labour needs (in the mill) are modest, ranging from 12 to 40 man-hours per ton. Fibreboard production can be based on a wide variety of coniferous and broadleaved species, including suitably blended mixtures, and is eminently suitable for utilizing residues (including even bark and sawdust) from other forest industries. There is a growing trend to the use of unbarked wood.

In recent years several dry processes for fibreboard manufacture have been developed. These processes may well come to have an interest for developing countries, since investment is somewhat lower and there is no need for large supplies of fresh water. Resins are, however, needed for bonding purposes.

Particle board The particle board industry is essentially a post-war development. Over the 1950–60 decade world production grew from about 15,000 tons to nearly 2 million tons. Like fibreboard, particle board can make use of a very wide variety of species, coniferous and broadleaved, as well as flax, bagasse, and wood residues; indeed, this industry developed in the first instance to make use of wood residues. It is, in fact, this tolerance in raw material requirements that confers on both these board industries a special attraction for countries with tropical forests, wherein frequently only a small proportion of the available timber (species and sizes) are suitable for the other major forest industries.

Investment in a particle board mill of intermediate size represents roughly half that in a fibreboard mill of comparable tonnage. Though there are economies of scale, relatively small mills can be economic, particularly if operating on locally available residues or serving a captive market. The average capacity of mills in 1956 in Europe, North America and the world as a whole was 4,200, 2,500, and 3,500 tons respectively. Investment cost ranges from about $12,000 to $30,000 per daily ton, depending on the process used and hence on the type of board produced.

There are fewer restrictions on location than in the case of fibreboard. Water is not needed. Power requirements are modest, 100 to 300 kilowatts per hour per ton of board, as are mill labour requirements, 5 to 20 man-hours per ton. A key consideration, however, is the availability and cost of resin, normally urea, or phenol resin. This bonding material, which represents about 5 to 8 per cent of the weight of the finished board, may account for 15 to 35 per cent of production costs, depending on the process used and the cost of resin. Thus resin costs may frequently exceed wood costs. Obviously, if resin has to be imported, this sharply diminishes the import-saving value of the project.

Miscellaneous and secondary forest industries

In addition to the major forest industries just discussed there are very many other smaller industries based on raw materials of forest origin. These are so diverse that no simple grouping is wholly satisfactory for classification purposes.

Though some of these smaller industries are little more than extensions of the sawmilling and veneer industries, they may be separately established, particularly where the existence of a suitable resource or the needs of a consumption centre make this advisable. In some instances the raw materials may even be imported. Wood-turning, with handles for agricultural implements and sports goods, wooden-ware and spools as principal products, is one example. The manufacture of match blocks in the form of sawnwood or veneer is another. Small plants (or units within larger plants) are suitable for producing shingles, pencil slats and briarwood pipe blocks, often for export, where appropriate raw materials are available. The manufacture of cooperage and other wooden containers and of wood-wool are complementary to certain food and drink exporting industries as well as to the shipping of many manufactured goods. The capital requirements per unit of wood consumed are of about the same order as those for smaller sawmills. Mills may, however, be quite small in size. A large proportion of the production costs are made up of charges for skilled and semi-skilled labour, but this varies considerably from industry to industry. Raw material costs tend to be quite important in the total.

The chemical distillation of wood yields a large variety of products, the more important of which are charcoal and methyl or wood alcohol. When coniferous woods are used various oils and tars are also produced. In addition to its common household and commercial uses for cooking and heating, charcoal has a number of important industrial uses, such as in steel manufacture, water purification and tobacco-curing. One of the developing countries has recently made a major use of charcoal in the manufacture of Portland cement. The capital requirements for wood distillation plants are not excessive. Charcoal alone may be produced in simple pit methods requiring no capital. The other products are, of course, lost in this case.

A number of extractives from wood and bark provide the raw material for several small but important industries. Some species of pine are suitable for the tapping of a resinous exudate used for the manufacture, by a distillation process, of turpentine and resin. A considerable amount of labour and little capital are required in the industry. The trees may also be used for their timber. Products of this industry are important in a variety of chemical industries.

The production of tannins, most important raw materials in the hide and leather industries, may be based on a great number of woody and herbaceous plants. The most important sources have been the wood of the quebracho, which is common in South America; the bark of the chestnut, oaks and hemlock, which were the important materials in North America and Europe; mangrove bark, common to many tropical coasts; and the bark of wattle, which has become an important plantation tree for this purpose. A wide variety of species found in the developing countries are suitable for tannin production. Export markets have been poor in recent years but domestic production for local leather industries is logical for most developing countries.

The final group of industries to be briefly summarized here are the secondary wood and paper manufacturing industries, which use as their raw materials the products of sawmills, plywood and veneer plants, board mills and paper mills. They may be closely associated with mills producing their raw materials or may, by contrast, be widely decentralized near consuming centres. Their products are most varied, supplying consumers, literally, from cradle to grave. Among the more important of the secondary wood-using industries are furniture manufacturing; joinery plants producing such things as doors, window sashes, mouldings, and even prefabricated houses; boat-building; manufacturing of vehicle bodies – wagons, lorry bodies, and so on. Although they may frequently do their own initial processing, wood-turning and container plants sometimes are simply secondary manufacturing units. Paper-using plants also produce a great variety of goods, including corrugated boxes, cartons, paper bags and sacks, waxed containers, envelopes, napkins and exercise books. These industries tend as a group to be labour-intensive – calling for a wide range of skills – and to use relatively high-cost raw materials. Capital requirements are generally modest to low. Plants can often be small and decentralized but there are some economies of scale for the more mechanized. These industries can often be developed as units in industrial estates. They are often well suited to developing countries because they tend to be labour-intensive, and can usually vary in size. Even in countries with little or no forest resource they can be operated on imported materials, saving appreciable foreign exchange on the value added. Many wood-deficient developing countries are now importing products of the secondary wood and paper industries to a value in excess of their imports of all other wood and paper products. By contrast some countries in this category, such as Israel and the United Arab Republic, have developed these secondary industries to a high degree.

Many of the characteristics of the forest industries which we have just discussed are determined largely by the nature of the raw material on which they operate and the conditions under which that raw material is supplied. Our assessment of the potential role of forest industries in developing countries would therefore be incomplete without at least a cursory glance at the forestry sector.

Supplying wood, the raw material of the forest industries, is the major function of the forestry sector of the economy. There are two fundamental phases of the timber-supplying forestry operation: logging, the felling and transportation of logs to the market or to the wood-user; and forest management, which is concerned with the provision of standing trees ready for felling. These two phases are intimately interwoven and, in turn, they often have a distinct bearing on the other major function of forestry – assuring the flow of non-timber goods and services inherent in the forest environment. The non-wood production of the forest is considered in a later section. Here we are concerned with the forest as the 'woodshed' of the forest industries.

Some characteristics of forestry

A most striking, although not always obvious, characteristic of forestry is the complexity and variability of the production function. The forest grows, not as the simple summation of trees growing as individuals, but in a competitive race for space and nutrients in which the development of each tree affects that of its neighbours. According to environment and to their historical development, forests vary from simple groups of trees of the same age and of the same species to heterogeneous mixtures of trees of many ages and of a vast number of species. Fairly homogeneous forest stands of a few conifierous species and of fairly simple age structure, which are typical of the more northern temperate areas, lend themselves well to the techniques and economies of mass-production logging. The tropical rain forest with its myriad diverse species, typical of many of the developing areas, demands, in its exploitation, either a search over sizeable areas for individual trees, or logging and processing techniques capable of handling most heterogeneous raw materials. Trees grow at vastly different rates, according to their species, their physical environment and the competition from their fellows. The age of felling depends not only on the numerous combinations of these factors, but also on the kind of product being cropped. Thus there may be pulpwood cut from fast-growing plantation species after six or eight years of growth, or veneer logs harvested from 200- to 300-year-old trees from the natural forest.

As a tree grows it builds upon its former frame, making it larger and larger, accumulating annual growth from year to year. Over any appreciable area, however, individual trees at various stages of their life fail to withstand competition and die. The rate of mortality is high when many trees of similar sizes are competing or when numerous individuals reach 'old age'. In the natural forest, except in times of epidemic losses due to disease or insects, the mortality losses balance the accumulation of annual increments and the net result of the dynamic change within the forest is little or no change in total volume of standing trees.

Natural forests do, however, represent an accumulation of past annual growths which have, generally, built up heavy volumes of large, old and frequently valuable trees. Such forests have often been exploited as a cost-free timber mine or reservoir of forest capital without regard to problems of replacement. In the early stages of development in many countries, this exploitation without renewal has enabled the accumulation of other forms of capital. Such a 'free loan' has often brought in its train the social costs of abrupt declines in local economic activity and of abandoned towns. Nevertheless, exploitation of the natural forest has played an important role in the development of these countries.

The use of natural forests without concern for replacement, that is, the liquidation of forest capital, can occasionally be justified – but only under very special conditions. Normally, where continuity of supply has to be assured, there must be provision for successive croppings from the same areas. Plans and schedules for this may take a variety of forms and involve different intensities of use.

These are largely conditioned by two inherent characteristics of the forest. The first characteristic is the identity of factory and product, a characteristic shared to some extent with meat production and fisheries. The act of cropping destroys a part of the forest capital (the wood factory), but in so doing harvests as a product an accumulation of annual 'interest' or growth'. It is thus possible to vary the actual volume and time of harvest within fairly wide limits – to delay the harvest, storing the crop as it stands, or to accelerate the cutting temporarily, borrowing from the capital. This flexibility of the harvesting period is a characteristic of forestry which offers distinct advantages. Of course, continuous harvesting in excess of growth potential will eventually destroy the forest. At the same time, the removal of trees does profoundly affect the growth of their neighbours or permits the establishment of new trees. Thus, within limits, harvesting can promote the net growth or rate of production of the forest.

The second characteristic concerns the very large areas upon which forestry is practised. This makes close supervision difficult, and the progress of production equally difficult to observe.

In its least intensive form forest management may differ from capital liquidation only in that it ensures a future crop, either from trees not felled at the time of the initial cut or from new trees. The most elementary approach to supply continuity consists of a simple progression of harvesting throughout the forest, returning to the first area of cutting when the next crop matures.

Most natural forests have such a variation in tree size that a complete cropping of commercial species at the time of initial felling is inappropriate. In such cases, two or more crops may be taken from a given area during the span of years that corresponds to a rotation.

Intensive management is characterized by more frequent returns to the same area. Not only are final crop trees removed; thinning, the removal of small and intermediate-sized trees, is also undertaken. This reduces potential losses through mortality and favours the growth of the remaining trees, permitting the annual growth to accumulate on fewer and larger individuals.

With increasing intensity of use come other measures, including protection from fire, insects and disease. Harvestable growth has been doubled or trebled in many well managed natural forests by means of a wide range of techniques including thinning, weeding, pruning, enrichment planting, seed source selection, and drainage.

Planting forest trees in unforested areas or within cut-over areas in the natural forest has, of course, long been a recognized technique. But plantation forestry has made spectacular advances in recent decades. Forestry genetics can assure high-quality breeding material. With the use of selected seedlings, by tilling and fertilizing the soil, plantations can produce as much as ten times the growth of the natural forest.

The shift to what are essentially agrotechnical methods presents many advantages: convenient selection of species and rotation period; a more homogeneous crop, lending itself to mass-production removal and processing techniques; co-use of the land with agricultural crops in the first few years after establishment; reduction of supervision and transport costs by concentration; and freedom to plan the sequence of age groups for orderly harvesting (as distinct from accepting the age patterns in the natural forest). Another distinct advantage is the possibility of complementing production from the natural forest.

Prospects for further development in plantation forestry are most promising. Incredible growth rates, particularly in tropical regions, have been obtained, sometimes with species which have done poorly in their native habitat. A promising area of investigation, as yet scarcely explored, is the application of fertilizers, trace elements and hormone compounds. Along with more widespread and better-organized research and experimentation, facilities for the exchange of information have expanded. It is the improved organization, no less than the increasing scale of research effort, which guarantees new breakthroughs.

An adaptation of plantation forestry – now commonly called linear forestry – has evolved in a number of countries, usually those with much land in agricultural use. Fast-growing species are planted in rows along roads, railways, canals, rivers, terrace edges and field boundaries. They have often been established as boundary markers and for their shade, windbreak and erosion control functions. These plantations have often supplied much industrial wood as well as fuelwood. In some areas, they have proved so profitable that they have led to forest plantations of the normal type on land formerly under agriculture.

The logging phase

Logging methods, in addition to being greatly affected by the nature of the terrain and by the climate, are also much influenced by the nature of the product harvested, by the structure of the forest and by the form and intensity of forest management. Methods vary from the most elementary of hand methods to heavily mechanized operations. Generally, the more highly mechanized operations have developed under one of two conditions – where a uniform forest and easy terrain encourage mass-production techniques, or where difficult terrain poses special problems. Although some measure of mechanization improves efficiency, there remain many instances where hand methods, or at least methods requiring little capital, are equally or even more effective.

Logging must often have a seasonal pattern because of rainfall and resultant ground conditions, because of snow or ice conditions, extreme fire hazards, or volume of stream flow. In many cases seasonal labour requirements for logging complement those for agriculture, some types of manufacturing, and building activity.

Some advantages inherent in forestry

The characteristics described above are those which are responsible for the flexible productive function in forestry (forest management plus logging), permitting ready adaptation to conditions which vary greatly in space and time.

On the one hand, output itself may readily be varied with little change in the nature or quantity of inputs. There is at any time a considerable choice of the form in which the output will be harvested. With new opportunities opened up by the technology of processing and changed economic conditions, a shift in the product can be readily accommodated. In this way, material originally planned or grown for veneer logs or sawlogs can be used, with few limitations, for pulpwood – even after being felled and transported to a mill. Wood considered originally only of fuelwood quality may, with technological improvements, be used as pulpwood or as raw material for particle board. Much pulpwood may even be used for sawlogs. The time of harvesting is flexible within considerable limits, permitting adaptation to short-term fluctuations in demand, without danger of spoilage or excessive problems of storage.

On the other hand, there exists marked flexibility and possibility of variation in the combination of inputs. Even in the exceptional case where forest capital is liquidated without planned replacement there is a variety of choices on land input (land here in the sense of land plus forest growing stock). One can harvest little from much land, or more from less; the choice determines the relation between direct and indirect costs of harvesting. The former choice means relinquishing timbers of marginal value; but it may serve an 'opening-up' function over and above forest exploitation.

If, as is normal, continuity of supply is the aim, then to the choice of variation in logging input are added numerous alternatives within forest management, as well as between the two major phases of forestry. Generally, the greater the input of land, the larger is the portion of wood cost made up by logging cost; the less the use of land, the larger is the portion composed of timber-growing costs. More extensive forestry over large areas calls for less labour for timber growing but more for the creation of what may be temporary infrastructure, and more for logging labour and transportation capital because of the greater distances. Plantation forestry is the extreme case of limiting land input.

In the growing of timber, time itself is an important input, which varies with the type of forest, the product and management intensity. The cost of time is interest on engaged capital; this is why the more intensive practices tend to be associated with a short rotation period.

Evidently the many choices available, both as regards combination of input and patterns of output, give rise to numerous problems of decision. What is relevant in our present context, however, is that they also offer a multitude of possibilities in the supplying of raw material for domestic industry or for export. This range means that there is virtually no country, whatever its stage of economic development, whatever its forest endowment, for which forestry is not an appropriate economic activity. Experience has shown that, even in countries with little natural forest of value, plantation and linear forestry can transform the situation speedily, opening up entirely new perspectives.

FEATURES OF FOREST INDUSTRIES RELEVANT TO DEVELOPMENT

A general appraisal of investment prospects in the forest industries sector can now be attempted. The question is: Given a decision to undertake industrial investment, to what extent can investment in the sector under review be recommended for its short- and long-term advantages?

The individual situations in the countries included in the group of less developed regions vary greatly. Therefore, arguments and conclusions will necessarily have to be stated in very broad and general terms. The general indication they provide will apply more to some countries and less to others: this indication, however, may provide an incentive to undertake more detailed country reviews to show how far the propositions of this chapter are relevant in individual cases.

Demand expansion and import-saving effects

A partial argument for investment in the forest industries of less developed countries arises from the present situation and future prospects of demand relative to present supply possibilities. As has already been seen, the group of less developed countries, in spite of their very low levels of income and per caput consumption, already now presents a substantial deficit in net trade of forest products, and this trade deficit is bound to increase very rapidly, at least in absolute terms, unless very large investment is undertaken.

Final and intermediate goods with an income elasticity of demand as high as that of forest products (and especially of paper and wood-based panel products) pose difficult problems to developing countries. One of the most important obstacles that these countries have to face in their growth process is their balance of payments situation, since they normally have a structural deficit on current account which is likely to become bigger and bigger as the growth process gets under way. The increasing deficit is normally due to imports of the capital goods necessary for industrialization, which may be compensated for by loans and grants restoring the equilibrium on capital account, and to imports of commodities the consumption of which increases in proportion or more than in proportion to income. In order to maintain the deficit within reasonable limits, without holding in check the growth process, imports of goods other than capital goods must be restricted with tariffs and quotas, and at the same time the domestic productive capacity of previously imported goods must be expanded, so as to deal with additional requirements.

The magnitude of the import-saving effects resulting from expanding domestic production of forest products is not by itself, however, a decisive argument for investing in the sector, since an equally relevant import-saving effect might be obtained by expanding the production of other goods with a similarly high income elasticity of demand. The heart of the matter consists in choosing which commodities should be consumed at the expense of others. Since the given amount of capital will not suffice for expanding domestic production of all goods, there will be some goods the consumption of which must be restricted in order to prevent a growing trade deficit. Hence the case for investment in forest industries cannot rest simply on the import-saving effect that an expansion of such industries would have, but should be supplemented by other arguments.

Of such arguments there are plenty, stemming from structural characteristics of supply and demand, in part already examined in earlier pages.

Characteristics of the raw material and locational factors

One set of arguments derives from the nature and properties of the raw material employed in forest industries.

First, wood is the only raw material that nearly all inhabited regions of the world have available and can reproduce from existing forests, or could possess by establishing plantations. It is a general principle of development policy that priority should be given to industries processing local raw materials, since the presence of the latter in part offsets the external diseconomies that have prevented industrialization in the past. Nevertheless, it is often forgotten in underdeveloped economies that their forests – which the very lack of development has in many cases helped to preserve – are as important a source of natural wealth as mineral deposits; if properly exploited, forests represent a most important incentive to the beginning of industrialization.

A second argument for expansion of forest industries, again connected with the characteristics of forest industries inputs, rests on location theory. Of all the major raw materials, wood is usually the most difficult to transport. Not only is forestry tied to extensive areas of land, so that transport can never start from a permanent position, as it does, for instance, in the case of coal; in addition, wood as cut in the forest is a bulky material varying in size and shape, and the extent to which these can be altered for the sake of easier transport is severely limited by the future use of the wood and by other factors. Finally, forest industries, as was shown above, are typically weight-losing, and the wood raw material accounts for a substantial proportion of total production costs.

Less developed regions, though already exporters of broadleaved sawnwood and plywood still export a considerable quantity of sawlogs, which are then sawn or felled in the importing countries. Here, evidently, there is a *prima facie* case for expanding sawmilling and plywood capacity by an amount sufficient to satisfy not only growing internal demand, but also to substitute exports of processed wood for exports of sawlogs. It is a case which, for once, could find support even in the traditional theory of international specialization, since this substitution of exports would result in a net decrease in costs owing to the saving in freight. This advantage has so far been insufficiently exploited, partly for certain technical reasons (which are not, however, insuperable), but mainly because of the lack of infrastructure which characterizes all less developed countries. This, however, should no longer be an obstacle if a consistent development policy is pursued: as has already been stressed, investment in forest industries is appraised in this chapter not in isolation but in the general context of an overall development policy which presupposes, as a preliminary step, the building of social overhead capital and implies the installation of industries also in different sectors. In this case the cost of infrastructure can no longer be considered as a cost to be borne for the sake of a single investment project in a simple sector: what was true for the colonial exploitation of one or very few export goods (and made it financially convenient to export the raw material rather than process it locally) does not apply with reference to the overall economic growth of a country.[14]

[14] The same reason suggests that in the long run, where possible, a policy of forestry development should be followed that aims at creating the supply of the types of wood (especially conifers) which are now lacking, in order to minimize the burden of necessary imports.

Location factors are similarly important for wood-based panel products and for pulp and paper. For the manufacture of many grades of paper, however, an admixture of long-fibre pulp is needed, and many developing countries at present lack indigenous sources of long fibre. In the long run, adequate forestry development can usually fill the gap; in the short run, long-fibre pulp has to be imported. In the meantime there are often excellent prospects for the local manufacture of short-fibre pulp to be combined with imported long-fibre pulp in the local manufacture of paper.

An even better utilization of local resources will, of course, be attained as technical progress leads to the substitution of the types of wood which are locally available for those which have to be imported – especially of broadleaved sawnwood and wood-based panel products for coniferous sawnwood and of short-fibre for long-fibre pulp in paper manufacture.

The technological advantages of forest industries

Another set of arguments in favour of forest industries rests on the characteristics of the technologies in use in the industries themselves. It was pointed out earlier that the wider the range of the production function and the greater the flexibility relative to scale, the more suitable a sector is for investment in the less developed countries. Forest industries, taken individually, present these advantages.

First, in the production of the raw material, expensive mechanization can often be postponed and unskilled labour used instead. Logging often takes place under conditions where expensive mechanization is not a pressing necessity, and is sometimes uneconomical owing to the heterogeneity of the environment and of the produce. Quite often, and especially in regions where it tends to be plentiful, manual labour assisted by animals or relatively cheap machinery can hold its own in competition with expensive machines. Thus the owner of a small forest industry is normally in a position to do his own logging without incurring heavy initial expenses; and, as long as labour remains relatively cheap, larger operators will also be able to postpone far-reaching mechanization in the forest. The possibility of postponing the use of expensive machinery in the production of raw material is distinctly helpful in less developed areas, since it reduces capital requirements while at the same time providing considerable employment possibilities for labour possessing only the types of manual skill commonly found in agricultural areas.

Secondly, the physical properties of wood render it relatively easy to work mechanically, so that many products can be manufactured adequately with the use of fairly simple machinery. The difficulty of transporting the raw material on the one hand, and the ease with which it can be worked on the other, make it possible for small, or fairly small, units to be economical in the manufacture of such basic products as sawn timber, veneer, and mechanical pulp: the proximity of raw material supplies, and sometimes also the possibility of selling locally a large part of the product, go a long way towards compensating for the disabilities of size. Where conditions are favourable, the manufacturing unit can be increased step by step, as additional capital and qualified manpower become available. Even certain types of integration are possible on quite a small scale. This possibility of growth by degrees is very useful in developing economies.

The demand for forest products:
indirect advantages and external economies

We have noted that a major problem of development policy consists in the sectoral allocation of a limited amount of capital and in deciding for which commodities production should be expanded and for which, instead, consumption must for some time be restricted in order to prevent a growing balance of payments deficit. Characteristics of supply, as examined so far, provide good indications for the choice; but also, independently of them, characteristics of the commodities and of the needs that they satisfy can be of help.

Many commodities with a high income elasticity of demand are consumption goods, introduced into advanced countries at relatively high income levels. These are also demanded in less developed countries in spite of lower average incomes, especially where, as is often the case, there are conspicuous inequalities in income distribution. Sometimes imitation or demonstration effects are at work. Such goods can, on all counts, be considered less essential since they satisfy less urgent needs. Admittedly this is a value judgement more than an economic evaluation; but hardly anybody would or should hesitate in the choice between better food, more clothes, and education on the one hand, and cars, radios and the like on the other. From this point of view there can be little doubt that the consumption of forest products in a country is as good an index as any of the standard of social, as well as material, development of the population: in the less developed areas the products of forest industries can help the attainment of some of the essentials of material well-being and of human dignity – ranging from suitable housing and furniture to the possibilities of instruction and the diffusion of books and newspapers. There can therefore be little doubt that the sector ranks rather high in the scale of priorities that should be established in determining for which goods production should be expanded and demand completely satisfied, and of which, instead, consumption should be restricted.

This consideration is reinforced by the consideration of other indirect effects of investment in forest industries on the economy as a whole, mainly consisting in the creation of external economies in a broad sense.

The first group of economies to be noted are not external to the sector, but concern the mutual relations between the industries within the sector: the installation of some forest industries tends to pave the way for complementary production within the area concerned and make the sector as a whole to some extent self-propelling. Forest exploitation commonly yields wood of different kinds and grades, and the mechanical conversion of wood usually leaves a substantial amount of residue that can be utilized by other branches of forest industry. With rising demand for wood products of different kinds on the one hand and increasing value of the raw material on the other, existing industries often provide the incentive to the establishment of new enterprises, and complementary types of utilization tend to develop. In sum, the heterogeneous nature of the wood resource, together with the versatility of wood and its unwieldy character in the raw state, tend to stimulate new industrial activities within the area, often within the same enterprise.

External economies of a most important type arise from the fact that forest industries should normally be localized as near as possible to the forests, and hence are normally decentralized in the hinterland of the regions concerned. This 'backwoods' character of forest industries creates a natural tie between them and various infrastructural undertakings. When a new road opens up forests to sawmilling and is used to transport sawn timber to the consuming centres, the economic benefits thus derived may contribute substantially towards amortizing the cost of the road; logging roads may help to extend the regional road system; the establishment of a hydro-electric plant may permit the building of a newsprint mill, which, once in operation, is bound to become a major customer of the electric plant; and so forth. This interrelation is an important feature of forest industries, notably in the early stages of development, and may be a very effective factor in preventing the occurrence of 'dualism' in economic growth, that is, of a cumulative differentiation between two parts of the same region.

A further indirect advantage arises in forestry from the high flexibility of forestry work, and from the consequent possibility of utilizing labour that is temporarily idle. Owing to the perennial nature of trees, neither intervention in their growth through silvicultural treatment nor the final harvest of the wood is tied to a strict time schedule; and although climatic factors associated with the seasons of the year affect different kinds of work in the forest, this influence is much less pronounced than in agriculture. Such flexibility is important in less developed areas. Since many kinds of forestry work are well suited to the employment of relatively unskilled labour, a labour potential which otherwise would be wasted can be utilized in current production or for the formation of savings in the shape of future yields of raw material.

But possibly the most important of the indirect effects of installing forest industries is of an eminently dynamic character. Forest industries can be considered a propulsive sector, that is, a sector the expansion of which is liable to induce spontaneous investment in other branches of production. This is due to the fact that the forest industries have a very strong forward linkage with other sectors. A high degree of linkage makes a sector a good starting point for industrial growth: investment there, by inducing demand and providing supplies for other sectors, widens investment opportunities in the economy as a whole and has a multiplier effect – not in the traditional sense of the word, which is based on final demand and on the consumption of income by the newly employed, but in the sense of increasing inter-industry demand.

Few of the advantages of forest industries that have been listed so far can be translated into a financial evaluation, since they are not liable to find expression in terms of money. This makes it difficult to attempt a quantitative comparison of costs and benefits and a precise assessment of social profitability. All the said advantages, however, should be taken into account by planners when making decisions on the allocation of available investment resources – with particular care, since, in the case of forest industries, social benefits may sometimes be as important as the financial profit.

A tentative estimate has already been made of the financial cost of an increase in productive capacity sufficient to prevent the trade deficit from rising. The capital cost per unit of additional production is but little greater than the cost per unit of imports. But the former cost would be borne once and for all over a period of years; the latter would be a recurring cost. The total investment required over the decade – some $5,000 million – is a forbidding sum. But this must not be conceived as a sudden lump-sum investment; it would be a gradual, progressively rising investment, spread over a number of years. Viewed in this light, there are no grounds for regarding such a target as unrealistic.

RESOURCES, TECHNOLOGY AND RESEARCH

Analysis here has so far brought out many cogent reasons why countries in the early stages of economic development should give special attention to the establishment or expansion of forest industries. These stem, essentially, from the structural and dynamic characteristics of the demand for forest products, from the flexibility and range of the production functions of forest industries, and from the fact that nearly all the less developed countries possess unused or insufficiently utilized forest resources, or could possess them within a short space of time.

The first two points have been amply demonstrated. The third, commonly taken for granted, requires examination, since the naïve assumption that unused forests spell industrial opportunity has in the past been the source and origin of much disillusionment and many disappointments.

The variety of forest reserves

It was pointed out earlier that in most developing countries the forest reserves differ considerably in composition and quality from those of the industrially advanced countries which have succeeded in building up important forest industries.

Natural conifers   Perhaps a score of these less developed countries possess significant areas of natural conifers. These consist mostly of pine species and, while some of these areas are readily accessible, others lie in remote places with difficult terrain. In general, given reasonable management, regeneration and growth rates are good – usually much higher than in the coniferous forests of North America, northern Europe and the USSR, but somewhat less than the rates achieved in the intensively managed artificial coniferous forests of, say, Denmark and the United Kingdom.

Planted forests   Quite a number of developing countries already possess substantial areas of planted forests – various types of pine, and such broadleaved species as poplar, willow and eucalypts. As has already been mentioned, phenomenal growth rates are frequently recorded in these plantations; more than five times the rate in the natural coniferous forests of the north temperate zone is quite common.

However, important as are these coniferous forests and plantations (important precisely because currently available technology is well adapted to their utilization), they are nevertheless exceptions in the less developed regions of the world. In fact, more than nine tenths of the forest reserves of Asia, Africa and Latin America consist of broadleaves forests, and these vary greatly in their nature, and consequently in the problems and prospects of their development. A brief summary of the major types will illustrate this point.

Tropical rain forests   Tropical rain forests represent perhaps the popular concept of underdeveloped forest resources. These occur in greatest abundance in high rainfall areas near the equator, particularly in the basins of the Amazon and the Congo and in the peninsular and insular areas of South-east Asia, but they also range quite widely in smaller concentrations over other parts of the tropics. They cover some 1,000 million hectares and comprise 40 per cent of the forests of the developing countries. The stands are dense and are composed of numerous species, only a few of which at present provide important commercial woods (such as the mahoganies, okoumé, wawa and greenheart). Of the total volume of growing stock, frequently no more than 5 to 10 per cent consists of currently marketable species. The buttressed and fluted bases of the trees, and the abundant growth of climbing vines and creepers, add greatly to the exploitation problem caused by the heterogeneity of the stands.

Moist deciduous forests   Moist deciduous forests are found in tropical and near-tropical areas which have seasonal variation in temperature and rainfall, often on mountain slopes. The stands are also dense but are less heterogeneous than the rain forest. Conifers are sometimes found in admixtures. This forest type is one which has been subjected to considerable population pressures (with consequent clearing for agriculture and shifting cultivation) as well as to the exploitation of a few desired species such as teak and podocarpus. This type accounts for about 200 million hectares – nearly 10 per cent of the forests in the developing regions.

Dry deciduous forests Dry deciduous forests are found in those tropical and sub-tropical areas which have limited rainfall. They are particularly abundant in eastern South America, south-central Africa and southern Asia. The density of the stands is greatly affected by the amount of precipitation, and in drier locations they become open and interspersed with thorn scrub thickets and frequent savannas. Many of these forests have been subjected to frequent burning and sometimes to over-grazing. Except in the moister locations where a few species have commercial value, the trees are very badly formed. These forests comprise about 800 million hectares or 35 per cent of the forests under discussion.

Temperate hardwood forests Temperate hardwood forests account for approximately 50 million hectares of the forest reserves of the developing countries. These forests, found largely in East Asia, parts of the Himalayas and southern Latin America, sometimes include conifers.

Mangrove and bamboo forests Miscellaneous types of more restricted distribution include the mangrove forests of tropical coastlines and bamboo forests. Bamboos are an important component of wet evergreen, moist and dry deciduous forests; they also are found at high altitudes and temperate climates in Asia, and pine bamboo stands frequently follow in the wake of shifting cultivation.

Over the greater part of these forests there has, as yet, been no systematic exploitation, but only a scattered and sporadic use of the forest by local populations for fuel and rudimentary constructional material. Even so, there are vast areas which have been commercially exploited in the past or are being so today. To a large extent this exploitation has been geared to the production of unprocessed wood for export. Progress in establishing local forest industries has been disappointing. And the reason is not that available technology has but limited applicability to the kind of forest reserves which these countries possess. This much is clear if we recall that several of the less developed countries do possess 'orthodox' coniferous forest reserves still undeveloped, reserves which differ little from, and are no whit inferior to, those resources which already sustain sizeable forest industries in the industrially advanced countries. These reserves remain an unrealized potential, even though their composition would readily permit industrialization on the basis of existing technology. Evidently, technology is not all.

In any case, currently available technology is by no means as irrelevant to the circumstances of developing countries as is often supposed. At this stage it may be useful to take a quick look at some of the technological trends which have been at work in the industrially advanced countries over recent decades.

Recent technological trends

Two basic trends can be distinguished, and both have intensified in the post-war period: the broadening of the raw material base for the forest industries, and the fuller utilization of the forest crop.

Both these trends have their origin in the particular circumstances facing established forest industries in the advanced countries. Thus limited availability, or rising costs, of the species preferred for mechanical pulping (spruce, fir, hemlock and pine) has led to the use for groundwood of poplar, aspen and eucalypts. Among the chemical processes, the earliest to be adopted on a large scale was the sulphite process, also suited mainly to the dominant species of the north temperate zone – spruce, firs, hemlock and some pines. Since the early 1930s, however, there has been a spectacular expansion in sulphate pulping capacity, an expansion due to the fact that this process, with greater flexibility and great tolerance to partially decayed wood and bark, can be used for pulping practically all kinds of fibrous raw materials. Finally, since the last war, there have been developed a number of pulping processes which combine mechanical and chemical action, offering higher yields than those obtained by pure chemical processes, and capable of substituting both mechanical and chemical pulps over a wide range.

Thus, over the last thirty years, the relatively narrow raw material base of the paper industry in the advanced countries has been expanded to include all the resinous pines (especially in the United States), birch (formerly a 'weed' tree in Scandinavia), most temperate hardwoods (alone or in mixtures) and various agricultural residues (notably cereal straw and sugar cane waste). For example, hardwoods accounted for 15 per cent of pulping raw materials in Europe in 1961, as against a negligible percentage in 1945. At the same time, much greater use has been made of wood residues from sawmills and plywood plants for pulping. The volume of residues so pulped in Europe rose from 4.5 million cubic metres in 1956 to over 11 million in 1961.

Though the technological progress which has brought about a broadening of the raw material base of the pulp industry has had its main impulse in the raw material supply situation in the advanced areas of the world, it has incidentally made possible the establishment or expansion of the pulp industry in the less developed areas which, by and large, are lacking in the coniferous species which constituted the industry's traditional material. The impact has come not only through the devising of new pulping techniques, but also from a modification of the traditional pulp furnish for the manufacture of different types of paper. It has become increasingly possible to substitute short-fibre pulp for the coniferous long-fibre fraction, without major sacrifice of quality and strength properties. Today there are very few developing countries that do not possess fibrous resources from which it is technically possible to make most grades of paper.

Similar considerations (supply and price) have prompted the remarkable expansion in the advanced countries since the war of the fibreboard and plywood industries, and have brought into existence a completely new industry – particle board – which has grown spectacularly over the last decade. Technical improvements have enabled plywood to replace sawnwood, the real cost of which has risen, in many end-uses. Fibreboard has made similar gains, thanks to improved properties, a broadened raw material base and an improved relative price. The case of particle board is even more striking. Initiated in wood-deficit Germany and making use mainly of mill residues, the industry was favoured by improved and cheaper synthetic resins and captured a large part of the market (for example, as furniture core) previously held by sawnwood. However, the product proved so competitive that it soon spread to the wood-surplus countries of northern Europe, to the United States and to many other parts of the world. Today, particle board plants exist in nearly fifty countries.

Even the sawmilling industry, which has seen no radical technical advance for half a century, has been affected to some extent by the trends just discussed: there is greater emphasis on precision sawing and high yield. Thanks to important advances in wood preservation techniques, less durable species hitherto despised can be given a reasonable life in service and hence find new markets.

These technical advances have been realized by means of research directed towards the solution of those problems which confront forest industries in the industrially advanced countries. The volume of research directed to the specific problems of the less advanced countries is still negligible. But an important incidental effect of these advances is that they have created immensely greater technical possibilities for successfully establishing forest industries in the less developed countries. If these possibilities have so far scarcely been realized, the reason is that as yet efforts to adapt and transfer existing technology to the circumstances of the developing countries have been sporadic, uncoordinated and often half-hearted. This, in turn, is due to the fact that the socio-economic context necessary for the adaptation and application of technology has only recently matured in many of the less developed countries and has still to mature in others.

Where research is lagging

The main need is for the adaptation of available technology, and for applied research rather than for basic research. This is not to deny the need for fundamental research, both for the discipline and training it provides and for the possibility it always offers of radical new discoveries. But, in terms of simple cost/benefits, efforts on a less exalted plane are likely to be more fruitful.

In research, as in technology, emulation of the organization and methods of the more advanced countries is seldom appropriate. There is usually much more to be learned from those countries which have themselves still to contend with serious problems of regional backwardness and are vigorously trying to face up to them. The special contribution which such countries can make is still insufficiently appreciated.

Because the forest resources of the developing countries differ considerably in location, composition and distribution from those of the more advanced countries, one of the most important areas for applied research and experimentation is into the economic and technical factors which bear on the cost of extracting the raw material supply for industry and hence on the raw material input cost per unit on processed output. For the most part these studies should be conducted on the spot, although there is great scope for the coordination of parallel studies on a regional basis. Some of the subjects requiring urgent attention are: minimum input techniques for attaining certain types of forest following exploitation of the original stand; inexpensive methods of protecting from fire, grazing, and so on, in ways that allow for the interests and traditional habits of the local inhabitants; plantation forestry as related to all species of possible interest (here time is important, and the need is for small-scale experiments to be started as soon as possible to gain time, without waiting for the funds needed for a comprehensive programme); suitable logging tools, and suitable combinations of different types of logging equipment with manual work and the use of animals, adapted to the local environment and labour supply conditions; and methods of low-cost forest-road construction and maintenance.

Another desirable area of research concerns problems of storage and shipment, both before and after conversion. So far inadequate attention has been paid to checking or controlling decay, warping, discolouration, and so on, under varying climatic conditions. Specially important are the problems involved in shipping processed wood overseas under different conditions.

Much work has already been done on the physical and chemical characteristics of secondary species, but this work has all too often been carried out in metropolitan countries and aimed at testing candidate export species. More helpful would be engineering studies of the usefulness of these species, with or without preservation, for local housing and non-residential construction, harnessing prefabrication techniques. More work is needed on the properties of plantation species and secondary hardwoods in relation to different pulping processes and for various board products. Cheaper and better glues and resins, where possible manufactures from locally available materials, are needed to improve the properties of plywood and particle board under severe climatic conditions. As regards research on pulp- and paper-processing, the great need is for scaling down the economic production of pulp within the known processes (notably the semi-chemical and the soda and sulphate processes), and for adapting plant design to semi-skilled labour. In sawmilling there is little need for new machines, but great need for improved plant layout as well as considerable scope for the introduction of modern methods of stock control.

These are but a few of the promising avenues for research and experimentation.

All require essentially an objective review of what is already known, and an intelligent adaptation of that knowledge to the specific conditions of developing countries – particularly as regards the local raw materials, the possible scale of operations, and locally available labour and skills.

A large part of the problem is an informational one. The volume of new and relevant information increases annually, and international and national arrangements for pooling, analysing, transmitting and receiving the relevant information are failing to keep pace. Awareness of what has been done elsewhere is a prerequisite for the successful exercise of the imaginative approach and flexibility which alone can ensure the effective adaptation of existing technology to the special circumstances of the developing countries.

Making capital go further

We have seen that several of the principal forest industries are capital-intensive, so far as the processing plant is concerned. It is a common characteristic of countries in the early stages of the growth process – at any rate, as soon as they have committed themselves to a conscious development programme – that capital is scarce and expensive. On the other hand, most of, though by no means all, the developing counries do possess a reserve of unemployed or under-employed rural labour, sometimes amounting to the equivalent of 30 per cent of the active rural population. There is, therefore, a clear need for economizing in capital, provided this is consonant with efficient and economic operation. It does not by any means follow that labour-intensive techniques are invariably to be preferred to capital-intensive ones.

While the choice of techniques must take into account the alternative impact on operating costs, other considerations will frequently bear on the final decision. Labour-intensive methods may be preferred because for political and social reasons it is necessary to create employment opportunities. What should not be overlooked is that factor availability can change rather quickly as the process of industrialization proceeds. Labour which is plentiful and cheap today will certainly, as it acquires skills, organization and an increased sense of dignity, become scarcer and dearer tomorrow. This is not a regrettable contingency; it is the very purpose of development. The corollary is that, in selecting techniques and designing mill layouts, labour-intensive methods should be limited to those stages of the process which lend themselves to ready mechanization at a later stage when it becomes economic. This applies above all to materials-handling operations at either end of the production process.

Forestry and forest industries provide many opportunities of absorbing under- and unemployed labour. Even in the developed countries almost all operations in the forest are carried out by manual labour. Afforestation, thinning, pruning, nursery work and some aspects of insect and fire control, for instance, do not lend themselves readily to mechanization: these operations are mechanized but rarely, and only in those countries where labour is extremely scarce and expensive. The same is true for many aspects of forest exploitation – save in those few instances where large log sizes compel mechanization. What should be emphasized here, however, is that limited or negligible mechanization should not imply primitive methods of work. In all these phases there is ample scope for spectacular increases in productivity by the provision of suitable transport and simple, well adapted tools. These tools should be designed to meet local conditions, and in many cases it will be possible to organize their manufacture locally in small workshops.

So far as the wood-processing plants themselves are concerned, it is to be feared that in the past many opportunities of capital-saving have been neglected. This may be due in part to the fact that it is frequently easier for an entrepreneur, contractor or consulting engineer to operate from established designs and layouts rather than think through every aspect with a view to capital-saving under local conditions. In mill construction, for example, manual labour can often be used in the substitution of expensive construction machinery for excavating foundations and road-making. Buildings can make use of cheap, local building materials and, if the climate allows, outside construction may be adequate for certain phases of the operations. Thorough advance planning by key personnel can do much to cut down actual construction time and hence capital costs. For example, a pulp and paper mill which might take eighteen months to construct in an industrially advanced country commonly takes three years or more in a less developed country; this alone adds 5 to 10 per cent to the investment cost. Seldom can the margin be cut down to zero, but effective pre-planning can reduce the margin and effect considerable savings.

Multipurpose machines offering flexibility in the production programme often have advantages over single-purpose machines where production series are small; this is relevant not only in paper-making, but in such industries as furniture and joinery manufacture. Shonfield[15] attaches much importance to good obsolescent machines, claiming that much of the equipment required during the early stages of industrialization can readily be provided second-hand. Certainly this is a source not to be scorned, for it should be recognized that the relative factor, the availability that made these machines obsolescent elsewhere, is very different from that in the developing countries. In fact, some of the important forest industries existing today have made their start with second-hand equipment. It would be a mistake, however, to exaggerate the part which second-hand equipment can play: (a) it is not always well adapted to local raw materials; (b) spares and replacements often pose major problems; (c) it tends to make excessive demands on skilled labour. It may be observed in passing that the recent trend towards automation in process control in the industrialized countries is very relevant to industrialization in the developing

---

[15] Andrew Shonfield, *The Attack on World Poverty* (London, 1960), pp. 163ff.

countries. There is nothing either bizarre or contradictory in installing electronic equipment inside the mill, where it can replace special skills that take many years of training and experience to acquire, and making lavish use of manual labour in the woodyard.

It is common knowledge that operating ratios (the relation between actual output and nominal or all-out capacity) are much lower in developing countries than in industrialized countries. This is one of the main sources of capital wastage. The most frequent causes of stoppages and high breakdown time are low standards of maintenance and delays in obtaining replacements and spares. Sustained effort can reduce these losses, for example, by special emphasis on planned preventive maintenance or by standardizing auxiliary equipment such as electric motors and pumps. There are, in fact, many types of auxiliary equipment common to forest industries and other sectors of industry. Careful study of joint requirements may well establish a case for domestic production of these items. This is not only a useful way of effecting import substitution; the fact of their being locally available can do much to employ fixed investment more effectively in all the industries served, by reducing shutdown time. Central repair shops, serving several industries, can also contribute.

Many of the forest industries – plywood, veneer, blockboard, joinery, furniture, paper conversion, to name a few – are suitable for operations on a modest scale and can be accommodated on industrial estates where all types of common services can reduce the capital needs for each individual venture and also assure efficient deployment of managerial and other skills.

Forest industries in developing countries often require relatively much more working capital than their counterparts in industrially advanced countries, for lack of effective coordination between production programmes at the mill and sales trends. Special attention to these problems, and the adoption of various simple systems of stock control which have now been developed, can help to reduce working capital needs.

The difficulties imposed on developing countries by the limited size of the domestic market have already been sufficiently stressed. At the same time it has been made clear that, so far as forest products are concerned, markets are in continuous, and often very rapid, expansion. All new ventures, therefore, should be planned from the outset with a view to subsequent expansion. This concerns not only the raw material catchment area, but also land, buildings, plant layout, and so on, as well as, in some cases, the selection of process plant. This may require slightly higher investment per unit of output in the first instance, but will lead to very substantial capital savings later – perhaps within two or three years. In the pulp and paper industry, for example, the new investment needed to add a given capacity expansion to an existing mill is generally only 50 to 70 per cent of that required to establish a separate mill of equivalent capacity.

This brief discussion of capital-saving possibilities is not, of course, comprehensive, but merely indicative. It serves to show, however, that many possibilities exist, not all of which have been realized in the past. One reason, of course, is that hitherto the total market for forest industry equipment in the developing countries has been rather small in relation to the annual requirements in the industrially advanced countries. The consequence has been that but few manufacturers have devoted much attention to the special needs of the developing countries. Over the next decade these equipment needs will represent a very considerable market in their own right. It was seen earlier that total investment needs in primary forest industries in the less developed countries could amount to $5,000 million up to 1970 if industrial development should take place to the extent needed to prevent imports of processed wood goods from rising. Two thirds or more of this sum would represent expenditure on forest industry equipment. It is clear that those equipment manufacturers who concentrate on designing and making what is needed, rather than on selling what they are accustomed to making, will be in the best position to take advantage of the opportunities this expanding market affords. It is clear, also, that the scale of expansion in many of the larger developing countries offers opportunities for the domestic manufacture of some, if not all, of the necessary equipment.

DETERMINING THE ROLE OF FORESTRY

The intimate interrelation between the forestry and forest industry sectors means that a coherent forestry plan is a prerequisite for the sound long-term development of forest industries. Planning forestry with due regard to the other economic sectors involves:

1 Estimating the future demand for wood and for the non-crop utilities that the forests can provide: this refers both to the forests already in existence and to those that may have to be created;
2 Estimating the size and the nature of the forest resource, and appraising the extent to which essential production factors might be available for forestry;
3 Determining the plan within the context of the economic needs of the country as also the measures for the execution of the plan.

Planners, especially in countries where the economy is in the early stages of development, will often find inadequate the data on which decisions are to be based. Such lack of data ought not to delay planning unduly. Plans, however, provisional, should be formulated and applied; they can be revised as additional knowledge becomes available. This is particularly important where tendencies hostile to forests are at work that may cause considerable damage in a brief span of time.

Estimating the demand for wood

Consideration must be given to the future internal demand for wood in all forms, ranging from fuelwood and saw timber to the wood component of elaborate products such as paper and board, and to plans for export, if any.

Projections of demand as conditioned by internal consumption and export possibilities must be made for the next fifteen to twenty years, indicating the size and composition of the demand at convenient intervals, for example, of five years. These demand projections (which specify roundwood needs from the forest) are derivations of the more detailed demand projections required to specify forest industry plans – both for the next industry planning period, be it three, five, or seven years, and for the perspective plan of fifteen, twenty or twenty-five years which, in this sector, should provide the frame for the shorter-term plan. Since many undertakings in forestry require considerably more time than fifteen or twenty years to reach fulfilment, changes in demand in the more distant future should also be considered. It is true that the possibility of relevant action within the period of the short-term plan may be limited, but this is no reason for disregarding likely long-term changes. The long-term prospects are particularly relevant to decisions concerning, and provisional measures directed to, integrated land-use policies, including questions of forest reservation.

Internal consumption and export are interdependent. They are complementary when leading to economies of scale, or when, by creating a more varied market, they permit a fuller utilization of the resource: as is well known, intensive forest exploitation commonly yields wood of different species, or of the same species but appropriate to different uses, or both, while the industrialization of the wood yields produce of different grades, and sometimes several joint products. On the other hand, there are also situations where export and internal needs cannot be reconciled, and planners must weigh the advantages of export earnings against future difficulties in supplying those needs.

In considering future demand, the possibilities of deliberately planned substitution should be appraised. Many products based on wood can be substituted by others that are not, and vice versa; in addition, there are important and steadily expanding possibilities for substitution within the field of wood proper. Kinds and qualities of wood that are relatively abundant or can be quickly grown in plantations may serve as substitutes for scarcer materials. Imaginative substitution can be of great importance to a growing economy as an import-saving or export-earning device. In certain cases it may be found worth while to use temporary substitutes that are to some extent inferior. Substitution may involve technical study and, in addition, inertia and bias may have to be overcome.

Estimating the demand for the non-crop utilities of forests

These utilities, nowadays often termed forest influences, may be grouped as follows, using a recent classification:[16]

1   Direct influences, roughly corresponding to mechanical effects, or rather to influences in which mechanical action appears to play a preponderant part. This category includes the protective action of the forest against falls of stone from rocks or scree areas lying above the forest, or against avalanches, and especially the manner in which it acts as a windscreen.

2   Indirect influences, comprising those in which the physicochemical influences play the principal, though not the only, role. These are the influences which, by modifying the environment, let the forest affect soil retention and the water cycle.

3   Psychophysiological influences – a category that apparently has to be differentiated, although, as for the other categories, the influences that may be grouped in this category are derived largely from mechanical or physicochemical effects. But they have now become so great, particularly in heavily industrialized countries where there is a marked population increase, that they cannot be ignored. These are the influences which directly interest man, since they provide him with a better environment: purified air, rest and recreation areas (green belts), tourism, sports, and so on.

Forest influences form part of the socio-economic infrastructure of a country; as might be expected, the general public is not aware of their usefulness to the same extent as in the case of infrastructural elements that enter the everyday life of most citizens, such as roads, schools or medical services. Also, scientific knowledge on some of the more complex influences of forests is relatively little advanced. Yet there can be no doubt that their overall importance to a community is enormous.

From the point of view of planning, forest influences must be appraised in relation to the economic and other sectors of life that these influences serve: the protective effects of a shelter-belt have no significance except in relation to the crops that are shielded from winds; the hygienic and recreational values of a green belt only acquire meaning when considered in relation to a town. In this sense, forest influences are the concern of the agricultural planner, the urban planner, and the like and it is their function to decide whether the aims that they have in view should be attained with the aid of forestry or through other means, whenever there is a choice of means.

---

[16] FAO, *Forest Influences*, FAO Forestry and Forest Products Studies no. 15 (Rome, 1962), pp. 248–9.

However, since forests rarely serve only non-crop functions – they nearly always also produce, or can be made to produce, wood at the same time – and since, on the other hand, every forest can acquire some of the non-crop functions under certain circumstances, these functions, or influences, of forests are inseparable from forestry planning. It is necessary, therefore, to estimate future requirements in relation to likely developments in farming, colonization, urban expansion, and so on. These appraisals are indispensable elements of the plan for the forestry sector, but they can be derived only from the other economic sectors and the overall needs of the region.

In planning the treatment of a forest, it is often difficult to decide whether a certain area deserves special consideration on account of the non-crop functions that it may be exercising or may come to exercise in the near future; common sense suggests that uncertainty in this respect justifies cautious treatment.

Estimating the size and the nature of the forest resource

This involves the perusal of the available data and the collection of new data by means of forest surveys and related studies. In regions possessing major forest resources, such surveys may require many years of work, yet some of the data may be urgently needed for planning. Often situations arise that call for no small measure of judgement in deciding on geographic priority and the degree of precision to be aimed at in surveys. It is convenient to distinguish three types of survey, of different intensity, each appropriate to different phases of planning.

Reconnaissance surveys are designed to furnish at low cost preliminary information concerning the location and extent of large areas of forest.

At the next stage, more detailed classification of forest areas is required, together with estimates of volumes of standing timber and some information about species and dimensions. Nationwide coverage at this intensity will eventually be required; in developing countries areas so inventoried can be considered as the first contributions to the national forest inventory. Though obviously more expensive than reconnaissance surveys, costs per unit area need not be high, and already provisional decisions, positive or negative, can be taken – so far as the timber supply is concerned – about potential projects.

For a final decision, and in particular for the working plan which will embody management decisions in relation to the timber supply area, more intensive inventories are required. Detailed forest maps will be essential, as will volume estimates, by species and diameter classes, and preferably also by quality classes. Costs per unit area will be a good deal higher than for national forest inventories and, *a fortiori*, for reconnaissance surveys.

Until recently, one of the most serious obstacles to forest industry development in the less advanced countries was the high cost of obtaining essential data concerning the forest resource. This state of affairs has now been radically altered. The tremendous advances made in aerial photography and photo-interpretation techniques – new high-precision cameras, wide-angled lenses, infra-red photography, improved films and electronic printers – have all played their part in producing better-quality aerial photographs from which more information can be extracted. Again, the application of modern statistical sampling techniques to forest surveys has made possible greater precision at lower cost. Finally, modern methods of data processing have facilitated the compilation and analysis of inventory data.

Information will be required not only on the physical nature of the forests – their area, location, composition, wood volume, growth, and so on – but also on their distribution according to ownership and the size of individual properties; these latter considerations may have a decisive influence on the pattern of subsequent development. The extent and methods of treatment and utilization, industrial and other, as also the non-crop functions of the various forest areas, must be checked.

Appraising the availability of production factors

The availability of land, manpower, and capital must now be appraised.

Land   Afforestation will involve occupying land at present not under forest. Conversely, some of the existing forests may have to give way to arable farming, pasture and townships. In either case, sound decisions on the most appropriate use of a given area of land cannot be made except within the framework of an integrated land-utilization programme.

The transfer of land from forestry to other uses ought not to be undertaken without sound reasons; such transfer has led to regrets in countless instances. The relinquishment of land from forestry may involve several losses. In the first place, the area concerned obviously ceases to produce wood. Secondly, total wood production in the locality may be lowered to the detriment of future supplies to the population or forest-industrial development. Thirdly, and in spite of good intentions to the contrary, important non-crop functions of the forest are liable to be impaired. In addition to all this, clearing very often involves appreciable waste of wood that is difficult or even impossible to avoid. Probable losses must be weighed against the benefits of transfer and, if the latter is decided upon, losses must be minimized as much as possible.

Needless to say, the withdrawal of land from forestry hardly makes sense unless it is permanently suited to the new use. Many of the colonization schemes of the past did not pay sufficient regard to the capacities of the soil and, now that the need for a more equitable distribution of farmland has become a pressing issue in many countries in Latin America and elsewhere, there is a danger that haste, expedience, or both, may lead to a repetition of past errors. Under certain circumstances, properly conducted colonization can help to ease agrarian problems. But, unless the land is right for the purpose, an extension of cultivation will not bring relief to rural misery but will only extend its bounds.

It is also worth bearing in mind that forestry can often assist colonization in a very direct manner: work in forests can help to equalize the distribution of the work of settlers throughout the seasons of the year, and can provide them with much-needed cash income; in certain cases, controlled grazing in the forest can benefit cattle while reducing the fire hazard to the forest; and so on. These aspects of forestry are sometimes overlooked in the clamour for more agricultural land.

Manpower   The treatment and exploitation of the existing forests and the establishment of plantations in new areas demand the application of manpower of various levels of skill. In underdeveloped economies, managerial and professional skills tend to be scarce, and so does skilled labour, while unskilled or semi-skilled labour tends to be abundant, although scarcities may occur locally or at certain seasons of the year. Often the availability of capable management is decisive. Where this can be found, a large proportion of the administrative and manual tasks in forestry can be broken up and distributed in a manner that permits economy of scarce or relatively scarce skills, while also facilitating training at different levels. Such training should avoid wasteful 'spreading out'; it should be confined to essentials, so as to build up rapidly the required manpower.

Although continuity of operations is very important in forestry, much of the manual work is not tied to a strict time schedule, so that it is possible to use seasonal surplus labour from agriculture, unemployed labour, and so on. These important possibilities must be taken into account.

Capital   The characteristic scarcities of capital in underdeveloped economies affect forestry in common with all other activities. Forestry needs to depend relatively little on foreign-exchange availabilities provided it is possible to substitute expensive equipment, which would have to be imported, by the use of labour, rendered more productive with the aid of suitable tools or of inexpensive small machinery.

Since public ownership occupies a very important place in forestry throughout the world, a large part of all forestry activity is in the hands of government departments, either central or local. Their finance usually follows the general budgeting procedures of the country or locality concerned; occasionally special funds or block grants are provided to cover departmental expenses over a period of years. Forest departments in most countries have come to be regarded as entities of a quasi-commercial nature; they are expected to show the highest possible financial return that is compatible with sound operation. However, it is unusual for a department to show surpluses in the early stages of work, even when it controls valuable forest resources, since considerable inputs are needed to bring the forests under proper management. Moreover, sales of

produce have to be carried out in a manner more conducive to forest-industrial development than to departmental revenue.

With the development of international finance designed to benefit the less developed countries, some governments have been able to obtain finance from international and bilateral funds, either in convenient loans or as grants. In this way, they have obtained infrastructural investments that have facilitated, or will eventually facilitate in a fairly immediate manner, the development of their forests. Such investments include the building of roads and of power plants within, or in the vicinity of, forest regions. There seems to be no palpable reason why similar finance should be impossible for certain investments in forestry proper, such as afforestation that may be required in order to supplement a local forest resource, where, for example, the latter provides a good basis for initiating a forest industry but planting by government is needed to assure long-term supplies. In a case like this, payment of interest and amortization of the principal may, in fact, be easier to perform than in the more conventional infrastructural loan, since the assurance of funds for afforestation will create the possibility of selling wood to industry from the existing public forests.

Credit capital plays an important part in the forestry of commercial companies; such finance is normally obtained for the sum total of their activities, of which forestry is one. In a number of countries, the government has made available special long-term credits to forest owners, communities and cooperative societies for such purposes as afforestation and the drainage of forests. Usually this type of credit is linked to certain measures of government control, and it can be a useful policy instrument for assisting, subsidizing and controlling non-state forestry.

Determining the plan and the measures to be adopted

In many of the less developed countries, forestry programmes will have to be judged to a very great extent by their overall effect on the balance of payments and the increase of national wealth as related to certain objectives. For instance, a forestry programme might be appraised by the extent to which, in providing the raw material basis for forest industries, it will contribute to the amount of capital available for such annual investment in the economy as is considered necessary in order to maintain a certain rate of economic growth. Whatever the criteria adopted, the quality of the decisions in determining the forestry plan will depend to a great extent on the knowledge and planning available for all the sectors of the economy, including the foreign trade related to each.

No matter what the total input assigned to the forestry of the region, the distribution of this input will vary according to the technical condition and the economic significance of forest stands; and intensity of treatment may range all the way from minimum protection against destructive agencies, notably fire, in remote areas, to the most intensive management and silvicultural treatment in the neighbourhood of wood-using industries. Normally, working plans will be drawn up, laying down the objectives and working procedure for each major area and its subdivisions.

In some cases, exploitation may be carried into virgin forest areas. In principle, the working of these areas is desirable, since it means mobilizing new resources and, where a fire hazard exists, it will facilitate control, by rendering these areas more accessible, creating settlements of forest workers that can be called upon in an emergency, and so on. However, there is also some danger involved. The opening-up of these areas may distract attention from the need for better utilization practices in those already being worked; it may mean the extension of undesirable practices of exploitation. Not infrequently it may be wiser to leave alone new areas of virgin forest until organization of forestry has progressed to a stage when they can be handled with relative ease.

Technically, afforestation work need not differ from the replanting of felled areas. Financially, there is often an important difference, since the latter type of planting is undertaken within a going forestry concern, whereas the former very often is not. In regions very poor in forest, afforestation is unlikely to alter the position radically within the normal span of the forestry plan. Yet a great deal can often be accomplished with relatively modest input, for instance, where wood from fast-growing plantations can supplement wood-waste from different sources to an extent permitting the establishment of a local industry.

Forestry occupies a somewhat peculiar position in the political thought of most developed countries, including those with liberal economies, in that public ownership or at least a large measure of direct or indirect intervention in private and other non-state enterprise has long been regarded as a necessity. In the course of time, a vast body of experience has been gained, under the most varied conditions, on methods of administration, organization, management, the exploitation best suited to public forests, the techniques of selling their produce, the role of the state in forestry education and research, and so forth, as also on the scope and the limitations of numerous techniques of state intervention through assistance and legislative control. In many cases, assistance by the state has proved more effective, and control less irksome, when exercised through the intermediary of cooperative and other associations of forest owners.

Those concerned with forestry in the less developed countries will be able to draw on this vast experience when considering methods of handling public forests and of ensuring overall coordination through public intervention. One word of caution is perhaps necessary: planning that overreaches itself, that fails to take account of local limitations, especially those imposed by the size and training of the professional and administrative staff of forest departments, is a travesty of planning. In the past there have been too many instances of forest laws enacted whose provisions have proved inapplicable in practice because of lack of means of enforcement and for want of popular acceptance. There have been concessions granted, containing admirable provisions for silvicultural measures to accompany exploitation, which provisions have been ignored in practice for lack of professional control. Ambitious planting programmes have been announced in a blaze of publicity, only to die a silent death as earmarked funds are quietly diverted to other uses.

The lesson is not that those responsible for the establishment and execution of forestry plans ought to lower their aims or stifle their sense of urgency. The lesson is rather that, unless provision is made within the framework of the plan for the creation of trained cadres and for the guaranteed career prospects that will ensure the forest service against wastage, the plan is incomplete.

PLANNING FOR FOREST-INDUSTRIAL DEVELOPMENT

In their general aspects, the problems of planning the development of forest industries have much in common with the problems of planning any industrial sector. With these general aspects of industrial development planning and programming we shall not concern ourselves here, since they are already reasonably well documented.

We shall, instead, content ourselves with drawing attention to certain special aspects of planning for forest industry development which stem from the particular characteristics of these industries and their relationship with other sectors of the economy.

The time horizons for planning

The forester and the industrial development planner inevitably differ in the emphasis they lay on the different time horizons for planning. We have already drawn attention to the long-term nature of many forest operations, and the consequent need for long-term projections of requirements, however approximate, to provide an order of magnitude of future demands on the forest in its capacity as a 'woodshed' for forest industries. Few other sectors of the economy have the same need to look so far ahead, since very long-term considerations, for example, to the end of the century, weigh less heavily on current decisions. The industrial planner, certainly, is concerned mainly with the current or imminent general economic planning period, whether it be three, five or seven years. In recent years there has been a trend to the use of perspective planning – setting out broad outlines and provisional targets for up to fifteen or twenty years ahead, as a background for current planning. The current plan, in these cases, is seen as the first instalment of the perspective plan. The perspective plan itself (as well as its second instalment, the next short-term plan) is progressively modified and adapted in accordance with new data on needs and possibilities – and in particular in the light of achievements of past plan periods.

Perspective planning has everything to recommend it, and it is significant that it is finding increasing favour both in centrally planned economies and in economies which rest mainly on free enterprise. However, the point that needs to be made in the present context is that, for forest industry development, perspective planning is mandatory. This much is evident from the characteristics of forestry as we earlier described them. To establish a pulp and paper mill in a given location in ten or fifteen years' time, it may be necessary to intervene in the forest now, to supplement the resource, or arrange for its eventual gradual replacement by plantations, or simply to ensure that the resource is still there when it is needed. But there is another consideration which argues for perspective planning. Some major projects in the forest industries sector may take from five to seven years to realize if, as is frequently the case, feasibility studies have to start with a detailed inventory of the forest resource. Such projects inevitably spill over from one plan period to the next. What is needed, therefore, is a forward planning group that can look ahead beyond the immediate plan period; this group can ensure that resources are not misallocated in the short-term plan. To meet the general targets which have been adopted, a series of specific projects should be under study. Some, as investigatory work is completed, can be immediately implemented; others will be discarded; others will be taken up as resources permit and the need arises. In other words, the short-term plan should not only include certain specific projects to be realized within the plan period; it should also include provision for data collection, pilot investigations and project planning needed for succeeding plan periods.

Getting and using resource data

It is clear that data pertaining to the forest resource, the forest inventory, represent an important category of information required in planning forest industry development. No prospectus for investment in forest industries can be prepared without this information. Some of the technical aspects of obtaining these data were touched on in the preceding section. The point to be stressed here is that this is the kind of information that governments must possess themselves. The cost of acquiring it, though very much cheaper than even a decade ago, is still considerable, and there may be an inclination to leave data collection to entrepreneurs and potential investors. This is a mistake. Unless governments have their own data they are in no position to weigh the pros and cons of various projects and pronounce on the validity of projects submitted to them. If concessions or contracts are eventually involved, they are unlikely to be able to negotiate these concessions or contracts on equitable terms. Moreover, even if privately obtained data are turned over to the government, the likelihood is that the inventory will have been tailored to the expected requirements (areas, species, dimensions) of the private party, and will therefore be unsuited or inadequate for use in assessing the prospects for alternative projects, perhaps in other branches of forest industry. This point is particularly important at the present time when technology is making rapid strides; the possibility always exists that species and dimensions presently unconsidered may be effectively utilized in the not distant future.

In the past a common feature of forest exploitation in the developing countries has been single-commodity exploitation. This has meant that much useful timber has been left in the forest, since it was not adapted to the purpose of the operator or, sometimes, that timber extracted has been put to uses lower than its intrinsic qualities merited. Instances of integrated forest industry development, with integral utilization of the forest crop, have been rare. But governments have a profound interest in the fullest utilization of the forest crop, for technical as well as economic reasons, and will seek to influence operators in this direction when negotiating concessions. This they can hardly do without adequate knowledge of the forest resource.

Planning demand

The broad indications of demand trends for forest products which suffice for establishing forest production goals will not, of course, be adequate for planning forest industry projects. Much more detailed investigations of present and potential markets for particular products and grades are necessary. In many developing countries the starting point for an assessment of current consumption will be an examination of the import statistics, since imports are the only present source for many processed forest products. Demand projections, based on such parameters as per caput income and demographic growth, can be helpful. But for considering specific industrial projects it is necessary to get down to further detail by investigating, for instance, the specific requirements of other sectoral developments, and particularly of major potential consumers such as of bags for cement, boxes and crates for fruit exports, of sawnwood and wood-based sheet materials for housing programmes, and so forth.

It was noted earlier that most of the demand for forest products consists of inter-sectoral demand rather than final consumption. In many developing countries a substantial proportion of the total demand may well arise either in the public sector itself or as a direct consequence of government programmes, such as railways and other utilities, housing, school buildings, works departments. Governments are thus well placed not only to encourage or promote the establishment of appropriate forest industries, but also to influence production standards.

This significance of this role will be appreciated if it is borne in mind that, in developing countries, construction, as distinct from equipment, may account for 50 to 70 per cent of total fixed investment. Thus housing and urban facilities have a large share wherever there is a substantial transfer of population from agriculture to industry, while the importance of public works and public utilities (roads, docks, transport, water, electricity, schools, hospitals and government buildings) is always great in the first decades of development, declining thereafter. The great importance of construction has not always been fully considered in development programmes, and the scarcity of building capacity has often been the principal obstacle to stepping up the rate of capital formation. A common error is failure to provide for the necessary output of building materials and components.[17]

Not only can the government, as major consumer, decisively influence the demand for sawnwood, wood-based panels and other construction timber; by properly planning its demand it can help industries to specialize in making parts and components, such as panels, windows, doors, staircases and bearing elements.

Skilled labour is often a bottleneck in expanding construction. For this reason special attention should be paid to labour-saving construction materials such as plywood, particle board, fibreboard and wood-wool board. In the developed countries, shortage of construction labour has been a major factor in increasing the demand for wood-based panels.

It is not necessary to discuss here the standard measures which a country may take to encourage industrial development: tax exemptions, tariffs, subsidies and the like. These are common to all industries, and here we are concerned only with aspects special to the forest industries. There is, however, one further point arising from the demand characteristics for forest products which is perhaps worth mentioning. It has already been noted that many of the forest products are broadly substitutive over a wide range of end-uses. This applies, for example, to the three major wood-based sheet material industries. If none of these industries exists at present, and if there are sound technical and economic grounds for preferring to develop one rather than the others, judicious import regulations can be helpful in both testing and priming the market.

The importance of infrastructure

The location of forests in relation to population concentrations, the transport volumes and distances involved in both raw material procurement and product distribution, and the technical requirements of forest industries, all combine to make the development of this industrial sector – perhaps more than that of

[17] It is interesting to note that, in the USSR, one of the main principles in planning the material and technical basis of construction is that its development should keep ahead of the increase in the volume of construction envisaged in the plan. To this end, a higher rate of growth is planned for the gross output of the building materials industry than for the total volume of construction. *See* A. T. Repenko, *The Material and Technical Implementation of Housing Programmes, report on the seminar on housing surveys and programmes with particular reference to problems in the developing countries* (United Nations, Geneva, 1962).

any other – heavily dependent on progress in creating certain basic infrastructural facilities: power, water, road and rail communications, and port facilities. At first sight, this fact might seem a discouraging one for developments in this sector. There can be no doubt that in the past it has had an inhibiting effect. Governments and private entrepreneurs, attracted by the idea of valorizing a particular forest resource by establishing a major forest industry unit, have often renounced the undertaking once it was realized that it would be necessary to create those forms of social overhead capital which already exist in the industrially advanced countries. The cost of providing these facilities, when shouldered entirely by an individual project, would add perhaps 50 per cent to the cost of investment.

Today the situation has radically changed. Not only has the concept of industrialization as a conscious and organized process won full acceptance in the developing countries; it is understood that successful industrial develop-ment can take place only if governments deliberately set about creating the necessary infrastructure. The important thing from the planning standpoint is that infrastructural investment plans should take full account of the forest industry development possibilities that they can provide. This applies when mapping out new roads and railways, siting power stations and power lines, or developing new or improved port and harbour facilities. Not only can judicious planning help to bring new forest industries into existence; the industries they generate will often represent the first major financial return on the infrastructural investment undertaken. In some cases, they may provide the decisive element in determining whether to undertake a particular infra-structural investment or not.

Planning for specific areas within a country

Next, a word on the area aspects of planning. The emphasis given to area planning, and the degree of initiative accorded to areas in both plan formulation and plan implementation, will vary from country to country. The central problem will always be how to harness most effectively local energies and enthusiasms without falling into inconsistency in aims and errors in phasing, both as between the several areas and as regards the relation between central and local targets. In large countries, of course, a considerable measure of de-centralization is inevitable if planning is to be effective.

Planning by area assumes particular importance for forestry and forest industries. It is at this level that the non-crop functions of the forest can best be appreciated and the social implications of customary rights in the forest fully understood. Moreover, from the industrial aspect, while there are certain forest industries that must clearly have a national range in order to prosper, there are other branches which can successfully operate on a smaller scale. From the standpoint of economic development (including industrialization), there is much to be said for studying the forestry and forest industry development possibilities of a country not simply in terms of the country as a whole, but also in terms of defined forest-economic areas within it. These areas should be defined not simply on the basis of existing or potential forest resources, but also by taking into account population concentrations, other physical endowments, current and future claims on the land, and so forth. This approach can be helpful in assuring a clear orientation of the aims of forest policy in each area. Thus certain areas will be clearly marked to become principal wood reservoirs for major forest industries serving the whole country. In others, an ordered transfer of forest land to agricultural use, while retaining sufficient land under forest to supply industries serving local needs and to assure maintenance of non-crop utilities, can be permitted. Finally, there will be areas where the main emphasis will have to be placed on protective forestry, with forest industries playing a subordinate and perhaps negligible role.

Autarchy or economic integration?

Some developing countries, oppressed by the prospect of a steeply rising import bill for forest products, have already resolutely undertaken programmes of forestry and forest industry development, and a careful examination of these programmes suggests that, in one or two cases, national self-sufficiency in forest products is the implicit, though seldom explicit, ultimate goal. The programmes already established do not overlook the fact that, in some instances, certain commodities produced from the indigenous forest resource will find difficulty in competing on even terms with the products of the industrially advanced countries. Justification is found in the pressing need to save foreign exchange, in the fact that industrialization in any sector is unlikely to suceed without a measure of protection, and perhaps even in the fact that a vigorous forestry programme is required in any case to assure the flow of non-crop utilities of the forest. Sound as these arguments may be, it would be a serious mistake to suppose that they can be held to justify the goal of self-sufficiency in forest products in all instances.

Mention has been made earlier of the fact that current moves towards economic integration among the less industrialized countries can favour the development of certain industries by extending the market and thus overcoming the obstacle presented by small national markets in branches of the industry where scale economies are pronounced (such as newsprint and chemical pulp). This in itself is a very strong argument in favour of the confrontation, and if necessary the adjustment, of national plans for forestry industry development on the part of countries participating in economic integration schemes. Indeed, without such confrontation and adjustment, there is danger that mutually inconsistent plans may be pursued and the avowed aims of economic integration frustrated.

But small national markets and economies of scale are not the only reasons for giving special attention to the forest industries within areas of economic integration. In the less developed countries, where economic integration schemes are already moving forward or are at present being discussed, there is often a wide disparity in the natural forest endowment and in the suitability for growing different types of timber. Moreover, there is often a large measure of complementarism in the nature of the forest resource held by different countries within the area, for instance, as regards short-fibred and long-fibred material for paper-making. It is only common sense that these disparities, and this complementarism where it exists, should be taken into account in any mutual agreement on these national development plans which will make for optimum regional economic development. The advantages lie partly in the programmed international division of labour, partly in securing the optimum utilization of the region's forest resources. In many cases the adoption of national self-sufficiency in forest products as the goal to be achieved will mean deliberately forgoing these advantages.

An organizational need

Whatever the role that may be accorded to public and private enterprise respectively in developing forest industries, there is, and must always be, an indissoluble link between the development of this sector and the forest resource on which it is to be based. This argues the need for a specially close and intimate relationship between those authorities responsible for the forests (usually the forest service, a department of the Ministry of Agriculture) and those responsible for planning and encouraging industrial development. Unless there is the closest coordination, the danger is always present that, on the one hand, the forester may forget that his function is to serve people, not to serve trees, while on the other the industrial developer may ignore, to the cost of the community, and perhaps to his own, both the dynamics of the forest and its important functions other than as a wood-provider.

It is a regrettable fact in most developing countries (and for that matter in several more advanced countries) that as yet no effective link exists. That this has led in many cases to reckless and wasteful use of the forest resource is widely recognized; its legacy is felt in the significant proportion of total forestry effort which has now to be devoted to what are essentially rehabilitation measures. What is perhaps less widely understood is that this lack of effective collaboration has been largely responsible for the failure to recognize, plan and realize hundreds of perfectly sound and feasible forest industry projects.

It is idle to imagine that this situation can be remedied merely by establishing formal links. If foresters, forest utilization officers, industrial economists and development planners are to reach a mutual understanding of each other's problems and to explore creatively the development opportunities that lie in the forests, working contacts must be multiplied at all levels. These are the considerations which have led some countries, in which forest industries already play or are clearly destined to play a key role, to concentrate responsibility for forestry and forest industries in the same department or ministry. This solution is not likely to be universally valid; but the problem of achieving an organic and creative working relation between the two sectors has to be solved if a vigorous programme of industrial development based on the forest is to be realized.

The choice

In the forgoing paragraphs we have referred to some of the problems of planning for forest industry development which arise from the peculiarity of the forestry and forest industry sectors and their relation with each other. The list is intended to be illustrative, not exhaustive. Each example quoted, however, implies a particular responsibility on the part of governments if these sectors are to be effectively developed. This could hardly be otherwise, given the nature of the resource itself. And this is true whatever the political philosophy inspiring government action, whatever the type and degree of planning undertaken by government to promote the welfare of their peoples.

It has been shown that the forests have a great potential as a source of human welfare, and that industrialization based on the forest can both contribute to and promote the general economic development process. Yet it must be acknowledged that the mobilization of the forest resource through the establishment of forest industries is not a prospect that brings unmixed joy to the hearts of many professional foresters. They know only too well that, if the forest is to fulfil its role, there must be exact knowledge of the resource, the forest must be brought under proper management, working plans must be devised, and extraction schemes worked out. Only thus can the resource base of industry be made secure. But these tasks require strong and effective forest services, and today forest services in many developing countries are still extremely weak. It is awareness of the danger this situation represents, not any mistaken attachment to the idea of conservation as an end in itself, which impels many foresters to don the mantle of Cassandra.

But it would be a mistake to cherish illusions on this point. And it is an illusion to suppose that there exists choice between mobilizing the forests now, and leaving them intact until forest services have been built up to the point where it is safe to open the forest gate. The technical and economic conditions for establishing new forest industries in the developing countries are maturing fast. In the course of the coming years many new areas of forest are inevitably going to be brought into use. The choice is between mobilization in the public interest based on sound planning and with adequate safeguards and with the forest services taking an active part and being built up in the process, and mobilization taking place in an uncontrolled and haphazard way, while weak forest services stand by helpless. This is the real choice.

It is in making this choice that the responsibility of government is engaged. For this is not a question which concerns a forest department alone; it concerns ministers of agriculture, economy, industry and trade; it concerns planning departments and development agencies; it concerns finance ministries and budget bureaux. Only concerted action on the part of all departments can ensure that forest industries play their part in the attack on economic underdevelopment, and that the immense contribution which forests, rightly used, can make to the development process is fully realized.

2

Prospects for Expanding Forest Products Exports from Developing Countries

This paper does not discuss the general problems of raising the economic growth rate in the developing countries. It takes for granted (a) that the growth prospects for the developing countries are closely linked to their ability to raise their foreign exchange earnings; (b) that at the present time they are highly dependent on a limited range of traditional exports of primary products, predominantly of agricultural origin; (c) that it is necessary to lessen this dependence by progressively developing and diversifying their economies and stepping up their exports of processed goods and manufactures.

This paper examines the possibilities for expanding exports of one particular commodity group, namely forest products, from the developing countries. It is argued that there are moderately good prospects in the short run, say, to 1970 or 1975, and very good prospects in the longer run. These favourable prospects spring from important readjustments which are now beginning to take place in the world forest and timber economy. Moreover, the establishment of forest industries to process these exports (and to satisfy rising domestic requirements) would have an important propulsive effect on the general development of the economies of these countries.

However, this development is not inevitable. If it is to be realized it must be planned for. That is to say, those developing countries which wish to take advantage of the opportunities which will arise must plan the development of their forest resources and forest industries to this end. In some cases a restructuring of existing forest industries will be necessary. The coordination of plans at the regional and sub-regional levels could help to avoid misinvestment.

Moreover, this consummation could be delayed, impeded, even aborted,

A paper prepared for the regional economic commissions of the United Nations by the Forestry and Forest Products Division of the Food and Agriculture Organization, February 1964, 41pp. Reproduced with permission of the author and the Food and Agriculture Organization of the United Nations.

by the developed countries – both those with a market economy and those centrally planned – unless they are prepared to recognize the fundamental changes taking place in the world forest and timber economy and are prepared to adjust their policies to these changes. Contrariwise, the developed countries can – at both government and industry levels – do much to facilitate the required development. Important progress could be achieved through bilateral trade/ development projects, for which the objective conditions in this sector are peculiarly propitious. Moreover, this type of project would be appropriate for, and would often require, support from international public financing institutions.

FOREST PRODUCTS IN WORLD TRADE:
THE DEVELOPING COUNTRIES' SHARE

The value of world trade in forest products in 1961, at f.o.b. export prices, was slightly more than six and a half billion dollars, and comprised nearly 5 per cent of all world trade. This total includes cork products, waste paper, and some manufactures of wood and paper, which are excluded from consideration in this paper. Table 2.1 compares the total of the main forest products exports (sawlogs and veneer logs, pulpwood and pitprops, sawnwood, plywood, woodpulp, newsprint, other paper and paperboard: these together account for nearly nine tenths of forest products exports) with total commodity exports by major economic regions.

Thus these main forest products represented, in 1959/61, 4.3 per cent of export trade in all commodities for the world as a whole, 5.3 per cent in the case of the developed countries, 3.0 per cent in that of the centrally planned economies, but only 1.7 per cent in that of the developing countries.

However, in relative terms, the trade in forest products of the developing countries in recent years has grown faster than has world trade in this commodity group: 8.6 per cent annually against 3.7 per cent. It has also grown faster than the developing countries' trade in *all* commodities (3.2 per cent). These are rather hopeful indications, but there is still scope for much improvement. Even in 1959/61, when the developing countries' share in world trade in all commodities stood at just over one fifth, their share in world forest products trade still remained below one tenth. Moreover, this is only one side of the picture. Imports of forest products into the developing countries also grew rapidly over this period, the increase averaging 6.6 per cent yearly. And because the forest products trade of the developing countries already showed a sizeable adverse balance in 1953/5, the more rapid *rate* of growth in exports was little more than sufficient to keep pace with rising imports. As table 2.2 shows, the developing countries' *net* imports of forest products declined only slightly, from $252 million in 1953/5 to $210 million in 1959/61. Since these values are in terms of f.o.b. export prices, the net trade deficit is actually greater by approximately $100 million of transport and other costs.

Table 2.1 Value of exports of main forest products and of all commodities

	Main forest products			All commodities		
	Average annual value ($ billions)		Average annual increase (%)	Average annual value ($ billions)		Average annual increase (%)
	1953/5	1959/61		1953/5	1959/61	
World	4.32	5.36	3.7	87.1	125.1	6.2
Developed countries	3.75	4.45	2.8	56.2	83.3	6.8
Developing countries	0.28	0.46	8.6	22.3	26.9	3.2
Centrally planned economies	0.29	0.44	7.1	8.6	14.9	9.5

Table 2.2 Net trade in forest products of developing countries, volume and value

	Average annual volume (million m³ roundwood equivalent)			Average annual value ($ million, based on f.o.b. export prices)		
	Exports	Imports	Net trade	Exports	Imports	Net trade
1953/5	9.5	13.7	−4.2	277	529	−252
1959/61	17.7	17.2	+0.5	465	675	−210

Table 2.2 shows that, in volume terms (expressed as roundwood equivalent), the trade balance substantially improved, and actually changed to a net export. The difference in the magnitudes of volume and value changes was due to the additional exports being mainly of unprocessed wood, while the additional imports were of higher-valued processed goods.

This is well illustrated by table 2.3, which shows by commodity group the value composition of exports and imports of the developing countries in 1953/5 and in 1959/61.

Table 2.3 Composition of forest product trade of developing countries

	% of value			
	Unprocessed roundwood	Sawnwood and plywood	Pulp and pulp products	Total
Exports 1953/5	39	56	5	100
1959/61	54	41	5	100
Imports 1953/5	5	34	61	100
1959/61	6	28	66	100

Forest products trade is often handicapped by the fact that many of the forest products are bulky in relation to their value. Some items, for example, fuelwood and rough poles, scarcely enter into international trade at all. Trade in some others, as pulpwood and pitprops, is largely confined to exchanges over limited distances. A large proportion of all forest products trade is, in fact, intra-regional – within Europe and inside North America. Evidently, the higher the value per unit weight or volume, the greater the exportable range (other things being equal) and the greater the proportion entering into international trade. The figures in table 2.4 show this, and also illustrate the diversity of the forest products.

Table 2.4 Unit values of forest products, and proportion of production entering into international trade, 1959–61

Commodity	Unit value ($ US per m. ton	Raw material index[a]	World trade as proportion of world production %	Remarks
Unprocessed roundwood			2	
Fuelwood	10	100	0.2	
Poles	30	100	2	Great variation in quality.
Pitprops	20	100⎫	6	
Pulpwood	15	100⎭	6	
Hardwood logs	35	100	8	
Utility grades	10			
Quality grades	50			
Coniferous logs	25	100	0.9	
Processed wood			11	
Sawn hardwood	75	195	6	
Utility grades	65			
Quality grades	110			
Sawn softwood	65	215	13	
Plywood	210	265	10	
Particle board	115	140	9	
Pulp and pulp products			16	
Fibreboard	90	140	19	Proportion in world trade has been stimulated by surplus capacity.
Woodpulp	125	310	16	Most production
Mechanical	65	165	7	directly converted
Chemical	130	330	20	to newsprint in integrated mills
Paper and paperboard	165	180	16	
Newsprint	135	190	54	Usually tariff-free; imports subsidized in some countries
Fine paper	230	240	7⎫	High import tariffs in many countries.
Paperboard	120	110	5⎭	

[a] Raw material index: tons of raw material required to produce one ton of product × 100; this depends on processing wastage, moisture difference and additives.

Unit values encompass a considerable range: from 1 to 20 or more. Weight reduction (on processing) ranges from zero up to 70 per cent. These elementary considerations naturally have some bearing on the extent to which the various products enter into international trade. Thus only about 2 per cent of all roundwood produced enters international trade. Of the products of the sawmilling and plywood industries (which are of somewhat higher value, having been subjected to a moderate degree of processing), some 11 per cent enters into international trade. The percentage rises to 16 for the higher-valued products of the pulp and paper industries.

But though these considerations (weight-losing, value in relation to weight or bulk) have had some influence on the location of forest industries and the consequent pattern of trade in forest products, this influence has by no means always been decisive. Indeed, it can scarcely be claimed that the present-day world distribution of forest industries (to which, of course, the pattern of trade in forest products is directly linked) represents the ideal compromise between the diversity and geographical dispersion of wood resources on the one hand and the geographical distribution of demand on the other. Geography has certainly played its part. The high figure in the last column of table 2.4 for newsprint is no accident. The production of newsprint, still most economically made in highly capitalized units from coniferous woods, is heavily concentrated in the northern temperate coniferous belt. Sawn softwood, which is traditionally preferred as utility and construction timber, originates mainly in the same areas, while many of the highly desired decorative and special-use hardwoods are logged in the tropical zones of Asia, Africa and Latin America. But a dispassionate arch-planner on a world scale, unencumbered by history and given a *tabula rasa*, would prescribe a somewhat different distribution from that which exists today.

In the course of the next decades the world will certainly move steadily towards a somewhat different distribution – the resource economist would say towards a more rational distribution. This shift will provide significant opportunities for the developing countries. But developed and developing countries alike have a common interest in ensuring that this shift takes place smoothly, with minimal misinvestment and dislocation of markets.

TRADE IN FOREST PRODUCTS: THE GENERAL PATTERN

The general pattern of the flow of trade in forest products in 1959/61 is set out in table 2.5.

Thus, no less than 71 per cent of all trade takes place between developed countries. We may note in passing that of this trade among the developed countries over one third consists of exchanges between the USA and Canada, while not far short of one half takes place between European countries.

Table 2.5   Total trade flow in main forest products, 1959/61
(average annual value in $ million)

Exports From	To	All Destinations	1 Developed countries	2 Developing countries	3 Centrally planned economies
All origins		5,357	4,413	675	269
1		4,452	3,813	505	134
2		465	345	117	4
3		440	256	53	131

The relative importance of trade flows between the three groups distinguished in table 2.5 is brought out in table 2.6, which includes, for comparison, the corresponding figures for 1953/5.

Table 2.6   Relative importance of trade flows in forest products,
1953/5 and 1959/61

Direction of trade flow	1953/5		1959/61	
	Average annual value (million $ US)	% of all trade	Average annual value (million $ US)	% of all all trade
Between developed countries	3,246	75	3,813	71
Between developing countries	92	2	117	2
Between centrally planned countries	131	3	131	2
From developed to centrally planned	87	2	134	2
From centrally planned to developed	138	3	256	5
From developed to developing	412	9	505	10
From centrally planned to developing	25	1	53	1
From developing to developed	184	4	345	6
From developing to centrally planned	1	–	4	–

Trade between the developed countries was only slightly less dominant in 1959/61 than in the earlier period (71 against 75 per cent of the total). Over the interval exchanges between developed and centrally planned countries have risen, both absolutely and relatively: from $225 to $390 million per annum, or from 5 per cent to 7 per cent of all world trade.

Exports from the developed to the developing countries have shown a marked rise: from $412 to $505 million. Trade in the reverse direction, however, has expanded even more rapidly, almost doubling from $184 to $345 million. Thus the net adverse balance of the developing countries' trade with the developed countries fell over the period, by nearly one third.

The developing countries' trade with the centrally planned countries evolved in a unilateral fashion. Exports to the centrally planned countries remained negligible, while the flow in the opposite direction more than doubled, from $25 to $53 million.

Finally, trade between developing countries showed but a slight advance in absolute terms – from $92 to $117 million; in relative terms the advance was negligible – from 2.1 per cent to 2.2 per cent.

In the following pages we shall examine in turn (a) the exports from the developing to the developed countries, (b) trade between developing countries. We shall discuss past and current trade flows in somewhat more detail and draw attention to opportunities for expanding both these trade flows. We shall also touch on the prospects for establishing a trade flow from the developing countries to those countries with centrally planned economies.

THE EXPORTS OF THE DEVELOPING COUNTRIES
TO THE DEVELOPED COUNTRIES

The principal trade flows from developing to developed countries are set out in table 2.7.

Table 2.7   Forest products exports of developing countries
to developed countries, 1953/5 and 1959/61
(average annual value in $ million)

	Total developed countries	USA and Canada	Western and Southern Europe	Australia, New Zealand and South Africa	Japan
1953/5					
Latin America	40	21	18	1	–
Middle East	1	–	1	–	–
Asia + Far East	68	9	22	7	30
Africa	75	6	67	2	–
Total developing countries	184	36	108	10	30
1959/61					
Latin America	40	21	18	1	–
Middle East	4	1	3	–	–
Asia + Far East	158	23	27	15	93
Africa	142	6	129	7	–
Total developing countries	344	51	177	23	93

This table reveals that of the total increase over the period ($160 million), no less than $125 million were accounted for by two particular streams of trade: Asia to Japan (up by $63 million) and Africa to Europe (up by $62 million). Exports from Latin America showed no improvement whatever, even though during this period exports from Asia to North America rose by $14 million. Both Africa and Asia exported additional amounts to Oceania/South Africa – $13 million in all.

Having noted that the near doubling of developing-to-developed forest products exports over this period had, in fact, a rather limited geographical character, we shall now examine this trade in somewhat more detail.

The forest product categories involved

Not only was the expansion of this trade flow limited geographically, it was also concentrated largely on one specific wood category. Table 2.8 shows that the main increase was in exports of unprocessed roundwood. Indeed, of the total expansion over the period, of $162 million no less than $121 million is attributable to increased exports of *broadleaved logs*. In fact, African exports of broadleaved logs to Western and Southern Europe rose from $45 to $99 million, while Asian exports of the same category to Japan rose from $30 to $92 million.

Table 2.8   Developing countries' exports to developed countries, 1953/5 and 1959/61, by wood categories (average annual value in $ million)

	1953/5		1959/61	
Roundwood	91		215	
Pulpwood		–		3
Pitprops		1		–
Coniferous logs		–		1
Broadleaved logs		90		211
Sawnwood and plywood	91		121	
Coniferous sawnwood		25		20
Broadleaved sawnwood		58		75
Plywood		8		26
Pulp and paper	2		9	
Woodpulp		–		4
Other paper and board		2		5
Total	184		345	

Exports of the products of broadleaved *sawnwood* and *plywood* (predominantly broadleaved) also showed a substantial improvement over the period: from $66 to $101 million. Exports of *coniferous sawnwood* from the developing countries to developed countries were virtually limited to pine sawnwood shipped from Central to North America and parana pine shipped from Brazil to Europe. The trends are shown in table 2.9.

Table 2.9   Latin American exports of coniferous sawnwood to developed countries, 1953/5 and 1959/61 (average annual value in $ million)

	To USA and Canada	To Western and Southern Europe	To Australia, New Zealand and South Africa
1953/5	10.6	13.9	–
1959/61	5.9	13.1	0.6

In addition, there was a very small export, valued at less than a million dollars, of coniferous sawnwood from East and South-east Africa to Europe and South Africa. Thus, while exports to Europe (mostly parana pine) were maintained, exports to North America (in fact to the USA) fell considerably as lumbering operations by expatriate companies in Central America declined.

The improvement in exports of broadleaved sawnwood was confined to Africa and Asia. As table 2.10 shows, Latin America failed to share in this expansion. The most important increases were in exports from Asia to Australia and New Zealand, and from African countries to South Africa.

Table 2.10   Exports of broadleaved sawnwood from developing to developed countries, 1953/5 to 1959/61 (average annual value in $ million)

From \ To	USA and Canada	Western and Southern Europe	Australia, New Zealand and South Africa	Japan
1953/5				
Latin America	5.0	2.4	1.4	–
Asia	6.9	19.6	5.1	0.1
Africa	1.8	14.5	1.0	–
1959/61				
Latin America	7.3	1.0	0.3	–
Asia	7.7	21.3	11.1	0.1
Africa	1.5	18.2	6.2	–

Plywood exports showed a handsome advance over the period: from $8 to $26 million. Table 2.11 shows volumes exported. The establishment of the important export of plywood from the Philippines to the United States is the predominant change.

Table 2.11 Changes in developing countries' plywood exports to developed countries, 1953/5 to 1959/61 (annual average in 1,000 m³)

Direction of trade flow	Exports 1953/5	Exports 1959/61	Increase
Latin America to North America	3	13	10
Middle East (Israel) to North America and Europe	5	18	13
Africa to North America	4	16	12
Africa to Europe	33	58	25
Asia to Europe	2	9	7
Asia to North America	3	164	161
Total: All developing countries to developed countries	50	278	228

Table 2.8 showed that the flow of the products of the pulp and paper industries from the developing to the developed countries was very small: 9 million dollars' worth only in 1959/61. This consisted of small quantities of woodpulp, mostly from North Africa to Europe, and of about 5 million dollars' worth of other *paper and board* from North Africa to Europe.

This brief survey of trends in exports of the various wood categories from the developing to the developed countries shows that the expansion which has occurred has been limited to certain areas in Asia and Africa: Latin America has had virtually no share; and it has been limited to one or two categories, and has consisted overwhelmingly of broadleaved logs. Europe is still the main market for forest products exports of the developing countries, absorbing more than half of the total. Japan has become extremely important, though only as an outlet for broadleaved logs. North America presently ranks next in importance, though in absolute terms the rise in exports to North America has been only slightly greater than those to Oceania and South Africa.

We shall next consider prospects for expanding exports to these markets for the several wood categories. Since, however, our attention will now turn on the expected changes in the requirements of the developed areas, we shall group the wood categories in a different way, recognizing that the final consumption needs of the developed countries can be met by the import of either unprocessed or semi-processed wood (to feed industries in the developed countries) or by the import of finished forest products.

PROSPECTS FOR EXPANDING THE DEVELOPING COUNTRIES' EXPORTS

The most promising prospects stem from the changing requirements/resources balance in some of the main developed regions and countries. The greatest potential by far lies in Western Europe, already the biggest market for forest products from the developing countries, and we shall first examine prospects in that region.

Prospects in Western Europe

A study recently concluded by FAO and ECE, *European Timber Trends and Prospects – A New Appraisal for 1950–1975*, draws attention to the rapid rise in Europe's wood requirements and to the rate at which Europe's current timber deficit will grow, should roundwood production in Europe rise no faster than is predicated by the forestry policies and plans presently being pursued. The study shows that, if the present targets for economic growth are achieved, Western Europe's annual *requirements* of industrial roundwood (or its equivalent in processed goods) will rise by about 90 million cubic metres between 1960 and 1975. This increase will be made up as follows:

million m³ roundwood equivalent

Sawnwood	17	(12 coniferous, 5 broadleaved)
Plywood and veneers	9	(nearly all broadleaved)
Pulp and paper	65)	
Particle board and fibreboard	7)	72 (40–50 in coniferous species)
Other industrial wood	–9	(decline)

The additional requirements for smaller wood for pulpwood, particle board and fibreboard are partly offset by the decline in the requirements for pitprops and other industrial wood, so that additional smallwood requirements might be about 65 million cubic metres – of which perhaps 20 to 25 million might be satisfied by broadleaved species.

Western European *production* of industrial roundwood, which rose considerably in the decade 1950 to 1960 (by about 33 million cubic metres), is expected to show a substantial further rise of 48 million cubic metres by 1975, according to the targets implied by current forest policies and plans. This increase is expected to be made up as follows:

million m³(r)

Large-sized logs[1]	21 (about 8 coniferous, 13 broadleaved)
Small-sized roundwood	27 (about 12 coniferous, 15 broadleaved)

[1] Very few are expected to be of veneer quality.

A comparison of the prospective increases in requirements and the additional removals foreseen to 1975 suggests the following potential shortfalls (which are, of course, additional to the volumes already being imported net in 1959/61:

million m³(r)

Sawlogs, coniferous	4
Veneer logs, broadleaved (largely tropical)	8
Small-sized roundwood, coniferous	25 or more

Although the quantity of large-sized broadleaved logs is adequate to supply the volume required for sawnwood, the make-up of demand will require that a large part be tropical sawnwood, say some 3 or 4 million cubic metres (r); this will be in addition to the 3 million cubic metres (r) imported in 1959/61 as sawnwood or logs for sawing.

A further curtailment of present coniferous sawnwood exports from Western Europe to other regions could make available for consumption in Western Europe the equivalent of 1 to 2 million cubic metres of coniferous sawlogs. Similarly, a reduction in exports to other regions of woodpulp and paper could result in the equivalent of 5 to 8 million cubic metres of coniferous pulpwood being made available for European consumption.

Thus, unless present forestry plans and policies are substantially revised in Western Europe, the following additional volumes of forest production – or their equivalents – will be required to be imported in 1975, over and above the volume imported in 1959/61:

million m³(r)

Veneer and plywood (or logs)	8 (of which 6–7 tropical broadleaved)
Broadleaved tropical sawnwood (or logs)	3
Coniferous sawnwood (or logs)	2–3
Long-fibre pulp (or paper)	20 or more

Let us now turn to consider what the exports of the developing countries to the Western European market have been, how they might be developed and what portion of the additional import requirements they might supply. First, we shall examine the broadleaved species market, where the developing countries have already established an important place.

It will be recalled that the present exports (1959/61) from the developing countries to Europe consist overwhelmingly of unprocessed timber. The volumes, and values, of exports of broadleaved wood products originating in each of the developing regions are set out in table 2.12. Volumes are shown, for comparative purposes, in raw material equivalents, that is, as though in the log form.

Table 2.12 Exports of broadleaved logs, sawnwood and plywood from developing regions to Western Europe, 1959/61

Exporting regions	Logs	Sawnwood	Plywood	Total value	Estimated total value if all had been processed before export[a]
		(1,000 m³(r))			*($ million)*
Latin America	52	29	5	2.8	4.5
Asia + Far East	260	663	21	27.5	38.0
Africa	3,860	613	133	122.3	260.0
Total	4,172	1,305	159	152.6	302.5

[a] The table excludes 3 millions dollars' worth of plywood exports from Israel.

In the final column of table 2.12 a very tentative estimate is made of what would have been the export value of this group of commodities had all been exported in 1959/61 in the processed form. The estimate is tentative, since no precise estimate can be made of the proportions of broadleaved logs which were destined for the production of sawnwood and plywood respectively. It is not suggested that the whole of this trade *could* necessarily have been transformed into processed goods. But undoubtedly a substantial part of it could have been, had appropriate measures been taken.

We shall discuss some of the problems relating to this transformation of trade later. Here we may simply note that already in 1959/61 there existed a theoretical scope for improving the export earnings of the developing countries for this group of forest products, *not* by expanding the trade flow but merely by converting a larger proportion before export.

Only the developing countries can export to Western Europe the additional volumes of tropical broadleaved wood and its products which Europe will require by 1975. These amount to approximately 10 million cubic metres in roundwood equivalent. If all were exported in the form of logs, export earnings would amount to roughly $250 million at 1959/61 prices. If all were fully processed into plywood, veneers or sawnwood, before export, earnings would amount to nearly $600 million. This is in addition to the 150 million dollars' worth of extra earnings that could accrue to the developing countries if all the present trade in this category were processed before export.

Summing up this phase of the discussion, we can say that by 1975 it should be possible for the developing countries to raise their earnings in Western Europe from tropical woods from $150 to $400 million *as a minimum*. If all the new trade were processed before export, then earnings would rise to $750 million. This implies, of course, that the additional processing facilities be established in the developing countries, not in Europe. Theoretically, the $750 million could be raised to $900 million by fully processing before export all the *present* trade. This would, of course, affect existing processing industries in Europe.

The other main wood categories which Western Europe will require in vastly increasing quantities by 1975 are coniferous sawnwood and long-fibre pulp or paper. These are already important items in Western Europe's import bill, as may be seen from table 2.13.

Table 2.13 Western European imports of coniferous sawnwood, pulp and paper, annual average 1959/61

Commodity	Net imports (+) Quantity[a]	Gross imports Quantity[a]	Value $ million by origin[b]			
			Total	1	2	3
Coniferous sawnwood	4.54	6.31	208	54	13	141
Woodpulp	0.06	1.15	160	133	4	23
Newsprint	− 0.14[c]	0.47	63	59	–	4
Other paper and board	− 0.76[c]	0.39	72	48	5	19

[a] million tons; for sawnwood, million m³ (s).
[b] *1* – developed countries; *2* – developing countries; *3* – centrally planned countries.
[c] Excess of exports over imports.

These imports originate almost entirely in North America and the USSR. The developing countries have presently but a negligible share. This is because in the developing regions coniferous resources are small and undeveloped at the present time. There are, however, reserves of certain promise in the form of Central American pine, exotic pine plantations in Chile and in East and South-east Africa, tropical pines in Indonesia and several other countries of South-east Asia. Moreover, in these areas – and in many other parts of the developing regions – soil and climatic conditions are such as to render possible the establishment of coniferous plantations on short rotations yielding from 15 to 30 cubic metres per hectare a year. This compares with 2 to 7 in the natural coniferous forests of the northern temperate zone, though on a few favourable sites and with intensive management these figures can be raised. In fact, many of the developing countries are better suited, by soil and climate, for the cheap mass production of coniferous fibre than are those areas of the world where the pulp and paper industries are presently heavily concentrated. At the present time this natural advantage is overlaid and outweighed by handicaps of an institutional and historical nature, but it will undoubtedly assert itself in time. How soon depends on how energetic are the steps taken to remove these handicaps.

Since the European deficit in both coniferous sawnwood and pulp and paper will continue to rise after 1975, and since there is considerable doubt whether the regions which presently make up Europe's deficit on these items – North America and the USSR – will be able to do so on the growing scale that will be required in the later decades of the present century, it would seem rational for the developing countries so to plan their forest and forest industry development that they can take some shares in this growing market already by 1975, with a view to becoming major suppliers of Western Europe's extra needs in the following decades. The share which the developing countries can gain by 1975 must necessarily be conjectural, and will indeed depend to some extent on the policies pursued by the developed countries themselves – both in Europe and on the part of potential suppliers in other developed regions – North America and the USSR. But it would seem not unduly optimistic to hope that by 1975 the developing countries could provide Western Europe with, say, 0.5 million cubic metres of coniferous sawnwood, 100,000 tons of newsprint and 250,000 tons of long-fibre pulp. At present export prices these would represent additional exchange earnings of approximately $60 million. Against the rather heavy Western European deficits foreseen for 1975, this may seem an extremely modest target. However, it does not represent the whole of the target at which the developing countries must aim. It has already been pointed out that Western Europe's present exports of coniferous sawnwood, pulp and paper – largely to developing countries – are likely to be absorbed within Europe. These imports the developing countries must replace. They must also expand their industries to take care of their own rising requirements to the year 1975. This alone, as we shall see later, will require a considerable effort. To achieve all this *and* to break into the competitive European market will be no easy task. It calls for the purposive planning of forest industry development – a planning that can look beyond the quick, easy but limited gains from import substitution to the more difficult but more enduring and more substantial earnings from exports.

If industry expansion in the developing countries is so planned, and if the development envisaged is favoured and not obstructed by the developed countries, then the modest target set above could conceivably be exceeded several-fold already by 1975.

Prospects in the centrally planned countries:
Eastern Europe and the USSR

It has already been noted that in 1959/61 exports of forest products from the developing countries to the centrally planned countries were very small indeed, amounting to no more than $4 million. This figure may slightly understate the true position, since it is believed that small quantities of tropical timbers did in fact reach Eastern Europe and the USSR via Western Europe. The fact that the current trade flow is negligible does not, however, mean that this group of countries could not in the future become an important market for the developing countries.

It is well known that the USSR is a timber-rich country. It has traditionally been an important supplier of timber to Western Europe, principally coniferous sawnwood, but also of smaller quantities of plywood, pitprops, pulpwood and sawlogs. It also helps to make good the wood deficits of some of the centrally planned countries of Eastern Europe. Today it is Europe's principal external supplier of coniferous sawnwood, this category accounting for more than half of its 240 million dollars' worth of annual exports to Western Europe in 1959/61. In addition, it exported pulpwood and coniferous sawlogs valued at $16 million to Japan.

The USSR's net earnings from forest products trade – which have continued to rise in recent years, as the figures in table 2.14 show – are derived mainly from processed wood (sawnwood, plywood) and industrial roundwood: in pulp and its products the USSR is approximately in balance, its exports to Europe and to some of the developing countries being almost exactly offset by its imports from Western Europe.

Table 2.14   USSR net exports, 1960–2 ($ million)

	Roundwood	Processed wood	Pulp and paper	Total
1960	55	162	6	223
1961	77	183	− 2	258
1962	110	202	2	314

A measure of the importance which the USSR has attained as a supplier of forest products to both Western and Eastern Europe is afforded by the geographical breakdown of USSR exports in 1962 shown in table 2.15.

In the centrally planned economies of Eastern Europe, timber requirements have risen very rapidly during the last decade, and they continue to rise. Hungary and East Germany, seriously wood-deficient, are heavily dependent on imports. In Poland and Czechoslovakia, both traditional exporters, the surplus available for export has declined steadily in recent years. Czechoslovakia's net export balance still stands at $35–40 million, but Poland's balance has fallen to below $10 million in recent years. Both Romania and Yugoslavia continue to have an important net export, but even in these countries vigorous efforts are being made to prevent this balance from being eroded by rising domestic requirements. In all these countries great emphasis is placed on

Table 2.15 Destination of USSR exports, 1962

	Units	To Western Europe	To Eastern Europe[a]	To all other destinations
Coniferous logs	1,000 m³(r)	510	440	1,495[b]
Pulpwood	1,000 m³(r)	1,645	1,070	550[c]
Pitprops	1,000 m³(r)	475	695	35
Coniferous sawnwood	1,000 m³(s)	3,405	1,985	610
Plywood	1,000 m³(s)	120	7	20
Woodpulp	1,000 m.tons	145	80	40
Newsprint	1,000 m.tons	10	35	60

[a] i.e. to the centrally planned economies of Eastern Europe.
[b] Includes 1,207,000 m³ to Japan and 222,000 m³ to mainland China.
[c] Includes 548,000 m³ to Japan.
Exports to Western Europe represented in aggregate some 9 million m³ (roundwood equivalent); to Eastern Europe, slightly over 6 million m³; to all other destinations about 3.5 million m³.

securing economies in wood use, in part through recourse to alternative materials, in order to limit import requirements or to preserve an exportable surplus.

The FAO/ECE study referred to above shows that, for the Eastern European centrally planned countries as a group, the rise in requirements between 1959/61 and 1975 will, as in Western Europe, outpace the estimated rise in forest output. These trends will give rise to the following additional approximate import requirements by 1975:

Roundwood equivalent in million m³(r)

Coniferous sawnwood (or logs therefor)	2
Broadleaved plywood and veneer (or logs therefor)	0.5
Long-fibre woodpulp (or pulpwood therefor, or paper)	10–12

These are roughly the additional quantities that will require to be imported on the basis of present plans. It is doubtful whether these extra amounts of coniferous timber or their derivatives can be obtained from either Western Europe or North America. The natural proximate source is the USSR. The USSR certainly has the resources to meet these requirements. However, some very long hauls would be involved, since much of the timber (or products) would have to come from newly exploited areas in Siberia. Moreover, the recent scaling down of the USSR's pulp and paper expansion plans, coupled with the pressure to raise paper consumption standards within the USSR, makes it doubtful whether the USSR will be able to establish a pulpwood, pulp or paper surplus equivalent to 10–12 million (r) by 1975. There seems, in fact, to be no reason why the centrally planned economies of Eastern Europe should not look to the developing countries to satisfy at least a part of these rising requirements.

In any case, the overall economic plans to the year 1975 have not yet been finally determined either in Eastern Europe or in the USSR, though some progress has been made with perspective planning. Central planning connotes the planning of trade. It would seem reasonable for those Eastern European countries which must look beyond their borders to meet their rising pulp and paper needs to diversify their supply sources by importing from the developing countries. Indeed, this might well prove more economic than the efforts presently envisaged to achieve integral utilization of forest waste.

In addition, there are certain policy measures which, if adopted in the centrally planned economies, could lead to export opportunities for the developing countries over and above those implied in the figures cited above. We have already mentioned the intense efforts made to achieve economies in timber use. If it were decided to slow down the drive towards timber economy and substitution – which has in certain instances perhaps been pushed beyond the economic limit – this, too, might afford new opportunities for the developing countries.

Finally, there is the whole question of the use of tropical woods and their products in the centrally planned economies and in the USSR. At the present time the consumption of tropical timbers in the centrally planned economies is negligible. The consumer's range of choice over a wide area of durable consumption goods, especially furniture, is limited to temperate species locally available. Should the present trend towards diversifying and improving the quality of consumer goods strengthen in the centrally planned economies, it would seem logical to import increasing quantities of tropical timbers (logs, sawnwood, plywood or veneers) from the developing regions.

In short, there is a variety of potential wood needs arising in the centrally planned economies which could be met partly through imports from the developing countries. If such trade flows were deliberately planned, this would in itself constitute a valuable instrument for the economic development of the exporting countries. Evidently, the extent to which this trade flow develops by 1975 will depend on decisions, both political and economic, yet to be taken, but it would seem reasonable to hope that by 1975 this trade flow may have reached the following proportions:

	$ million
Broadleaved logs, sawnwood and plywood	40
Pulp and paper	60

Prospects in North America

Canada and the United States, in aggregate, are in a very substantial net export position in their timber balance. The region is a net exporter of all important forest products except plywood and broadleaved logs, and only in the case of the former have net imports into the region reached the importance of 3 or 4 per cent of consumption.

Total gross imports of the most important products from outside the region amounted annually in 1959/61 to $195 million, and of this $79 million was pulp and paper products from developed countries. Of the remainder, $108 million is accounted for by broadleaved plywood, sawnwood and logs. Imports of these items are summarized in table 2.16.

Table 2.16   Imports of broadleaved logs, sawnwood and plywood into North America, 1959/61 ($ millions)

Origin	Broadleaved logs	Broadleaved sawnwood	Plywood	Total
Western Europe	–	–	9	9
Japan	–	11	46	57
Latin America	3	7	2	12
Middle East	–	–	1	1
Asia + Far East	2	8	13	23
Africa	3	2	1	6
Total developing countries	8	17	17	42
Total	8	28	72	108

A comparison with 1953/5 imports shows that log imports indicated little change, that sawnwood imports increased modestly from $20 to $28 million. In the case of plywood, imports rose from $25 to $72 million. The main increases were in imports from Japan ($17 to $46 million) and from the developing countries of the Far East ($0.4 to $13 million, largely accounted for by exports from the Philippines).

Since 1950, imports of hardwood plywood into the region have increased by more than twenty times. The share of tropical species has risen greatly. It is therefore most difficult to forecast the probable requirements for plywood imports far in advance. However, a reasonable estimate might be for import requirements to further expand by 1975 to two or three times their present level – to about 1.3 million cubic metres (s) or the equivalent of about 3.0 million cubic metres (r) of logs. Of the additional 0.8 million cubic metres (s) required, 0.6 million cubic metres (s) might be expected to come from developing countries. In addition, developing countries might be expected to supply

0.3 million cubic metres (s) of coniferous sawnwood, and 0.7 million cubic metres (s) of broadleaved sawnwood. At 1959/61 prices this would make 1975 exports of developing countries to North America approximately $150 million compared with the present $50 million.

Prospects in other developed countries

There are, in other developed countries, potential markets for forest products from developing regions. In some cases, there are growing deficits in the overall wood balance; in others, there is an increasing demand for special qualities which can be supplied only by the developing countries.

Japan's internal consumption of forest products has expanded at a rapid rate. At the same time exports of certain processed forest products have also increased rapidly. A substantial proportion of the production of these goods has been based on unprocessed roundwood imported from the developing countries. Despite the fact that industrial removals from the Japanese forests have nearly trebled in a decade, the wood deficit has steadily increased. In 1959/61, industrial removals were in the order of 55 million cubic metres (r) annually. At this time the net trade deficit amounted to about 5.5 million cubic metres in roundwood equivalent, having increased from 1.3 million cubic metres in 1953/5. The wood was imported largely as broadleaved logs.

By 1975, industrial wood requirements are expected to reach 90 to 95 million cubic metres (r), while industrial removals will increase less rapidly. Consequently, the net deficit will have to be met by the import of the roundwood equivalent of approximately 20 million cubic metres (r), that is, by additional imports of about 15 million cubic metres (r). Of this additional requirement, about 4 million cubic metres (r) will be broadleaved veneer logs or the equivalent in veneer or plywood, perhaps 4 million cubic metres (r) broadleaved sawlogs or their sawnwood equivalent, a further 4 million cubic metres (r) coniferous sawlogs or their sawnwood equivalent, and 3 million cubic metres (r) long-fibre pulpwood or pulp and paper.

In 1959/61, the average import of broadleaved sawlogs and veneer logs was valued at $94 million (f.o.b. export prices). Of this, more than 92 million dollars' worth came from developing countries of Asia. Practically no broadleaved sawnwood, and no plywood, was imported. A significant proportion of the plywood made from imported logs was exported. The additional requirements of broadleaved plywood made from imported logs was exported. The additional requirements of broadleaved plywood and sawnwood foreseen by 1975 could represent a market for developing countries of $400 million, provided a reasonable proportion were furnished in processed form.

This may seem a high target. But it must be borne in mind that Japan's imports are rising at a very rapid rate indeed, a rate which scarcely emerges from the 1959/61 average figures just cited. A clearer picture of the most recent trend is shown in table 2.17, which gives some details of imports into Japan of the five main imported wood categories for the years 1960 to 1962.

Table 2.17   Japanese imports of certain wood categories, 1960–2

Commodity	Unit	Quantity (million units)			Value ($ million)		
		1960	1961	1962	1960	1961	1962
Broadleaved logs	m³(r)	4.75	5.86	6.68	124	142	179
Coniferous logs	m³(r)	1.23	2.67	3.16	33	82	99
Pulpwood	m³(r)	.19	.41	.46	3	6	8
Coniferous sawnwood	m³(s)	.15	.59	.65	7	24	28
Woodpulp	m.tons	.14	.17	.23	26	31	38
Total					193	285	352

All the coniferous sawnwood, and about 50 per cent of the coniferous sawlogs, originated in North America, as did most of the woodpulp. Doubtless a good proportion of the woodpulp from the USA came from Alaska mills in which Japan is financially interested. Given the sizeable undeveloped reserves of tropical conifers in South-east Asia, and bearing in mind reverse trade possibilities with Latin America, it seems not unreasonable to hope that by 1975 the developing countries could be providing Japan with a significant part of its immense coniferous needs: say, one million cubic metres or coniferous logs or the equivalent in sawnwood and 200,000 tons of pulp and/or paper. This would mean a new market for the developing countries of some $40 to $50 million.

Unlike other wood-deficient countries of the developed region – most countries of Europe, and Japan – in recent years, *Australia, New Zealand* and *South Africa* have prevented their net timber import balance from increasing either in quantity or in value. This has been accomplished by the development of coniferous plantations and the resultant reduction of imports of coniferous sawnwood and by limitation on requirements of pulp and paper products from other regions, all of which had come primarily from developed countries. By contrast, imports of broadleaved logs and sawnwood, largely from developing countries, more than doubled – from less than $11 million annually in the 1953/5 period to more than $23 million annually in the 1959/61 period. Over this period annual imports from the developed countries remained relatively unchanged at about $58 million.

It is expected that these countries, at least in total, will continue to approach self-sufficiency in coniferous sawnwood and pulp and paper products, although by 1975 the equivalent of 1 or 2 million cubic metres (r) will probably still be imported in the form of sawnwood and pulp products. Some 50,000 cubic metres (s) of coniferous sawnwood and 30,000 metric tons of woodpulp might be supplied by developing countries. The deficit of nearly 1 million cubic metres, roundwood equivalent, of broadleaved species is expected to widen to 3 million cubic metres. This will be essentially all provided by developing countries. In 1959/61 prices this would amount by 1975 to some $130 million more than the present level, provided the imports were largely processed.

Prospects summarized

Western Europe is destined to remain the principal prospective market for the developing countries. The additional trade by 1975 should amount to at least $300 million and might well run to twice this sum or more. The next most important market is likely to be Japan, a rapidly expanding, high wood-using economy which is progressively running into wood deficit. Here additional markets may be found to the value of $400 million or more; however, the likelihood is that a substantial part of the additional trade will be in log, rather than processed, form so that actual earnings for the developing countries might lie somewhere between $200 and $300 million. There are also prospects of important expansions in the centrally planned economies, say $100 million, and in North America, say another $100 million. Other developed countries in aggregate might provide outlets for a further $100 million.

In sum, by 1975 there should be not far short of a billion dollars worth of new trade in forest products to be won by the developing countries. Given favourable developments, this sum might be considerably exceeded.

It may be charged that these are hypothetical figures. Of course they are. But, assuming that the trends discussed above have been correctly discerned, the realization of these targets depends mainly on the ability of the developing countries to deliver the goods; but also, and this in quite a large degree, on the willingness of the developed countries to make room for them. That is to say, outside the main deficit areas – Eastern Europe and Japan – there is scope for about 300 million dollars' worth of extra trade by 1975 in the developed countries.

Trade between the developing countries

We have seen that, taking into account current and expected changes in the resource/supply/requirements complex of some of the industrialized regions and countries, there are undoubted prospects for expanding exports of forest products from the developing to the developed countries. Though these opportunities may be limited in the short run, in the longer term they could become extremely important. Meanwhile, however, the developing countries as a group still have a very sizeable adverse trade balance on their forest products account *vis-à-vis* the rest of the world. We noted earlier on that this deficit did diminish somewhat between 1953/5 and 1959/61. The difference between the inflow and the outflow actually fell from $252 to $210 million. But it was noted that, since all these figures were recorded at f.o.b., the actual trade deficits of the developing countries probably ran about $100 million higher than these figures.

Moreover, we should not lose sight of the fact that the expansion of exports from the developing countries was limited and localized. Thus, if we disregard the increase in the export of tropical logs (West Africa to Europe, South-east Asia to Japan, $125 million in all), it becomes clear that the dependence of the developing countries on the rest of the world for imports of the forest products categories they consume actually *rose* over the period, by some $80 million.

Trade between developing countries in 1959/61, at $117 million, represented less than one fourth of all their trade in forest products. Moreover, of that $117 million, no less than $110 million occurred within individual regions; inter-regional trade between developing countries amounted to a paltry $7 million.

Forest products trade between developing countries, 1959/61, was as follows:

	$ million
Between Latin American countries	49
Between Middle-Eastern countries	1
Between Asian countries	49
Between African countries	11
Inter-regional	7

In this period, more than two thirds of Latin America's intra-regional trade in forest products was in coniferous sawnwood. Among the major exporters, Brazil accounted for about 90 per cent, with exports concentrated towards Argentina; Honduras accounted for most of the reminder, with exports to Venezuela, with Chile's share at about 3 per cent directed largely towards Argentina and Peru.

Almost half (47 per cent) of the trade in forest products between the Asian countries was in broadleaved sawlogs and veneer logs; most of the remainder (32 per cent) was sawnwood. In the unprocessed roundwood category, about 40 per cent were Philippine exports to Taiwan and South Korea; 34 per cent Borneo exports to Hong Kong; 15 per cent Sarawak exports to Hong Kong; of the remainder less than 10 per cent were Indonesian exports, largely to Singapore. Exports of sawnwood, originating mainly from Malaya, Thailand and Burma, were distributed among a wide range of Asian countries.

Of the $11 million in forest products exports within African countries, over one half was in sawnwood and plywood, with most of the remainder in pulp and pulp products. The bulk of the sawnwood was of broadleaved species which was exported from Ghana to South Africa and other African countries, and from the Congo to Nyasaland.

The presently low levels of trade in forest products between the developing countries (both intra- and inter-regional) and the growing dependence on imports from the developed world noted above are in fact related phenomena. Considerable efforts have been made since the war, especially in Latin America and parts of Asia, to establish domestic forest industries and reduce national dependence on imports of processed wood. Almost invariably, however, these efforts have been conceived within the narrow frame of import substitution at the national level. Countries have been obsessed with the 'dollar saved equals a dollar earned' approach in its crudest form. Confronted by the dilemma of narrow national markets on the one hand and very pronounced economies of scale on the other, countries have established many import-saving – but uneconomic and high-cost – mills which have required continuing high protection, instead of seeking to resolve the dilemma through effective regional and sub-regional collaboration. The result has been that in the countries where mills have been established, the further development of the forest industries has been retarded or frustrated, while neighbouring countries which might have drawn their supplies from an efficient plant within the region have had to look to the developed countries for rising imports to meet their rising domestic needs.

This trend has not, of course, been confined to forest industries: it applies to many industrial sectors. It has been particularly regrettable in the case of forest industries because there are many instances where the forest resources of neighbouring countries are complementary, and hence where considerable economies could have been achieved by economic cooperation. However, the faults of the past (which were not necessarily avoidable) are now widely recognized, and there is an increasing disposition in the developing world to emphasize mutual aid in the form of common market arrangements and coordinated development programmes.

It is not possible, of course, to set targets for the volume of forest products trade between developing countries. This would require, in effect, an estimate for each individual developing country of that part of domestic requirements which could best be met from native production and that part which could most economically be met from trade. All we can do is to point to the current and expected future level of requirements, in each region and in the developing world as a whole. This will give some indication of the tremendous scope that lies ahead for developing intra-regional trade.

If we start from the assumption that the current flows of trade from the developing to the advanced countries should be maintained and strengthened, then we may direct attention first to those imports which the developing countries are receiving from the developed countries.

The figures in table 2.18 are all at f.o.b. prices. The actual cost of these imports to the developing countries was over $600 million.

Studies recently conducted (and presently under way) by FAO in collaboration with the regional economic commissions of the United Nations show that in all these regions wood requirements will rise sharply by 1975. Table 2.19 gives an indication of the additional requirements (over and above 1959/61) of each of these regions by 1975.

Table 2.18   Exports from developed[a] to developing countries, 1959/61 ($ million)

To	Roundwood	Processed wood	Pulp and paper	Total
Latin America	–	17	206	223
Middle East	1	19	44	64
Asia + Far East	2	33	142	177
Africa	2	50	42	94
Total	5	119	434	558

[a] Including centrally planned countries

Thus by 1975 the developing regions will require annually about 3 billion dollars' worth of forest products over and above their current (1959/61) needs.[2] This is additional to the imports (well over half a billion dollars) they are currently receiving from the advanced countries. Regardless of the important prospects already noted for expanding exports to the developed countries, their own rapidly rising requirements offer opportunities for a rapid expansion of forest industries which, if properly directed, will enable them to ensure the establishment of efficient units, taking full advantage of wider markets and the complementarity of their forest and other fibre resources. An industry securely based on a sound domestic and local market is much better poised to enter the arena of intercontinental trade than one which has no such base on which to gain experience and from which to expand. It is imperative that future planning of forest and forest industry development in the developing countries should take full account of the wider potential markets now in the offing. Otherwise there is little hope that the potential new earnings to which attention has been drawn in this paper can be realized.

Prospective capital needs and trade balances

A very substantial amount of capital will be needed if the developing countries are to achieve the required expansion of their forest industries. This is one of the biggest problems the developing countries have to face. Attention has already been drawn to the expected increase in requirements of forest products that will arise by 1975 *within* the developing countries. If all these extra requirements were to be imported from the developed countries, the annual import bill of the developing countries would rise by just over $3 billion. If all these extra requirements were to be produced within the developing countries, then the capital investment that would be needed, in forest industries and in the associated forest operations, would cumulatively amount to $5.5 billion by 1975.

[2] Calculated on the basis of world average import (c.i.f.) prices in 1959/61.

Table 2.19 Additional annual forest products requirements of developing regions by 1975 over 1959/61

Region	Sawnwood		Plywood		Fibreboard + particle board		Paper + paperboard		Total ($ million)
	(million m³)	($ million)	(million m³)	($ million)	(million m. tons)	($ million)	(million m. tons)	($ million)	
Latin America	12.3	560	.16	25	.78	100	4.59	1,050	1,735
Middle East	.77	35	.16	25	.11	15	.61	140	215
Asia + Far East	3.9	175	.89	150	.24	30	2.55	590	945
Africa	1.5	70	.08	15	.08	10	.40	75	170
Total	18.5	840	1.29	215	1.21	155	8.15	1,855	3,065

This is not, be it noted, a 'self-sufficiency' target: it presupposes that imports from the developed world will continue at their current level of $500 million.

If, in addition to holding imports at their current level, the developing countries were to establish a further capacity to enable them to expand their exports to the developed world to an annual figure of one billion dollars, then an additional investment (cumulative to 1975) of $900 million would be needed. Thus, a total investment of $6.4 billion would have converted their current net import of $200 million to a net export of $800 million.

It is unlikely that so bold a target can be attained. Even were capital in these amounts forthcoming, it is unlikely that the immense research and training programme and the considerable infrastructural development that would have to accompany this investment could be realized. Moreover, it may be doubted whether such a target for the developing countries is economically sound.

A more realistic alternative might be that summarized in table 2.20. This rests on the assumptions that by 1975 the developing countries will have established capacity to (a) cover their own extra needs of all categories save pulp and paper, of which they would import about one quarter of their extra needs, processing themselves the other three quarters and some 2 million cubic metres (s) of sawnwood, and (b) raise their exports of processed forest products to the developed world by one billion dollars annually.

For this target their aggregate investment requirements would amount to $5 billion. Though their pulp, paper and sawnwood imports would have risen by $600 million, their total trade balance on the forest products account would have improved from a current net import of $200 million to a net export of $200 million, and a sound basis would have been laid for a rapid and progressive rise in net export earnings in the subsequent years.

THE RESPONSIBILITIES OF THE DEVELOPED COUNTRIES

The foregoing description and analysis of the trade pattern in forest products reveals some of the opportunities with respect to increasing the export earnings potential of the developing countries. The responsibilities for realizing this potential devolve upon both the importing and exporting countries. Without a broad, many-sided approach to this problem it is unlikely that the volume of trade, its composition and its pattern of flow can be changed significantly so as to foster the growth of a more broadly based industrialization of the developing countries and the expansion and diversification of their export trade. In this and in the following section, attention is focused on various measures which can be taken by the developed and by the developing nations, individually and jointly.

Table 2.20 Tentative estimates of additional annual production, and investment to 1975, associated with forest industries in developing countries

| Commodity | Additional annual domestic requirements within the developing countries | | Additional annual production of developing countries | | | Additional annual imports from developed countries | | Additional investment required cumulatively from 1960 to 1975 | | |
| | | | A for domestic requirements | B for export to developed countries | | | | A for domestic requirements ($ million) | B for export to developed countries ($ million) | Total ($ million) |
	Quantity[a]	Value at import prices ($ million)	Quantity[a]	Quantity[a]	Value ($ million)	Quantity[a]	Value ($ million)			
Roundwood	[b]	[b]	[b]	10.0	220	–	–	[a]	50	50
Sawnwood	18.6	840	16.7	4.0	225	2.2	100	240	60	300
Plywood and veneers	1.3	210	1.3	3.5	500	–	–	150	400	550
Woodpulp	[c]	[c]	[c]	0.60	80	0.6	100	[c]	270	270
Paper and paperboard	8.2	1,850	6.4	0.18	25	1.8	400	3,600	110	3,710
Fibreboard and particle board	1.2	150	1.2	–	–	–	–	140	–	140
Total		3,050			1,050		600	4,130	890	5,020

[a] Quantity figures are represented in the following units: (1) roundwood million m³(r); (2) sawnwood million m³(s); (3) plywood/veneers million m³(s); (4) woodpulp million m.tons; (5) paper and paperboard million m.tons; (c) fibreboard and particle board million m.tons.
[b] Included in sawnwood, plywood and veneers and board products.
[c] Included in paper, paperboard, fibreboard and particle board.

Increasing access to markets

Any hope for expanding and diversifying the export trade of the developing countries must, in the first instance, rest on increased access to the markets of the developed countries. Removal of any obstacles to such trade must, accordingly, be a matter of high priority. The prevailing level and structure of tariffs present a formidable barrier to the expansion and broadening of the trade flow in forest products from developing to developed countries. This is evident from the following examination of existing tariffs imposed by the major industrialized countries on the principal categories of forest products entering international trade.

In most of the industrialized countries, there are no import tariffs on un-processed wood in the round: sawlogs, veneer logs, pulpwood, pitprops and various miscellaneous items. Some countries, notably Japan and Australia, do, however, have tariffs on some species as high as 20 per cent to 27.5 per cent. There are usually no tariffs on most types of unplaned sawnwood. Where they still remain they are seldom over 10 per cent, although minor instances do exist of tariffs being as high as 20 per cent, 30 per cent or even 60 per cent. Until recently the United Kingdom and France maintained tariffs on both round-wood and sawnwood (6 per cent to 20 per cent), designed to give preference, through exception, to the British Commonwealth or to French colonies and ex-colonies.[3]

Tariffs on veneers and plywood are sufficiently high to have a distinct effect on the feasibility of establishing processing plants outside the importing countries. In few of the developed countries are tariffs on veneers very low or non-existent. In most cases they are from 10 per cent to 20 per cent, but in some cases, as in Canada and Australia, they are as high as 25 per cent and 37.5 per cent respectively. Tariffs on plywood are usually between 10 per cent and 20 per cent, but several countries have higher tariffs – one as high as 57.5 per cent. Fibreboard and particle board tariffs are usually in the range of 10 per cent to 20 per cent, but are as high as 70 per cent in the case of New Zealand.

Woodpulp and newsprint are generally tariff-free or have only low tariffs applied to them. On the other hand, tariffs on other papers are generally in the order of 10 per cent to 20 per cent. For certain types of partly manufctured paper (for example, paper cut to letter size or treated paper), tariffs are much higher, *ad valorem* rates of 40 per cent to 60 per cent being not uncommon.

The effect of this tariff structure has been particularly prejudicial to the

---

[3] The EEC countries were in the process of changing tariffs to establish a common external tariff of 5 per cent or 8 per cent on most logs and 10 per cent or 13 per cent on most sawnwood, when other developments brought about an agreement for a change more favourable to developing countries. From 1 January 1964, EEC countries and the United Kingdom have abolished tariffs on logs and wood roughly sawn for thirty-five tropical species.

development of processing plants[4] in the developing countries and to the expansion and stabilization of export earnings of these countries.

The removal of tariffs from tropical products, including tropical forest products, has been included as a short-term objective of the GATT Programme of Action undertaken within the framework of the GATT Programme for the Expansion of International Trade.[5] Some progress has been made in eliminating tariffs on tropical forest products. However, many tariffs on a wide range of processed forest products remain to limit access to the markets of industrialized countries. Evidently, measures which would facilitate the entry of processed goods are considered to run counter to the short-term interests of some industry and trading groups in the developed countries. Given the long-term interest of all the developed countries in increasing their imports of processed products from the developing countries, it is not likely that these sectional interests will prevail. Appropriate policies designed to ease the necessary readjustments to the increased flow of imports will doubtless be instituted, as is usually done in every dynamic economy to soften the impact on sectors adversely affected by secular changes in trade and technology. It is likely that the governments of many of the developed countries will accelerate this process of tariff reduction in the forest products sector.

There are two further aspects of the tariff question that may be noted. One is that the removal of tariff barriers tends largely to benefit other industrialized countries which can rapidly expand their output of forest products. The other is that the largest deficits or impending deficits occur in Europe and Japan, and there are also grounds for expecting that the supply of tropical hardwood to North America and the centrally planned economies might expand. Special measures will be needed to ensure that exports from developing countries may expand to take advantage of these markets made available through the removal of tariff obstacles.

These measures may take the form of selective reduction of the tariff barriers in such a way as to assure the developing regions of an expanded market. This preferential treatment accorded to developing regions may not, however, suffice to give the developing countries a foothold in this market, unless other complementary measures are taken.

The range of possible lines of action apart from tariff reduction which the developed importing countries themselves might take to encourage an increasing volume and altered pattern of trade with the developing countries is best surveyed in relation to various categories of forest products. Clearly, measures appropriate for tropical woods and their products (of which the developing countries are the exclusive suppliers) must differ from those appropriate for pulp

[4] The establishment of export capacity in pulp and newsprint, commodities not subject to high tariffs, has been inhibited by other factors.

[5] See GATT, *Basic Instruments and Selected Documents* (Paris, 1959).

and paper and coniferous sawnwood. Likewise a distinction should be made between increasing the volume of trade in the products in crude or semi-processed forms and in processed or manufactured forms. That is, of course, significant not only in terms of the value per unit of trade flow: it also affects the stability of the trade, the value added, and the contribution of trade to the industrialization and diversification of the economy of the exporting countries.

Tropical hardwoods and their products

The potentialities for expanding the flow of trade in tropical hardwoods rest not only in increasing the present volume of trade but also in diversifying its pattern in terms of both production and markets. The overwhelming bulk of trade in tropical hardwoods consists of exports from West Africa and Southeast Asia, but other countries of these regions and of Central America and South America have reserves which could be mobilized.

Here the problem is not merely one of expanding the market for these commodities, but also – and more importantly – one of increasing the proportion of processed products in the export flow from the developing countries. There are some special difficulties for the developing countries in establishing a completely new chain of integrated operations, from logging to the sale of plywood, veneers and sawnwood, in the light of the fact that it is usually market-originating capital which has in the past undertaken such vertical integration on the basis of assured markets. It is easier for the investors to 'back up', so to speak, to their sources of supply than for the suppliers to expand production and hope to win new markets. Accordingly, the most feasible, though not necessarily most desirable, approach might be to induce the manufacturers, distributors and users of processed wood products, such as wholesalers, plywood- and furniture-makers, to extend their operations to the countries producing or capable of producing tropical hardwoods, through financing wood-processing industries and the associated forest operations.

The centrally planned economies are in a position through their state trading organizations to assist the developing countries in expanding their forest operations, and in establishing processing facilities, through negotiating long-term trade agreements which assure a large and sustained market for the processed products and thereby the financial viability of processing plants. The Eastern European and USSR markets, which today accept but a negligible volume of tropical woods, represent an important potential. All these economies are laying greater emphasis on diversifying the range and improving the quality of their durable consumer goods, including furniture. At the present time their per caput consumption of tropical hardwoods is very low compared with that in Western Europe. Should they decide to plan deliberately for a steadily rising utilization of tropical woods, they could provide a new and important trade flow, most of which could and should be in processed form.

Coniferous sawnwood

The developing countries play only a minor role in world trade as a source of coniferous sawnwood. Europe constitutes the most significant international market for the trade in this important type of wood. Most of Europe's import needs are drawn from the USSR, with varying quantities purchased from Canada, which is able to provide dimensions not readily available in Europe or the USSR. As the only other significant flow, Brazil supplies Europe with parana pine.

The likelihood of the developing countries making a greater contribution towards meeting Europe's deficit in sawn softwood is worth some attention. Though in the aggregate they may never constitute a major source of supply for Europe's import needs because of the scattered nature of their reserves of suitable resources, the possibilities of such expansion which do exist bear mention since they will, for the particular countries involved, offer opportunities for export earnings. The crucial issue will centre on price and quality and, in this respect, some developing countries may prove competitive.

Sawn softwood from Chile, produced in low-cost plantations of radiata pine located close to shipping ports, is being marketed in Argentina and Peru. Some shipments to Europe have been made. It might perhaps win a place in the European market if its price could be brought down sufficiently to offset high freight costs and quality differences. The same prospect holds for plantation conifers of East and South-east Africa, which are favoured by lower freight costs than Chile for the Mediterranean market but which are less favourably located in relation to ports. For the tropical pines of South-east Asia, a possible market prospect might be developed in meeting Japan's needs for sawnwood imports. Central American pine also holds some promise of export expansion.

It would be rash to expect any substantial increase in the flow of coniferous sawnwood exports from the developing countries to the developed countries of Europe which constitute the major wood-deficit area. Even Brazil's exports of parana pine to Europe, which have an established market, cannot be expected to increase, despite increasing demand. The sustained supply is not sufficient to meet both the growing demand in Brazil itself and in the River Plate area and that of overseas importers. In any case, the USSR and Canada, as traditional suppliers with great supply elasticities, enjoy more favourable prospects of meeting Europe's increasing import needs than the developing countries as a whole.

To expand the exports from developing countries to any significant degree would call for measures which discriminate in their favour. Since existing tariffs on sawnwood are negligible and the Western European market is very competitive and somewhat variable, fluctuating with year-to-year trends in construction activity, the most promising approach to expanding these exports from developing countries would take the form of bilateral trade arrangements. Under

such agreements the developing countries might be assured of a foothold in the European market. On this basis the increase in exports might be maintained beyond the initial contractual period, provided appropriate measures were taken in the interval by the developing countries themselves. Greater possibilities exist, however, for trying new patterns of trade between the developing industries themselves under bilateral agreements and regional arrangements (which are discussed in a later section).

Pulp and paper

The prospects for establishing a substantial export trade in pulp and paper from the developing countries to the European market are very favourable in the longer term, although circumstances for entering the market are not propitious for the immediate future.

At the present time Scandinavia is supplying the bulk of woodpulp which other European countries import to feed their growing paper industry, as well as providing newsprint, kraft and other mass-production grades of paper. Canada supplies substantial quantities of newsprint; and Europe itself is a net exporter of pulp products to other regions. However, conditions are changing rapidly. In Western Europe, for example, between 1949/51 and 1959/61, production of paper rose by 93 per cent and that of pulp by 73 per cent. Yet over this period Western Europe's net export, of pulp and paper combined, to other regions fell from 1.83 to 0.69 million metric tons. The trend in Eastern Europe was not dissimilar. These trends may be expected to continue. There are now but few unutilized coniferous reserves in Europe capable of sustaining additional pulp and paper capacity. Indeed, the rather anomalous current *excess* of capacity in Western Europe stems largely from a race between companies to pre-empt the remaining sizeable reserves of conifers. This is why many mills, especially in Northern Europe, are presently restricting their operating ratios and why several new projects are being deferred. This situation will not endure. Towards the end of the decade, demand will have caught up with present (and projected) capacity, and in the seventies the European deficit will steadily grow.

To meet this situation steps will undoubtedly have to be taken to extend the available resources in Europe: in the short term, by diverting more fuel-wood to industrial use, by pulping more hardwood, by intensifying the use of thinnings, and by shortening rotations; in the longer term, by undertaking vigorous programmes of forest improvement, quick-growing plantations, and afforestation on lands becoming available as a result of the technical revolution which is taking place in European agriculture. These measures, however, can only modify – they cannot fundamentally transform – the outlook. Moreover, it would be economically unsound to push the effort too far, since beyond a certain point the costs of creating additional resources in Europe would greatly exceed the cost of developing existing resources, or creating new ones in other regions. It may be noted that European production of *short-fibre* pulps, making use of low-grade hardwoods, straw, reeds and eucalyptus plantations, can be expanded to meet a part of this need.

Is it possible for the developing countries to take advantage of this situation? The developing countries, in their bid to capture part of the growing pulp and paper market in Europe, start off with many disadvantages such as lack of capital, know-how, managerial and technical skills, of cheap power and chemicals in some instances, and of distance to the market. However, some countries have one decisive advantage wshich may offset all these disadvantages, namely, a rapid rate of growth. In Chile, Brazil and parts of East and Central Africa, coniferous fibre is being grown at five to ten times the rate (per hectare per year) that is possible in the cool temperate zone of the northern hemisphere, where pulp and paper production today is heavily concentrated. And there are many other areas, in Africa, Latin America and Asia, where new resources – in the shape of plantations of quick-growing conifers – could be created in suitable locations. Similarly, with respect to short-fibre pulps, some extra-European sources might be developed as cheaper sources of supply, as for example, eucalyptus pulp from Madagascar or North Africa, okoumé pulp from Gabon, bagasse pulp from the United Arab Republic or from Central and South America.

One important aspect of this overall problem is how to enable the developing countries to valorize their coniferous resources when they lack the financial and technical means to do so.

Multilateral and bilateral aid possibilities

The situation described above clearly suggests the need not merely for the removal of all trade barriers but also for measures which would go further and promote expanding exports from the developing countries. To achieve this purpose there is great scope for bilateral agreements which would open new channels of trade and thereby expand the flow of trade. These bilateral trade agreements need not only provide assured markets but, of no less importance, they can provide the basis for both bilateral and multilateral capital flows for individual projects and for infrastructural investments. These would be necessary in order to increase the supply from the resources in the developing countries and, as far as possible, augment that supply in the most fully processed form, in order to increase value added per unit of resource and thereby the export earnings of these countries.

The scope for bilateral trade/development agreements (which may, but need not necessarily, include an aid element) rests on the mutual interest both developed and developing countries have in establishing new trade flows. There is a mutual interest at the governmental level. There is also a mutual interest at the sector level – on the part of both industry and trade.

Consider, for example, the prospective shortage of long-fibre pulp in Europe. There is something anomalous about a situation in which we have on the one hand perhaps a dozen European countries anxious to locate and assume new, continuous supplies of long-fibre pulp and, on the other, perhaps as many developing countries anxious to valorize their coniferous resources but lacking the technical and financial means to do so. Obviously, a series of bilateral development/aid projects could confer mutual advantages. The prospective importer would furnish part of the capital, some or all of the equipment, technical and managerial services, and assist in getting the mill established and running, providing the requisite training and advising on the associated forest operations. Repayment would take the form of long-term contracts for part or all of the pulp produced, the selling price of which could be reviewed periodically in the light of trends on the international market. Government short- or medium-term credits could help to tide the sponsoring agency or group over the installation and running-in period. Should third-country expenditures be required (for example, for part of the equipment, or for specialist services), this would be suitable for financing by such international lending institutions as the IBRD or IDA. The sponsoring agency in the prospective importing country might be a state agency in a centrally planned country, or, in the market economy countries, a consortium of existing paper industry interests and equipment manufacturers. It would often be appropriate to include a considerable aid (as distinct from commercial) element in any such bilateral arrangement. The important thing to note is that any aid element in this type of project is one that leads directly to trade.

We have been considering long-fibre pulps, but clearly the same type of project would be valid for other categories, for example, for newsprint. Here newspaper publishers in the prospective importing countries, as well as paper merchants, might well be interested. Integration between newsprint manufacture and newspaper publishing is already very common and widespread. Similarly, kraft paper production would present considerable interest for paper importers and for manufacturers of packaging containers.

We have focused attention on the scope for bilateral arrangements between European countries and developing countries leading to new export flows in pulp and/or paper. But this is only one example. All other developed countries with a present or prospective wood deficit have an equal interest in such an arrangement. And the pulp/paper sector is, of course, not the only forest products category lending itself to such an arrangement. Plywood, veneers, coniferous and broadleaved sawnwood, even board products, all offer the possibility of mutually advantageous trade/development arrangements.

Vestiges of the old prejudice against bilateral trade agreements, as unnecessarily restricting the normal expansion of trade on multilateral lines, still remain in some quarters. But the type of trade/development arrangement which has been outlined in the foregoing paragraphs is in no sense restrictive. On the contrary, it represents an instrument for the constructive expansion of trade, since without the capital flow built into this kind of arrangement, the export capacity cannot be created.

We have considered above the various methods of financing the establishment of forest industries (including essential transport and communication systems as well as industrial plants), but the long-term improvement of the developing countries' forest resources, especially in the field of coniferous plantation establishment, must not be overlooked. Here attention centres not so much on the kind of financial arrangement (whether bilateral or multilateral) but on the source of finance. Neither private capital from outside nor that specifically associated with forest industries development is likely to be available to finance plantations, the production from which cannot be related to a definite project. Nor can developing countries afford to lock up scarce investment funds for periods of twenty years or more. But it is clear from what has been said that there is a very strong case for establishing coniferous plantations in suitable locations in developing countries. Though the returns are long delayed in relation to investments in manufacturing industry, the eventual yield is high. Additionally there are important external economies to be reaped through such investment, since virtually all the investment generates income within the developing country; it relieves underemployment, it diversifies the sources of rural income and thus exerts a high multiplier effect. How then are such plantations to be financed? Here surely is a sphere where private financing could and should make a distinctive contribution. While both multilateral and bilateral arrangements are possible, international sources such as IBRD and IDA must be ready to help finance such projects.

Multilateral agencies might play a key role in relation to infrastructural investment for transport, surveys and training, and in particular for undertaking inventories of existing forest areas and increasing the degree of utilization through improved management practices and control. The assistance of such agencies may be of two kinds. One concerns the provision of survey data, technical know-how and training, while international lending organizations can finance necessary investments in the physical infrastructure.

Another type of arrangement for providing assistance might involve utilization of the current surplus capacity for pulp and paper (including newsprint) in Europe and North America. While this excess and unused capacity exists in several of the developed countries, in many of the developing countries consumption is being artificially depressed through inability to devote sufficient precious foreign exchange to imports of these products. Shortages weigh heavily on newspaper size and circulation, on textbooks and exercise books for schools, and even on paper for commercial and packaging purposes. These two elements – surplus capacity and latent demand – could be merged through bilateral or multilateral development/aid programmes analogous to the use being made of food surpluses for development purposes, as in the World Food Programme.

It is, of course, less simple to devise suitable arrangements in the case of a commodity such as paper. Firstly, paper surpluses are potential, not actual. Secondly, recipient governments might need assurance that acceptance of aid in this form would not involve a curtailment of aid in other, less specifically tied, directions. Donor governments would doubtless wish to be assured that grants of paper would not affect current commercial exports. These problems are similar to many that have been overcome by existing programmes. It might be proposed that in the donor country the paper could be acquired by the government from the producers at marginal cost, while in the recipient country, the paper granted could be disposed of either in the public sector (for example, for educational purposes) or commercially, receipts being placed in a counterpart fund to be applied to development projects. Paper aid for development is not a novelty; such grants have been made in the past by both Canada and Sweden. The information presently available to FAO and Unesco (the latter organization being intensely interested in the development of mass media and the availability of paper for educational purposes) suggests that the government of any developing country which can establish a clear need for paper grants and is prepared to formulate a suitable request will be able to evoke a positive response from one or more of the developed countries with present and potential paper surpluses.

This form of aid has an important side-effect. In most developing countries the national market is extremely small, too small to support a domestic mill of economic size. Paper aid can serve as a market-primer, bringing nearer the day when the establishment of domestic production facilities can be seriously contemplated.

Paper is not the only forest product for which capacity in the developed world is currently in excess of requirements and where this type of aid might be given. Aid in the form of woodpulp may also be contemplated in certain instances, as when non-integrated mills in the developing countries have had to curtail operations for lack of foreign exchange with which to import pulp. Similarly, particle board and fibreboard could be given to the programmes for the building of schools, hospitals, and so on. Here too aid programmes utilizing surplus capacity in the developed countries could make a constructive contribution to development, while serving an important function as market-primers.

The measures, from tariff removal to special trade agreements, which have been mentioned in the foregoing pages as appropriate steps to be taken by the developed countries to foster an increased flow of exports in forest products from the developing countries are not in themselves adequate. Even if all the measures suggested here were to receive swift endorsement and early implementation, this would still not dispense with the need for aid on an increasing scale. The slogan 'trade, not aid' is a spurious one since in this sector, at any rate, the required expansion of trade cannot be secured without an increasing flow of aid, not only in the form of investment capital but also in the form of

professional and technical skills, with provision for training, and in the form
of research and adapted technology.

Assistance in training and research

The need of the developing countries for professional and technical skills will
undoubtedly be met in time as they advance economically and can provide
the requisite teachers and facilities. In the short run it is therefore clearly vital
that the developed countries offer assistance in this sphere. For the immediate
future the pressing needs are for qualified professionals and technicians in the
various key sectors of the economy, including the forestry and forest industries
sectors. The United Nations Special Fund, as well as the technical assistance
programmes of the UN and its specialized agencies, are paying particular
attention to this problem, though the present scale of effort is hardly commen-
surate with the need, even taking into account the many bilateral programmes.

However, the vital importance of training as part of an assistance programme
is increasingly recognized. Under arrangements of the Expanded Programme
of Technical Assistance and the Special Fund of the United Nations, FAO has
initiated a crash programme on forestry education to assist countries in
planning, establishing and strengthening the training facilities necessary to
provide qualified personnel at all levels. Since 1962, forestry faculties, departments or schools have been developed or assisted through multilateral projects
in several countries, and more projects are in preparation. Training centres
on special subjects are being continually sponsored. But these efforts are severely
handicapped by the shortage of qualified personnel in the developed countries.
To increase the supply of qualified personnel and to make effective use of them
calls for national as well as international measures, and coordination of technical
assistance programmes. There is a need to devote many more resources to
financing schools and special training projects. Special incentives to universities
and companies may be needed if experts are to be released to undertake
assignments in the developing countries.

The responsibility of the developed countries for adapting and transferring
suitable technologies to the developing countries is widely acknowledged.
Indeed, the whole problem was discussed at length in the 1963 United Nations
Conference on the Application of Science and Technology for the Benefit of
the Developing Countries. Here the United Nations and the several specialized
agencies are already making a useful contribution. In the forestry and forest
industry sectors the work programme of FAO has in recent years been heavily
oriented towards facilitating this transfer of know-how.

However, experience to date has shown that there are considerable difficulties
in achieving, firstly, the required switch of research effort in the developed countries, and secondly, appropriate means for applying the findings in the developing
countries. Research efforts are scattered among a variety of institutions, public

and private; in all institutions the resources available for research fall short of the needs of existing programmes, so that it is difficult to secure any diversion of funds and personnel to attack problems of main interest to developing countries; and the coordination of research between research institutions in the developed countries is seldom satisfactory – even at the national level.

A review of the situation in the forestry and forest products sectors makes it clear that the need is not for exhortation. Goodwill is not lacking; governments and institutions, both public and private, have signified their readiness to cooperate. As yet, however, it has proved possible in only a few instances to secure the necessary concentration of effort.

One means of securing faster progress might be a more general acceptance of the principle of 'problem adoption' by countries; that is to say, a given developed country would agree to accept as its responsibility the solution of a particular problem of key importance to a group of developing countries. The adopting country would establish the necessary organization and feed in funds where necessary to ensure the orientation of research institutes, training institutes and industry towards the solution of this problem. Where appropriate it would award fellowships, both for research and for in-service training, for candidates from the developing countries. It would collaborate with the developing countries in carrying out tests *in situ*, promoting pilot operations, and so forth. Finally, given an economic breakthrough and a solution to the problem tackled, it would assist the developing countries in setting up commercial operations.

In the forestry and forest industries field there are many urgent problems which might be solved along these lines. For example, an important problem for many developing countries is the development of low-cost housing programmes based on prefabrication techniques, making use in some instances of conifers, in others of secondary hardwoods. The solution of this problem calls for a many-sided attack: materials-testing, preservation techniques, design of suitable units; industrial organization of the supply of elements from the producing plants and their assembly into units; organization, financing and credit of a housing agency; and so forth. There are several developed countries with considerable experience in all these aspects; if their experience to date were brought to bear, and if current research programmes were but slightly modified and supplemented, it should be possible within a short space of time to produce a solution – technically, economically and organizationally appropriate to the circumstances of the developing countries.

Another problem which might be tackled along similar lines is the economic production and practical application of satisfactory glues and resins from locally available animal and vegetable resources. In the plywood and particle board industries up to 20 and 50 per cent respectively of the manufacturing cost may be made up by synthetic resins which, at the present time, have to be imported from advanced countries with sophisticated chemical industries. It is believed that recent technical progress in at least two advanced countries has made possible the economic production of phenol-type resins from a variety of tannin materials. As yet, however, no steps have been taken to make this new technology available to the developing countries which are in a position to make good use of it. Here again, problem adoption might be the best means of ensuring that this new technology is radiated and applied in practice.

These are but two examples; it is not necessary to extend the list here. None of these problems is being completely neglected. But none is moving towards a rapid and practical solution, simply because efforts are not being concentrated for the purpose of specifically assisting the developing countries. If the principle of problem adoption by countries were accepted, this would at once lend purpose to many bilateral aid efforts – which at present are less effective than they might be – and at the same time secure that concentration which could lead to an early solution.

The more specialized efforts of a problem adoption scheme are not alone enough. There must also be a greatly intensified programme of sub-professional and professional education, as well as the adaptation and application of research findings. These must be fostered mainly by international agencies, but can well be supported by bilateral arrangements.

THE TASKS AHEAD OF THE DEVELOPING COUNTRIES

The measures that need to be adopted by the developed countries, namely, the reduction and removal of trade barriers, the increase of capital flows and technical assistance in survey, training and research, and the arrangements for bilateral trade and long-term investment agreements, will avail little unless there is energetic action on the part of the developing countries themselves. These countries face a host of problems in trying to utilize their forest resources effectively to increase export earnings and accelerate the process of industrialization. In the first place, they generally lack an adequate data infrastructure indicating in sufficient detail the extent and nature of their resource endowments and the economic factors upon which to base forest development planning. Thanks to recent advances in survey techniques, it is now possible to obtain the essential data relating to the forest resource much more quickly, and much more cheaply, than was possible but a few years ago. This obstacle has thus become less formidable, though there is still a shortage of experts versed in the new techniques, particularly as applied to heterogeneous tropical forests.

The transport and communication infrastructure in these countries is generally very weak, a matter of special importance to the increased utilization of their forest resources. These resources are sometimes geographically scattered, and usually remote from the urban concentrations, from potential markets and from ports. Heavy investments in road, rail and water communications, in port and harbour facilities, may be required if these resources are to be valorized, as well as social investment at the site. Much of this investment will inevitably be multipurpose, and the forestry and forest industry sectors cannot be expected to bear the whole cost.

It may be observed in passing that the remove location of the forest resource also has a positive aspect. The creation of new forest industry complexes away from the present urban concentrations will provide new poles of development so badly needed in many developing countries. The establishment of new forest industries, and the bringing under effective control and management of the forest resource, will call for a wide range of managerial, professional and technical skills. This, of course, is a problem common to all sectors.

We saw earlier that the development of the forestry and forest industry sectors will call for a very considerable capital investment in the coming years. In the preceding section mention was made of various ways in which capital inflows could be directed into these sectors. But it must not be forgotten that the bulk of the capital needed for developing these sectors must, as for all other sectors, be mobilized by the developing countries from within their own economies. Foreign capital inflows can only be supplemental to domestically generated capital. On a global basis, in relation to the requirements of the developing countries, the current capital flow from developed to developing countries is inadequate both in total and in its geographic and sectoral distribution; it is likely to remain so for many years to come. This applies to both private capital flows and to bilateral and multilateral grants and loans.

Given the chronic scarcity of capital, what are the arguments for affording priority to these sectors? Some have already been expressly stated; others have been implied. They can be summarized briefly as follows: high elasticity, with respect to income, of the demand for forest products, especially at low income levels; high import-saving effect; considerable export potential; the multiplier effect of investment in these sectors; the considerable external economies achieved; the considerable flexibility of the wide range of forest industries in relation to scale of operations and factor requirements.

It has been pointed out previously that the prospects for foreign capital entering these sectors are bright – brighter than for many other sectors of the economy. This is because many of the developed countries will have a direct interest in promoting forest and forest industry development in the developing countries. This very fact at once warrants and is likely to encourage the direction of domestic capital into these sectors: warrants, because it stretches the total capital resources available; encourages, because domestic capital, public and private, will see advantage in being associated with foreign capital and the know-how and skills it can bring to the development of these sectors.

It is important that, within the sectors, the capital investment be wisely directed. The developing countries have a responsibility to assure this. In the past there have been serious cases of misinvestment. Sometimes, in their alacrity to realize substantial import savings, projects have been undertaken without regard to the sustained availability of the raw material. In other cases insufficient attention has been paid to other production factors – water and chemicals, for example. In still others, unsuitable technologies have been selected.

The dangers of misinvestment are greater than ever today precisely because, in all parts of the developing world, there is a growing conviction of the need for a regional approach to problems of development. The case for a regional approach in the forest industries sector is particularly strong, since in many branches, especially newsprint, chemical pulp and fibreboard, scale economies are very pronounced, while many national markets are still too small to support mills of economic size. A coordination of national plans is necessary if efficient, low-cost industries, capable of entering the export market, are to be established. Moreover, such coordination will certainly facilitate the flow of capital to the sector.

There are other considerations which favour a regional approach. It makes possible the rational use of complementary resources available in neighbouring countries (long-fibre and short-fibre material, paper-making fibre and processing chemicals, cheap hydro-power, veneer logs, wood waste and synthetic resins, and so on). It favours the establishment of integrated forest industry complexes. Given a regional approach, it is possible to make economic use of scarce managerial and technical skills and to coordinate research facilities. The common tariff, a feature of all regional economic integration schemes so far proposed, is evidently but the first step. It may facilitate but it cannot of itself assure, that the advantages of the regional approach are realized.

Some of the advantages mentioned can, of course, be realized without formal regional planning and even without a common market. The confrontation, and where appropriate adjustment, of national development plans for this sector by pairs or groups of developing countries which have trade links or common trade interests can have positive results.

All that has been said points to the urgent need for developing countries to establish closer policy links between the central planning authorities concerned with overall development policy and those concerned with forest and forest industry development.

As yet, few of the developing countries have been able to establish the planning structure and to find or train the requisite qualified administrative and professional personnel. However, there are indications of progress, with policies for forest industry development being more clearly defined in the context of overall development policy, with administrative structure and processes being strengthened, and with programmes for gathering and interpreting relevant information as a basis for policy being more effectively carried out.

The need for close links between those responsible for the sectors we are considering here and those responsible for overall planning is sufficiently clear. Even more obvious is the need for the maximum coordination between those responsible for the management of the forest resource and those responsible for the development of forest industries. Yet it is precisely here that we have, in very many developing countries, a critical hiatus. This lack of effective collaboration hampers the efforts to realize soundly based forest industry development. There are strong arguments at any rate in those countries in which forest industries already play or are destined to play a key role, for concentrating responsibility for forestry and forest industries in the same department or ministry. Apart from the impetus this can give to forest industry development, it is the best means of ensuring that the non-crop values of the forest are not neglected, and that unwise exploitation does not bring in its train floods, erosion and water shortage.

The sooner the appropriate planning machinery and institutional arrangements just discussed are established, the sooner they can become effective. The technical and economic conditions for establishing new forest industries in the developing countries are maturing fast. Those governments which are alive to the situation are already taking the initial steps, often seeking technical assistance from appropriate multilateral agencies, especially the Special Fund of the United Nations, the Expanded Technical Assistance Programme and FAO, as well as from bilateral programmes. Thus essential resource data are being assembled and analysed, present and potential markets are being investigated and in some cases deliberately planned, the needed cadres are being trained, and pilot plans for demonstration and training established. Steps are being taken to secure the forest estate, and to bring key areas under effective management. Feasibility studies are being conducted, and medium- and long-term development plans adumbrated.

Nevertheless, having regard to particular opportunities offered by the forest and forest industries sectors, especially for building up a substantial export to the developed countries, it is to be feared that the pace of these developments is still too slow, and that many countries which do possess the necessary resource endowment have thus far failed to see the opportunities that lie ahead.

In this paper emphasis has been placed on the export opportunities that will arise for the developing countries by the year 1975. But the developing countries must not limit themselves to this time horizon, which has been selected here only for expositional purposes. It is clear from the trends which have been delineated that export opportunities will further increase in the closing decades of this century. The conditions exist for a progressive and profound modification of the pattern of international trade in forest products in favour of the developing countries. How far these opportunities are realized, by 1975 and in the decades to follow, depends on the speed with which the developing countries shape their policies in the years immediately ahead to take advantage of them.

3

The Forester as Agent of Change

If there is one charge that cannot be levelled against professionals, it is that of taciturnity. Professionals, as a group, tend to be rather vocal, even voluble – certainly more vocal than most ordinary members of the community. From time to time, they even become eloquent. Indeed, I suppose they are never more eloquent than when they are striving to convince the community that what they conceive to be their own interests are identical with the interests of the community. Recent history provides us with many examples. I recall the resistance of some religious groups to the secularization of schools, or even the introduction of non-denominationalism into schools; the resistance of the legal profession to certain forms of legal aid; the resistance of the medical profession to Medicare. These are but some examples, but the list could be extended almost indefinitely. Indeed, even members of the supposedly 'silent' services have been known to break into speech or print, or to trigger off informed voices or authorized sources, when weapons systems, and weapons contracts, are under discussion.

Maybe all these actions are fully consonant with the view that is sometimes put forward: that the distinguishing mark of the professional is that he invariably puts his client's interest above his own. But it is my impression that, when there have been apparent collisions between professional groups and the community at large, the community, at any rate, has not always been convinced that the motives of the professional were entirely altruistic. This ought to put us on our guard during this present conference, since I think we must admit, if we are honest with ourselves, that the professional is coming increasingly under suspicion. The nature of that suspicion is perhaps best summed up by George Bernard Shaw's terse dictum: 'All professions are conspiracies against the laity.' This present conference is a conference of professionals, organized by professionals, but not – if I read the minds of the organizers aright – *for* professionals.

A paper for the Centennial Year of the University of California, Professional Schools' Programme, Berkeley, May 1968.

It is concerned rather with those services which the professional renders to the community and how those services can be improved. And it is particularly concerned with those communities that find themselves lagging in the development race. I do not know whether this conference will come to any findings or conclusions. But if it does, I sincerely hope that they will be set forth with sufficient clarity and frankness to disarm the suspicions of the laity, and to make it apparent that, during these three days at least, the professionals were concerned with the interests of the community rather than with their own.

When I was first invited to join this conference, I felt a good deal of sympathy for the organizers. This was not because, given the attribute of professionals to which I alluded earlier, I envisaged a talkathon, a veritable outbreak of logorrhea. It was because I realized that the organizers would have to solve, if possible without offending anyone, a difficult puzzle which has often intrigued me, namely: what constitutes a profession? A simple solution, of course, would have been to admit, as professions, those disciplines represented in the professional schools on the Berkeley campus. But I suppose that not even Berkeley's academic eminence would have justified such a self-consciously parochial solution. The problem arises in part because of the recent proliferation of professions. Once we leave the 'archetypal' professions (and let me say in passing how grateful I am to EDUCATION AND WORLD AFFAIRS for this adjective!), it is really very difficult to know where to draw the line.

It seems to me that, in endeavouring to determine what constitutes a profession, there are certain identifiable elements:

1 A profession consists of a group of persons whose contribution to society comprises not material goods or commodities, but services which they render to society. These services may be rendered to society as a whole, or to individuals, groups or classes within society;

2 The adequate rendering of these services is deemed to require advanced training in a certain group of related disciplines, and/or some kind of in-service training or apprenticeship over a shorter or longer period;

3 In most instances, perhaps in all instances, it is the group itself which takes the initiative in describing its services as a profession, which lays down the necessary conditions or desiderata governing entry into the profession, and which wins consent, which may be active or tacit, from society for the action it has taken.

Thus, most professions are, in fact, self-proclaimed. In most societies there is no screening committee for adjudicating the merits of the self-proclaimed professions. That the services which the professional renders should be useful to society is not a necessary condition for professionalism. Historically, there have been societies in which some contemporary professions would have been irrelevant. Equally, future societies may deem some of our contemporary professions irrelevant.

The recognition of a new profession comes seldom by a single act of state. Rather, an emerging profession wins minor acknowledgement in a series of preliminary skirmishes, enlarges its foothold through sporadic *ad hoc* decisions, which may be executive or judicial decisions, and eventually stands forth in full autonomy and splendour, often to the mystification of the community at large which had failed to recognize the new invader.

My sympathy for the organizers of this conference sprang exactly from the fact that most professions are self-proclaimed. Had the organizers taken a truly catholic view, then I would not have been at all surprised to see, given the introspection that pervades all professions today, figuring among the papers submitted to this conference, titles such as: 'The brewer faces the future', 'Morticians at the crossroads', and 'Dry-cleaning in the space age'. However, the list of invitees that reached me a few months ago suggested that the organizers had agreed on a somewhat narrower definition of what constitutes a profession.

It might be thought that, since those of us who have been admitted to this conference have somehow or other survived the attention of some kind of credentials committee, we should be content to let the matter rest, and get down to the theme to which we have been asked to address ourselves. However, I feel that I must labour this point a little longer, not because I want to invoke your sympathies for those unfortunates who have been left outside the door by the organizers, but because the profession with which I am most intimately acquainted has become somewhat concerned of late over its own credentials. I speak of the credentials of the forestry profession, not of my own personal credentials: these latter, in fact, will scarcely bear examination, since I can only claim to have become a forester through absorption. Typical of the self-doubt which characterizes the forestry profession today is the guest editorial which appeared in the official organ of the Society of American Foresters, contributed by no less an authority than the Dean of the Berkeley Forestry School, John A. Zivnuska, under the title, 'Forestry: a profession or a field of work?'.[1] Before commenting on Zivnuska's case, which relates essentially to the contemporary American scene, it is perhaps germane to glance at the early origins of the forestry profession. For forestry, though by no means one of the 'archetypal' professions, is certainly not a recent upstart.

Ordinances governing the use of the forest have a venerable history. There were many paragraphs in Roman Law, for example, which dealt with forest property and forestry offences. If the first interventions by public authority had to do with the religious functions of the forest, in subsequent centuries questions of grazing rights in the forest attracted most attention. Mounting pressure on the forests in Europe through the Middle Ages led to a series of ordinances aimed at conserving the forests and their use for hunting. In

[1] John A. Zivnuska, 'Forestry: a profession or a field of work?' *Journal of Forestry*, 61:5 (1963).

fourteenth-century France, Charles V introduced the first forest code, designed to bring about some form of management into the forests since he wanted to build a strong navy. But the most momentous and far-reaching step came with the publication of Colbert's ordinance in 1669, which set forth general aims (which took into account navigable waters, hunting and fishing, as well as timber production), prescribed management methods (designed to conserve the forest capital, but also to produce clean, straight oak stems for shipbuilding), and laid down penalties. England had long had similar preoccupations, but desultory measures taken by successive English monarchs, often in imitation of the French kings, did little to stop forest depletion. Even the publication of John Evelyn's *Sylva*, in 1664, brought little improvement. Norwegian timber, which had begun to reach England already in the thirteenth century, was largely used for rebuilding London after the Great Fire of 1666, and the first North American timber was brought in by Samuel Pepys, Charles II's Secretary to the Navy, in 1668.

But the true beginnings of forestry science, and hence the roots of professional forestry, were in Germany. The first significant technical publication was *Jagd und Forstrecht* (1561), By Noe Meurer, adviser to the Palatine Elector. This was followed by two important works by Johannes Colerus, of Brandenburg, late in the century. But even before forestry science started to make progress, forest services were building up, correlated to some extent with the varying exigencies of the wood supply situation which characterized the several principalities. Thus, already in the fifteenth century, Tyrol had an *Obrist-Forstmeister*.

After the setback of the Thirty Years War, German forestry science really began to blossom. The practical knowledge about the forests accumulated since classical times began to be interpreted scientifically and applied systematically to suit man's needs. After the publication by Carlowitz of *Economic Sylviculture* in 1713, Moser and others established the first management plans. The work of Oettelt, who applied mathematical calculus to the determination and control of forest production, gave rise to the foundation of the early forestry schools, the first of which was established in Ilsneburg by Zanthier in 1768. The most successful and famous one was established by Cotta, first in Zillbach (1795), and later transferred to Tharand in Saxony (1811). The Tharand Forestry School flourished quickly and attracted many foreign students, who later founded new forestry schools in other countries, such as France (1825) and Spain (1848).

Thus, one can say that forestry as a profession was born in Germany in the second half of the eighteenth century. For it was here that theoretical work in a number of relevant disciplines led to an understanding of practical forestry, an understanding which was broadened by systematic research and disseminated through a body of students who felt that they belonged to a learned trade.

In Austria and Russia, German progress was being followed very closely, and schools were also established in the early years of the nineteenth century. Also, at this period, Hartig published his famous work on how to obtain a predetermined sustained yield and how to treat the forest so that it could attain an ideal status, according to observation and experience. It was a German who first headed the Indian forest service, and the Dehra Dun School was established in 1878, some years before the first Chair of Silviculture was established in Britain. The first modern forestry administration in Japan, in 1875, was headed by Matsuno, who had attended the Eberswalde school, while it was a Prussian immigrant, Bernhard Fernow, who, by his appointment as chief of the Division of Forestry in the US Department of Agriculture, may be said to have introduced scientific forestry to North America.

This short historical excursion, for which I apologize, will perhaps have served to show that forestry as a profession, while not 'archetypal', is far from 'arriviste'.

At the latest count, the world has 185 forestry schools of university level. Of these, 56 are in Europe (including the USSR), 44 in North America, and 34 in other developed countries: Japan, Australia, South Africa and New Zealand. This makes a total of 134 in the developed world. The developing world has 51 professional forestry schools. Twenty of these are in mainland China, 16 in Asia, 12 in Latin America and 3 in Africa.

The annual outturn of all these forestry schools is around 7,000. The present world force of professional foresters is estimated at around 88,000, of which 32,000 in Europe (including the USSR), 30,000 in North America, and 9,000 in other developed countries. This makes 71,000 or about 81 per cent of the world force, operating in developed countries. Of the remaining 17,000, working in the developing world, no less than 11,000 are in mainland China, 4,000 in Asia (excluding Japan and mainland China), 1,500 in Latin America and 500 in Africa. Taking the world as a whole, probably two thirds of all foresters, around 60,000 in all, are employed in the public sector, and the overwhelming majority of these will be concerned mainly with public forests of one kind or another.

Like most other professions, the world force of professional foresters is heavily concentrated in the developed countries. It is not, compared with many other professions, a particularly numerous profession. Yet it does occupy a certain strategic position, firstly by virtue of the fact that so many of its members are employed in the public sector: this enables them to have, provided clear and far-sighted forest policies have been adopted, a more direct impact on events than have some of their sister professions; secondly, by virtue of the extent of the lands, mainly public lands, in their charge. The significance of these points from the development angle may perhaps be better appreciated if we recall that, whereas in Western Europe and the USA only 35 per cent and 27 per cent respectively of forest lands are in the public domain, in the developing world as a whole (excluding mainland China), no less than 67 per cent of forest lands are publicly owned. In fact, most developing countries subscribe to the views on basic natural resources enshrined in Resolution no. 2158 (XXI) of the General Assembly of the United Nations, the relevant paragraphs of which read as follows:

PERMANENT SOVEREIGNTY OVER NATURAL RESOURCES

The General Assembly. . .

Recognizing that the natural resources of the developing countries constitute a basis of their economic development in general and of their industrial progress in particular,

Bearing in mind that natural resources are limited and in many cases exhaustible and that their proper exploitation determines the conditions of the economic development of the developing countries both at present and in the future,

Considering that, in order to safeguard the exercise of permanent sovereignty over natural resources, it is essential that their exploitation and marketing should be aimed at securing the highest possible rate of growth of the developing countries,

Considering further that this aim can better be achieved if the developing countries are in a position to undertake themselves the exploitation and marketing of their natural resources so that they may exercise their freedom of choice in the various fields related to the utilization of natural resources under the most favourable conditions. . .

1   *Reaffirms* the inalienable right of all countries to exercise permanent sovereignty over their natural resources in the interest of their national development, in conformity with the spirit and principles of the Charter of the United Nations and as recognized in General Assembly resolution 1803 (XVII).

1478th plenary meeting,
25 November 1966

Thus, during the post-war period, one of the first initiatives taken by many newly independent nations has been to take legal and administrative steps to characterize the forest as a national resource. This has often meant bringing forests into the public domain.

So far I have evaded giving a direct answer to the question: wherein lies the professionalism of forestry? Here it is convenient to refer back to the article by Zivnuska, which I mentioned earlier. This article starts out with the statement: 'The practice of forestry involves the management of forests and related wild lands for the various ends of society. A forester is a manager of forests and wild lands for these ends.' This, I think, brings us close to the heart of the matter, though I am not completely convinced that Zivnuska, in developing his theme, has rigorously pursued all the implications of his opening formulation to their limits.

The forester is a resource manager. The resource with which he is concerned includes not only forests but also related wild lands, lands marginal to, perhaps held in reserve for, settled agriculture. This resource ought, in principle, to belong to the community. But even if, for historical or ideological reasons, the resource does not belong to the community, it should be managed in conformity with the long-term interest of the community. The social values which this resource can yield are by no means limited to timber production. Proper management of the resource consists in giving due weight to the whole range of goods and services which forest lands can provide, producing them in the blend needed by the community, without unduly restricting the options for the future.

What kind of man is fitted to discharge this responsibility? Only a man who has received the necessary training in the related basic and applied sciences and in the relevant social sciences, together with some kind of in-service training. This is the kind of man that all professional forestry schools worth their salt set out to form. If they are today failing, if they are afflicted with self-doubt, it is largely because they have become so absorbed by, even hypnotized by, the many-sided advances on the scientific front which have brought the technological revolution to forestry, and by the need to assimilate and apply all this new knowledge, that they have overlooked the basic truth: that forestry is as much about people as it is about trees.

Forestry is by no means as closed a profession as some of its sister professions. The accreditation activities carried out by some professional forestry societies (of which perhaps the Society of American Foresters affords the best example) are aimed rather at improving educational standards than at excluding oddballs and amateurs. In no country as yet is a *professional* licence necessary before one is permitted to approach a tree. This tolerant attitude, I believe, springs less from a fear of the revolt and chaos that would attend any attempt to lay down and enforce standards than from a deep appreciation of the contributions made to professional forestry by other disciplines, and a recognition of the signal contributions to forestry made in the past by oddballs and amateurs. My hunch is that, with the changing tasks of forestry, the profession in the future will become less, rather than more, self-contained, and that practitioners of other disciplines, together with oddballs and amateurs, will be more, rather than less, welcomed in its ranks. Yet, for all that, there is something special about a forester. It is inherent in the characteristics of the resource with which he is concerned, in the disciplines he must summon to apprehend that resource, and in the relationship between the resource and the community. Every forester, through his training, comes to recognize the long-term public interest and the points at which this interest conflicts with the short-term interest, public or private, and he is expected to set the former before the latter. He is expected to serve as the public conscience on matters of resource management and resource use. This is the forester's version of the Hippocratic oath in medicine.

THE FORESTER'S STOCK OF KNOWLEDGE

The stock of knowledge which the forester requires to have at his disposal (by which I mean he should know where to find it, and how to use it when he has found it) is increasing exponentially. This is the main reason for the contemporary critical reappraisal of the content of forestry education.

The problem is partly bound up with the changing tasks of the forester. One reason (though not the only reason) why these tasks are changing fast is that the full implications of the principle of multiple use are now beginning to be understood. For many years now there have been few to quarrel with the notion that the forest is capable of producing, besides a variety of crop values, of which timber is the most important, a wide range of other benefits, some physical and tangible, others aesthetic and intangible, but no less prized. Since the principle of multiple use became enshrined in the forester's terminology at the Fifth World Forestry Congress, held in Seattle in 1960, we have seen sharp changes in the social preference scales in very many countries. Concern about adequate supplies of clean water; anxiety to stem rural depopulation; the upsurge in recreational demand: these and other factors have focused more attention on the previously less regarded roles of the forest. In a growing number of countries, and in a growing number of zones in most countries, the timber crop functions of the forest are already subordinate to the other functions of the forest, and the objectives of forest management are continually changing – so much so that in several industrialized countries production forestry as an economic activity is already adversely affected. Indeed, foresters have much yet to learn about the economics of providing these non-timber values from the forest. Until they have done this, they are hardly likely fully to convince society of the need to underwrite the costs of social forestry, of providing community benefits.

But even within the narrow context of timber production, the array of technical and economic knowledge which the forester needs to have within his reach is growing with incredible rapidity. The technological revolution concerns the growing of wood, the harvesting and transport of wood, and the industrial transformation of wood. Here the problem which faces the forester is akin to that which faces all other professionals, though it is perhaps possible that the problem is more acute for the forester, since the range of disciplines which feed into forestry is immensely wide, and since the technological revolution has reached forestry rather late. Only a few in the profession have as yet truly comprehended the significance for the profession of the computer, of the radio-isotope, of the earth satellite, for example.

Progress in the managerial sciences is also beginning profoundly to affect the outlook of the forester. Increasingly, forestry literature is studded with references to operations research, systems analysis, linear programming, critical path analysis, and so on. The new managerial techniques are being increasingly invoked by foresters, as their attention shifts to what we might term the macro-economics of the forestry enterprise. A good deal of attention has been paid since the war to the micro-economics of forestry, but it is only quite recently that the profession has started to give serious consideration to the question: what intensity of management pays? Simulation models, based on new data-handling facilities, permit precise estimates of the effect of various interventions, so that, for example, data derived from the forest inventory can now be used not simply for medium- and long-term working plans, but also for day-to-day management decisions.

Finally, the forester, who has always been addicted to planning in his own sector, has come to realise the imperative necessity for his plans to be articulated with those for other sectors of the economy. There is thus a growing interest on the part of foresters in the relationship between what happens in their own sector and what happens in the economy at large. I shall have occasion to touch on the nature of this relationship a little later on. For the moment, I would simply point out that this question of inter-sectoral relationships is one that was for long neglected by foresters.

Perhaps I have already said enough to demonstrate that the stock of knowledge on which the forester must be able to call is growing rapidly, partly as a result of the forester's changing tasks, partly as a result of the acceleration in research and technology. Thus the conscientious forestry educator has repeatedly to pose himself the question: how much of what I am currently teaching is already obsolete, and how much will be obsolete by the time my charges take the field? And if he is intelligent as well as conscientious, he must necessarily ask himself the even more basic question: is it my job to help them develop their brains, or merely to fill them? Much of the controversy, and most of the confusion, in the sphere of forestry eduction today could be avoided if this question were explicitly put and explicitly answered. There is scarcely a forest faculty board anywhere that does not have its annual tug-of-war around the curriculum. The lecturer in wood anatomy needs an extra semester hour; the silviculturalist needs two additional semester hours; the professor of forest management needs extra time, and so forth. So fast are their disciplines advancing and changing, they argue, that unless these claims can be accom-modated, their protégés will go forth naked into the world. So, three-year course become four-year courses; four-year courses are expanded to five years; and the case is advanced for a sixth year. Meanwhile, the timetable of the poor student becomes more and more crammed with class and lecture hours, until he is caught in the toils of these formal aspects of education for thirty-five and forty hours a week or more. This pretty well ensures that he gets no time to think, and, in particular, no time to think up awkward questions for his mentors. Obviously, this problem of keeping pace with rapidly advancing science and technology is not soluble by prolonging and cramming the curriculum. That way madness lies – not merely because it is patently absurd to hope to absorb and relay the expanding pool of knowledge; but because the essence of professionalism lies not in storing up knowledge, but in knowing how to recognize what is relevant, how to track it down, how to analyse it, and how to apply it. If we fail to understand this, then we may as well write off forestry as a profession; we are relegating it to the level of a technical vocation. Though our schools may turn out well trained technicians, these are not the men and women who will be capable of discharging the responsible tasks which face the professional forester today.

This problem, of getting the true meaning and purpose of professional forestry education back into focus, is particularly important when we come to consider training professionals for work in the developing countries, whether we are speaking of young men from the developing countries who come to Europe or North America to study, or of our own young people who intend to spend part of their career overseas. For, as I shall show presently, the tasks which confront the young professional in the developing country are infinitely more delicate and complex than those that confront a young professional here, and the responsibilities he has to bear are infinitely greater.

FORESTRY BECOMES INTERNATIONAL

If foresters today are looking more and more beyond their national boundaries, and showing greater concern with international forestry, this is not simply a reflection of the scientific need, common to all disciplines, for a greater international exchange of national experience. This need certainly exists, and in the forestry field it is reinforced by three particular considerations. Firstly, forest types have nothing whatever to do with political boundaries. Secondly, new resource/people situations are continually arising which, though perhaps novel in the national context, frequently have marked similarities to situations already encountered elsewhere. Thirdly, the man-made forest is coming to play a greater and greater part in providing for wood needs, and a significant proportion of man-made forests makes use of exotics.

However, the rising need for an international exchange of national experience is not the only factor enlarging the forester's horizon. The acceleration in the world's industrial wood consumption since mid-century, accompanied by radical changes in the pattern of wood consumption, has brought increasing pressure on the available wood resources of certain regions. These current shifts in regional wood resource/requirements balances are steadily leading to a somewhat different international division of labour in the world forest and timber economy. Thus the proportion of the world's wood needs met through international trade has increased, and is destined to continue to increase. In the new pattern which is emerging, many of the developing countries will have an important part to play, since they are so favoured by soil and climate, by land and labour availability, that they can grow industrial wood at many times the rate, and at a fraction of the cost, as can the developed areas of the world where forest industries are presently concentrated. The new international division of labour will in many respects be a more intelligent one than the present one. It will represent a more effective use of existing resources; it will require the creation of new resources according to a sensible pattern.

The changes which are taking place in the world forest and timber economy have been summarized in a recent FAO study, 'Wood: world trends and prospects'.[2] The conclusions flowing from this study present an indispensable frame of reference which individual countries have increasingly to take into account as they redefine their forest policies and lay down forest production goals. There is no country today which can regard its forest economy as a closed one. Each country, in establishing its forest production goals, must have before it some clear concept, and if possible a quantified concept, of its future place in the world forest and timber economy. It must have some idea of the extent to which it intends to rely on imports to satisfy its future wood needs. It must have some notion of the extent to which it intends or expects its own forest resources to contribute to the wood needs of other couontries.

Obviously, it is no easy matter to define the degree of self-sufficiency a country should aim at, say, in twenty or fifty years' time, or the size of the exportable surplus it should aim to create. But an obvious starting point, in deciding how much investment to direct into the forest sector in order to raise national industrial wood production by a certain amount by a given target date, is to consider how the cost of generating additional wood supplies (and valorizing them) compares with the costs of generating extra wood supplies in other parts of the world. As yet, an adequate information basis for tendering sound advice to public authorities is woefully lacking, and this is because only quite recently have foresters understood that this is a matter which concerns them. But today more and more foresters are coming to understand that each national forest resource is but part of a global resource, and that it has to be developed and managed in an international context. This, then, is another important reason why forestry is steadily becoming more international in outlook.

But there is a third reason, and this is directly connected with the problem that has brought us together in this conference. Though we may inhabit one *physical* world, economically, socially and politically we live in two worlds, and these two worlds – the affluent, technologically advanced, developed world, and the poorer, more populous, technically backward, developing world – are getting farther apart. The affluent North – individuals, statesmen and governments – feels a sense of responsibility and obligation towards the South in this situation. We would be less than honest with ourselves if we failed to acknowledge that motivations are mixed on the side of the affluent North. In

---

[2] *Unasylva*, Vol. 20: (1–2) Numbers 80–1 (1966). Revised as FAO *Basic Study No. 16* (1967).

part, this obligation stems from common humanity. In part, it lies in the feeling that moral debts piled up in a century of colonial exploitation of the South by the North are now due for repayment. In part, it is rooted in the fear of the social upheavals that may sweep away its way of life if something is not done quickly. Those of us who are professionals, and who have greater occasion to draw on the universal pool of knowledge, and perhaps more frequent opportunities for observing the disparities between the two worlds, have a special responsibility. Indeed, one would hope that, in the spectrum of our motivations, the higher wavelengths predominate. It is my impression, though I admit I have no solid grounds for asserting this, that, among professionals, foresters are more than averagely sensitive to this responsibility. If this is so, it doubtless springs from the fact that the notion of service to the community plays a somewhat more important role in the formation of foresters than in the formation of some other professionals. But whether or not this is true of the forestry profession as a whole, it certainly seems to be true of the rising generation of foresters. In recent years I have met and talked with forestry students on many campuses, in North America, in Western and Eastern Europe. Everywhere I have been struck by the numbers who were aware of the problems which have brought us together today, and by their earnest desire to see their professional skills harnessed to some form of international service. Some time ago I was informed (and there may be those in this conference who can confirm whether this is still true) that the percentage volunteering for the Peace Corps was highest among forestry students. Certainly, scarcely a day passes that does not bring to my desk in Rome a letter from a senior forestry student or a recently graduated forester asking what opportunities there are for international service and how he can best fit himself for such a career.

The following extract gives a clue to the outlook of young foresters today. It is from a letter written by a young Californian forester (unknown to me), to the *Journal of Forestry*, the journal of the Society of American Foresters. It runs: 'We youngsters can't get all worked up about professionalism, the 'image' problem, etc. These things are becoming irrelevant to us. What does matter, I believe, is how we can meaningfully involve ourselves in our social and physical environment and discover new worthwhile goals that modern society is forcing us to search for.'[3]

FORESTRY AND THE DEVELOPING COUNTRIES

It will be evident to you, from what I have already said, that the tasks which face the forester today and tomorrow in the developed countries are much more complex, and much more responsible, than those which faced him yesterday.

[3] *Journal of Forestry*, Vol. 66: (1), (1968).

He will be much more concerned with what I have loosely termed social forestry, the management of the forests to provide an expanding flow of those physical benefits and social values which the forests are capable of generating for the community, and he must seek to do this at minimum cost for the community. At the same time he must grow a timber crop, as economically as possible, for a wide range of forest industries which, because of technological progress and changing patterns, are bringing about radically different calls on the forest. But all this, you will say, is equally true of the professional forester in a developing country. And indeed it is. But there are two important differences. The first is that the professional forester in most developing countries has, practically from the outset of his career, to resolve issues of such complexity, and to take decisions of such moment, as his colleague in the developed country will probably not be called upon to take in the first ten years of his professional service, if, indeed, he is ever called upon to take them. The second is that the professional forester in the developing country is obliged to be development-oriented.

Most foresters entering their professional career in the developed countries take service with a public forestry authority, with private forestry estates, or in the forests of industrial companies. Their first years are still years of apprenticeship. This is when they learn to become 'dirt' foresters. They carry out a variety of technical, and often menial, assignments. They absorb the wisdom of their elders and betters in the profession. For many young foresters these are the years of disillusion, of complaints that their technical knowledge and mental capacities are under-utilized. These are the years of maximum fall-out from the profession. The plain fact is that in most developed countries professionals are under-utilized and uneconomically deployed. Many of the tasks on which they are engaged could equally be carried out by competent technicians. Those professionals who survive this period of their service (and a surprisingly high proportion do) are given new assignments of progressively increasing responsibility, and eventually get the opportunity of applying the problem-solving and decision-taking capacities they carried out of school, if in the meantime these capacities have not atrophied.

But in many developing countries, so acute is the shortage of professional foresters, the young forester starting his career is likely to find himself plunged immediately into tasks involving heavy functional or area responsibilities. The problems that come across his desk, or that confront him in the field, are frequently of a complexity that his training and limited experience have ill equipped him to resolve. Moreover, many of the problems are different in kind from those which faced his expatriate predecessors in pre-independence days. He is now compelled to approach all his tasks with a development orientation. This is because governments in the developing countries are coming to understand that the forestry sector is capable of making a special contribution to the process of overall economic growth. The reasons for this, which derive from our improved understanding of the relationship between the forestry sector and other sectors of the economy, can be briefly summarized as follows.

Firstly, the forest and forest industry sector has significant backward linkages and important forward linkages; thus, expansion of this sector has a repercussive effect through the economy generally.

Secondly, income elasticities of demand for many forest products are rather high, especially at low income levels; other things being equal, sectors with dynamic demand characteristics warrant priority in development programmes.

Thirdly, forest industries rank high as import savers, and can be potential export earners.

Fourthly, forest industries are based on locally available raw material, a consideration justifying priority in development programmes.

Fifthly, forest industries represent a wide range of factor inputs, scales of operation, and technologies. Few other industrial sectors offer such flexibility and choice of alternatives.

Sixthly, much of the demand for several important forest products arises in the public sector. In developing economies, consumption and production facilities can be planned in harmony.

Seventhly, the forestry sector reaches back into rural areas and forward into the industrial sector; it can therefore facilitate the diffusion of industrial skills and absorption of underemployed rural labour necessary in early stages of development.

Eighthly, under certain circumstances, frozen forest capital can be transformed into liquid capital, feeding the development process.

Ninthly, because most forest industries are located near the raw material source, their establishment can provide new poles of development in developing countries, curbing the rising social costs of excessive urban concentrations.

Finally, the optimum contribution of the forestry and forest industries sectors to economic growth will come only if forest development plans are closely integrated with national economic development plans.

As these facts become more widely understood, governments are understandably loth to face rising import bills for forest products essential for economic development and cultural advance, or to see their forest wealth disappearing in unprocessed form overseas, where the value added in manufacture accrues to industries in the developed countries. Thus the pressure is constantly on the forester to do something to rectify this situation. No longer can he content himself with being a tree-tender. He has to become a forest-mobilizer, and set about managing, developing and industrializing his forests in the interests of the total development effort. Hence, a senior forester in a developing country is called upon daily to explain to, argue and negotiate with, planning officers, development institutions, finance and trade ministers, potential investors, industrial consultants, equipment suppliers, bankers, and so forth, and must strive to do this in language which all these can understand. And the pity of it is that the forestry school at which he graduated probably had no concept of how important it would be to him to get acquainted with this language. Not surprisingly, his judgement often errs. But the miracle is that so many of this new generation of foresters in the developing countries learn to swim so quickly and so well in seas that would daunt their contemporaries in the developed countries. The miracle is all the more astounding when we bear in mind that the senior forester in the developing country does not have at his beck and call the massive institutional support, research services, specialized staff and documentation facilities that his fellows in the developed countries enjoy. And we must never forget that he normally has to operate with forces that are under-trained and inadequate in numbers, and on a shoestring budget. In short, the job of a professional forester in a developing country is not only different; it is a good deal tougher. Once we appreciate this, we can begin to get some understanding of what is wrong with the education we give him in our institutions in North America and Europe. We can also get a glimmering of the kind of people we need to send from our own ranks to help him in his tasks.

However, before discussing what steps can be taken to remedy present deficiencies in the formation of professional foresters for service in the developing countries, it will perhaps be useful to turn for a moment to some of the disappointments that have been experienced in technical assistance programmes – disappointments that have led to disillusion. Disillusionment is, of course, a necessary precondition for effective action. Most of us concerned with the development business have started out with a number of illusions. The important thing is to shed these illusions, to shed them as quickly as possible, and to do so without losing one's faith and purpose. But much disappointment would be avoided, and a great deal of time saved, if we could reduce the number of illusions we start out with.

Failures of technical assistance

I have already touched on one illusion which is widespread: the notion that the job of the professional in a developing country is somehow simpler and easier than that of the professional in the developed country. Another widespread illusion is the notion that the expatriate professional in the developing country is, or can be, a principal agent of economic and social change.

How did this illusion arise? It arose, I think, because we assumed that, of the various shortages holding back development, capital and know-how were the most important. This has proved to be an erroneous assumption. But from this assumption we mistakenly deduced that injections of walking know-how would somehow transform the situation. The early days of technical assistance (and perhaps I should interject at this point that I am speaking mainly of multilateral aid programmes in forestry and forest industries, the only area in which I can claim detailed, first-hand knowledge) were the days of the expert adviser. These were the days when the shelves of ministers, senior administrators and senior professionals in the developing countries began to fill up with impressive technical reports, containing masses of noble advice. A large number of these reports have been collecting dust ever since, largely because the means necessary to implement this advice have not been available.

Not all advisory missions of this kind were failures, of course. There were many successes to report. But the degree of success was more closely related to the objective capacity to implement advice than it was to the quality of the expert. Though we speak glibly of developing countries, there is a world of difference between Mexico and Paraguay, between the UAR and Rwanda, between India and Laos.

In those countries which have already advanced some way on the developmental path, and have already acquired some institutional strength, it is relatively easy to identify and define problems, and most of the problems have a substantial technical content. In these circumstances, it is not too difficult to tender suitable advice, and there is some assurance that the advice, once tendered, can be implemented. In such cases, technical assistance advisory missions did succeed in removing many significant impediments to development. But the more general case was that it was not easy to identify the problem, or, if the problem was identified, it was seen to be intimately related with a host of associated problems, the solution of which was a prerequisite for the solution of the original problem. Moreover, most of the associated problems were institutional rather than technical in character.

It was a realization of the severe limitations under which the Expanded Technical Assistance Programme was working that led to the establishment of the Special Fund of the United Nations. Special Fund operations permitted a more sustained attack on a broader front on many of the development problems. Parallel developments took place in the bilateral aid fields. What, basically, happened was that technical assistance moved from the 'tell me' phase to the 'show me' phase. This change of emphasis speedily led to a considerable increase in the developmental impact of multilateral aid, an improvement far more than proportional to the actual increase in the scale of multilateral aid. Each Special Fund project is the subject of a tripartite contract, between the United Nations Development Programme, who supply the funds, the executing agency, and the government concerned; it may last from three to six years, and involve an expenditure of from one half to 2 million dollars, with counterpart funds and facilities contributed by the government. These Special Fund operations are now merged with technical assistance operations in the United Nations Development Programme, conferring a much greater degree of flexibility on multilateral aid programmes. These projects are designed to remove the obstacles to investment. Thus, they generally fall into one or other of three categories: pre-investment surveys, designed to obtain resource data and other essential information for investment; education and training institutions, at various levels; and applied research. However, the scope of these projects is steadily widening, and more and more pilot and demonstration projects are included.

But, though there has been a marked increase in developmental impact, there is no doubt that the success ratio has fallen short of the hopes that were entertained when this side of the programme was first developed.

The main failings have been, firstly, the tardiness or complete absence of investment follow-up on projects of a pre-investment type; and, secondly, the non-durability of some of the institutions which have been established or strengthened, once external support is withdrawn.

As regards the former, there is no doubt that part of the blame lies with the aid agencies, for failing to adequately design and implement projects. Frequently the data collected were not analysed or presented in a manner calculated to attract the interest of financing agencies, public or private, native or foreign. Here let me hasten to add that, though I am speaking of shortcomings in multilateral aid programmes, I know from personal observation that bilateral aid programmes have been equally remiss in this respect. Strenuous efforts are now being made to remedy these shortcomings. We in FAO, for example, have given considerable attention to the better preparation, design and implementation of projects, and, to facilitate investment follow-up, have established cooperation with the World Bank and several regional banks, as well as a cooperative programme with industry.

Nevertheless, the fact that some projects have been badly designed and poorly implemented is but a minor reason for the failure of investment follow-up. There is simply not enough capital ready and available to take up the thousands of sound investment projects ready and waiting. Moreover, capital, particularly private capital, is incorrigibly conservative and demanding; it is not in the least adventurous. It seems no inconsistency in, on the one hand, demanding a series of political and commercial guarantees that will virtually eliminate risk, and, on the other, insisting on a rate of return calculated to cover all those risks. Witness the repeated insistence on the part of investment capital on the need for political stability. In the context of most developing countries, this is a nonsensical demand. For development means change, and above all a change in social relations, and social relations in the last analysis are changed only through political action.

But it is not my purpose to rail at capital, which, after all, has its own laws. The fundamental reason why investment follow-up is often long delayed is that the local political, economic and social conditions have not sufficiently matured. I therefore do not share the view that lack of immediate investment follow-up means failure. I can quote a case in point from the sector with which I am mainly concerned. We started pre-investment work as long ago as 1953 in a certain Central American country, and a series of missions and projects have followed. This year, a very substantial investment will take place, one which will undoubtedly have a significant impact on the economy of the country concerned. Until quite recently, had we been cynical, we could have counted all our past effort wasted. But in fact, without the preliminary work over the years, the investment would not have taken place today. On these matters it is necessary to take a philosophical, long-term view; then one understands that patient pre-investment work is necessary to prepare the ground for future investment, even though the follow-up is not immediate.

Concerning the non-durability of institutions, and here I am thinking particularly of professional schools and research institutes, it is a common, though by no means universal, experience that standards are apt to fall, and the scope to narrow, if external support is prematurely withdrawn. This is because we have failed to appreciate how heavily such institutions depend on environmental factors: for example, relationships with and support from other institutions, governmental and non-governmental, the adequacy of the educational infrastructure, as well as accumulated experience and tradition. In a developed country, we are apt to take these things for granted. But it is now clear that in most developing countries viable and durable institutions will require more sustained support than they have received to date, a support which can taper off gradually, and perhaps be given through university-to-university and institute-to-institute relations.

This question of continuity in aid is becoming more important. In this respect, some of the bilateral programmes are still hampered by dependence on annual votes, and the need to commit expanditure in fixed fiscal periods. Not only does this inhibit intelligent forward planning of assistance; it also tends to give projects a 'do it for me' shape, instead of a 'do it with me' shape, so that training aspects are neglected, and there is little left to show when the operation is completed.

Both the failings to which I have referred have their roots in failure to appreciate the socio-economic context within which aid has to be rendered. This failure is often associated with an unwillingness, on the part of governments and frequently on the part of individuals, to accord the developing countries the right to be eclectic in their approach to solving developmental problems.

It is perhaps inevitable that, for some time to come, many of the bilateral aid programmes will continue to be subject to political and trade considerations. Many regard this as a pity, but it is a fact that the number of studies, as, for example, that by Hyson and Strout in a recent issue of the *Harvard Business*

Review,[4] which aim at demonstrating that the developed countries do well by doing good, is steadily multiplying. But even if much aid has to have strings, there is no reason why such aid should not correspond to what is really wanted and what can be most effective. And aid can never be effective if it is a vehicle for exporting ideology, either consciously as a matter of donor government policy, or unconsciously through the preconceived notions of its agents.

Here is one more important respect in which the expatriate professional serving in developing countries is frequently ill prepared, and part of the blame for this lies with the educational institutions in the developed world.

Another aspect of this aid problem, one which has received considerable publicity of late, and one which is often counted as a failure of aid programmes, is the brain-drain, from the developing to the developed countries. A strikingly high proportion of men and women who move from developing countries to the United States for graduate or postgraduate training do not return to their own countries. The same phenomenon certainly occurs in the other developed countries, but the percentages may perhaps be lower. My impression is that the percentage in forestry is considerably lower than in other professional fields, though it is certainly not negligible, especially on the industry side.

This is a matter on which it is easy to become emotional. One hears talk of lack of patriotism, lack of loyalty. But investigations have shown that only one in four of the brain-drain have stayed abroad for material reasons – reasons of salary, earlier promotion, and so on. A few have stayed abroad for political reasons. The majority have stayed abroad because the facilities for working, particularly for research, are incomparably superior. Too often men have returned to their own country, and after two or three years of frustration have migrated again.

But this problem of the brain-drain from the developing to the developed countries has to be seen in a wider context. All the world over, the more affluent and technologically advanced centres are bleeding the less affluent and more technologically backward centres of badly needed expertise. And this encompasses not only international flows, as between Western Europe and North America, or between Canada and the USA; it also encompasses brain flows within countries, for example, from the south to the north of Italy, from the north to the south-east in the UK, and I am sure there are similar flows in the North American continent. Within national borders, these flows tend to widen existing regional disparities. They can only be halted or reversed by decisive measures of public policy, which will involve not only material incentives, but also investment in infrastructure and other facilities to create the environment which will attract and hold the badly needed brains.

As regards international flows, it has always been my view that the developing

[4] Charles D. Hyson and Alan M. Strout, 'Impact of foreign aid on US exports', *Harvard Business Review* (January–February 1968).

countries cannot afford free trade in brains. In fact, I have a good deal of sympathy with the viewpoint expressed a few months ago by the eminent scientist Dame Kathleen Lonsdale, President of the British Association for the Advancement of Science. She referred to the estimate which has been made of the capital value of a Ph.D., in terms of new ideas and influence, as at least three quarters of a million dollars. She argued that, since brains and skills are exports and imports, she did not see why they should not be paid for by the importing government on a commercial basis. She pointed out that, so far as the UK was concerned, a thousand scientists or engineers transferred to the United States at their own request, and paid for at $9 million a dozen, would easily equalize Britain's balance of payments. 'After all, race horses and footballers have to be paid for; why not scientists?', she asked.

She went on to say that the poorest nations, through the export of brains, would benefit by legitimately earned capital with which to build and equip schools and colleges for the production of more exportable scientists and engineers.

If any justification is needed for adopting Dame Kathleen's proposal, it can be found in the words used by Dean Rusk in introducing the 1965 Immigration Law: 'Our country has the rare fortune to be able to attract from abroad immigrants of high intelligence and capacity: immigration, if it is well administered, can be one of our greatest natural resources.'

Though many of us will have a certain sympathy with Dame Kathleen's point of view, it would be unrealistic to suppose that her proposals are likely to be adopted in the near future. Meanwhile, what is to be done? It seems to me that those who go overseas for training on government-assisted or aid-assisted schemes should be under some sort of an obligation to return. At the same time, one ought to ensure that any training they receive abroad is training which can be adapted to the circumstances of their own country, and not something utterly remote from the conditions they will experience on their return. The most sensible way of sending people overseas for training is to send them as a part of a comprehensive project in their own country which ensures that, on their return, there will be a continuing job to do, a job in which they will be given real responsibility, and where they will receive facilities which will enable them to do that job. The point I am trying to make is that it is not enough to blame the brain that migrates. There is a responsibility on all of us: on the service in the country from which he comes; on those responsible for his training in the country to which he goes; and on those in the aid agencies that have the responsibility for making appropriate arrangements.

From this very cursory review of some of the problems arising under technical assistance programmes, it is clear that there are serious deficiencies in the professional education we are giving, both to men and women from the developing countries who are to return to take up professional careers in their own country, and to men and women in the developed countries who intend to spend part of their careers working overseas. But before commenting on the content of educational and training programmes, I would like to emphasize another point that emerges from our discussion. All that we have said so far indicates that the fruitfulness of a professional forester's contribution to economic and social progress is at least as much dependent upon the institutional context, the outlook of the individuals and groups with which he is working, as it is upon his own intrinsic and acquired qualities. In circumstances where investment regularly suceeds advice, where the people as a whole are involved in building for their own benefit, where a determined assault on nature is being made in the interest of man, the professional appears not as a forlorn proselytizer of development, but as an invaluable accelerator and lubricant of the development process. He is there to ensure that the effort of the people is used as economically and productively as possible.

It would be naïve to suppose that these hopeful conditions exist in most low-income countries. From this it does not follow, however, that our professional is a creature born before his time. To understand why, we must turn our attention for a few moments to some features of the present conditions of low-income nations. Many of them have large populations; most of them have extensive and under-utilized natural resources; all of them have, in all senses except that of realized demand, huge and pressing needs. As against this, they still produce and consume relatively little. They share a world with nations which have achieved, over two centuries of turbulent and aggressive social history, a stage which has been dubbed that of high mass consumption.

These nations have not become noticeably less turbulent or aggressive, and they show at the moment few signs of extending their mass consumption to the low-income countries. It would be both simplistic and pessimistic to expect the process of development in low-income countries to be broadly a repetition of the recent history of the metropolitan nations. Nor is it possible to predict what course the development path will take. It has been truly said that men make their own history, but in conditions that they do not choose. But we do know something about these conditions today.

It seems to me that, in the total development context, there exist three important sources of tension: between needs and production in the low-income countries; between conditions in the developed as against those in the developing countries; and between the needs of people and the preoccupations of governments within the low-income countries. It is clear that any alleviation of the first, most basic, pressure is going to require a degree of change in the second two conditions. And here may well lie the importance of our type of ideal professional – who seems, at times, prematurely present on the scene. For in attacking as best he can the gap between needs and production in the low-income countries, he cannot fail to highlight the need for change in these other respects. If at times his work seems to be frustrating, if often his advice is pigeon-holed, he may nevertheless be a living advocate of greater investment and transfer of resources from the developed to the developing countries, and a carrier in his own person, and by a limited example, of the possibilities of really fruitful use in the low-income countries of both indigenous and imported resources. To serve well in this role, it is unnecessary for him to be equipped with any particular credo or ideology: rather he should approach his work with a determined agnosticism, and a lively sense of how broad his role can be.

I have referred to the contrast frequently encountered in the low-income countries between the needs of the people and the preoccupations of their governments. George D. Woods, retiring President of the World Bank, made this point forcibly in New Delhi a few months ago, when he said:

There are many leaders in the less developed countries today who are courageous, selfless and devoted; but unhappily there are some who are not. We see instances of personal aggrandizement; we witness waste through conspicuous and unproductive public expenditures: we see attempts to evade responsibility by blaming internal problems on other countries; we see failure to advocate and enforce necessary steps involving effort and a measure of sacrifice. And how to accomplish peaceful changes in the distribution of political power is a problem that in many of the less developed countries remains unsolved.

One of the serious liabilities of some poorer countries, in short, is leadership that does not lead. And one of the results is likely to be public apathy and cynicism instead of the ferment of enthusiasm and the hard work needed for economic progress.[5]

All of us who have been in the development business for any length of time are keenly aware of the truth of this. And though public apathy and cynicism are likely to be one of the results, other results are even more likely. I am reminded of the sign that welcomed entrants to a neighbourhood grocery store when I was a boy: 'God helps those who help themselves; but God help those found helping themselves here.' Another result, implicit in what George Woods said, is that people will start to help themselves.

One of Latin America's outstanding economists, Celsio Furtado, has pointed out that 'the speed with which modern technology must penetrate the underdeveloped world in order to overcome initial resistance and ensure continuity of development inevitably provokes a series of social reactions incompatible with the preservation of most of the pre-existing structures.'[6] One of the permanent headaches of all those who are seriously engaged in development assistance is that their efforts are intended to help peoples, whereas their dealings are for the most part with governments. At the end of the day, the

---

[5] Address of George D. Woods, President of the World Bank, before the United Nations Conference on Trade and Development, New Delhi, 9 February 1968.

[6] Celsio Furtado, *The World Today*, 'US hegemony and the future of Latin America' (1966).

professional has to decide whether he is for stability or for development, whether he is for order or for justice. Having reached his decision, he has by no means acquired a licence to intervene directly in the political life of the country to which he is assigned. But he will have acquired a depth of view which will enable him to see where his efforts can best be applied, and what emphasis he should give to his work, to ensure that they have a lasting impact. He will achieve this depth of view only if he has taken pains to acquaint himself with the true nature of the economic, social and political tensions that rend the country in which he is to serve, has rid himself of preconceived notions, and has won through to a sympathetic understanding of the problems which are going to frame his own particular mission.

The touchstone for judging the success or failure of technical assistance is how much it contributes to improving the capacity of the social and institutional order for utilizing as fully as possible the creative and productive capacities of the population. Technical assistance is only really successful if it is geared to promoting development from within. It is not simply a question of transferring skills; these skills have to become firmly rooted, capable of growth, and attack a wide front.

If I may use a bellic image, usurping the privilege of ivy-covered professors with ivy-covered walls, the development battle is not won by an invasion where 'progress' establishes its bridgeheads in a backward land; it is rather won by helping the local liberation army to remove stagnation, to destroy the structures that perpetuate underdevelopment, and to keep growing and building up its own command.

This tells us much about the qualities needed in the professional who is to join the development battle. Obviously he must be honest and competent; but he must also be free from preconceived ideas, he must be adaptable to unfamiliar circumstances, he must be sympathetic to strange ideas, and he must be tolerant of the shortcomings of others. In short, he must have the curious, open and fresh mind of the truly intelligent, and this means that he must be young, if not in years, at least in heart.

How successful are our professional forestry schools in preparing this type of man and woman?

PROBLEMS OF FORESTRY EDUCATION

There is no doubt whatever that a useful trickle of the kind of people we are looking for is emerging from the institutions of higher forestry education in Europe and North America. But, given the present orientation, curricula and methods of these institutions, it might be truer to say that these people are surviving the educational process rather than being formed by it. If an adequate flow is to be assured, some important changes are needed. It should not be too difficult to bring about these changes, since, for reasons which I have explained earlier, some of them are needed in any case if the new generations of foresters are to cope successfully with the changing tasks that confront them in the *developed* countries.

I shall try to indicate some of the general changes I would like to see. I shall resist the temptation to be specific, because the way in which these changes are brought about will depend very much on the traditions and aims of particular institutions. There is a world of difference in tradition and purpose between professional forestry schools in the United Kingdom, Germany, France and the United States, for example, and even between individual institutions within these countries.

Firstly, the temptation to lengthen the first degree course and to cram the timetable should be firmly resisted. The battle to bring within the students' ken the scientific advances in all the disciplines that go towards a forester's formation is not only a losing one; it is a mistaken one. The timetable for some of the traditional subjects must be curtailed, partly to make way for new material, partly to give students more time to think and discuss.

Secondly, the economic content of the forestry course must be broadened and enriched. This concerns not only the courses in forest economics, which should encompass, besides the micro-economics of forestry, an understanding of the relationship between the forestry and forest industries sector and other sectors of the economy, and some notions of development theory and development planning. It also means that economic aspects should receive more attention in other taught courses, as, for example, silviculture, logging and harvesting, management, and wood utilization.

Thirdly, an attempt should be made to weld together those elements of the present curriculum which are concerned with aspects, other than timber production, of the forester's role as resource manager. These elements include (since not all are customarily taught) watershed management and torrent control; range management; soil conservation; forest influences; wildlife management; recreation. To these elements might be added new material, for example, on land-use planning, rural sociology, and so on. The aim should be to broaden the scope, to teach in an integrated way, while forgoing much of the depth. The course will not produce watershed managers or wildlife managers. Depth treatment and specialization would be deferred for a second degree.

This approach would succeed in giving a better framework within which students could fit knowledge of all aspects of resource management; it would also serve as a stimulus to fill out that framework. There will certainly be some objections from traditionalists to this approach. The charge will be levelled that graduates will be less well trained, less technically competent, than their predecessors. This is certainly true; but progressively greater reliance should be placed on sub-professional, technical grades, for many of the duties, which professional foresters are today performing in the early stages of their careers.

Fourthly, all forestry students should have, at an early stage in their education, say in their second year, an exposure to world forestry problems. This course should not be an encyclopaedic treatment of world forest resources, international trade in forest products, and wood-using industries. Rather it should be treated as a problem analysis course, setting out selected resource/people situations in their total social and economic context, highlighting similarities and contrasts.

It will be apparent to all that no professional forestry school is going to be able to move in the desired direction unless it has on its faculty a fair sprinkling of staff who have acquired international experience.

All the foregoing changes would help to improve the forester's preparation for future work in his own country. The last would serve to stimulate the interest of young men and women to undertake overseas assignments, and enable them, in consultation with their tutors, to tailor their subsequent training to this end.

I should perhaps interject a word here about those, whether on the faculty or among the students, who are destined to take up teaching posts in the developing countries. Here I share the views of Professor S. D. Richardson,[7] who, after emphasizing that *what* is taught is less important than *how* it is taught, goes on to say:

In making appointments to teaching posts, the quality in a candidate to which university authorities appear to pay least regard is his ability to teach...In developed countries, the practice is less hazardous than it appears, because the many adjuncts to communication which are freely available (adequate textbooks, audio-visual aids, an environment and traditions conducive to independent enquiry on the part of the student, etc.) reduce the need to rely on personal teaching ability. But in countries where these facilities are non-existent – and particularly where teacher and student are separated, racially, socially, culturally and by language...the art of effective communication is of overriding importance and demands a rare quality in the teacher. The ability to accept and identify himself with the aspirations of his students, a strongly developed social conscience, patience, and an open-minded pragmatism in his approach to socio-cultural customs (and standards) which may be quite foreign to his own traditions and experience, are essential components of this quality.

The question is often asked whether short-term training schemes to prepare professionals for work overseas can serve any useful purpose. Indubitably they can, but only if certain conditions are set. In my experience, most young foresters who are going out on an overseas assignment take great pains to improve their knowledge of the country where they are to work, and readily accept and act on any suggestions as to how they may best do this. A training course can help in strengthening the young forester's awareness of the complexities

[7] S. D. Richardson (Professor of Forestry, University of Wales) 'Recruitment, education and training in forestry: some qualitative needs in developing countries', a paper submitted to the Ninth British Commonwealth Forestry Conference, 1968.

he is likely to encounter. This will only happen if his instructors are such a mixed bag that the interplay among them, and between them and the participants, reveals that all is not black or white, that there are no ready-made answers, that the only valid approach is the open-minded and pragmatic one. To put the matter in blunt terms, while every professional serving overseas must be, in a sense, an ambassador, he should be an ambassador for his people, not an arm of his Foreign Office. In any such training course, obviously, refresher or crash language courses will be included.

What are the changes that are desirable in the formation we give, in the professional forestry schools of Europe and North America, to students from the developing countries? Before developing this point, I would urge that it is in the interest of the developing countries that as few as possible of their would-be foresters go overseas for first degree work. This, of course, can only be achieved by a considerable strengthening of existing institutions in developing countries, and perhaps, in some instances, by the creation of new ones. This strengthening will undoubtedly lead to a further increase in unit costs per student, but I think we must admit the necessity of this, recognizing that in the long run it is likely to be economical. The strengthening I have in mind relates not merely to increasing faculty staff, but also investment in the ancillary facilities that make for the success of a higher educational institution. In particular, a real effort should be made to decentralize, not necessarily to universities, but to associated institutions in the developing countries, a good part of the research presently being conducted in metropolitan institutions on problems relevant to developing countries.

I would like, with your permission, to offer a short aside on this question of research. The components of research are, as a rule, hardware, brains, skills and labour. The almost universal trend in research is towards a higher hardware component. This has led many honest administrators and researchers to argue as follows: because research is becoming more expensive, because it is more dependent on costly hardware and sophisticated supporting facilities, and because resources in the developing countries are so limited, it makes economic sense to concentrate basic research in the developed countries, and to concentrate in the developing countries on cheap, practical programmes of applied research, furnishing research direction from the developed countries. This is a plausible argument, especially when it is illustrated by examples of misconceived prestige projects in the developing countries, and of research facilities under-utilized. But a moment's thought will suffice to realize that this is simply a neocolonialist approach to research. If we had more and better research institutions in the developing countries, and if scientists and professionals from the developed countries, especially those concerned with problems germane to the developing countries, felt an obligation to strengthen such institutions, spending a good deal of time there, not only would the flow of useful research findings expand, not only would nearby teaching be strengthened, but the lamented brain-drain would be stemmed.

Students who receive their university education in their own country, or in a country presenting similar forestry problems, are less apt to lose their identification with their own country in the course of their training. Their education can be matched more closely to the needs of their own countries, and the practical work they carry out during their course will permit them better to apply what they have learned.

Even so, it would be over-optimistic to expect that, in the course of the next decade, professional forestry schools in the developing countries will have been strengthened, and will have multiplied, to the point where there is no further need for students from those countries to travel to North America or Western Europe for first degree work. Indeed, I would expect the numbers to remain somewhere near their present level. If this is so, how should courses be adapted to make them of greater value to the student from overseas? I believe that the suggestions I have already made will contribute greatly to better prepare them for the tasks they will face on their return. But the actual content of the taught courses is, in my view, far less important than the effort which the teaching staff is prepared to put into avoiding the greatest peril that lies in the path of the student from overseas: that of alienation, of progressive loss of identification with the problems of his own country. As a rule these students are a small minority in the class; they often have serious problems of personal adjustment; sometimes they have language difficulties; frequently their background in basic sciences and mathematics is not all that it might be. I know of no reputable forestry school where the teaching staff does not go out of its way to render special help to such students, often at a considerable sacrifice to themselves. But the best schools are those where the teaching staff welcomes the presence of these overseas students as a heaven-sent opportunity to open new windows on the world for the other students in the class, and who can so present their material that students of all nationalities are drawn together in partnership in recognizing the true nature of the forestry problems arising in the several countries, and in discussing those problems within the limits of the knowledge they have so far acquired. It is through first-class teaching that the overseas student wins through to a better understanding of his national resource problems, of his own importance, of the responsibilities and opportunities that lie before him. It is through first-class teaching that he becomes eager to return to his own country, in a spirit of determination and confidence, to join his own front in what is a global battle for resource development, a battle in which he is already assured of sympathetic allies on other fronts in many lands.

I concede that, if this approach is followed, the young North American forester may end up knowing more about the ravages of the goat in Turkey, or the habits of shifting cultivators in South-east Asia, than about the peculiarities of the Christmas tree market in Pocahontas County. But I believe North American forestry will survive this check.

Overseas students need a much more liberal allowance of out-of-classroom time from the teaching staff than many faculty members are presently prepared to give them. But these hours, where confidence is established and both personal and professional matters are freely discussed, are the most important in the overseas student's life. The teacher who takes this side of his work seriously will certainly have fewer published papers to his credit at the end of the academic year, but his long-term impact on world forestry will be both more vital and more durable. His superiors, hopefully enlightened by this present conference, will ensure that he does not suffer for his shorter publications list.

The key to preventing alienation is involvement: involvement on the part of the teacher, that creates involvement on the part of the class, and thereby compels involvement on the part of the overseas student. This process is facilitated if the personal involvement is part of a wider involvement, if some kind of special relationship exists or is being created between the professional school and the country of origin of the overseas student. This may take many forms: technical ssistance, special studies, research projects; these may be operated under direct university programmes, or within the ambit of bilateral or multilateral assistance programmes. If the will to get involved is there, means can usually be found.

I fear that the organizers of this conference will be bitterly disappointed that, on this question of the orientation of forestry education, I have had so little to say that is new, and certainly nothing that is revolutionary. But the fact is that the problems we are considering are not exactly new, and many of them have been under discussion now for some years. Many of the changes I would like to see are already being canvassed, sometimes tentatively, sometimes boldly; indeed, one or two are already being implemented. I believe that they will be adopted at an accelerated pace in the course of the next decade, and that as a result of these changes the professional forestry schools will be better able, in the words of Hardy Shirley 'to develop in their students a capacity for leadership and a willingness to accept the responsibilities of leadership.'

4

World Forest Development: Markets, Men and Methods

With your permission, I shall start with a quotation. It is taken from a 1964 issue of *Pulp and Paper*. The heading for the 1964 world review reads as follows: 'Canada plunging ahead with one of the greatest expansion booms of the industry; one sixth of the world's woodpulp – over 12 million tons – now made in Dominion'. That's the heading, and, if you will bear with me a moment longer, I would like to give you a little of the text. It runs as follows:

It is doubtful whether any region in the world has shown such a concentration of interest in the building of new pulp and paper mills as was evident in Canada's west coast province during early 1964. There was a period from March to April that witnessed the entry of a prospective new mill almost every week-end, and big mills too, most in the 500-ton-plus category costing up to $45 million each. With so much new capacity in the planning stage, it was little wonder that leaders felt it was prudent to inject a note of caution. Surely, they agreed, the world could consume only so much pulp even in an area of dynamic population growth and economic expansion. But for the most part the voice of Cassandra was drowned out by the roar of diesel shovels and tractors as foundations were laid for new pulp production.

That ends the quote, and maybe we should pause here to get the full flavour. I particularly like the piece about the voice of Cassandra being drowned out by the roar of diesel shovels; that really has an audio-visual impact. Mind you, a classicist might boggle at the imagery. When Apollo bestowed upon Cassandra the gift of prophecy, this was against a pledge of reciprocal favours on Cassandra's part. When Cassandra failed to keep her part of the bargain, Apollo did not recall the gift; he simply added a condition – that whenever Cassandra prophesied, no one would believe her. So essentially Cassandra was rather a miserable and lonely person. This does not quite square with what the journal

H. R. MacMillan Lecture in Forestry, University of British Columbia, February 1965.

says. There seems to have been more consensus than would really justify the Cassandra metaphor. But perhaps it is unfair of me to cavil, to deny the journalist his licence. Should we not rather thank *Pulp and Paper* for injecting a little needed colour into our lives?

But I believe that the above quoation sheds some light on why you have invited me here today from so far away. If I have understood the situations aright, some of you are just a little concerned about where you are going to sell the additional output that is going to flow from the expanded capacity. And you would like me to try to tell you exactly how much of what you will be able to sell, where you will be able to sell it, and how soon. In short, you want a tranquillizer with an FAO label on it.

Alas, contrary to what you may have heard, we in FAO have not been visited with the gift of Apollo. It is true that we do attempt from time to time to peer into the future, basing ourselves on our study of the past and present. And if some of our efforts have met with success, this – as any statistician will tell you – constitutes no guarantee for the future.

Thus, I am not at all sure that I can bring you the comfort and joy you would like to have from me. Instead, I shall endeavour to direct your attention to some important changes that are taking place in the world forest and timber economy. My aim is to give you a sense of the present as history. If I succeed, this may help you towards a better understanding of your own problems.

Today we are almost a third of the way through the second half of the century. I think it has now become clear that, since the middle of this century, there has been an entirely new dynamism about forest products consumption. Let me give you one striking example. The rise in the consumption of industrial wood in Europe over the decade 1950 to 1960 (64 million cubic metres) was more than twice as great as the whole expansion that had taken place in the previous forty years.[1] Similar, if somewhat less striking, figures could be adduced for other regions. We have seen a quickening in the pace of economic growth since mid-century: an aftermath of the Keynesian revolution. Forest products, increasingly versatile, penetrate into many sectors of the economy. The demand for them is thus very closely linked with the progress of the economy.

If this is understood, we get a different perspective of the likely level of industrial wood needs, say, towards the end of the century. Plainly, both the foresters of the world, and governments, have to give more thought to meeting the world's future needs.

---

[1] FAO, *European Timber Trends and Prospects: A New Appraisal 1950–1975* (New York, 1964), p. 207. Subsequent references to Europe are also taken from this study.

THE CHANGING PATTERNS OF WOOD CONSUMPTION

The *pattern* of forest products consumption is also changing very rapidly. Consider the following changes that took place over the period 1950 to 1963.[2] World sawnwood production: up by 44 per cent. World paper and board output: almost exactly doubled. World plywood output: up from 6 to 20 million cubic metres. Fibreboard: from less than 2 to well over 5 million tons. Particle board: from a negligible figure to nearly 3.5 million tons. Thus, whereas in 1950, pulp products and panel products taken together represented about 36 per cent of the value of all forest products, by 1963 they represented about half. And, of course, these trends will continue. To give another example from Europe: whereas, in 1950, 60 per cent of total roundwood consumption was required in sawlog sizes, it is estimated that by 1975 this percentage will have fallen to 49. With a steadily growing proportion of the total crop destined for final use in reconstituted form, the goals of forest management must progressively change.

What makes these problems particularly urgent is the fact that wood consumption is already pushing hard on the forest resource in several parts of the world. Europe perhaps presents the best documented case. I have already mentioned the steep rise on consumption that took place in Europe during the fifties. What is even more surprising is the fact that over the same period Europe's own production of industrial wood rose by nearly 40 million cubic metres, something which few European foresters thought possible at the beginning of the decade. But even though Europe's industrial wood supply grew during that decade almost three times as fast as it had done during the preceding half-century, nevertheless the decade saw a drastic change in Europe's timber balance. At the beginning of the decade Europe was a net exporter of around 4 million cubic metres in roundwood equivalent. By the end, she had become a net importer to the tune of 21 million cubic metres.

What of the future? The forest policies presently being pursued do envisage a substantial rise in forest output up to 1975, though a sizeable part of the increase which is foreseen will be in species and sizes that connote rising marginal costs, unless prodigious efforts are made to keep costs down. Nevertheless, a gap is envisaged, which by 1975 may be of the order of 40 to 70 million cubic metres, depending on the rate of economic growth which will have been achieved, as compared with the 1960 gap of 21 million cubic metres. Moreover, this is a gap which can be expected to grow in the succeeding decades. When I speak of Europe I am excluding the USSR. But what I have said applies to both Eastern and Western Europe.

It may be of interest to you if I spell out in somewhat more detail the probable pattern of the additional markets that are likely to arise in Europe over

[2] FAO, *Yearbook of Forest Products Statistics* (Rome, 1964), pp. IXff.

the coming years.[3] Let us take Western Europe first. If we match the additional wood supplies that are likely to become available from Western Europe's own forests against the extra requirements, and if we assume that a certain proportion of the coniferous sawnwood, pulp and paper presently exported to other regions is retained in the Western European market, then we are left with the following shortfalls. (For ease of comparison I express all figures in roundwood equivalent (r).)

Veneer and plywood (or logs therefor)	8 million m³(r) (of which 6–7 tropical broadleaved)
Broadleaved tropical sawnwood (or logs therefor)	3 million m³(r)
Coniferous sawnwood	2–3 million m³ (r)
Long-fibre pulp (or paper)	20 or more million m³ (r)

Evidently the bulk of the first two items must originate in the developing countries. The extra sawn softwood will clearly come mainly from Canada or the USSR, though it is likely that one or two developing countries may be able to claim a token share. But the massive extra market will be in the long-fibre pulp or paper made therefrom. For these supplies Western Europe will have to look mainly to North America, and principally Canada. There will, I believe, be some additional imports from the USSR, but I would not expect these to be substantial. And I think we may assume that by then there will be the beginnings of a flow of pulp to Western Europe from newly established mills in favourable sites in certain developing countries. But the major part of these new requirements, if they are to be met at all, must be met from North America.

Turning to the centrally planned economies of Eastern Europe, here the wood balance has sharply deteriorated, in spite of tremendous efforts to reduce the intensity of wood use. Unless even more drastic steps are taken to hold down wood consumption, then additional import requirements (again in terms of roundwood equivalent) will arise by 1975 of the following order:

Coniferous sawnwood (or logs therefor)	2 million m³(r)
Broadleaved plywood and veneer (or logs therefor)	0.5 million m³(r)
Long-fibre woodpulp (or pulpwood therefor, or paper)	10–12 million m³(r)

[3] The figures that follow are based on a geographical breakdown of material summarized in FAO, *European Timber Trends and Prospects: A New Appraisal 1950–1975*.

The proximate source for the coniferous sawnwood and for the woodpulp or paper is the USSR. So far as the sawnwood is concerned there should be no great problem. But it may be doubted whether the USSR will be able to furnish all these extra pulp and paper requirements in Eastern Europe by 1975. As you know, the Russians encountered certain difficulties in expanding their pulp and paper capacity, and the original targets set for 1965 in the Seven Year Plan had to be revised drastically downwards. My impression is that the lessons of that period have been learned, and that it is likely that the new targets now set for 1970 will be achieved. We may certainly expect plans for a substantial further expansion in the subsequent quinquennium. It would be surprising, however, given the pressing need to raise paper consumption levels within the USSR, if they were able to generate within the next decade an export surplus of the order of 2 to 3 million tons of pulp or paper. Bearing in mind the serious gap in supplies there will be by that time in Eastern Europe, I would doubt whether the USSR will enter the Western European pulp and paper market on a really massive scale within the next decade. The fact remains, however, that the USSR is fully aware of the rapidly rising pulp and paper import requirements in Western Europe – and elsewhere, for that matter; that she is fully conscious of her own immense undeveloped resources; and that she will not be content in the long run to remain a supplier of coniferous sawnwood and small-sized roundwood.

Among the industrialized nations outside Europe, the one with the most striking wood deficit is Japan. Japan's imports of five main wood categories rose from $190 million in 1960 to $470 million in 1963. This latter figure included nearly half a million tons of woodpulp. In Japan, cuttings of industrial wood have risen very rapidly in recent years, and will continue to rise. But here, again, they are failing to keep pace with rising wood needs. By 1975 there may well be an additional import need of up to 15 million cubic metres, nearly half of which would be required as coniferous sawnwood and long-fibred pulpwood or pulp and paper.

I have rattled off a lot of figures, in a rather glib fashion. I must refer you to various of our publications[4] for the factual data and reasoning that underlie these figures. I will repeat what I said at the outset of my talk. We have not been visited with the gift of Apollo: we could therefore well be wrong. But the figures I have cited are directly linked to the assumptions we have made about economic growth rates in various parts of the world. So far as Europe is concerned, for example, we assumed that the growth targets set by the Organization for European Cooperation and Development – of which Canada

[4] E.g., in addition to those already cited, FAO, *Timber Trends and Prospects in the Asia–Pacific Region* (Geneva, 1961): FAO, *Latin American Timber Trends and Prospects* (New York, 1963); *World Outlook for Forest Products* (*Unasylva*, 16(2): 63–74, 1962); and *Expansion of Exports of Forest Products from Developing Countries* (*Unasylva*, 18(1): 3–11, 1964).

is a member – would be achieved, though we covered ourselves by working out probable requirements on the basis of a somewhat lower rate of growth; for Eastern Europe we extrapolated, with some downward adjustments, past and planned growth rates. The *trends* I have delineated, however, would seem to be incontrovertible. Depending on the economic growth rates actually achieved, the magnitudes I have mentioned might be reached a year or two before 1975, or a year or two after.[5]

Perhaps I should also add another caveat. Though the forest products industries are growth industries, and the long-term trend in demand and markets is upwards, it would be surprising if there were not in the future, as there has been in the past, a certain zig-zagging around the upward trend line. If we also bear in mind that extra capacity in pulp and paper, for example, may take up to three or four years to come into operation, we should not be surprised, nor unduly excited, if temporary imbalances arise from time to time. Indeed, occasional imbalance is probably inevitable in growth industries operating under these technical conditions. Herein lies one of the difficulties of investigating *short*-term market prospects. Steps we can take to avoid excessive fluctuations include keeping ourselves fully informed on capacity expansion plans, and keeping demand trends under continuous review.

What I have said so far will perhaps have given you the feel of a world forest and timber economy in a stage of rapid evolution, with changing patterns of production, consumption and trade, and further changes still to come. We should also bear in mind a further general point.

Since mid-century, the growth in population, and the accelerated consumption of *all* resources that is accompanying it, has brought a shift in the attention of scientists and statesmen from resource conservation to resource planning and management. This is particularly true of the land resource, and the forester should have, indeed must have, a vital say in land-use decisions. The problem presents itself under very different aspects in different parts of the world. In the industrialized countries the growing pressure of urbanization, communications and recreational demand have to be reconciled with the multipurpose concept of the forest, the forest as a generator of a broad stream of tangible and non-tangible benefits over and above the timber crop. The forester must justify in economic and social terms his claim to every hectare. Oddly enough there are signs that in many of these countries the pressure of agriculture on the forest may be relaxing. One result of the technical revolution in agriculture is that considerable areas of land marginal to agriculture are becoming available for forestry, and some of these lands are potentially more productive than

---

[5] Thus the first major regional study FAO, *European Timber Trends and Prospects* (Geneva, 1963) underestimated industrial wood consumption in 1960 mainly because the assumption it contained about the growth in the European economy over the decade were too low. In effect, the situation foreseen for 1960 came about approximately already in 1958.

most of the lands presently under forest, provided suitable techniques are developed. This has been happening already for some time in the USA, though I do not have exact estimates of the areas likely to become available for conversion. In Europe it is estimated that over the next ten years up to 10 million hectares may be so freed. This compares with a present forest area of 140 million hectares.

But in many other parts of the world the pressure is acute, and this in spite of wide disparities in the man/land ratio. Sometimes the alienation of forest land to agriculture is a mere buying of time, an evasion of needed reforms in the agrarian structure. Where such transfers involve land unsuited to permanent agriculture, as is often the case, the outcome is a trail of misery and a squandered resource. Elsewhere, as in some of the dry savannahs, proper management of the forest land sector needs a complex, multi-discipline approach lest the disturbance of delicate ecological balance leads to disaster. Problems of shifting agriculture; of mountain depopulation; of hill–plain conflict: none of these are new problems, but they are all problems which are becoming more acute. Foresters must learn to solve them, working with related disciplines.

The points I have made so far would all seem to suggest that the forester's problems have not only multiplied but also become more complex since the mid-century. But the weapons in the forester's armoury have also multiplied and become more powerful. Thanks to improved financing, and better co-ordinated effort, there has been acceleration in both forest science and forest industry technology, with a swifter translation of research findings into field practice.

One of the most significant, to my mind, is process diversification, with its consequent broadening of the raw material base, in forest industries, thus permitting more integral utilization of the forest crop. Of course, there is still a long way to go. The problem of mixed temperate forests is only partly solved, and that of the heterogeneous tropical broadleaved forest scarcely touched. Indeed, in relation to these last, we have made only limited progress. High hopes were entertained at one time that the forest wealth of the tropics would be speedily valorized by a kind of scissors movement: on the one hand, technological progress permitting fuller utilization; on the other, enrichment or conversion through silvicultural measures. So far insufficient progress has been made on either flank to produce economic solutions of general applicability to the problems posed.

Another weapon that has assumed much greater importance in recent years is the man-made forest: artificial plantations of quick-growing, often exotic, species. Of course, neither the idea nor the practice is new. What is new is the scale and systematization of research and experiment. Quick-growing plantations offer special hope to many of the developing countries whose existing forest resource is insufficient or unsuitable. Moreover, many of these countries can, thanks to favourable soil and climate, produce in this way wood fibre at five to ten times the rate per hectare a year as can be done in the natural forests of the present forest industry centres in the cool, temperate zones. It is perhaps significant that, by 1964, over 4 million hectares of quick-growing plantations had been established in the developing countries of Latin America, Asia and Africa, most of them since the war; and that the current annual rate of planting is over 300,000 hectares. Moreover, I believe we are still only at the beginning of what might be termed 'agro-silvics'. For example, the use of fertilizer is still in its infancy. Some recent experiments suggest that judicious application will prove economic in natural, as well as man-made, forests.

However, I must not tarry to embroider these themes: the forester's new responsibilities and his new capabilities. The point I want to make is that this is an exciting time to be entering the forestry profession or to be joining forest industry. Moreover, it is a challenging time to have responsibility for the preparation of foresters.

THE NEEDS OF THE DEVELOPING COUNTRIES

Let me now say something of the evolution of forest products markets in the less developed countries of the world. I speak now of the countries of Africa, Asia and Latin America, excluding Japan and the Republic of South Africa. In all these countries, too, the need for forest products is rising fast. It would be rising faster if these countries could succeed in raising their economic growth rates. Indeed, for many forest products the response of consumption to income growth is greater at lower incomes than at higher incomes. But here comes the rub. In the two decades that have elapsed since the end of the war, growth rates in these countries have come up neither to hopes nor to expectations. Instead, we are confronted with the problem of the widening gap: that growing disparity between the 'have' and 'have not' nations, which constitutes the central problem of our age. Fortunately, some of the reasons for the failure of the developing countries to achieve hoped-for-economic growth rates are now better understood than they were but a few years ago. This is not the time and place to pass development theory under review, but there are two particular aspects I would like to mention since they are relevant to my theme.

First, there is a much clearer understanding of the interdependence of the industrial and agricultural sectors in the development process. Those who have insisted on the priority of industrialization plans, almost to the exclusion of efforts in the agricultural sector, have come up against several unpalatable facts. In the first place, given the low level from which industrialization starts in most of these countries, the employment opportunities created are inadequate to induce automatically required changes in agriculture. Moreover, without very careful planning, the vaunted spread effects of industrialization are unlikely to be realized. What we have witnessed, in case after case, is a serious industrialization effort that has become progressively bogged down, bringing about a limited industrial enclave surrounded by a backward and stagnating agricultural economy.

This is not to deny the importance of industrialization. Obviously the underdeveloped countries must do their utmost to build up industry with all possible speed. But this can only succeed if simultaneous efforts are made to achieve a substantial rise in the productivity of agriculture. However, the required rise in agricultural productivity cannot be obtained simply by making the farmer aware of the existence of better techniques. He needs the incentives which will induce him to master and apply techniques. The new technical inputs, whether they be improved seed, tools, machinery, fertilizer or water, must be brought within his economic reach. He needs the assurance of markets for his additional output. He may need new credit facilities. In short, a large number of institutional changes have to be brought about, if agricultural productivity is to be raised. In particular, progress in the agricultural sector is itself largely conditioned by progress in the industrial sector, particularly as regards the supply of certain agricultural inputs coming from the industrial sector and as regards markets for agricultural output.

In the light of this interdependence of the industrial and agricultural sectors in the development process, forestry and forest industry activities take on a particular significance. At one end they reach back into the rural economy; at the other, they penetrate into many branches of the industrial sector.[6] The flexible range of forest industries, with their considerable variation in requirements of capital, skill, raw materials and other production factors, means that most developing countries, provided they have a suitable raw material base, are in a position to develop one or more of these industries on an economic scale. Moreover, these industries can exercise a propulsive influence on the whole economy, frequently permitting the establishment of secondary and conversion industries. At the same time, the forestry activities associated with the establishment of these industries exercise a beneficial influence on the rural sector, relieving under- and unemployment in the countryside, and in general diversifying the rural economy. For these and many other reasons (including their high import-saving effect, and the fact that they valorize indigenous renewable resources), forest and forest industry development has a rightful claim to high priority in the development plans of many underdeveloped countries.

There is another aspect of the development process which is better understood today. I refer to the intimate relationship now seen to exist between development and trade. One critical determinant of the economic growth rate in the less developed countries is the capacity to import. This import capacity is largely conditioned by exchange earnings. At the present time, most developing

---

[6] See also Jack C. Westoby, 'Forest industries in the attack on economic underdevelopment', *Unasylva*, 16(4): 67 (1962). See this volume, chapter 1

countries are heavily dependent, for their exchange earnings, on the export of a rather narrow range of primary products, mostly food and agricultural raw materials. Efforts to stabilize and raise earnings from the export of these products are frustrated by a variety of factors: the low – sometimes negative – income elasticity for certain products in the industrialized countries; protective agriculture in many of the industrialized countries; the substitution of synthetic for natural raw materials; and so forth. The United Nations Trade and Development Conference held in Geneva in 1964 recognized the problem, considered various measures proposed for dealing with it, and recommended the establishment of a permanent organ to keep the problem in its various aspects under review. One of the conclusions that emerged clearly from that conference was that if growth rates are to be speeded up in the developing countries, it will be necessary for these countries to expand their exports of manufactured goods, of processed goods; clearly, special steps will be necessary in the industrialized countries if this is to come about.

For many industrial products, the prospects of the developing countries winning new markets in the industrialized countries are far from bright – even if they were allowed to compete on level terms. But forest products, at least in certain developing countries, appear to offer exceptionally favourable prospects provided forest industries can be established on sound economic and technical lines. I should point out that wood costs can be decisive in overcoming some of the cost disadvantages from which these countries presently suffer. In a paper published in 1963 by Nils Osara,[7] it was pointed out that in East Africa, for example, plantation pulpwood could be produced at a price on the stump representing roughly 10 to 15 per cent of the delivered price which European mills are currently paying for pulpwood. This seems to leave ample margin to cover, not only harvesting and transport costs from stump to mill, but other cost differences as well. Moreover, case studies we in FAO have recently conducted, and which are to be published shortly, show that to certain selected favourable sites in Africa and in Latin America, coniferous pulpwood can be made available at a delivered cost of $5 to $6 per solid cubic metre, under bark. This gives a very significant margin when compared with current European, including Scandinavian, costs – which run to $14 or more. It compares favourably with Eastern Canada and with the southern pine belt – even when allowance is made for density difference. And it stands comparison with British Columbia costs, both tidewater and interior.

I have quoted one or two typical figures by way of example. I wanted to make it clear that the establishment of important export-oriented forest industries in certain developing countries is not only possible – it corresponds to

---

[7] Nils A. Osara, 'Expansion of forestry and forest industries in underdeveloped countries', *Unasylva*, 17(3):70 (1963).

the need of those countries to expand their exports of manufactured goods. It also corresponds to the need which will be increasingly felt in certain of the industrialized areas of the world for growing imports of forest products.

Studies which we in FAO have made in recent years in collaboration with the Regional Economic Commission of the United Nations enable us to give certain indications of the possible trend of forest products markets in the developing countries. Assuming rather modest rates of economic growth up to the year 1975, we estimate that the developing world as a whole will require forest products additional to their consumption in 1960 to the value of about $3 billion. Rather more than half of this will be in the form of paper and paperboard, somewhat less than a third in the form of sawnwood, and the balance in various wood-based panels. This is over and above what they themselves were producing and consuming at the beginning of this decade, and is additional to the imports they were then receiving from the advanced countries – well over half a billion dollars. It may be doubted whether it is feasible for these countries to create amongst themselves by 1975 the additional productive capacity that would enable them to satisfy all these additional requirements. But it should prove possible, providing sufficiently energetic steps are taken soon, to take care of virtually all the additional requirements of wood-based panels, most of the extra sawnwood required, and up to about three quarters of the extra paper and paperboard needs.

When I say 'create amongst themselves', I mean, of course, to establish the necessary capacity within the developing world. I do not mean to imply that each individual country or even any geographical area within the developing world should aim at self-sufficiency. Indeed, the successful establishment of forest industry capacity is in most cases dependent on a very rapid expansion of trade between developing countries, and will probably require considerable further progress in the establishment of regional and sub-regional common markets. Here I should perhaps point out that one of the striking anomalies of the present-day pattern of international trade in forest products is the abysmally low level of trade between developing countries. No less than 80 per cent of all trade in forest products takes place between the developed countries. (I include here both those with free market economies and those with centrally planned economies.) Eleven per cent flow from the developed to the developing countries; 7 per cent in the reverse direction – from developing to developed; and only a bare 2 per cent between the developing countries themselves. By and large the trade links of the developing countries in forest products still reflect an essentially colonial-type relationship: an outward flow of unprocessed or partly processed wood to industrialized countries – often to the former metropolitan power; and a reverse flow of higher-valued fully processed forest products.

The tentative, but to my mind realistic, target I have mentioned was suggested in a paper FAO submitted to the United Nations Trade and

Development Conference.[8] It would mean that by 1975 the developing countries would be covering themselves most of their additional forest products needs. They would still require, however, if their increased needs were to be fully satisfied, additional imports (pulp, paper and perhaps a little sawn softwood) from the advanced countries to the value of $600 million. Whether this potential market will ever become a realized market depends, of course, on whether by then their economies and export potential have been built up to the point where they can afford to pay for these extra imports. It cannot be emphasized too strongly that assistance rendered by the advanced countries to the under-developed countries in their developmental effort is not a matter of building up competitors; it is a matter of building up customers.

I have spoken of rising forest products needs within the developing countries. But there are very real prospects for these countries to find extra markets in the advanced countries. We have estimated that it should be possible for these countries by 1975 to find additional markets in the advanced free market and centrally planned economies for about 1 billion dollars' worth of forest products. For the most part this would consist of broadleaved logs, broadleaved sawnwood, veneers and plywood. A striking feature of the last decade has been the consistent rise in the demand for tropical woods in the industrialized countries. Special efforts and measures will be needed to ensure that a greater proportion of this expanding trade flow is processed in the countries of origin. But in addition to the enhanced flow in broadleaved wood products, there should also be the modest beginnings of an export trade in pulp and paper.

Should all these developments I have mentioned come about (and they would require a cumulative investment up to 1975 of the order of $5 billion) then we should see established through the developing world soundly based forest industries capable of taking care of most of the developing world's own needs, and poised to enter the export market on an increasing scale in subsequent decades. This would correspond to the manifest needs of the advanced countries. At the same time the present adverse trade deficit of the developing world on the forest products account of about $200 million would have been converted to a positive balance of roughly the same order.

THE IMPLICATONS FOR CANADIANS

Let me now try to draw together some of the points I have made so that we may examine their implications for Canadians.

1   In the less developed countries of the world – that is to say, in the countries of Africa, Asia and Latin America, excluding Japan and the Republic of South Africa – the demand for forest products is rising

[8] See Chapter 2 of this book.

fast. These countries may need by 1975 some 3 billion dollars' worth more of forest products than they consumed in 1960.

2   Many of these countries already possess, while others could quickly create, resources that would enable them to satisfy most, if not all, of their rising needs of forest products.

3   For these countries which have suitable resources, there are powerful arguments in favour of assigning a high priority to investment in the forest and forest industries sectors.

4   In addition, a number of these countries offer exceptionally favourable possibilities for the establishment of sizeable export-oriented forest industries.

5   At the same time, the changing resources/requirements balance in some of the industrialized areas of the world makes it clear that these areas will have to import forest products increasingly in the future. The additional needs of these areas will already be substantial by 1975, and will continue to rise thereafter.

6   The developing countries are doomed to failure in their efforts to achieve self-sustained economic growth unless they can succeed in expanding their exports, particularly of manufactured goods, to the developed world. In many industrial sectors prospects are far from bright for them. But in the forest industry sector, both history and geography are on their side.

Most of the estimates I have adduced have related to 1975. But the trends I have noted will persist and intensify in the subsequent decades. We are, therefore, faced with the need to bring about, between now and the end of the century, nothing less than a substantial modification in the existing international division of labour in the world forest and timber economy. If this is to come about, then the groundwork must be laid in the next ten years. It is in the interest of developing and industrialized countries alike that this required transition takes place smoothly.

If forest and forest industry development in the developing world is to be accelerated, there is urgent need for a greatly expanded, and continually expanding, flow of capital, aid, know-how, and professional and technical skills. A special responsibility lies with all those associated with forestry and forest industries in the advanced countries. And it seems to me that in this task of encouraging and assisting forest and forest industry development in the less industrialized countries a very special responsibility lies with Canadians, particularly with British Columbians, and perhaps most of all with this university. Earlier I spoke of the characteristics which distinguish forestry and forest industries as a dynamic propulsive sector in the development process, but this is something that British Columbians will understand from first-hand experience. For, as Mr McKee, Deputy Minister of Forests of your province, once stated:[9] 'British Columbia's economic and social history is forest history. This is a forest land, the so-called forest province, of a forest nation.'

How can you help? I would like to offer one or two tentative suggestions for your consideration, based upon the experience we have acquired in FAO over recent years. Here I would like to make it plain that I am now speaking to you as British Columbians. I do not speak of the wider obligation that the Canadian government is undertaking or has pledged itself to undertake. Canada is by no means at the bottom of the league when it comes to international cooperation and technical assistance programmes. And I know from personal experience that the Canadian contribution, both under bilateral and the several multilateral programmes, is highly appreciated for its technical quality. But Canada's rightful place, so far as international cooperation in the forest and forest industry sectors is concerned, is near the top of the league. British Columbians can ensure that she gets there.

First, the output of trained foresters and forest industry specialists needs to be stepped up. This you must do anyhow, if your own growing needs are to be met. But the aim should be to achieve, or create, an institutionalized surplus. The federal and provincial authorities, the larger private companies, and the faculty too, should aim at manning tables which facilitate a liberal policy of secondment and loan. Establishment rules should be such that service overseas is regarded as *premium* service, and rewarded accordingly – not penalized, as so often at present. Those private companies that adopt progressive policies in freeing their professional and technical staff for overseas assignments should receive the gratitude and esteem of all Canadians. The recalcitrant few that choose to adopt dog-in-the-manger policies should be held up to scorn as operating against long-term Canadian interests.

In passing, both your public authorities and private companies might care to consider, as so many forest services and companies in Europe are presently doing, whether part at least of the current shortage of professionals may not be due to the fact that the existing stock of professionals is being uneconomically used.

How to ensure that growing numbers of young foresters will feel the urge to spend at least part of their career overseas? I believe that it is important that every forester, quite early in his training, be given a sense of the growing interdependence in the world forest and timber economy; that he be made aware of the similarities and the contrasts between the basic forestry problems in different parts of the world; that forestry be recognized as one of the most international of professions. Even those who do not eventually opt for an overseas career will bring to your own problems here a breadth of background that cannot but be beneficial. It may be objected that foresters whose forestry

[9] R. G. McKee, 'Canada's Pacific forests', a paper submitted to the Fifth World Forestry Congress, Seattle, 1960.

theory and practice are acquired in the predominantly coniferous forests of the cool temperate zones may have little to contribute over much of the underdeveloped world. I do not agree, though I admit that narrow experience limits their usefulness. Several European countries, alive to the current shortage of foresters with tropical and sub-tropical experience, are helping to fill this gap by sponsoring Associate Expert schemes. Canadian authorities may wish to consider whether this might not be a very worthwhile use of technical assistance funds.

Of course, the developing countries are struggling to step up their own output of trained foresters, and many new faculties have been established in recent years. There is much to be said in favour of these people getting their basic forestry training in their own country, or in a neighbouring country where similar forest conditions obtain, though it is often advantageous to pursue certain postgraduate studies overseas. But these institutions need, at any rate in their early stages, expatriate teaching staff and various forms of support. There are here great opportunities for collaboration between some of these newly established faculties and senior institutions in the industrialized countries. This partnership could embrace not only secondment for teaching, perhaps on a rota system, library assistance, help with teaching materials and equipment, but also postgraduate training, research projects on key forestry problems in the country of the junior partner, maybe even student exchanges.

What kind of foresters do the developing countries most need? Certainly, there is a need for intensively specialized, single-discipline foresters. But even greater is the need for foresters who can guide, help, and above all *work with* the local foresters in the tasks of policy formulation, planning, management and administration. In these tasks, a detailed knowledge of highly specialized disciplines is much less important than a competent grasp of several related disciplines. For historical reasons, the forestry cadres in many of the newly emergent countries belong mainly to what I might term the biological stream of forestry. These cadres urgently need supplementing on the economic and utilization side and, I would say also, on the ecological and land-use side.

Perhaps the most acute shortage at the present time is of forest economists, but of forest economists of a new type. A more appropriate term would be forest development officers. The ideal forest development officer would have a reasonable basic knowledge of forestry, which included an awareness of techniques available, their limitations and costs. He would therefore need a good groundwork in economics, some acquaintance with development theory and an eclectic grasp of planning methods and techniques. He would not necessarily have a detailed technical knowledge of forest industries, but he would have to undersand the quantitative and qualitative raw material requirements of each, other factor requirements, and in general have a good notion of all the considerations that influence investment and production costs. He should have a particular understanding of the factors determining logging and transportation

costs: this is the key phase in forest development in most of the developing countries. He should also know something about marketing methods, including not only organization and promotion, but also the planning of forest products demand in the public sector. Above all, he must be able to determine the kinds of data needed for decision-making, be able to assemble and analyse them, and have acquired the habit of taking decisions.

There are several good textbooks now on forest economics. As yet there is not one ideally suited for training forest economists for work in developing countries. Nor is there any centre of training and research which fully meets the present need. What is required is a centre for forest development studies, where research and postgraduate training go hand in hand. Formal teaching would play a minor role. There would be more emphasis on seminar-type instruction. But most of the work, especially in the second year of the two-year course I envisage, would consist of cooperative case study work, moving on from fairly simple hypothetical problems to concrete case studies.

A school of this type would require a major interdisciplinary effort. It would have something in common with certain higher schools of business administration. It would produce foresters capable of talking to, and negotiating with, ministries of agriculture, of trade and commerce and of industry, planning boards, potential investors, concessionaires, buyers – in the language which these people understand. Such men would be worth their weight in gold in the developing countries today. They are badly needed if forestry is to play its role effectively in our rapidly changing world economy.

Along with the need for a shift in the pattern of forest education goes the need for a shift in the pattern of forest and forest industry research. The valorization of the forest resources of the developing countries presents many special problems, problems related to heterogeneity, accessibility, climate, markets, and so on. Insofar as these problems are presently being solved by advances in technology, this is for the most part a by-product of research directed specifically to the problems faced in the industrialized countries. The amount being spent on research specifically aimed at solving the problems of the developing countries is pitifully small. As was made clear during the United Nations Conference on the Application of Science and Technology, held in Geneva a couple of years ago, the problem is less one of seeking fundamental technological breakthroughs than adapting technologies already available. Research institutions in the advanced countries must start to apply at least a fraction of their resources towards solving the specific problems of the developing countries.

RESPONSIBILITIES FOR THE FUTURE

My time is up. And though I may not have exhausted my theme, I fear I may already have exhausted your patience.

A few days before I left Rome I was privileged to read a summary of 'Guideposts to Innovation', the report of your president's Committee on Academic Goals. The following words, taken from the foreword to that report, made an exceedingly deep impression on me.

The University of British Columbia is sensitive to its changing responsibilities. It is aware of its changing role in response to the great issues of our time, the impact of the scientific revolution, the new dimensions of power, the gigantic contrasts of feast and famine, over-population, the surge of under-developed countries, the massive threats to individuality.

These are noble words indeed, and I look forward to the day when every institution of higher learning will have the wisdom and courage to frame its academic goals in terms of such explicit humanism.

These words show that British Columbians not only know how to interpret their own past; they are also fully aware of their responsibilities for the future – responsibilities that reach far beyond the borders of this province. This is why I have taken the liberty, in my talk today, of putting forward certain suggestions which you might care to take into consideration when you come to decide how best to shoulder these changing responsibilities.

5

One-World Forestry: New Zealand's Role

When I was invited to participate in this phase of the New Zealand Forest Service's Golden Jubilee celebrations, I accepted with alacrity. I must confess that my eagerness to accept was prompted rather by a personal wish to satisfy my long-standing curiosity about these islands, than by any thought of the personal contribution I might be able to make to the celebrations. Thus, my reaction to the invitation was a purely selfish one.

However, as the months passed, I became increasingly perturbed as almost to repent my decision. I read some of the proceedings of the Forestry Development Conference, and more recently received the forestry sector report to the plenary session of the National Development Conference. It is evident that during the past year the problems facing the forest industry sector in this country have been ventilated with a thoroughness that all countries must envy. Broadly representative committees, of high competence, have examined every phase of the sector's problems. I have no doubt that many decisions have already been taken, and are in the course of implementation.

In view of all this, it is quite evident that there is very little that I can add to the illuminating dicussion that has already taken place. What I have to say must therefore necessarily be marginal, and perhaps inconsequential. I beg you therefore to consider the remarks I am going to make as more of a footnote speech than a keynote speech. My footnotes will be mainly directed towards shedding further light on the progressive insertion of New Zealand into the world forest and timber economy. The title I have chosen is more than a catch-phrase. We in FAO are pretty well placed to observe the progressive internationalization of forestry, at several different levels.

First, at the rather obvious level of trade and markets, the world forest and

A public lecture delivered at Rotorua, New Zealand, October 1969; first published in the *New Zealand Journal of Forestry*, 15:1 (1970), pp. 9–24.

timber economy is steadily becoming more integrated. You are probably all well familiar with the tremendous acceleration in the consumption of forest products that has taken place since mid-century. This was most spectacular in Europe, where the rise in wood consumption in the first post-war decade was twice that in the previous half-century. A similar acceleration, though less spectacular, is evident in other regions of the world. This phenomenon is, of course, associated with the higher economic growth rates that have prevailed generally since the war. What is perhaps less generally realized is that a growing proportion of total consumption is satisfied through international trade. Thus, around 1950, forest products traded internationally represented 19 per cent by value of total forest products produced and consumed. By 1967, this percentage had risen to 24. Over the period the total volume of forest products traded had risen by 150 per cent, and the value by 80 per cent. Moreover, it is quite apparent that international trade in forest products will continue to increase, certainly in absolute terms, and probably in relative terms – relative, that is to say, to global consumption. This is partly because in several areas of the world rising demand is pressing hard on locally available resources, and there must be increasing recourse to imports. A contributing factor is that rising living standards have brought about a sharp increase in the demand for tropical hardwoods, a preferred constituent of many durable consumption goods. Another notable feature of the last two decades has been the increasing importance of those forest products which involve reconstituted wood, such as fibreboard, particle board, and the whole range of pulp products. This is leading to steadily changing calls on the forest, and hence to modification of forest production goals. Since this trend is also accompanied by rapid technological advance which serves to broaden the raw material base of the industries reconstituting wood, the price of wood is tending to become more decisive and wood quality less decisive. This naturally opens up great possibilities for those countries suitably endowed to produce wood cheaply and quickly.

These factors – the growth in wood consumption, the changing pattern of demand, advancing technology, and greater emphasis on price – together mean that it becomes increasingly necessary for each individual country, in establishing its own forest production goals, to take account of the international context. That is to say, each country, in deciding how much to invest in forestry, and what the pattern of that investment should be, must take into account, not only its own future needs, but also the extent to which it will be more sensible to meet part of those needs from imports, and also how far it ought to provide a margin to satisfy needs arising elsewhere. This, then, is one sense in which forestry is becoming more international; one sense in which we stand today squarely in front of one-world forestry.

There are still some countries, I fear, which have failed to reslize the direction in which the world forest and timber economy is evolving, which have not started the task of reappraising their forestry production goals in the changing international context, and which have not understood the importance of continuing studies of present and prospective future production costs in their own country as compared with other countries. In the light of the recent National Development Conference, I think New Zealand can reply 'not guilty' to this charge.

But if some forest administrations have been slow to understand, some of the major forest industries have been less slow. We have witnessed during the last decade international capital movements, and new company links, in this sector, on an unprecedented scale. Product diversification and security of raw material supplies have been two of the principal motivations in this trend.

But not only is forestry becoming more international at the obvious level of trade and markets, it is steadily becoming more international at the technical level, in terms of science, research, and the applications of science and technology. This applies both on the growing and harvesting side, and on the processing side. Successive congresses of the International Union of Forestry Research Organizations demonstrate that forestry, too, shares in the contemporary information explosion. Increasingly, funding authorities, when reviewing the work programmes and budgets of forest research organizations, insist on sensible answers to two elementary questions: what proportion of your effort do you devote to ensuring that you are making full use of research carried out elsewhere, and avoiding useless duplication and replication? And what proportion of your effort do you devote to ensuring that any useful findings get promulgated and applied? Twenty years ago the first of these questions would hardly have been necessary. Save in very limited fields, the volume of research being conducted was not sufficiently considerable to give rise to real dangers of duplication. Over the last twenty years, the number of forest research institutes in the world has almost doubled. The IUFRO Congress in Rome in 1953 was attended by about 150 scientists; that in Munich in 1967 was attended by 750 scientists.

Nor is it simply a matter of more work being conducted, of more facts and findings becoming available. A growing proportion of applied, as well as basic, research is becoming internationally relevant. This is not simply because forest types do not respect political frontiers, or that similar man/resources/relationsips occur in widely separated countries. It is rather because, first, the accelerating evolution of the man/resources relationship poses country after country with problems which have already been faced elsewhere; and partly because the economic and intellectual climate for adapting and exploiting technological breakthroughs has radically altered. Multiple-use forestry is a good example of the first; the whole area of tree improvement is a good example of the second.

A corollary of the two trends towards one-world forestry that I have outlined is that the forestry profession itself is becoming more and more international. More and more foresters are coming to realize that a stage overseas is not only desirable; it is necessary. This is particularly true of the younger generation of foresters, many of whom are in fact looking forward to spending a substantial part of their careers overseas. Their movitation is of the highest. They recognized far better than do my contemporaries, that the principal problem of the mid-twentieth century is the growing gap between the have and the have-not nations. They believe that development assistance can help solve this problem. And they find professional and moral satisfaction in devoting themselves to this cause.

But, leaving aside those who seek careers in international forestry, we are reaching the stage where it can be truly said that the education of a forester is incomplete without some international experience. And the real gain from service overseas and from multiplying international contacts lies less in techniques and gadgetry than in the intellectual cross-fetilization which enables the forester to think about his own problems in new and different ways and, in particular, to see them in the light of a world perspective. This is particularly important at a time when the tasks of the forester, both in developed and in developing countries, are changing with a rapidity never previously experienced. In the advanced industrialized countries the forester is perforce becoming more cost-conscious; he is seeking to get to grips with advances in related disciplines, and notably in the managerial sciences; he is striving to meet the rising demand on the forest for values other than the timber crop – the complex range of protection and recreation values that it is convenient to term social forestry; and in some countries he is already planning for the forestry use of land liberated by agriculture following the current green revolution. The forester in the developing countries has to face most of these problems too, but in addition he is under far stronger pressure to pursue a development-oriented forestry, directed to cutting down his country's timber bill, earning foreign exchange, providing employment opportunities, and broadening his country's industrial base.

These are, in fact, new and exciting days for forestry, perhaps as exciting as any since those distant years when forestry as a science was becoming established. This is why the stay-at-home forester is beginning to be regarded as the half-educated forester. I doubt whether this accusation can be levelled at the foresters in New Zealand, who are well known to have itching feet. I believe the peripatetic foresters of New Zealand have brought back to these islands many of the ideas which have contributed to the healthy state of New Zealand forestry today. And already, in a large measure, New Zealand forestry is repaying some of the debt in ideas it owes to the rest of the world. Today there are splendid opportunities of enriching your own experience while helping those less fortunately placed. I am surprised, for example, that New Zealand has not as yet devised some kind of associate expert scheme, whereby young graduate foresters acquire international experience by working alongside experienced men in multilateral and bilateral programmes. I can only think that this is because New Zealand does not yet appreciate how much it has to offer in this field, and how much it could gain.

You will notice that I have used the phrase 'the healthy state of New Zealand forestry'. There are plenty of signs that New Zealand forestry is in a healthy state: the jubilee celebrations, the Forestry Development Conference, the ceremonies which have taken place in this town today, the high acclaim which New Zealand forestry has won all round the world, the growing number of forestry pilgrims that come to these shores. What is perhaps most surprising is the extent to which many New Zealand non-foresters are beginning to look upon forestry as the white hope of these islands, the most important diversification measure in the economy, the best insurance against the manifold perils that seem to beset New Zealand agriculture. Now I am no agricultural expert myself, and I am in no position to pronounce on the prospects of New Zealand agriculture. But I have the distinct impression, if I can rely on informed gossip, that some people are seeking to bury New Zealand agriculture before it is dead. There is much talk again of the possible entry of the United Kingdom into the European Economic Community; this would tend to affect some New Zealand exports dramatically, but you have succeeded in making the special problems which such an event would pose for your country well understood by the main parties. My expert colleagues tell me that wool is by no means a finished commodity, in spite of the inroads of synthetics. And the vigorous development of wool-processing in New Zealand in recent years suggests that this country is finding a way to hold on to a share of the market. Many people in Asia are tasting New Zealand mutton for the first time. Given the shortage of animal protein in the world, there seems to be no reason why more should not do so, and it should prove possible to introduce many consumers both in Europe and Asia to the delights of New Zealand lamb. The prospects for meat generally seem to be quite favourable. The immediate outlook for butter is certainly less promising, but if New Zealand's initative to seek some international regulation of the market is successful, and productivity here continues to reach even higher levels, there should be brighter days ahead for this industry.

Thus, is seems to me that there is no question of forestry replacing agriculture as New Zealand's main export-provider. Rather it is a question of forestry supplementing agriculture, and helping to keep the ship moving in those times when the winds of agricultural trade falter. Certainly, as of now, there seems to be no need for any sizeable shift of land resources from agriculture to forestry. The National Development Conference has recognized that enough land, of the right quality, in the right place, is available to meet the future needs as foreseen without trespassing significantly on the agricultural estate.

As you celebrate your forestry jubilee, the balance sheet of the last fifty years must look pretty good. The old-timers in my audience must feel considerable satisfaction, perhaps tinged with surprise, at having seen the forestry sector in this country grow up from infancy to lusty maturity in the space of a few decades. You have created one of the largest concentrated man-made forest resources in the world, and one with exceedingly high growth rates. On the basis of this resource, modern processing plants have been established, well located and of economic size. Consumption of forest products has steadily grown, so that New Zealand has today the world's highest per caput consumption of sawnwood, though, in relation to income, New Zealand remains an under-consumer of most other forest products. Though the home market is heavily protected, a growing export trade to Australia has been developed in some forest products – but it must be observed that these do not necessarily correspond to the most dynamic elements in the Australian forest economy, since they are largely limited to newsprint and sawnwood. And of late, a very important log trade has developed with Japan.

What sort of launching pad does all this give you for the next fifty years? As far as the first two decades are concerned, the targets set in the forestry sector report to the national Development Conference (and implicitly endorsed by the NDC, since all the relevant associated recommendations were accepted) reveal great confidence in New Zealand's future as a forest products exporter. The target for 1979, $96 million, at constant prices, as compared with $51 million in the calendar year 1968, is based (I quote) 'on a realistic assessment of future market opportunities overseas and New Zealand's ability to produce the required output and meet competition from other countries'.

The export targets from 1980 on, to the end of the century, are not specifically endorsed in the forestry sector report, but again, in accepting the relevant associated recommendations, the volume export targets originally set out in the 1969 National Forestry Planning Model have been implicitly endorsed by the NDC.

Now I did not have the pleasure of participating in the NDC, nor have I seen the summary records. But the impression I get from these quotations is that the sense of the conference was broadly as follows: up to 1979 we think we can see the markets; from 1980 on, we can't, but we think they ought to be there; in any case, we feel we ought to plan as though they will be.

Now, if I were a New Zealander, I think I would endorse this broad strategy. I would do so in spite of certain doubts and misgivings. I would do so because it seems to me that in the present situation, it is imperative for New Zealand to keep as many options open as possible. To renounce the targets set, or to scale them down considerably, would, in fact, mean closing off one very important option.

You will expect me to give an account of my doubts and misgivings. Let me, at the outset, make it plain that I have full confidence that world demand for forest products will continue to expand, and that between now and the end of the century any incursions which other materials may make in the forest products field will be more than offset by new applications we shall discover for wood and its products. Like my colleague Dr Steenberg, Assistant Director General of the Forestry Department of the FAO, 1970–74, who was privileged to address the Forestry Development Conference earlier this year, I do not envisage a 'world without wood'.

We in FAO are presently attempting to carry out consumption projections forward to the year 1985. Table 5.1 sets out figures of global consumption of the principal forest products in 1955 and 1965, with some very tentative estimates of future consumption in 1975 and 1985. These last figures are taken from our current work on the Indicative World Plan, eked out with a number of guesses. Since our work is still proceeding, they may be subject to considerable modification in due course. This is why I stress that, at the present stage, they are very tentative indeed.

That there has been a considerable expansion in the consumption of forest products between 1955 and 1965 is clear from table 5.1. Moreover, we think that the estimates are sufficiently reliable to show that this expansion will continue through the two decades 1965 to 1985. In the final column is shown the expected percentage rise over this period. You will note that the reconstituted woods show the highest percentage increases. Over the period 1965 to 1985 we expect global consumption of sawn softwood to go up by about 60 million cubic metres, and that of sawn hardwood by some 45 to 50 million cubic metres. Thus, by the end of the period, the proportion of hardwood in the sawnwood total will have risen from 22 to 27 per cent.

Now one of the items we have not yet felt able to quantify with any precision is the future hardwood component of the pulp sector. This will be a disappointment to you, as it is to me; indeed, this is one of the points which would cause me some concern if I were New Zealander. We are pretty sure that hardwood pulp in the future is going to be much more important than it is today, as the economic and technical advantages of hardwood pulp become more widely appreciated. Hitherto most of us have tended to think of long-fibred coniferous wood as the ideal pulping material; and that, provided there was enough of it, and it was cheap enough, there would be no need to look around for hardwoods. The situation today is very different. There is every indication that the shortage of hardwood will soon be as pressing a problem as was the shortage of softwood some ten to fifteen years ago. Already a quarter of Europe's pulpwood *production* consists of broadleaved species. The proportion ranges from 8 per cent in Austria to 97 per cent in Italy. This represents a big change over recent years. The trend has been similar in the United States, where the consumption of hardwood (including roundwood, chips and residues) rose from 14.4 million cubic metres in 1955 to 31.4 million cubic metres in 1965; that is, from 17 to 24 per cent of the total wood furnish. But even this performance is overshadowed by the striking changes which have taken place in Japan. In 1955, the Japanese pulp industry consumed only 0.8 million cubic metres of hardwoods; 85 per cent of its wood consumption in that year

Table 5.1 World consumption of forest products

Item	Million units	Actual consumption		Estimated consumption		Increase			
							Volume percentage		
		1955[a]	1965[a]	1975	1985	1955–65	1965–75	1075–85	1965–85
Sawnwood	m³	303	384	424	485	81	40	61	26
Plywood	m³	10.4	25.7	44	65.2	15.3	18.3	21.2	154
Fibreboard	m.tons	3	5.6	10.9	15.2[b]	2.6	5.7	4.3	171
Particle board	m.tons	0.5	5.2	16.5	23.6[b]	4.7	11.3	7.1	354
Woodpulp	m.tons	46	74	130	215	28	56	85	191
Newsprint	m.tons	11.2	17.2	26	37.8	6	8.8	11.8	120
Printing and writing	m.tons	10.1	17.5[b]	32.4	53.9	6.4	14.9	21.5	208
Other paper and board	m.tons	35	63[b]	104	180	28	41	78	185

[a] Three-year averages.
[b] Estimates allowing for incomplete data.

consisted of round softwood pulpwood. By 1967, round softwood pulpwood
accounted for only 15 per cent of the intake. No less than 58 per cent of the
intake consisted of hardwood, of which rather more than half was in the form
of hardwood chips. I think you will understand, from the figures I have quoted,
why it is difficult for us at this stage to give any firm prediction of the role
of hardwoods in the world's pulp industry by 1985. Any prognostication made
on technical grounds must necessarily be conditioned by the availability of
economic supplies.

Similarly, if we look at the other reconstituted woods – particle board and
fibreboard – we see that there are no established patterns in wood furnish, which
increasingly depends very largely on supplies available. It is clear that hardwoods and softwoods are substitutes over a very wide range of wood products,
and that they are capable of replacing each other to an extent that we certainly
did not foresee twenty years ago. The likelihood is that technological progress
will still further reduce the technical differences between hardwoods and softwoods, so that as time goes on countries will tend more and more to use what
they have available or what they can get. I imagine that already, given the
technological trends in pulping, New Zealand is reviewing the possibilities
offered by some of its native hardwoods, and the desirability of supplementing
them by planting exotic hardwoods.

Now I would not like anybody to conclude, from what I have said, that we
think the day of first-class long-fibre pulp is finished. What I am trying to suggest
is that it is no longer the premium material that we used to think it was a decade
ago. If it is cheap enough it will still find a market. For certain purposes it
will continue to be needed as a blend. And certainly there are several countries
in Asia which, in the course of the next two decades, will want to set up their
own manufacturing facilities, basing them on the raw materials they have
available in their own country. Several of these will doubtless be looking for
long-fibre pulp as part of their furnish, to complement the qualities innate in
their indigenous materials. I believe that they will be all the more ready to
do this if they have the prospect of importing, along with the long-fibre pulp,
some technical know-how and perhaps capital aid. If New Zealand wishes to
move in this direction, it will require a purposeful campaign by government
and industry in partnership. In these affairs industry cannot move alone, and
government can accomplish nothing without industry. Some years ago, when
disillusion spread at the limited impact of aid programmes, the cry went up:
'trade, not aid'. This was a false slogan, since both trade and aid are necessary,
and bilateral arrangements which marry aid to trade are those most likely to
speed the development process.

Another misgiving which doubtless many New Zealanders must share stems
from this country's unfortunate geographic situation from the standpoint
of trade. A latitude in the forties and a longitude in the 170s may be fine
for growing radiata pine; but it does not offer the best access to the world's

principal forest products markets. And there seems little likelihood of early changes in freight patterns that would go very far to offset this eccentric location. Geography, it seems to me, has already decided what New Zealand's principal market for forest products will be, now and for always. It is an expanding market, and New Zealand's share in it will be determined, as much as anything, by its ability to convince her Australian friends, inside and outside the trade, that New Zealand is capable of supplying them with a sustained and expanding supply of forest products at a price they cannot hope to match. The political frame for developing a complementarity between the forest economies of Australia and New Zealand has already been established. As Polonius might have advised, had he been around: 'The friends thou hast, and their adoption tried, grapple them to they soul with hoops of radiata pine.'

The situation of the Japanese timber economy is such that Japan's timber gap will continue to rise, certainly until towards the end of the century. There are few signs that Japan will renounce her preferences for importing logs and wood chips, at least until such time as these raw materials become too hard to get. This, it seems to me, is unlikely to happen, given Japan's ingenious use of hardwood, and the hardwood resources in and outside the region still waiting to be developed. The situation may change, of course, if labour costs rise fast in Japan, or if international pressure persuades Japan to modify its tariff structure. Meanwhile, however, New Zealand's share in this trade will depend very much on price and freights. And if the day does come when Japan is willing to accept more processed products, New Zealand will face strong competition from the west coast of North America and from the new industries being set up in Soviet Siberia with Japanese help. Here again, geography will favour New Zealand's principal competitors.

China, in spite of her vigorous plantation programme, will remain a wood-starved country for several decades. How far this wood famine will be translated into a wood import trade it is difficult to estimate. I myself would not expect a substantial expansion in imports save in the context of a general political and trade agreement, but such an agreement is not to be excluded.

I have mentioned already the possibility of New Zealand cooperating with Asian countries in helping to develop local forest industries, requiring the import of capital, know-how and some long fibre. It is conceivable that such developments could be stimulated were New Zealand to diversify her imports, and offer to her own consumers a wider range of forest products by importing more tropical woods.

But with all this, it seems to me that the principal lesson which New Zealand must learn from its geographical position is that its long-term export prospects for the forest industries, apart from Australia, must lie in the direction of high-value, sophisticated products with a longer export range, rather than relying on lower-value, mass-grade products on which freight bears heavily, and in relation to which there will always be serious competitors.

As I see it, New Zealand's problem is a very simple one. You have versatile, cheap raw material. And you can easily create more of it. But so can some others, better placed for world markets. How can you beat geography? By moving towards high-value lines and by getting ahead and keeping ahead in the whole field of product research, design and development. So what really matters is how much money and effort government and industry are prepared to put into research, design and development in the next years. In this respect, I find the research targets set by the NDC, bold as they are, to be somewhat disappointing. They imply that forest products research will not double until eight years have passed. But these eight years may well be decisive for the whole future of New Zealand's forest industries. Certainly, the new facilities opened today[1] at Rotorua represent a great step forward. And of course I heartily endorse the NDC conclusion that the scale of research increase has no direct relationship to the scale of production increase aimed for. But the considerations which I have set before you do seem to me to require a very special effort in the area of product diversification and product development.

I know that many of the possible export lines are already developing or under study – collapsed, prefabricated houses, non-housing structures for assembly, knock-down furniture, laminated beams. I am sure, too, that with the rapid trend towards containerization of sea freight, and with more bulk moving out of New Zealand than moves in, the possibility of a massive export of once-used containers is under examination. Perhaps it will be a New Zealander who first designs a sastisfactory modular wooden house, one that can change and grow with the changing family pattern. But perhaps the more important possibilities lie in products not yet designed or invented, and here there is an ample field to be pioneered. I am convinced, for example, that in the paper field there are innumerable high-value disposables waiting to be invented and patented.

The point is that this is the time when those concerned with New Zealand's forest industries should be ceaselessly scouring the world for ideas. Here it is as well to remember that most of the true innovations spring from the lunatic fringe of research, so that the approach in sanctioning research should be neither earthbound nor conservative. This is the time to attract to these shores the crackpots who are crying in the wilderness in other countries. This is the time to give every encouragement to your own crackpots. And this is certainly the time to keep under continuous study the advances being made in the technology of other materials, to see how these can be adapted to or married to the forest products field.

If I have emphasized this point about research, it is because I believe that the forest industries in these islands are going to need energy, imagination, inspiration and a dose of genius if they are to defeat geography. And the next

---

[1] Stage 1 of the new Forest Research Institute buildings, mainly comprising the forest products laboratories.

years will be crucial. It is just conceivable that the forest industries in New Zealand would be more energetic in this direction if they were not so comfortably ensconced in their own domestic markets. It is rather disconcerting to note how, for example, the consumption of wood-based panels has stagnated in New Zealand over the last decade, as compared with the progress made in other countries of comparable income level. The salient facts are set out in table 5.2.

Table 5.2   Increases in *per caput* consumption of wood-based panels in selected countries, 1955–66

Country	Relative national income per head, 1966	Plywood (1,000 m³)	Particle board (1,000 m³)	Fibreboard (1,000 m³)	Total (1,000 m³)
USA	178	34	3.5	2.6	43.8
Sweden	134	6.5	12.5	17	53.7
Switzerland	116	4.7	13.3	2.5	30
Canada	112	34	3.8	–	40.1
Denmark	103	4.1	13.3	6.3	35.5
New Zealand	100	1.4	2.3	1.1	6.9
Australia	100	–0.4	5.5	1.1	10.1
German Federal Republic	86	6	17.4	3.4	39.3
Britain	86	8.2	3.6	2.1	17.4
Japan	45	19	1.4	2.5	25.2

Table 5.2 shows the extra volume of wood-based panels sold to every man, woman and child in 1965 as compared with 1955. New Zealand, as you see, is at the very bottom of this league of selected countries. Is this because the New Zealand consumer clings conservatively to his home-grown sawn softwood? By no means, because, although it is true that New Zealand remains at the top of the world table of per caput sawnwood consumers, in several of the other countries listed in the table the rise in wood-panel consumption has been accompanied by a sharp rise in sawnwood consumption.

New Zealand is also a serious under-consumer (in relation to income, that is) of paper and board, other than newsprint. In 1965, both Germany and Britain, with per caput income one seventh lower than that of New Zealand, consumed per caput one third more of these grades, while Japan, with per caput income less than one half of New Zealand's had around the same per caput consumption as New Zealand. In fact, on the basis of income (and there is a pretty good correlation between income and paper consumption in the world as a whole), New Zealand ought to be consuming about 100,000 tons more of these grades a year than she does at present.

It may come as a surprise to some of you to learn that the New Zealander apparently reads less, writes less and wraps less, as well as using fewer panels, than his fellows in other parts of the world enjoying about the same living standards. I simply state the fact – I don't pretend to explain it – although doubtless some observers will ask themselves whether this might not be associated with the relatively high degree of protection enjoyed by the New Zealand forest industries. If I have mentioned the matter at all, it is because it leads me to pass two other observations. First, the technical innovations and breakthroughs that will carry New Zealand forest products to the ends of the world are more likely to come from a vigorous, expanding forest industry than from a stable and sheltered one, resting on its laurels. Secondly, if New Zealand is presently an under-consumer, one must necessarily ask whether it will remain so, staying under the global trend lines for the next decades, or whether it will tend to catch up. The per caput consumption targets set out in the 1969 National Forestry Planning Model seem to assume that, for many forest products, New Zealand will remain an under-consumer, in relation to income. Let me give one or two examples. On the basis of the income growth rates postulated in the planning model, New Zealand will have, by the year 2000, an income per caput about 50 per cent higher than the USA had in 1966. But the year 2000 target for per caput consumption of all grades of paper and board other than newsprint is 172 kilos. Actual consumption of these grades in the USA in 1965 was 179 kilos per caput. The plywood target for New Zealand for the year 2000 is 47 cubic metres per thousand of population: the comparable figures for Canada, USA and Japan were 74, 68 and 24 already in 1965. This comparison is perhaps not altogether fair, since the three wood-based panel products are to a considerable extent interchangeable. But if we take these three panel products aggregated, the New Zealand target for the year 2000 is 118 cubic metres per thousand. Already in 1965 Canada was consuming 100, Sweden 95, and the USA 93 cubic metres per thousand of population. The targeted expansion of these products in New Zealand is certainly considerable, but it may be doubted whether it is sufficient to enable the targeted fall in per caput consumption of sawnwood to take place.

These figures suggest that those who constructed the planning model have assumed that New Zealand will continue to trail behind other wood-rich countries of similar income as a forest products consumer. Should this assumption not be realized, then domestic needs to the year 2000 may well be somewhat higher than has been predicted, and the surplus available for export correspondingly less. One thing is certainly clear: continuing study of domestic trends in demand, and international comparisons, will be as necessary as continuing study of supply trends in ensuring that rational goals are set in successive reviews.

With the rest of the programme proposed by the Forestry Development Conference I have little serious quarrel. Moreover, I am confident that the research programme outlined will succeed in holding costs to a reasonable level, and in securing a better integration of forestry objectives with overall land-use problems. However, it does seem to me that there is one particular area which might have received more attention. It is customary to speak nowadays about the revolution in transport. Revolution there certainly is, but the revolution does not go as deep as to diminish radically the limitations set by freights and distances on commodity trade. I think it is already becoming clear that the movement of persons is going to entail more revolutionary implications than the movement of things. And I would respectfully suggest that the forestry sector report to the NDC has not taken sufficient account of the revolutionary implications of moving persons.

I would like to dwell on this point for a moment, because all the indications are that some of the greatest changes in store for forestry over the next fifty years will spring precisely from the rapidly rising movement of persons. The one-world forestry I spoke of will also encompass something like a one-world forest. It is a fact, confirmed by films, photographs, and the little I have managed so far to see, that these islands, from the standpoint of tourist potential, are incomparable. Glaciers, alpine peaks, mountain-ringed lakes, warm fiords, active volcanoes, hot springs, unique native culture, salmon and trout fishing, deep sea fishing, hunting, limitless space and verdure. These are the things people want to see. And these are the things which, thanks to growing affluence and more equitable distribution of wealth, more and more people can afford to see. And not only the rich and the upper middle classes; also the teachers, clerks, tradesmen, tram drivers. With the jumbo jets already here, the present trickle can become a flood – that is, if you want it to become a flood. Potentially, tourism can become New Zealand's number one foreign exchange earner. But you have to make up your minds whether or not you want to share the delights of your country with others. It is not easy to discern from the forestry sector report to the NDC whether you do or not. When I read the recommendations emerging from the work of the working party on multiple-use forestry, I got the impression that your answer to this question is a reluctant, grudging yes. Thus, I find the references to tourism in the relevant sections of the forestry sector report (paras 132–40, with the associated recommendations) almost laconic, as if scant consideration had been given to some of the cogent material submitted to the Forestry Development Conference. Moreover, the report of the tourism committee to the second plenary session of the NDC seems to give, in its relevant recommendations (32 and 33), less than full recognition to the tourist potential of forest lands and the role of the Forest Service. This may spring from the fact, as I have noted with astonishment and regret, that no member of the New Zealand Forest Service served on either the main committee on tourism or on any of its working parties. I therefore suspect that the economic significance of managing forests for recreation is still underrated. Yet there are already considerable areas of forest, both in North America and Europe, where tourism, whether it be in the form of camping, boating, fishing, hunting, nature trails, pony tracks or what have you, is already yielding more direct revenue than when the forests were managed for timber production. As the concept of multiple-use forestry has developed, in the changing world, we have come to understand that the management of particular forests must be directed towards a major use, with other uses subordinated. Already the leading schools in the West are revising their curricula so that more foresters are capable of managing their forests to draw full advantage from the world's fastest-growing industry: tourism.

Should New Zealand decide to give great emphasis to the development of her forests for tourism, we in FAO would have a very special interest. It is precisely from countries with a large proportion of marginal and unused lands that we can hope to see the most important advances in our understanding of how to manage those lands. Countries like New Zealand are in no way inferior to Canada or the USA when it comes to the potential multiple uses which may be developed on lands now wild and under the control of the Forest Service. Already there is a large and growing literature on assessing tourist potential in forest lands, on various forms of fish and wildlife management, and on methods for assessing the value of these non-timber products of the forest. But much more needs to be done. In developing new areas, there is much to be gained by assessing potential non-timber values at the same time as the initial forest inventory is made, so that both types of data can be made available to forest and land-use planners. So we in FAO have a selfish interest in seeing how you tackle these problems here. But perhaps the most important consideration, from New Zealand's point of view, is that deliberate planning towards this end would keep open for New Zealand forestry another option, an option which will surely be of growing economic significance, and one which might ultimately become, as it has already done in certain areas of the world, the most important forest-based industry.

It is worth while reflecting on what tourism can mean in economic terms. The NDC target for exchange earnings from tourism is $70 million by 1979 – a figure which strikes me as somewhat conservative. This excludes any income New Zealand might earn from carrying tourists back and forth. Adding New Zealand's share of tourist transport, the exchange earning target rises to $110 million – a figure already somewhat higher than the export target for the forest industries. So, in economic terms, tourism is certainly not chicken-feed.

Now of course the responsibility of getting these people here does not rest wholly on the Forest Service. But the Forest Service will have an important part, indeed a decisive part, to play in shaping the facilities and attractions that will bring them here. The point I am trying to make is that forest management for tourism, in all its manifold aspects, is neither a sideshow nor an incubus. For many forest areas and most marginal lands under the control of the forest services, it is becoming the major management objective. The

Americans and Canadians have discovered this. So have the British. Several European countries learned it some time ago.

Now of course these aspects were not neglected at the Forestry Development Conference. But I do think that they were underemphasized, and appeared to lean heavily on the potential and needs of domestic tourism. I have the distinct impression that the participants may have failed to appreciate the significance of the facts that world spending on travel abroad has been rising three times as fast as total national incomes, and that the impending revolution in passenger transport is going to offer many more strangers the chance to visit these distant shores.

This is really all I have to say. I cannot claim to have shed much light on New Zealand's role. The scattered comments I have made have, as I stated at the outset, really been in the nature of marginal footnotes to the forestry sector report to the NDC. This conference, and the way it was prepared, the way it was conducted, impressed us deeply in FAO. We believe there are many countries in the world which, at the present stage in the development of their forests and timber economy, could greatly benefit from similar initiatives.

So far as New Zealand's forestry sector is concerned, the conference has charted the course in a very general way, and has made some important preparations for the voyage. Much remains to be done. You have to keep alert to changes in the weather. You have to keep an eye on the seaworthiness of the boat. And sooner or later you have to decide on your exact ports of call. But it seems to me, from what I have been able to learn of your forestry and forest industries, that there is nothing wrong with the crew.

I wish you all *bon voyage!*

PART II
Rethinking

6
The Changing Objectives of Forest Management

WORLD WOOD TRENDS

Since the middle of this century the world's consumption of industrial wood has been growing at an unprecedented rate. It is not easy to document this with precision for the world as a whole, since for most parts of the world there are no adequate statistics available for the period before the First World War. But in Europe, for example, industrial wood consumption rose between 1913 and 1935–8 from 138 to 173 million cubic metres, that is, by 35 million cubic metres, or by 1 per cent a year on average. In 1950, consumption had not quite recovered the pre-war level, standing at 169 million cubic metres. By 1965, however, consumption had risen to 264 million cubic metres, a rise of 95 million cubic metres in fifteen years – an average annual increase of 3 per cent. In the USA, consumption of industrial wood actually fell sharply between 1913 and the late thirties, from 264 to 185 million cubic metres, largely because of the declining use of wood in solid form. But since the war, as a result mainly of the rapidly expanding use of wood in reconstituted form, consumption has risen sharply, and by 1965 had reached 331 million cubic metres.

This *acceleration* in industrial wood consumption since mid-century is, of course, associated with the acceleration in economic growth rates. The total product of economic activity has risen somewhat more sharply, taking the world as a whole, since mid-century. This perhaps reflects the post-war preoccupation of economists and governments with problems of growth and development, as against their pre-war concern with problems of stability and equilibrium.

Forest products penetrate into every sector of the economy, and the demand for them is linked in a hundred ways with the process of economic growth. It is therefore not surprising that the consumption of forest products is rising faster than ever. However, the link between economic growth and industrial wood consumption is not a simple and direct one; it is very much conditioned by the

Address to the Ninth Commonwealth Forestry Conference, India, 1968. Reproduced by permission of the author and the Food Agriculture Organization of the United Nations.

pattern of forest products consumption. That pattern has been changing rapidly since the war, as table 6.1 shows.

Table 6.1   Change in recorded world use of wood products, 1950–2 to 1965

Wood products	Million units	1950–2	1965	Change: 1951–65	
				Index (1950–2 = 100)	Average annual increase
Sawnwood	m³	266.1	368.7	139	2.4
Paper and paper board	m. tons	44.3	95.8	216	5.6
Plywood	m³	6.8	24.0	353	9.4
Fibreboard	m. tons	2.2	6.1	275	7.5
Particle board	m. tons	0.04	5.2	(over hundredfold increase)	
Roundwood	m³	129.2	116.4	90	−0.8

This table shows that the use of wood industrially in round form (as posts, poles and piling) is steadily declining. The consumption of paper and paperboard is rising rapidly – by about 3 million tons every year. Sawnwood consumption continues to increase, in spite of economies in intensity of use, and in spite of steady displacement in certain end-uses by other products, notably the wood-based panels: plywood, fibreboard and particle board, all of which have shown very high rates of growth over the last fifteen years.

Broadly speaking, these trends are expected to persist in the future. In 1966, FAO completed and published a study[1] in the course of which they updated, completed and integrated a number of earlier studies on wood consumption. This study developed projections to 1975, using average consumption for the years 1960–2 as benchmark. These projections, both for the several wood products and for the wood raw materials required to produce them, are set out in table 6.2.

According to these estimates, consumption of the products of the several forest industry groups over the next decade or so is expected to increase at more or less the same relative rates as has occurred over the last fifteen years, that is, a continuing rapid increase in consumption of the wood based panels, continuing substantial expansion in the consumption of pulp products, a slower but steady growth in the consumption of sawnwood, and a further decline in the consumption of industrial wood used in the round. Global consumption of wood used directly as fuel is expected to continue to grow, though but slowly.

Should these estimates prove well founded, then by 1975 the world will be using some 560 million cubic metres more wood than in 1961. Of this extra wood, some 450 million cubic metres will be used industrially. Of this additional industrial wood, well over half, close on 270 million cubic metres, will be required for pulp

[1] FAO, *Wood: World Trends and Prospects*, Basic Study no. 16, 1967.

Table 6.2 Estimated change in world consumption of wood and wood products, 1960–2 to 1975

Wood products	Million units	1960–2	1975	Increase: 1961–75	
				Volume	Index (1961 = 100)
Sawnwood	m³	346	427	81	123
Pulp products	m. tons	78	162	84	208
Panel products	m³	31	76	45	245
Roundwood	m³	188	185	– 3	98
Fuelwood	m³	1,088	1,199	111	110
Wood raw materials					
Sawlogs and veneer logs	m³	629	815	186	129
Pulpwood	m³	226	493	267	218
Other industrial wood	m³	188	185	– 3	98
Total industrial wood	m³	1,043	1,493	450	143
Fuelwood	m³	1,088	1,199	111	110
Total		2,131	2,692	561	126

and for fibreboard and particle board, that is, for those products which represent reconstituted wood. These industries seek different qualities in their raw material supply from those sought by the sawmills and the plywood mills; in particular, they can accept, indeed they prefer, wood in smaller dimensions, grown on a shorter rotation. Table 6.2 shows that the share of small-sized wood in total industrial wood, 22 per cent in 1960–2, will have risen to 33 per cent by 1975. This trend will certainly continue, and the proportion may well have risen to half by the end of the century.

Most of the extra industrial wood which the world is going to need by 1975 will be required in the presently advanced areas of the world, and this in spite of the fact that consumption is rising faster, relative to economic growth, in the less advanced parts of the world. This is because levels of wood consumption are very much higher in the industrialized regions than in the less developed regions. Though industrial wood consumption is expected to rise by 72 per cent in the low-income countries up to 1975, as against 37 per cent in the high-income countries, nevertheless over three quarters of the additional industrial wood, 335 million cubic metres, will be required in the high-income countries: Europe, North America, USSR, South Africa, the Pacific area and Japan.

Finally, we should observe that the figures I have given relate to consumption trends up to the year 1975. All the indications are that these trends will continue, though in somewhat attenuated form, through the succeeding decades.

Much of what I have said so far will doubtless already be familiar to you. My object in recapitulating it here is to bring home to you the historically novel nature of the contemporary wood supply situation. The world's industrial wood consumption is rising more rapidly than ever before. The pattern of that consumption is changing, entailing different calls on the forest. Most of the rise will occur in the developed regions, but the rate of growth is higher in the developing regions.

Let me say, parenthetically, that I am well aware of the vulnerability of these requirements estimates: the cavalier assumption about income and population growth; the paucity of information on trends in supply costs; the inadequate treatment of prices; and the almost intuitive assumptions regarding technological change. The actual levels of consumption realized in 1975, and succeeding decades, may well differ considerably, both globally and regionally, from those which have been projected. Nevertheless, no one has as yet seriously challenged these main conclusions, as concerns the direction of the major trends, their orders of magnitude, and their relative importance.

PRODUCTION GOALS: THE INTERNATIONAL CONTEXT

General though these conclusions are, they nevertheless present an indispensable frame of reference which individual countries have increasingly to take into account as they redefine their forest policies and lay down forest production goals. There is no country today which can regard its forest economy as a closed one. Already a very significant proportion of the world's wood needs is being satisfied through international trade. That proportion is destined to increase. Each country, in establishing its forest production goals, should, and in many cases must, have before it some clear concept, and if possible a quantified concept, of its future place in the world forest and timber economy. It must have some idea of the extent to which it intends to rely on imports to satisfy its future wood needs. It must have some notion of the extent to which it intends or expects its own forest resources to contribute to the wood needs of other countries.

Obviously, it is no easy matter to define the degree of self-sufficiency a country should aim at in, say, twenty or fifty year's time, or the size of the exportable surplus it should aim to create. The problem would be difficult enough even if all countries could agree that their national targets should be worked out on the basis of some single unifying doctrine, on the basis, say, of comparative costs. That is to say, a given country, in deciding how much investment to direct into the forest sector in order to raise national industrial wood production by a certain amount by a given target date, should consider how the cost of generating additional wood supplies (and valorizing them) compares with the costs of generating extra wood supplies in other parts of the world. Such an approach would give considerable intellectual satisfaction to a global planner, if such an animal existed. It would run into the difficulty that an adequate information basis is woefully lacking. Nevertheless, some data do exist, and they are being added to daily. It is right and proper that much more attention is now being given, at the national level, to the cost of stretching wood supplies in one's own country as compared with other parts of the world.

However, the fact that one has to proceed on the basis of partial knowledge does not mean that one cannot proceed at all. The point is that, even on the basis of the inadequate data at our disposal, one can usually designate a reasonable range of action. In real life, the situation which usually confronts us can be exemplified as follows. Imagine four alternative sets of measures, A, B, C and D, of progressive scope and intensity, each with its associated level of necessary investment. These sets of measures are designed, respectively, to produce, by say the year 2000, an extra 5, 10, 15 and 20 million cubic metres of industrial wood. It is usually possible to make some general observation on each of the points in this scale, as, for example:

With A, we cannot go wrong;
B   would seem pretty safe too, but there is some slight risk of over-production in relation to demand and taking into account what we think we know about the costs of alternative supply sources;
C   could pay off, but only if every factor, internal and external, in the total situation were to work out favourably;
D   is very chancy indeed.

This, I submit, is the way in which the case will usually be presented to the policy-maker, once the economist has been persuaded to jettison his jargon. And we know, from experience, that the policy-maker will usually opt for a line of action that lies between A and B, somewhat closer to A than to B. The object of forest economics research is, in fact, to get rid of as many ifs and buts as possible, and to quantify the remaining ifs and buts as far as possible.

Our hypothetical global planner, who would like to see forest resources developed and created in a way that ensures the optimum economic utilization of those resources, is hampered not only by the fact that he is not omniscient, that his data base is inadequate. He is also hampered by the fact that a variety of institutional frictions will limit the extent to which he can do the obviously sensible thing. For example, capital scarcity, alternative claims on investment capital, as well as political risks, mean that for many years to come it will be easier to finance 6 per cent forestry in a developed country than to finance 12 per cent forestry in an underdeveloped country. And this is only one example of the institutional frictions that abound.

The existence of these institutional frictions has two corollaries which should not be overlooked. Let us, for the time being, retain this notion of an omniscient global planner, anxious to ensure that the world's forest resource is developed, and where necessary expanded, in an optimum economic way. Let us further suppose that national planners are disposed to develop their national plans in conformity with his master plan. The transition to the economic optimum will not be achieved by the full play of economic forces, though economic forces may tend in the long run to move events in the desired direction, sporadically, uncertainly, and with a considerable time lag. This is because of the institutional frictions to which I have referred. The second corollary is that, because of this inevitable lag in the optimization process, the developed countries will frequently be able to safely invest more than the global planner would have wished. Thus, referring back to the earlier case, a developed country, confronted with the A, B, C, D alternatives, may often be able to opt safely for B or B + , instead of A + or B − .

I used the phrase 'institutional frictions'. This is, of course, a euphemism, but if I had recourse to euphemism it was not that I wanted to hide reality, but that I did want to pause at that point to spell out the reality. The reality is that, though we may inhabit one *physical* world, economically, socially and politically we live in two worlds, and these two worlds − the affluent, technologically advanced, developed world, and the poorer, more populous, technically backward developing world − are getting farther apart. The euphemism I used was thus simply a convenient shorthand to indicate a whole host of problems inherent in the complex web of trade and development interrelations that characterizes our age. The basic conflict of the second half of the twentieth century is not the East−West conflict − the politicians who continue to twitter in these terms have been left behind by history. It is the North−South conflict.

There are many in the affluent North − individuals, statesmen and governments − who feel a sense of responsibility and obligation towards the South in this situation. Their motivation is mixed. Their sense of responsibility may stem from common humanity. It may lie in the feeling that moral debts piled up in a century of colonial exploitation of the South by the North are now due for repayment. It may be rooted in the fear of the social upheavals that may sweep away their way of life if something is not done quickly. But the motivation does not matter. What matters is that fair deeds should match the fair words that have rained on us increasingly in the post-war decades.

All this may seem a cry from the adumbration of forest production goals, but it is not.

In the trade development context, we know that a necessary condition (though not a sufficient condition) for starting to narrow the gap between the two worlds is that the developed world must facilitate and accommodate a substantial import of manufactured and semi-manufactured products from the developing world. We know, too, that one of the sectors where this can be accomplished with least effort on the part of the developing countries and leading to least stress and dislocation on the side of the developed countries is the forest industries sector. This being the case, national forest production goals in those developing countries which are suitably endowed should be tailored to provide an expanding flow; at the same time, national forest production goals in the developed countries should be so fixed as to provide markets for this expanding flow of trade. In other words, the concept of global economic optimization which inspires our hypothetical global planner is not enough. The contemporary scene requires something that goes beyond this. Moreover, it is not sufficient to write these ideas into national forest production goals. This action has to be supplemented and reinforced by a wide range of actions in the areas of trade, tariffs and developmental aid.

GOALS FOR NON-TIMBER PRODUCTS

So far, in what I have said about forest production goals (which are essentially the translation of forest policies into action programmes) I have limited my remarks to wood production targets. I have said nothing about goals for the production of other forest-created or forest-derived values: watershed values, benefits conferred on agriculture, socio-economic support for the rural communities, wildlife, recreation and amenity values. In this, I follow an illustrious line of predecessors, all of whom have been careful to draw attention to the limitation in their approach; all of whom are emphatic in stressing the importance of the values they have omitted, conceding that in many instances these values exceed in importance the wood production function of the forest; and all of whom explain their omission by pointing to the dearth of quantity and value information about these benefits.

I have little that is new to say about these non-wood products of the forest. But there are one or two observations I would like to make. First, I would remark on the irony of the present situation. On the one hand, very rapid progress has been made in the last decade in emptying some of the witchcraft out of our thinking on the wood production function of the forest. Wardle's paper to the conference shows the major contribution which operational research can make to the decision-making process. Grayson's paper shows how these powerful new techniques of calculation and analysis are being widely applied in the management of enterprises, and makes a plea for extending these techniques to the higher levels of decision-making, including the formulation of forest production goals. But as yet, at least so far as I am aware, these techniques, which aim at analyzing the economic or financial consequences of various courses of action, are applied solely to the wood production function of the forest.

On the other hand, we are all painfully aware of the rise – the almost exponential rise – in the relative importance of the non-wood products of the forest. The pressures to step up the flow of these physical protection and social benefits from the forest get more insistent day by day. Thus, the irony is that, as our production models get better and better, they get more and more out of touch with reality. No one has yet elaborated a model which is of much service to multiple-use forestry. Will this be possible in the foreseeable future? I do not believe so. I see very little prospect of accumulating the necessary data and learning how to feed them into the model. Taylor's paper to this conference shows, for example, what a long way we have to go in the field of recreation. We are not even sure yet what we ought to be counting!

To my mind, however, the search for such a model is a vain one. The hunt is misdirected, for at the end of the day the Snark will inevitably turn out to be a Boojum.

My views on this vexed problem are simple, clear and yet, I fear, heretical. So far I have found few of my colleagues disposed to accept them. I can sum them up in a series of elementary propositions:

1   A distinction can be drawn, conceptually, between production forestry – forestry which aims at producing wood for industrial or household use – and social forestry, forestry which aims at producing a flow of protection and recreation benefits for the community.
2   In principle, production forestry should pay.
3   The starting point for establishing the goals for production forestry should be the current and expected future costs of producing wood, as compared with current and expected future costs elsewhere, all in relation to expected future demand. Many other factors, including political considerations, will have to be taken into account in deciding on final goals, but the starting point should be the one I have mentioned.
4   The goals for social forestry should be determined by the amount of investment the community is prepared to allocate to secure the desired social benefits.
5   The fact that wood and the physical protection and social benefits are frequently joint products does not rule out this approach; it merely means we must start keeping our books in a different way.

PRODUCTION FORESTRY AND SOCIAL FORESTRY

Permit me to elaborate some of these points. As growing emphasis is placed on procuring from the forest a flow of physical protection benefits and social values, the constraints and limitations imposed on the forester as an economic producer of industrial wood steadily multiply. This problem is going to intensify. This is one important reason why a number of countries in the developed world are becoming relatively high-cost wood producers. Charges are being borne on the wood-producing account which represent services rendered to the community at large no less essential than education or basic health services. Those charges, the costs of social forestry, should be borne by the public purse. Only then will it be possible to get the books straight for production forestry, to get an idea of the real cost of producing wood for industry.

I fear that foresters themselves may have been responsible for certain mis-understandings and confusion which have arisen in the minds of some of the public and in some governmental circles. They have preached the gospel of the multiple role of the forest, have stressed the flow of non-crop benefits which the forest can provide, and have, perhaps unwittingly, encouraged the idea that the forest can provide all these goods and services – industrial timber, physical protection benefits and social values – simultaneously and economically.

A few months ago I tried to illustrate this problem by means of an analogy.

We would all of us hesitate before buying an electrical gadget which purported to serve as hair-drier, washing-up machine and standard lamp. We would suspect that full efficiency in one of these uses could only be secured by some sacrifice of efficiency in the others. Yet foresters, perhaps a little mesmerized by the multiple-use concept, have been slow to admit that proper management for one product will adversely affect the output of other goods and services.

Exception may be taken to this analogy. It will be claimed that for any forest truly managed on multiple-use principles there will be an optimum product mix, and the mangement plan designed to produce that optimum product mix will be the optimum one. Indeed, I suppose that even for the novel electrical gadget I mentioned there could be an optimum design. But the real problem is: for whom are the several goods and services produced and who is to pay for them? It is as if our electrical gadget were destined to dry the hair of the family, wash up the pots of all the neighbours, and provide street-lighting for the whole street.

My good friend Ed Cliff, Director of the US Forest Service, took great exception to this analogy, and referred to the gadget as 'your infernal machine'. He construed my plea as an attack on multiple-use forestry. But my attack is not against multiple-use forestry, in which I firmly believe. It is against confusion of aim and purpose in forestry, which sometimes goes as far as sheer obscurantism.

When funds have been sought for forestry in the past, projects have often been justified on the basis of their major use, with the subsidiary uses thrown in, either as an offset to low profitability or as some kind of premium. This, of course, sidesteps the problem of having goods and services paid for by those to whom they accrue. Yet surely the volume of forest-derived physical protection benefits and social values which a nation is to have should be determined on the basis of what the nation can afford to pay, having regard to other calls on the public purse. It should not be determined by what the forestry sector is able to provide in the ordinary way of business without going into the red. A protective afforestation scheme is a matter for public discussion, public decision, public financing, just as much as the raising of the school-leaving age.

Evidently, it will never be possible to get the accounts for production forestry and social forestry completely separate. But if the principle is accepted, it should make for clarity in concept and somewhat greater precision in costing than we have today. So far we have paid far too little attention to these problems. In this respect we are lagging far behind our fellow-workers in the USA. I believe the accounting aspects of these problems can be solved. I believe they have to be solved if we are to ensure an adequate level of investment in forestry in the future.

In several of the populous, industrialized, advanced countries the role of the forest as a wood-provider is already subordinate to its role as a provider of physical protection benefits and social values. Even in those countries where the wood production function still dominates, there are certain areas where this function has already become secondary. These areas will inevitably extend and multiply, as the demands for clean water, for recreation and amenity, for support to rural communities, mount. Dawkins, in a recent paper, saw the day fast approaching when, in the forest, aesthetics would be all, and wood production an anachronism, associated with a technology that had become historically outmoded. By aesthetics, I understand him to mean the whole gamut of non-timber products of the forest. I do not share his view. But it is certainly true that the community need for these products is rising even faster than is the need for wood. It will become increasingly difficult to pay for social forestry out of the revenues from production forestry. Only in rare and exceptional cases will social forestry be self-liquidating from the revenues it generates (camping fees, park admissions, and the like). Therefore, unless we can win public authorities to the idea that the social services performed by the forest must be paid for by public funds, we shall progressively fall behind the level of investment required to ensure those services.

But if there are dangers of under-investment in some countries, in others there is the danger of over-investment. We in FAO are frequently called upon to comment and advise upon the forestry plans of developing countries. Typically, these have three elements: development of the natural forests, industrial afforestation, and protective afforestation or improvement work, for example, in watersheds, on sand dunes, and so on. This last element is normally non-self-liquidating on any financial reckoning, though of course it may be well worth while on the basis of a comprehensive, economic cost–benefit evaluation. We have had occasion to remark, in some instances, that the volume of investment earmarked for this last element seems excessive in relation to the country's financial resources, taking into account other urgent claims such as education, sanitation, infrastructure, and so on. And there have been cases where we have felt it necessary to counsel a reduced investment in protection forestry. I hope this admission does not send a shiver down the spine of those directors of forest services presently bracing themselves for the annual battle of the budget. The cases I have mentioned may not be typical, but they are less rare than one might suppose.

I have tried to explain why I think that it is time for foresters to launch an educational campaign designed to enlighten public opinion and public authorities on the distinction between production forestry and social forestry, and on the need to render unto Caesar the things which are Caesar's. Yet, as I hinted earlier, I find many of my colleagues reluctant to accept the necessity of such an approach and of such a campaign. This reluctance, it seems to me, is rooted in fear: a fear which, to my mind, is groundless. Over the years the forester has come to regard himself as the keeper of the public conscience in matters of resource conservation and resource use. It is a role for which he is peculiarly fitted, since his training teaches him to set the long-term public interest over the short-term interest, public or private. It is a role which has fallen to him largely because of the lack of practitioners of other disciplines with a similar breadth of view. George Bernard Shaw once said that 'all professions are conspiracies against the laity.' It would be truer to say of the forestry profession that for generations it has been a conspiracy *for* the laity, in the sense that it has consistently, in the interest of that wider community which includes the unborn generations, fought against abuse of the forest resource. The fear of which I spoke, and which has tended to make foresters conspiratorial, is twofold: first, that the isues involved are too complex to be readily grasped by the man in the street, the administrator and the politician; second, that even if the issues were understood, neither the man in the street, nor the administrator, nor the politician would care enough.

These fears are baseless. The man in the street can be brought to understand. And once he has understood he will lash the administrator and the politician into action.

I have heard it whispered that one reason for the dislike on the part of some foresters of this conceptual dichotomy between production forestry and social forestry is the forester's traditional horror of book-keeping. I treat this malicious whisper with the contempt it deserves.

One recent event encourages me to believe that the ideas I have advanced about social forestry being a social service which should be paid for out of public funds are neither unreasonable nor unrealizable. You all know that, in the United Kingdom, British Railways have been in the red for many years. As a matter of fact they went into the red about the time I ceased to work for them. *Post hoc, non propter hoc,* I assure you. Over the years many measures have been adopted in an effort to get them out of the red and back into the black. These measures included the curtailment of certain services, the closure of branch lines, and so forth. Due procedures were laid down: notice of closure; time for appeal; public enquiry; ministerial decision. Progressively, unprofitable activities were lopped off. But protests grew, particularly from those areas where alternative transport means were inadequate. This year, for the first time, the government has specifically allocated £50 million sterling for the purpose of keeping in being certain transport facilities which, though unprofitable, are deemed essential social services. The principle underlying this step is, I submit, one of capital importance. And I think it is highly relevant to the case for sustaining social forestry from public funds.

THE RENEWED INTEREST IN FOREST MANAGEMENT

The redefinition of forest policy, the establishment of new forest production goals, requires a reassessment of forest management, the plans for achieving the set goals at the enterprise level. And in fact there has been a renewal of interest in forest management, together with a certain change of emphasis, in recent years. Richter, in 1963, reported how 130 or so studies on management, intended in the main for forestry students, were spread out in time between 1750 and 1950:

	per cent
1750–99	17
1800–49	29
1850–99	37
1900–50	17

Thus the golden age for management planners was the second half of the nineteenth century. These figures are surprising. What is more surprising is that, according to Richter, in Germany, the country to which forestry science owes so much, only three books on management have been published in the last thirty-five years.

The revival of interest is quite recent, and it is perhaps most marked in the USA, the UK, Scandinavia and the Eastern European countries. This revival of interest stems partly from the need to reconsider traditional forest management, partly from the overall progress being made in managerial sciences. Changing concepts are reflected in changing titles. Thus in the Anglo-Saxon countries we can note the replacement of the world 'management' by 'management planning', which conveys better the idea of production organization, or by 'forest development', which is a more complete idea than that of organization of production. In France, more and more the word 'aménagement' is replaced by the word 'gestion', a notion broader in scope and more flexible.

SOME CONTEMPORARY PROBLEMS IN MANAGEMENT

Perhaps the greatest change that has come to forest management at the enterprise level is that, in determining the objectives, national and even international considerations have come to weigh more heavily, while purely local considerations have come to weigh less heavily. This is in part a reflection of the fact that we live in a planning age. We are all planners now, whether we subscribe to *dirigisme* or whether we prefer to align our action to indicative plans. But it is also a reflection of the fact that technical advances in forestry have widened the range for positive interventions and have rid us of some of the former constraints. Even the forestry enterprises in the private sector tend to turn more often to governmental bodies for guidance. The management plan has to interpret the objectives of the national plan, and for this appropriate machinery must be devised. Frequently the regional or provincial plan is an essential link. Various formulae have been devised for assuring this connection between the management plan at the enterprise level and the national plan. In Europe, significant contributions have been made by Fromer in Poland and Klepac in Yugoslavia. Even so, this institutional question of the appropriate machinery – transmission machinery, one might say – is one that needs much more thought and discussion than it has so far received. Looking ahead, the changing product mix required from the forest, with the growing emphasis on non-timber values, is going to subject existing machinery to ever greater strain.

Another change that is coming about in forest management is our growing preoccupation with the question: what intensity of management pays? Almost everywhere we note the tendency to multiply those measures designed to raise productivity per hectare. It must be admitted that, whatever the intensity of management, there is a biological limit to total productivity, which has to be taken into account. The better the soils, the more capable they are of responding, the more we can step up our inputs. Obviously, in the man-made forest, where we can totally transform the site (through soil cultivation, irrigation, fertilizers, improved plant material), the perspectives are different; here it is a matter of ensuring that the several interventions are carefully coordinated and phased to give satisfactory financial results. This trend towards man-made forests is one of the essential forestry characteristics of our time. But between the two extremes, the natural forest with conventional silviculture and the man-made forest with complete site transformation, a large number of intermediate formulae are possible. All these questions are now under intensive study. Quite rapidly we are filling the gaps in our knowledge of what might be termed the micro-economics of the forestry enterprise. We are getting answers to such questions as: how much, of which fertilizer, should be applied when? What frequency, what intensity, of thinnings?

But we also have a new concern, about what might be termed the macro-economics of the forestry enterprise. And this concern comes to us from observing the progress made in managerial sciences and techniques in other sectors. There are scale economies in management. We have to think more about, not only management costs per hectare, but also management costs per cubic metre. We have to examine, more attentively than we have done hitherto, the notion of an optimum economic size for the management unit. In Europe, current ideas are moving towards an area of from two to three thousand hectares as the most viable management unit in economic terms.

This trend immediately brings us face to face with two related sets of questions. What are the most suitable institutional arrangements for grouping and consolidating small forest holdings into viable management units, capable of harnessing new techniques? What are the optimum managerial inputs, professional and sub-professional, quantitatively and qualitatively? And this in turn compels us to re-examine the scope and aims of forestry education.

There is one other changing aspect of management I must single out for mention. More and more the management plan has to look beyond the growing of wood to the harvesting of wood. Here I refer not to the need to grow those species and dimensions for which market outlets will be available. That need is fairly obvious, and is now generally recognized. I refer rather to the need to ensure that the wood that is grown can be harvested and taken out economically. The most vulnerable phase, the economically decisive phase, in the whole chain to the final consumer, is the stage from stump to mill gate. All efforts to raise standing stock and growth are doomed unless there is an equivalent effort to ensure that the resource can be mobilized in economically favourable conditions. The growing shortage of labour for forest operations, and the increasing unwillingness of labour to undertake physically heavy and dangerous tasks, means inevitably that the machine is going to take over much of this work. There will be new machines: heavier machines, more complex machines, more sophisticated machines. The forest, the trees, the wood material that the new generations of machines cannot handle will be left unutilized. More and more the organization of the management unit will come to focus on how the wood can most economically be felled and extracted. This invasion of the forest by the machine will not be halted, even though the machine brings with it damage to the standing stock and soil deterioration. There are already many instances where experts are satisfied that the economies realized in exploitation more than compensate for the losses entailed and for the cost of soil restoration.

Thus forest management has increasingly to reckon with harvesting costs; hence the tendency to group within the same enterprise the functions of wood production, wood harvesting and wood transport, and to so integrate these functions as to achieve maximum profit on the totality of the operations. Hence, too, in those countries where some or all of the manufacturing facilities have yet to be created, the trend towards *combinats*, bringing under a single management all phases from wood production to the integral utilization of the forest crop.

THE ROLE OF THE COMMONWEALTH FORESTRY CONFERENCE

In the foregoing pages I have tried to set before you a general international frame of reference which must be taken into account in establishing national forest production goals. I have mentioned some of the political factors that influence the setting of goals. I have touched on some of the problems we face when we come to translate these goals into action programmes and into management plans. And I have drawn your attention to some of the changes which are taking place in our thinking about management objectives.

I suspect, though I have really no means of knowing, that it was much easier to be a forester forty years ago than it is today. So many things were simpler, so many things were clearer, than they are today. Yet I do not think a single one of us would like to go back forty years. In spite of all the uncertainties, doubts and unresolved questions, no generation of foresters has faced a situation so full of excitement, adventure and challenge as that which faces us today. The excitement lies in the technological revolution in which forestry is finally caught up. The challenge lies in the understanding we have achieved of the potential contribution which forestry can make to development and rising welfare. For, contrary to what many outsiders believe, forestry is not, in its essence, about trees. It is about people. It is about trees only so far as they can serve the needs of people. In determining how forestry can best serve the needs of the people, this Commonwealth Forestry Conference has a special role to play. This conference encompasses elements of the two worlds I alluded to earlier, and it links these two worlds by professional and cultural bonds. Both worlds today have need of such bonds, such bridges.

7
Forestry Education:
To Whom and for What?

Once nature dominated man. Today man threatens nature. Man's ancient fears were starvation, disease and carnivores bigger than himself. His contemporary fears are unemployment, war and pollution. Having made considerable progress in disposing of one set of enemies, he has succeeded in producing another set out of his own back pocket. Because some of the old enemies are not finally routed, anxiety about the new ones is as yet far from universal. It is hard to worry about space-ship earth if tomorrow's bread or rice is not assured.

The new enemies are the consequence of economic growth. The products of human labour have increased, and continue to increase, with the ever more intricate organization of production and the progressive incorporation of technological advance into the production process. One aspect of this is specialization. I am now connected, in almost every commodity I use, with men half a world away: men who produce it, or produce the things necessary to its production, or the things necessary to their production. Behind the complexity of the production process lies an infinite web of people-to-people relationships. Side by side with the division of labour, specialist education has become an essential ingredient of modern production.

In differentiating himself, by training and activity, more and more from his fellows, man as an individual has become more and more dependent on himself as a species. Individuals in general – and therefore the species as a whole – are ever more frequently the victims (and sometimes the beneficiaries) of human action over which they have no control and of which they have often no knowledge. No one today disputes that man's power to affect nature, both in the ordinary processes of production and in other avenues, such as warfare and space exploration, is outstripping his social capacity for controlling, planning

A paper for the World Consultation on Forestry Education and Training, Stockholm, October 1971. Reproduced by permission of the author and the Food and Agriculture Organization of the United Nations.

and safeguarding his overall relations with nature. As with many adolescents, his strength is outdistancing his ability to coordinate and control his actions.

We are beginning to learn, in the industrially advanced societies, how weak is the link between expanding output and social welfare. We are beginning to understand the magnitude of some of the external diseconomies which accompany economic growth. More and more are rising personal incomes consumed in an attempt to escape or alleviate intolerable social conditions: pollution, noise, delinquency and violence.

Small wonder that a recent report[1] stresses the urgent need for 'technology assessment', to

evaluate the social costs of existing civilian and military technologies in the form of pollution, social disruption, infrastructure costs, etc., and to anticipate the probable detrimental effects of new technologies, to devise methods of minimizing these costs, and to evaluate the possible benefits of new or alternative technologies in connection with existing or neglected social needs.

But the growing interdependence of man and the fragmentation of knowledge are not unrelated phenomena. There is a relationship between developments in technique and the way in which knowledge is developed, organized and distributed. The form and content of human knowledge – that which is transmitted by education – is bound up with the way in which real life is organized. If man has succeeded in developing sometimes to a terrifying extent, his particular technical limbs, this goes along with the trend to specialization, professionalism, closed shoppery. As science and technology progress, there comes a greater and greater pressure on the individual student, teacher or practitioner to make himself master in an ever narrower field.

While it is not the case, as some economists would have us believe, that the expansion of the various phases of formal education has been called into being solely by the demands of the labour market – this would be to ignore the decisive influence of popular pressure – there is no doubt whatever that these demands have had an overwhelming influence in shaping the form and content of formal education. To the increasingly specialized and sophisticated production techniques correspond the division, the re-division and, in many cases, the jealous enclosure, of area after area of human knowledge and discovery. Theodore Roszak,[2] in his introductory essay in *The Dissenting Academy*, comments bitterly on the transformation of the American university into 'an emporium of marketable skills'.

Roszak, in his essay, looks back with regret to a kind of 'golden age', when 'academic' values reigned supreme on the US campus. But, like most golden

---

[1] *Science, Growth and Society: A New Perspective*, report of the OECD Secretary-General's Ad Hoc Group on New Concepts of Science Policy.

[2] *The Dissenting Academy*, ed. Theodore Roszak (New York, 1967).

ages, this one never really existed. He ignores the historical changes in the scope and purpose of higher education. With few exceptions – exceptions which rather go to prove the rule – the institutions of higher learning, secondary and tertiary, have historically drawn their candidates from the upper strata or classes in society, and the output of these institutions has been destined either to keep the institutions in being or to fill those key posts in society which the upper strata or dominant classes deemed important if their dominance was to be maintained.

Historically, then, the universities have always been training grounds and indoctrination centres for the elite, and this function they still retain, though others have been added. The same applies to the various categories of para-university institutions that have multiplied during this century. Both the new institutions and the new functions of old institutions had their roots in the changing needs of society, as political and economic organization became more complex and as the incorporation of technology into the production system accelerated.

It was the need of industrial society for literate factory hands and clerks that ushered in compulsory primary education, accelerated and extended through popular pressure. The same needs and the same pressures, manifest under both capitalism and socialism, have brought about a progressive raising of the school-leaving age, which now, in principle, ranges from fourteen to eighteen in the industrially advanced societies, though in most of these societies the prescription is more effective in the urban than in the rural areas.

The mushrooming of university and para-university institutions that started with this century and has accelerated since the last world war is closely bound up with the increasingly complex organization and technology of advanced industrial societies. The established universities leapt, with different degrees of alacrity, to meet the new demands. Where there was reluctance, new institutions were created. Thus the institutions of higher learning have become more directly instrumental than in the days when they had been solely or mainly elitist, elite-training institutions.

Clearly, the fragmentation of knowledge which goes hand in hand with developments in technique contributes strongly, within certain limits, to the progress of individual disciplines. But this process has two consequences: one obvious, the other perhaps less obvious. Firstly, it generates problems for the social system as a whole, problems of the kind I mentioned earlier. Secondly, acting through the educational system itself, the process erodes the capacity and even the conscious will to solve the problems it has thrown up. Some would argue that it imparts the capacity *not* to recognize that problems are being thrown up.

Wherein lies the solution? If we cry for the return of the intellectual polymath, we cry in vain. That creature is already extinct, and not all the shadow-boxing conducted on our television screens by exponents of the 'two cultures' can bring about his resurrection. I do not have the solution, but I shall hope to provide some pointers to the direction in which a solution may be found.

So far as forestry education is concerned, we can all fervently share the plea of Stephen Spurr and Keith Arnold[3] that 'tomorrow's forester must have an holistic approach.' But there are tremendous problems in achieving this. Moreover, I think we have to go further than this. Do not forget that once upon a time the forestry profession, and forestry education, had a decided streak of the holistic approach –much more than most professions. Drawing on a wide variety of disciplines, the final stages of a forestry education sought to draw these together in order to prepare a 'compleat forester'. But this end-product of formal forestry education has become rarer and rarer, partly because the rapidity of development in the several disciplines has crowded out the integrative phase, partly because inadequate provision has been made for those new disciplines appropriate to the forester's changing tasks. If return to the holistic approach is necessary, what are the prerequisites?

Spurr and Arnold, in the course of their paper,[4] set out pretty clearly, and accurately to my mind, the sort of tasks the forester of tomorrow will have to undertake. Some of those tasks are very different from the ones he performs today. If the student is to develop an holistic approach, he must be allowed ample time for reflection and integration.

An encouraging feature of the contributions to this consultation is that there does seem to be a greater understanding of the fact that forestry is not about trees but rather about how trees can serve people. But this is still better understood on the whole by students than it is by the educators. It is true that the Roanoke symposium[5] revealed a consciousness of the failure to give students an opportunity to comprehend the socio-economic context within which they will have to employ their brains and exercise their skills. But there was nothing like a consensus about which of the social sciences were most relevant, and a widespread reluctance to jettison or curtail traditional features of the curriculum.

Evidently, a return to an holistic approach in forestry education is not going to solve those larger problems to which I have alluded: problems of growing interdependence coupled with alienation and helplessness; problems of the fragmentation of knowledge and its integration in application. As regards the latter, many contributions to this consultation have stressed that the responsible forester of tomorrow will increasingly have to work as a member of a team. How far he can succeed in this, and even give leadership in such teams, will depend on the degree to which forestry education can eliminate the myopia and parochialism of specialization. The establishment of multidisciplinary teams

---

[3] 'The forester's role in the face of social and economic change' Stephen H. Spurr and R. Keith Arnold, (FO: WCFET/71/3 July 1971).

[4] Spurr and Arnold, ibid.

[5] National Symposium on Undergraduate Forestry Education, Roanoke, Virginia, 12–13 February 1969, sponsored by the Society of American Foresters and the National Research Council.

is not of itself any answer to the problems of fragmentation and integration. In the words of Philip H. Coombs, former Director of Unesco's International Institute for Education Planning:

Look at what happens when a collection of specialists of virtually any brand is put together in an operational agency – such as a bilateral aid agency, a specialized international agency or a national ministry. In short order each subgroup of specialists creates its own box on the chart, spawns its own sacred doctrines and begins displaying aggressive tribal tendencies of the most unscientific sort.[6]

A more hopeful line of attack lies in what Guy Benveniste[7] has termed the metadisciplinary approach. This means training an expert with a solid grounding in a given areas of expertise and with a general knowledge of a problem area. He thus becomes a specialist in terms of his expert knowledge, and a generalist in terms of a set of problems to which he becomes committed. In the meta-disciplinary approach, it is the common problems to which the team members are committed that help them bridge the intellectual barriers of expert knowledge. This concept of the metadisciplinary approach, I suggest, is well worth bearing in mind when we approach the task of curriculum revision in forest faculties.

What about the other set of problems? – the increasing marginal utility of collective needs, the failure of governments to identify and satisfy them; the external diseconomies, or social costs, of economic growth; the growing inter-dependence, and at the same time the growing helplessness, of individuals? Where the welfare economists have so signally failed, it is conceivable that the professional, and in particular the professional forester, can succeed?

I would not argue that the professional forester can solve these problems. I would argue, however, that he can make a very important contribution. The word 'ethic', I am happy to see from the contributions to this consultation, is creeping back into use. I believe the time has come to redefine the ethic, to affirm the social responsibility of foresters, to set forth the social objectives of forestry. The forester of today needs to be re-dedicated, in the widening area in which he is called upon to exercise his judgement and his skills, to the principle of upholding the long-term community interest against short-term interest, public or private. If the *social* responsibility of foresters were not only acknowledged by foresters, but set forth proudly, it would be a tremendous source of strength for the individual forester in resolving the ethical dilemmas which confront him regularly in his working life. This is indeed perhaps the only sense in which professionalism is today acceptable.

[6] Philip H. Coombs, 'Education on a treadmill', *Ceres*, 3. 1971.

[7] Guy Benveniste, 'Metadisciplinary or interdisciplinary: the experience of the Professional School Committee at Berkeley', *International Development Review*, 11 (1969).

Social responsibility involves not only responsibility as a professional; it involves responsibility as a citizen. And here it must be conceded that the mainstream of the forestry profession has been lax, notably in relation to current environmental issues. It has been said that foresters are not eleventh-hour environmentalists, that they were showing a genuine and constructive concern for the environment decades before the contemporary upsurge of interest. But there is still a widespread illusion that most environmental blunders stem from ignorance, and that a combination of research, education and goodwill will set matters right. Some blunders do, but most do not. I am not persuaded that space-ship earth will become a better, more liveable, more viable place simply by persuading people to carry home their empty beer cans. Most serious environmental issues are direct collisions between long-term community interests and short-term vested interests, whether public or private. If these issues are to be resolved, the enemy has to be identified and isolated, allies have to be mobilized, and battles fought. This is the task of every responsible citizen. The forester, too, must be an active and responsible citizen, not just a professional adviser. Social responsibility is not merely a guiding principle; it is also a battle cry.

In the evolution of the forestry profession, as of any other profession, two distinct threads can be discerned. One is to protect and advance the status and material interests of its members. The other is to reassure the community. This latter is based on the premise that the adequacy of the services provided by the professional (and the professional is a provider of services rather than a producer of commodities) cannot be safely judged by the layman but only by fellow professionals. Almost inevitably, this standard-setting function tends to fall into the hands of respected, senior members of the profession, among whom sensitivity to change and openness to innovation are not always the most conspicuous characteristics. As often as not, once the professional has got his licence to practise, he is let loose on society for ever. There is no opportunity of challenging his fitness to practise, even though the problems of today may require a body of knowledge and an assembly of skills that did not exist when he was licensed.

If I may be permitted a digression, it seems to me that foresters would have made a much better showing on these environmental issues if the forestry profession had had the wit and the will to draw on all the intellectual resources available to it.

Has it ever occurred to you that one significant pointer to the backwardness of the forestry profession and to the inadequacy of forestry education is the paucity of women foresters? We can elect women to the presidency of the most illustrious scientific societies, we can make women prime ministers, we can send women whizzing through space. But we cling to male supremacy in the forest as if it were man's last refuge. I commend the forestry profession as a worthy target for the attention of 'women's lib'. Doubtless they will bear in mind the astute words of John Stuart Mill, writing just over a century ago:

The concessions of the privileged to the unprivileged are so seldom brought about by any better motive than the power of the unprivileged to extort them, that any arguments against the prerogative of sex are likely to be little attended to by the generality, as long as they are able to say to themselves that women do not complain of it.[8]

When I enquire of heads of forest services and on forestry campuses, 'Where are the women foresters? Where are the women forestry students?', I am given the most extraordinary explanations. Can anyone really believe that any professional forester today spends most of his time dodging two-hundred foot stems crashing about his ears? Can we seriously afford to cut ourselves off from the potential intellectual input of one half of humanity because of the problems involved in establishing separate toilet facilities in summer camps?[9]

I hold no brief for women's lib. I think that women are going to be liberated when the rest of us are, no sooner and no later. But I am firmly convinced that if we had a greater proportion of women foresters among us we should be making much less heavy weather of some of the problems that now face us – notably, in adapting our forestry thinking and forestry practices to the changing needs of society, and, in particular, in reconciling the needs of productive forestry with the growing concern for environmental quality. If I argue in favour of a greater contribution to forestry by women, I am not pleading for women. I am pleading for forestry.

Looking into the future, I think we perhaps ought to reflect on some of the quantitative aspects of the recent accelerated expansion in tertiary education. The proportion of the eligible age-group today entering into tertiary education is now over one in three in the United States.[10] In other industrialized free

[8] John Stuart Mill, *The subjection of women* (London, 1869).

[9] Further on, in ibid., J. S. Mill says: 'When we consider the positive evil caused to the disqualified half of the human race by their disqualification – first in the loss of the most inspiriting and elevating kind of enjoyment, and next in the weariness, disappointment and profound dissatisfaction with life, which are so often the substitute for it – one feels that, among all the lessons which men require for carrying on the struggle against the inevitable imperfections of their lot on earth, there is no lesson which they more need than not to add to the evils which nature inflicts, by their jealous and prejudiced restrictions on one another.' Since there are few pursuits that give a more 'inspiriting and elevating kind of enjoyment' that the management of the forest resource, is it not high time that foresters rid themselves of 'their jealous and prejudiced restrictions' against women?

[10] Percentage of eligible age-group in 1967 entering:

	Primary education	Secondary education	Tertiary education
Advanced free enterprise economies[a]	96	73	21
(USA only)	(103)	(95)	(36)
Centrally planned economies[b]	105	55	19
Developing countries[c]	40	9	2

enterprise economies, and also in the centrally planned economies, it averages
around one in five. In the developing world it is about one in fifty. But
everywhere the proportion is rapidly increasing, and the situation which is now
developing in the United States foreshadows the situation which will assuredly
develop soon in Europe. In the United States, over the last century, the
percentage of the eighteen to twenty-four -age-group enrolled in full-time
degree-credit courses has doubled every fourteen to eighteen years.[11] If this
trend were to continue, then by the end of the century the whole of the eighteen
to twenty-four age-group in the US would be undergoing formal tertiary
education. The United States is moving from mass to universal tertiary education. Along with this rising enrolment goes a rising drop-out rate.[12]

One thing is clear. The rising output of tertiary education, including that
of specialists, no longer corresponds to the market demand for graduates. This
is brought forcibly to our attention when any faltering in the economic growth
curve sharply cuts back the market demand for graduates; or when the merger
of two conglomerates tips hundreds of graduate professionals, administrators
and managers on the labour market at the stroke of a pen. The outlook for
the graduates of 1971 in many of the industrialized countries is worse than
that for any graduating class since the depression of the thirties. And this
situation will intensify with popular pressure for more tertiary education.

A somewhat analogous situation is arising in the centrally planned economies.
In the USSR, pressure on the limited availability of places for tertiary education is, if anything, more intense than in the West.[13] If tertiary education
expanded to meet this demand, it would seem that problems would arise in
placing the output in the Soviet economy in positions where they could effectively deploy the skills they have acquired.

It is surely evident that here we are up against the basic question: what is
formal education, especially in its tertiary phase, all about? It is preparation
for making a living? Or is it preparation for living? Had we better not face
the fact that the skills market as we knew it is on the way out in the affluent
free enterprise societies? We may have obediently transformed our universities
into 'emporia of marketable skills', but now the market system is collapsing
round our ears. Not only that, but we can confidently expect that also in the
richer planned economies the insistent demand for tertiary education as the

Peculiar figures for primary education in the US and centrally planned economies stem from duplication and recruitment outside the defined age-groups. The main point is that primary education is universal.
Country grouping is as follows:
[a] North America, Western Europe, Japan, Australia and New Zealand;
[b] USSR and Eastern Europe;
[c] Asia (less Japan and mainland China), Latin America and Africa.
Source: UNESCO
[11] Sir Eric Ashby, in The Times of 5 April 1971, commenting on the Kerr Commission Report.
[13] *Bulletin of the Institute for the Study of the USSR*, 17:11 (1970), pp. 39–45.

planned economies the insistent demand for tertiary education as the key to a richer life will in due course make nonsense of some of their present notions of manpower planning. A moment's reflection will show that there is much more in heaven and earth than is dreamt of in the philosophy of the educational economist. Look at the low correlation between student options and expected salaries. Look at the widespread dissatisfaction in the new student generations – the demand for social relevance rather than enhanced earning capacity.

What does this new phenomenon, which I am convinced is not merely a temporary one, mean for the forestry schools? Should we continue to accept only those who have a clear intention of practising our profession? Or should we broaden our concepts and provide also a range of options that will render the forestry school clearly superior to the liberal arts school as a preparation for responsible citizenship and a richer life?

This is one issue which this consultation should confront. Another is the response of forestry educators to the concept of lifelong education. Though learning may not be living, living is learning. Informal, or non-formal, education is a continuous, lifelong process. Formal education, with which we are mainly concerned in this consultation, takes up a much smaller proportion of the lifespan. It is usually characterized by the concentration of the educatees in time and/or in place, and by the use of professional educators. Formal education is accepted as something to be designed, planned and carried out with definite aims in mind – though these aims need not necessarily be vocational. Conventionally, formal education, in all its stages – primary, secondary and tertiary – is concentrated towards the beginning of the lifespan. There are powerful reasons why that convention should be discarded and the need for injections of formal education through the lifespan recognized. One reason stems from the accelerating accumulation and rate of obsolescence of knowledge. Time was when the individual emerged from formal education with resources that would see him through his effective working life. This is no longer true. As Zivnuska put it in 1966: 'The half-life of knowledge is falling sharply. Much of what we are presently teaching in our forestry faculties is already obsolescent'. This is one reason why continuing education, including formal education, is today a necessity.

But there is another, more basic, reason. For it is not simply a matter of going back to the 'knowledge' supermarket and helping oneself to the goods that were not on the shelves at the time of one's last visit. It is perhaps more correct to regard formal education as an accelerator, or better still, as a catalyst, raising the educatee's capacity to absorb and apply informal education. From this standpoint the purpose of continuing formal education is to renew this catalytic function, which tends to decline with the passage of time.

At this point I would like to apologize to those of my auditors who represent the majority, those who come from the underdeveloped world where two-thirds of the world's people live. Some of what I have said so far must sound to them

like a discourse from another planet. Some of the problems I have touched on
are problems they encounter only in their dreams. What advice can this consultation offer to the foresters and forest educators from the underdeveloped world?

The Third World is not a separate, unrelated problem, since the roots of
its backwardness lie in the wealth of others, just as surely as do those of the
backwardness of the Calabrian peasant or the Mississippi black. However, the
debt of the rich to the poor who made them rich is going to be a long time
a-paying. Therefore those leaders in the developing countries who have the
welfare of their peoples at heart must necessarily concentrate on 'operation
bootstrap'. With resources scarce, their approach to secondary and tertiary
education in general, and to forestry education in particular, must necessarily
be instrumental: instrumental, in the sense that forestry education must be
geared to national needs, trained on local realities, and consonant with national
possibilities. This consultation should convince you from the developing
countries, if you were not convinced before, of the uselessness of imitating
overseas institutions or of copying their curricula. Many of the overseas institutions do not know yet where they are going. You cannot afford *not* to know
where you are going. If the forestry sector, taken in its widest sense – as spelled
out by some of the contributors here – is or ought to become a significant
element in the national economy, then you will be wise to create your own
institutions for forestry education. Remember that there are few overseas
institutions indeed that possess the understanding *and* the resources to make
the studies of your nationals relevant to your own goals, to prevent them from
becoming alienated, to strengthen your students' sense of involvement in, and
commitment to, your national aspirations.

But at the same time do not underestimate what it will cost you to establish
and develop your own institutions. A successful forestry education institution
is not simply a matter of a cluster of physical facilities and a nucleus of teaching
staff. The forestry student in North America or Europe has access, not only
to these, but to infinite library possibilities, a network of research institutions,
all kinds of workshops, a galaxy of experience from public and private life.
Little of this can you hope to replicate until many years have passed.

Do not assume that it is obligatory to emulate the academic standards of
overseas institutions. It is not, and certainly not in the early years of a new
institution. It may well be more appropriate to have more men in the field
now, half-prepared, than later, fully prepared. But this required that you build
into your plans provision for future upgrading. In most overseas countries there
is a pattern of primary-secondary-tertiary education without pause. This is
not necessarily the most suitable pattern for you. There is much to be said
for a two-year in-service training after secondary education, before proceeding
to tertiary education. Not only does it strengthen the sense of involvement and
identification; it greatly enhances the value of formal tertiary education. You
will wish, as soon as possible, to add postgraduate education and research to

your institution, partly because of the contribution which research can make, partly because of its impact on the quality of undergraduate teaching. But again, there is great virtue in a pause, for in-service experience, before proceeding from graduate to postgraduate study. Until you have this postgraduate centre, and for some fields even after you have it, you will wish to send some officers overseas for postgraduate work. Send them only when they are mature and committed, when they have the experience and the capacity to shop for what is relevant. Do not send them for the ready-made formal postgraduate packages offered by some overseas institutions if these packages have no relevance to your needs. An institution that does not have the flexibility to tailor its offering to your requirements should be written off as far as you are concerned. Do not, above all, fall for cartolatry. By cartolatry I mean the worship of pieces of paper, in particular masters' and doctors' diplomas. The future of your country depends on people, not on the pieces of paper they have framed.

Doubtless you will get offers of aid, from both multilateral and bilateral sources. Examine the strings – all aid has strings! If the strings are in any way going to knit you a straitjacket, reject the aid. Aid is not necessarily worth having simply because it is free, or because it costs very little. If aid wants to mould you in its image instead of helping you to create your own, you are better off without it.

I hope my remarks will not be misunderstood. I do not condemn aid. I firmly believe that aid, including technical assistance, will be needed for many decades yet, and that it will progressively become more mutual. The participation in this consultation is sufficient evidence of the powerful contribution which aid, both multilateral and bilateral, has made to forestry education in the developing countries over the last two decades.

Most of my remarks so far have been addressed to tertiary education. But for the developing countries the preceding phases of formal forestry education are perhaps even more important, and I hope that this consultation will give close attention to these. I have only one piece of advice to offer. Get rid of the term 'sub-professional', with its implication that those phases of formal forestry education which precede the university level are somehow less important, even subhuman. Never forget that the three-tier system of forestry education that obtains in much of the developed world harks back to a class-structured society. You and I know more about human nature, and about human potential, than to assume that because a man or woman has only three O levels he or she will never be capable of doing anything other than that which he or she is told to do. So keep the ladder open, and make all necessary provisions and allowances to ensure that it is open. Your aim must be to give every man a chance of reaching his full potential. Don't copy the rigidities of the developed world in throwing away usable talent.

I have said nothing so far about worker education. Yet it is at this level that forestry education, by raising forest-consciousness and imparting new skills,

can provide the greatest rewards. Moreover, there is no surer way of revealing
and releasing those energies that are decisive for the development struggle than
by inserting the worker into the educational pyramid.

I spoke earlier of the trend in the affluent societies to, first, mass and then,
universal, education. A corollary of this is that the days of elitism are numbered.
Looking ahead into the future, it is clear that the day will come when men and
women no longer peel off the educational pyramid at predetermined points in
order to take up assigned slots in the forest hierarchy. We must eventually move
to a single-ladder system in forestry (and in other professions, for that matter),
against the background of lifelong education, abandoning our present notions of
the time mix of formal and non-formal education. There will continue to be selection, but hopefully it will prove possible to devise methods of selection other than
academic tests which institutionalize success and failure. At the same time, the
content of education will change so as to ensure an alert and informed citizenry.

I have made this somewhat naïve excursion into education futurology simply
in order to emphasize a point which I consider relevant in planning forestry
education in the developing countries. If I am right in supposing that some
of the formulae used in the developed countries are on the way to becoming
outworn, there is no virtue in copying them, even though the temptation to
do so may be strong, given the fact that scarce resources render even the aim
of universal primary education difficult to achieve in the near future. The
solution would appear to lie in the direction of greater attention than has been
accorded in the past to worker-level and intermediate-level training; continuing
and upgrading courses at all levels; and the utmost encouragement of mobility.

It is time I returned to my principal theme – Forestry education: to whom
and for what? I would summarize the purpose of forestry education as follows:

To help men and women (mostly young, but not exclusively so) prepare
themselves so that they may:

  1 Advise on the formulation of resources policies, especially in
    relation to forests and related wildlands, which reconcile the short-
    and long-term needs of the community for the goods and services
    which those lands can provide;
  2 Translate those policies into plans; and
  3 Implement those plans,

and, more generally, to provide a sufficient range of options for any
student who may be interested in acquiring the background that will
enable him to judge and pronounce, as a responsible citizen, on resource
issues.

You will observe that, in describing my 'for what?', I have also defined my
'to whom?'.

All this requires a radical reshaping of the forestry curriculum, and a re-education of the forestry educator. The forestry educator cannot inculcate the theme of social responsibility of the forester unless and until he feels it intensely himself. Once he has it, then he will seek, as does any good educator:

> To help the student to discern what knowledge is relevant, where to find it, and how to use it;[14]

> To bring the student to an understanding of the interrelatedness of phenomena, and the interpenetration of the various disciplines;

> To cultivate in the student a sense of responsibility – responsibility for his own actions, responsibility for the welfare of others;

> To inoculate the student against received doctrine;

> To help the student to overcome the problems, and taste the joys, of cooperating unselfishly with others.

None of this is new. You may even think it trite. But I fear that some of it has at times been forgotten or overlooked. It is time to put it squarely back in the centre.

---

[14] This involves rather more than is implied by the analogy used by Edmund Leach, Provost of King's College and Reader of Social Anthropology in the University of Cambridge, in the Reith Lectures of 1967: 'Education is the process by which the human computer is programmed to handle the data. Data storage – that is to say, the memorizing of facts – is entirely secondary.'

8

Quo Vadis? A Note for Discussion

HOW HAS OUR PHILOSOPHY EVOLVED?

Up to the early sixties the philosophical consensus underlying the work of the Department, then a Division, probably ran as follows: that international understanding was enhanced, and mutual benefit promoted, by the international exchange of technical and scientific information, and that there were a number of problems which could be solved through international cooperation. Development assistance was in its infancy. That there were striking gaps between nations was recognized. The reasons for backwardness had only just started to be analysed. One obvious reason, however, was lack of know-how. It was as a channeller of know-how that FAO first set foot on the path towards becoming a major development agency. Know-how was embodied in the 'expert'. As funds became available, and requests multiplied, we despatched walking know-how to the far corners or the earth. Only slowly was the fatuousness of this procedure recognized, as hundreds of expert reports accumulated, gathering dust on government shelves, containing thousands of earnest and well meant recommendations, most of which governments were powerless to implement.

By this time the Division was nearing completion of its cycle of regional timber trends studies. A clearer picture of the world forest and timber economy was beginning to emerge. At the same time interest grew, and work was done, towards achieving an understanding of the development process and of the contribution which the forest and timber economy could make to overall economic growth.

I think it can be said that by the mid-sixties the philosophical consensus of the Division had grown and become more precise. What did we believe in then?

An internal memorandum to all professional staff of the Forestry Department, FAO, April 1973.

That economic growth would bring with it a steady expansion in the need for a wide variety of goods that could be produced from the renewable resource of the forests; that the resources of some of the world's industrialized regions were no longer able, or would soon become unable, to satisfy their own growing needs; that many of the developing countries had substantial forest resources that could and should be brought into play, as well as soil, climate and labour conditions suitable for the creation of man-made industrial forests; that the intimate relationship between the forest and timber economy and other sectors of the economy rendered this sector capable of making a special contribution to the overall development process; that, therefore, in many developing countries this sector deserved special consideration in overall development planning.

As this philosophy began to take hold, our field programme expanded and our regular programme, similarly, took its main thrusts from that philosophy and from our accumulating experience in field operations: resource surveys, feasibility studies, market studies, education and training, and so forth. We have tried to persuade countries to embark on, and then to help them carry out, projects of the kind that would help to overcome identified obstacles to development. Our projects have had far more impact than in the old 'expert' phase. We have helped to train people by working with them, instead of simply telling them. We have got a little closer to some of the real problems, and we have tried to change the content of our programme in the light of the lessons we have learned. Hence our new emphasis on the content of training and education. Hence our emphasis on development planning. Hence our preparation of manuals. But we are still working on the consensus we developed in the mid-sixties. From time to time we reiterate it, almost in a perfunctory way. But some big holes are beginning to show in that philosophy. Progress has not been as rapid as we thought we had a right to expect. Were we expecting too much? Have we been working along mistaken lines? It is time to take stock of the world as it is actually evolving and consider whether we need to move towards a new philosophical consensus.

SOME OF THE HOLES

What are those holes? Let us admit at the outset that there is a more widespread interest in the potential of the forestry sector than there was ten or fifteen years ago. Our expanding field programme is sufficient demonstration. The steady permeation of our philosophy has contributed, but it has not been the only factor. Another important factor has been progressive disillusionment consequent on the failure to come to grips with the complexities of the agricultural sector, which has led to a shift of interest towards the forestry sector as one more likely to yield early and visible results. And sometimes unfortunately this shift of interest has been no more than a resolve to cash in quickly on forest wealth, in utter disregard of the long-term consequences.

Even less comforting are the following facts:

> Very few countries have developed a perspective plan and development strategy for the forest sector;
>
> Very few countries have achieved any articulation between forest-sector planning and overall development plans;
>
> Though there has been a considerable expansion in trained manpower for the sector, the cadres are still insufficient and their formation woefully inadequate;
>
> Regional and sub-regional integration plans for the sector have made but little progress;
>
> There has been but little progress in establishing domestic processing facilities, and not all the progress which has been made is sound;
>
> Social forestry, where the returns are economic but not financial is still at a standstill and we have failed to mobilize either external financing or internal community effort.

If we were to take any of these six criteria as yardsticks of our progress we would have to admit that it has fallen far short of some of our earlier hopes. Nevertheless, we must not run away with the idea that we have achieved nothing. We have, in fact, achieved quite a lot. For example, two decades ago, only a sprinkling of developing countries had anything that could be described as an indigenous forest service. Today, very few of them are without at least a nucleus. We have had a big hand in this, for in forestry development assistance FAO has been a senior partner, with the most widespread and sustained programme – unlike agriculture, where the FAO effort has been but a fraction of the total effort.

Even so, the limited progress to date as measured against the above criteria must be a matter of concern to us. Moreover, if we delve deeper into the way in which our programme has developed over recent years, we must admit to ourselves that there are several major areas which give grounds for disquiet. Let me mention a few.

Man-made forests   The area under man-made forests continues to grow, many countries (mainly those which are either wood-deficit or long-fibre-deficit) are espousing sizeable industrial afforestation schemes, and one or two have (with our help) succeeded in getting international financing. Are we going to need all this wood? Is it being put in the right places? Are we right in encouraging (or assenting to) the liquidation of slow-growing mixed hardwood forests and replacing them by fast-growing plantations? What happens to the global thermal and atmospheric balances? Are we losing sight of the trees in our preoccupation with the wood? Much of the impetus for fast-growing plantations comes from our predictions of wood shortages. A moment's arithmetic convinces us that the world's wood needs for decades to come can be met from concentrated industrial plantations which would represent a world forest cover of only one or two per cent. Ought we not to be getting more excited about the role of the forest in the biosphere before we let everybody jump on the man-made forest bandwagon, which we have done so much to foster?

Tropical forests   We have advanced only a few inches towards the goal of integral utilization of the mixed tropical forests through progress in harvesting and processing technology. Nor have we made any real progress towards enrichment of the tropical forests through silviculture treatment. The famed scissors are as far apart as ever, and in case after case we have to fall back on complementing or replacing the tropical forests by planting pines and eucalypts. Have we given up the tropical forests as a bad job?

Wildlife management, recreation, national parks   Our expanding programme in these areas hinges on tourism and foreign exchange earning, with protein from game for the locals a faraway second. We are egged on at every step by the loud cheers of the affluent conservationists and the animal-lover freaks. What about the quality of life for the indigenous peoples of the developing countries? And for the city ghetto-dwellers of the heavily industrialized countries? Who are we working for? Who should we be working for?

Education and training   At the Stockholm Consultation on Forestry Education and Training all kinds of new ideas were ventilated: concerning the forester and his tasks, concerning appropriate formation and curriculum revision, concerning pedagogics, concerning continuing education. Out of this welter and ferment new ideas and new approaches for our education and training programmes should have emerged, and our field projects afforded ample opportunities for trial and innovation. Has this really happened, or are we continuing essentially with the mixture as before?

Environmental impact   Our input into the UN Conference on the Human Environment, Stockholm, 1972, has brought a pay-off in the shape of the promise of financial support for a number of proposals we there advanced, and doubtless in the course of the next half-year we shall be shaping up our plans for world forest appraisal, new work on forest gene resources, and so on. But what about the environment aspects of ongoing and new projects? Environmental concern, like charity, should begin at home. We ought to be setting an example, blazing a trail. But are we?

Forest industrialization   We can draw considerable satisfaction from the fact that, after years of steady work, some major projects, involving multi-million loans, are now coming to fruition: Honduras, Malawi, Malaysia, Turkey, Yugoslavia. This is fine, even spectacular. But at the other end of the investment scale, what have we to show in the shape of sawmills, panel mills, preservation plants, joinery shops and so on? A few demonstration sawmills and joinery shops in our field projects, but that is about all. Is our help not needed? Or have we been putting less effort into these less spectacular, primarily domestic-oriented, projects? Maybe the time has come to draw up a balance sheet of our efforts to assist in establishing forest industries over the last decade, and consider where and how our impact might be raised.

It seems to me that, in the areas I have mentioned (and some others), the time has come to stand back and take stock.

We must constantly remind ourselves, too, that the conditions under which we operate are changing all the time. For example, such measure of success as we have achieved has brought new problems. At the outset of our development assistance efforts, it could be said confidently that every headquarters professional who visited a developing country had something new and positive to contribute. This is no longer true. In many of the developing countries today there are men at the helm in the forest service as competent, as knowledgeable, as sophisticated, as any of us. We should try not to forget this.

SOURCES OF DISILLUSION

These are difficult days for the multilateral agencies, and for all those engaged in development assistance work. Not a day passes but one statesman or another reminds us that the climate for development assistance has deteriorated sharply in recent years. There is a real danger that the enthusiasm and idealism of our team may be steadily eroded by a number of factors external to the organization. This can best be avoided if we stand back and examine the objective situation coolly and dispassionately, and then make up our minds where we stand.

One source of disillusionment is that we have so often seen many of the little gains registered by countries in the uphill battle against backwardness, a battle in which multilateral and bilateral efforts have supported the countries concerned, thrown away overnight in wars and political upheaval, for example, the Indo-Pakistan war, the Central American 'soccer' war, the Middle Eastern battles, and overshadowing all else, the sorry Vietnam affair. What is the use of all our efforts, some of us have thought, if years of patient work by nationals and expatriates can be erased at a stroke, and the development effort put back to square one? Earthquakes, floods, draught, and similar natural disasters we can comprehend. They are just bad luck, and do not constitute any reason for renouncing the development struggle. And even if we do pick up the struggle again after cataclysms which are plainly man-made (and therefore, our reason tells us, avoidable), yet, somewhere inside us, the question 'Is it worth while?' pricks us incessantly.

It seems to me that shattering events of the kind I have mentioned can sow disillusion and discouragement only in the minds of those whose approach to development problems is politically naïve, who are so professionally blinkered that they have come to see the conquest of backwardness as essentially a technical task, failing to understand that the development process is a highly political one, full of complexities. Those who are seriously discouraged should get out of the development business, now, because nothing is more certain than that the next decade will bring many more such shattering events. The rest of us will soldier on, as best we can, striving to understand the problems we meet in all their political complexity, and probing to direct our efforts where they can have durable impact.

Another external source of disillusion springs from the basic dilemma confronting all who are engaged in development assistance efforts. Our allegiance is to, and our efforts are on behalf of, faceless hungry peoples in the developing countries. But our dealings are with governments. In how many instances, for example, is it possible to give unequivocal positive replies to the following four questions:

1 Do the actions of government representatives convince us that they are sincere when they speak of their determination to improve the lot of the common people?
2 Is there any sign of readiness to initiate and carry through the structural transformations that are a prerequisite to development?
3 Are the actions presently planned likely to lead to that more equal income distribution to which governments are pledged?
4 What signs are there of readiness to promote widespread participation in the development process?

Of course, many of us would be happy if we could limit our development assistance activities to those countries where a positive response could be given to those questions. Alas, as an intergovernmental agency, we have about a hundred and twenty masters, and we have to serve all these masters equally. And we are obliged to serve them even if it is increasingly borne in upon us that there is a marked divergence between the bold, visionary speeches which government representatives make at intergovernmental meetings and the policies and procedures they follow back home.

We feel those things particularly in forestry. For while it is true that forestry, being a semi-insulated sector, largely in the public domain, is further away from the political nerve-centres of the development process, we are nevertheless intensely aware of the kind of intensive pressures to which the honest, poorly paid forester is subject. Thus, we are aware of the rate at which concessions are being awarded, of the unrecorded costs of obtaining and running concessions, of the one-sided character of many concession agreements, of the inadequate control and supervision of concessions. And we sympathize with the local foresters faced with the alternative of either sticking their necks out (and losing their livelihood), or turning a blind eye to the corruption and malpractice of national and local politicians, of local and foreign companies.

Another discouraging fact, stemming in part from the foregoing, is the wastage of trained people in the developing countries. Some of the brightest and best, despairing of making the development contribution of which they are capable in their own country, opt out and join the brain-drain. Some of the shrewdest, with an eye to the main chance, leave government service and carve out lucrative careers.

We all know that corruption and malpractice are widespread (though how many of us remember, as was pointed out by a delegate at one of our recent sessions, that these phenomena are not confined to developing countries?). But this does not absolve us from the responsibility of pushing on with the development task. The day *will* come when most of this corruption will be swept away by political developments. The lesson for us is that we should do more than we have been doing to succour and fortify the honest and dedicated elements, and keep firmly in mind that, in much of what we are doing in many of the developing countries, we are building slowly for the future, a future which will certainly come.

Another source of disillusion springs from the transition to country programming. Each country now is master of its IPF (Indicative Planning Figure), and is free to insist on projects which we may consider inappropriate, and to reject projects which to us seem sound and timely. Some of us feel that we have thereby lost power. But our power to influence government choices never rested, basically, on our (or the United Nations Development Programme's) control of the purse-strings. It rested on our capacity to persuade and convince. This capacity springs from a healthy, directed, properly explained, regular programme. We *have* had a decided influence in the past. If we keep our regular programme alive and properly oriented, we shall extend that influence in the future. Here it is as well to remember that the power of corrupt operators and short-sighted politicians to promote or connive at actions which constitute crimes against the resource heritage and offend long-term community interests is curbed not only by statutes and by countervailing power; it is limited even more by the prevailing ethos. This means, surely, that we must put much more effort than heretofore into creating and diffusing this ethos as it concerns the forest resource, at all levels of society.

Some of us are nettled by the predilections, fads and fancies of cooperating donor countries, each of which has its own favourites, as to disciplines, as to countries, and whose readiness to support us does not always coincide with priorities as we see them. These fads and fancies, which may change overnight, are, however, a fact of life. It is *we* who must learn to discriminate. We need to approach the whole question of government cooperative programmes in a more positive and discriminating way: not racking our brains to think up projects they might finance, but limiting ourselves to projects we consider truly coincide with developmental priorities.

Perhaps a main source of external disillusion is the disenchantment and disarray which has been the aftermath of Sir Robert Jackson's Capacity Study. But it is quite wrong to blame all that has happened on Jackson. Jackson was not responsible for the world monetary crisis, for recurrent balance of payments problems in some of the leading industrialized countries, for the series of 'stop-goes' in economic growth, for the internal and external repercussions of Vietnam. There are all part of a single crisis shaking some of the main pillars of the contemporary economic–political system, and the questions raised by Jackson provided a heaven-sent opportunity to castigate the UN system and stem the expansion of the international development effort. What we should have learned from the past few years is that the liberal ideas which underlay much of our development thinking had no basis in reality. There is, in fact, little – perhaps no – community of interest between rich and poor nations. The history of tariff negotiation, of commodity agreement, and so forth, over the last two decades is sufficient demonstration. It is poor against rich, and within each country it is poor against rich. We may have to go on paying lip-service to the myth, but each of us has to decide, for himself, which side he is on.

Earlier I mentioned the gap between words and deeds in the developing countries. But what about the gap between words and deeds in the rich countries? You will recall that, for the achievement of the targets of the second development decade, the developed countries were called upon to increase official development assistance on concessional terms to 0.7 per cent of their GNP by 1975. Even half of this target now seems out of reach. Only three countries (Netherlands, Sweden, Norway) seem likely to reach the target. The USA is expected to fall from 0.32 per cent in 1971 to 0.24 per cent in 1975. Moreover, the grant element (as against loans) is diminishing, and as a consequence debt service payments are rising annually by about 20 per cent. Thus, it is not simply the multilateral development agencies (which account for a very small proportion of the total development assistance flow) which are being squeezed.

If we believe that true development means a great measure of self-reliance, a willingness to initiate basic social and structural transformations, a determination to diminish some of the present inequalities, a readiness to involve ordinary people in the development process; and if we admit to ourselves that the present signs of this coming about are rather scarce in many of the countries with which we deal: does this mean that all our present efforts are nugatory? By no means. Because many of the things we do and can do are building for the future, are helping to prepare the ground for the day when the political will exists, helping to bring that political will into existence. This applies particularly to resource data of every kind, including feasibility studies, education and training in all its aspects; development planning and depth analyses with a policy orientation, whether at the country, regional or global level.

There are internal sources of disillusion, too. Because they are close to us, because they irk us every day, we spend much of our energy railing against these: cumbersome administrative procedures; the inordinate amount of time spent on planning and reporting on our work, instead of doing it; reorganization mania; uneven career development opportunities, and career uncertainties stemming from budgetary constraints and economy measures; and so on – the list would go on for hours. Perhaps the most serious is that we have never succeeded in scaling down our programme to the means actually available. Hence the permanent excess work pressure, the worst consequence of which is that it limits our opportunities of getting to know each other and of learning from each other.

I do not minimize the importance of these internal sources, but it seems to me that many of them are, in fact, the consequences of, or reflections of, the external sources of disillusion which I discussed earlier.

I have spilt many words over this question of sources of disillusion. This is because I firmly believe that it is of the utmost importance that each and every one of us fully recognizes the constraints and limitations of multilateral development assistance, and shares the will to achieve whatever can be achieved within these constraints. Admittedly, there is a good deal of truth in the dictum that once decorated the office of some of our Trust Fund staff: that development assistance 'is a device for taking from the poor in the rich countries to give to the rich in the poor countries'. But it is not only that. It is something more, and more positive. If we understand this, and accept to work within the limitations imposed on us, then we can rebut the cynics outside and among us. They are the worms in the apple.

WHAT DO WE BELIEVE IN NOW?

A good deal of what we presently believe in has now found expression in the Final Declaration of the Seventh World Forestry Congress. This declaration will repay careful study, as much for what it omits as for what it includes. That which is included may be taken to be the highest common factor of world forestry opinion in 1972. Even this consensus could probably not have been reached in the forestry world twenty or even ten years ago. It includes some evasions (for example, on developing countries' trade, and on the true significance of *Limits of Growth*, and so on). Nevertheless, it is a milestone.

But we, of course, believe in much more than is stated in the declaration. And we have many reservations which are not there exposed.

For example, we would take the 'one world' principle much further. Had we the time, resources and power, we could produce a master plan for the regional development of the world's forest resources in the interest of all the world's peoples. We are not going to prepare and publish such a plan. But we are going to pursue analyses which bring out the interrelatedness and interdependence of all countries on the global resource, and we are going to bring to bear whatever influence we can exercise to ensure that national plans and objectives do not conflict and do not injure others. So, until the world is ready, we keep the 'master plan' concept up our sleeve, well hidden, but we bend our efforts in the sense that we are custodians of a resource of global import. But even though the world is far from ready to assign to us the role of global forest planners, there is another role which we are compelled to exercise – not because it has been formally assigned to us, but because that role is recognized as necessary and no one else can exercise it.

We are the world forestry conscience.

On all major issues arising from man's relationship with the forests and related wildlands, both governments and the forestry profession look for a lead from us. In no other sector of activity does FAO carry such stature and enjoy such confidence. We have grown steadily into this role over the years. Not one of us, individually, deserves this role. Collectively, perhaps we do. But whether we do or not is irrelevant. It is a role we cannot abdicate. We have to make ourselves worthy of it. Insofar as we have inherited this role, it has not been due to the outstanding intellect or charisma of any of us or of our former colleagues. It is the consequence of patient, dedicated, thoughtful, often anonymous teamwork over a couple of decades. We have not, so far, been rich in individual genius. But the capacity of each one of us has been magnified by his relationships with his colleagues and his ties with our member countries.

How do we exercise this role?

> We seek to define and illuminate, in objective, not partisan, terms, the several functions of the forest, and to spread awareness of these, especially at opinion-forming and decision-making levels;

> We foster the notion of the national forest resource as part and parcel of the global forest resource, and seek to influence national plans and policies in this sense;

> We seek to strengthen, among individual foresters and in forest services, the forestry ethic: the notion of social responsibility, and the paramount need to safeguard the long-term community interest;

> In judging policies, plans, programmes and projects, we keep uppermost in our minds the probable impact on the lives of ordinary people.

I fear that the immediate reaction of many of my colleagues to such a formulation will be: these are vague and ill defined generalities. Heaven knows that life in a multilateral organization like ours is an ideal way to develop an allergy towards generalities. But I believe that these particular generalities, if brought to bear on every aspect of our programme, can be translated into very concrete terms, and provide valid criteria for judging the worthwhileness of each element of our programme. If we are the world forestry conscience, this has to permeate our whole programme.

If we recognize this role, which derives from collective strength transcending individual weakness, we should see the need for humility. But we should also understand that we are fortunate to be where we are, and doing what we are doing. For we have a purpose greater than ourselves, a purpose which is the envy of all who can be brought to understand it.

We know now that the development problem is nothing like as simple as many of us thought ten years ago. It is nothing like as simple as the Buenos Aires declaration would lead us to believe. This is evident from our discussion of sources of disillusion. But we must continue to build up men and institutions for the future, fully recognizing that in many cases the pay-off will be long delayed.

WHAT SHOULD BE OUR PRIORITIES?

When I first started to draft this note, I had the idea that I would wind up with a list of priorities as I saw them, as a basis for discussion with my colleagues. On reflection, I see that this would be unwise, mainly because it might canalize or inhibit discussion. I do have my own ideas, and I shall be pleased to contribute them later on if anyone is interested. But I think it much more important that there be free discussion within the Department, at all levels, on some of the issues I have raised, and that from this discussion there springs eventually something like a consensus of views on what should be our main tasks and how we should approach them.

9

On Behalf of the Uninvited Guests

Just over fifty years ago, at the beginning of May 1922 to be exact, D. H. Lawrence set foot in Australia, landing at Perth. By 29 May he was installed in a bungalow some thirty miles south of Sydney. By 3 June he had started on his Australian novel. One hundred and fifty thousand words and five weeks later, *Kangaroo* was finished, and the following year it was published.

My own interest in Australia, like that of many people from 'up-over', is inevitably episodic rather than continuous. This is why I feel the need to preface each of my visits to this continent with a little background reading. This explains why, a few weeks ago, I found myself re-reading *Kangaroo* after an interval of forty years. I understand from Australian friends that Lawrence is not the most popular of writers in Australia, nor is *Kangaroo* the most popular of novels. Nevertheless I enjoyed re-reading it, and I commend it to those of you who have not read it recently. Though far from the best of Lawrence's novels, it is remarkable for the freshness, the actuality, of its descriptions of the Australian scene. Though Lawrence is perhaps somewhat less happy in dealing with Australians, there are nevertheless some insights which have an almost contemporary flavour.

Take, for example, Harriet's observations soon after her arrival in Sydney: 'Oh, but it's a wonderful harbour. What it must have been like when it was first discovered. And now all these little dog-kennelly houses and everything. . . . Is this all men can do with a new country? Look at those tin cans!' That cry of Harriet's – 'Is that all men can do with a new country?' – did not find so many echoes fifty years ago. But as the years have passed it has been taken up by more and more Australians, and I have the impression that in the last few years it has become a deafening chorus. Implicitly, if not explicitly, it is one of the dominant themes of this Forwood Conference.

Re-reading Lawrence also reminded me sharply of some particularities of the Australian character, and hung out a warning signal for me. During the first

Keynote address to the Forestry and Wood-Based Industries Development Conference, Commonwealth of Australia Government, Canberra, April 1974.

encounter of Somers, the hero, with two new Australian friends he is asked to lend his book of essays, but is reluctant to do so. Says the first Australian: 'Let me try. We're a new country – and we're eager to learn'. Whereupon the second Australian chips in: 'That's exactly what we're not. We're out to show to everybody that we know everything there is to be known.'

There is a similar interchange when Somers meets the proto-Fascist leader, the great Kangaroo himself.

'You have come to a homely country,' says the Kangaroo.
'Certainly to a very hospitable one,' replies Somers.
'We rarely lock our doors,' says Kangaroo.
'Or anything else,' chimes in the Kangaroo's henchman, Jack Callcott.
'Though of course we may slay you in the scullery if you say a word against us.'

This split-mindedness about and towards the foreigner, on which Lawrence puts his finger in these two exchanges, is something which I have had occasion to observe myself during my visits to this country. It does not seem to have changed drastically over the last fifty years. Thus, in accepting your invitation to speak at Forwood, I put myself in grave danger of being 'slain in the scullery'. However, this is not the first time I have put my head in Kangaroo's mouth. If I have emerged relatively unscathed from previous encounters, it is because Yorkshire lignin is pretty indigestible stuff. So I am keeping my fingers crossed over this encounter.

It seems to me that the most useful contribution I can make to Forwood is to say a few words on behalf of those parties whom you have failed to invite to Forwood or whose views, in my estimation, have received insufficient attention in the preparations which have been made for this conference. I will identify those parties in due course. But first I would like to make it clear that I am now very optimistic about Forwood. Not so much about the immediate outcome – on this I still have doubts and reservations, though I hope that some of these will have been dissipated by the end of this week. But rather I am optimistic about the long-term impact of this conference – for Australians, and for their future relations with one of their basic resources: the forest.

Three months ago this was not so. At that time I had received none of the Panel reports.[1] But I had seen examples, from both the popular and the professional press, of the kind of preliminary skirmishing that was going on, and of the way in which the many rival and conflicting interests were setting about drawing up their battle lines. What I read dismayed and depressed me. According to the blurb which was sent me, you are all here (and I quote) 'to analyse the conflicting demands on the forest and to recommend a series of

---

[1] The Forwood organisers divided the field into six or so topics and commissioned a panel of 'experts' in each topic, to prepare a report on the situation, the issues and the solutions. These Panel reports then became the discussion papers around which the Forwood Conference was organized.

integrated policies which will ensure continuous supplies of raw material in perpetuity from vigorous forest resources, while at the same time having regard for all forms of conservation, the environment and recreational requirements'. These are fine and bold words. I truly hope that this is why you are all here. But the impression I got, from some of the pre-emptive manoeuvring which I read about, was that some of you at least saw Forwood as a golden opportunity for either:

> Squeezing more money out of the federal government for forestry in your state; or

> Squeezing more out of federal or state governments in the way of direct or indirect subsidies for your industry; or

> Knocking some business sense into the heads of unrealistic foresters and forest industrialists; or

> Exposing the environmental irresponsibility of timber-oriented forest services and forest industrialists; or

> Showing up some of the activists in the conservation lobby as impractical fanatics; or

> Educating the general public about the lofty aims and irreproachable practices of foresters and forest industrialists.

Thus, way back in Italy I could hear the knives being sharpened, and it needed little imagination to picture the blood that would flow here in Canberra, starting on 1 April. At that stage I was tempted, not to stay away, but severely to limit my participation.

I had the following bright idea. So far as the *disputes* were concerned, I would stay on the sidelines. So far as the *disputants* were concerned, I would tell all I knew. Now this would have been no idle threat. It so happens that, of all the non-foresters in the world, I am probably the one with the widest and most intimate knowledge of foresters. I know most of the heads of forest services, some of them fairly intimately. I know thousands of rank and file foresters. I have a wide acquaintance in the forest academy and among forest researchers. And for the last twenty-odd years I have lived and worked on intimate terms with foresters from a hundred countries. Thus I think I can claim to know their strengths and weaknesses.

I have also had a good deal to do with forest industrialists, ranging from the backwoods sawmiller turning out a few cubic metres a day to the presidents of multinational giants whose annual turnover exceeds the GNP of many developing countries and whose word is capable of toppling governments.

I am also familiar with many of the shades in the rainbow motley of the environmentalist camp: the fundamentalist preservationists, masquerading as conservationists, whose slogan is 'Whatever was, is right'; the extremist wildlife nuts who love animals more than people, but some of whom spend half their time protecting animals and the other half shooting them; the ecological super-optimists who, conceding that ecology does not have all the answers, are sure it will have them tomorrow, and that therefore all we have to do is to stop the world from turning until the answers are ready; as well as all those serious and concerned groups, professional and among the citizenry at large, who are convinced that many things can and must be done more sensibly than they are at present.

By giving my appreciation of the sociology and aetiology of the disputants, it seemed to me, I would be providing the decision-makers with some useful clues concerning the weights that ought to be attached to the various conflicting views put forward by the disputants.

This, then, was my bright idea. But I renounced it, for two reasons. Firstly, because, after studying the Panel reports, I realized that some very significant steps had already been taken during the preparatory stages towards resolving some of the major disputes that threatened to turn this coming week into a slaughterhouse. Secondly, because I realized that some things had not been said that ought to have been said, and that no one would say them if I didn't.

Forwood has been conceived as a step in planning the rational development of forestry and forest industries in Australia. When we say rational, we mean a form and level of development which is consistent with the facts of life and with the outlook for the future, as well as we can visualize it. Thus we need to know what those facts are, and we need to think rather deeply about the future. For making a plan, as Sir Arthur Lewis has said, is above all an exercise in imagination.[2] We have to try to imagine almost everything concerned with the future. What are people going to want from the forests in ten, twenty, fifty years' time? How many people will there be? How will they live? How will they communicate, travel, work, relax? How will they regard other people, and what sort of dealings will they have with them? How will all these things affect the demand for wood and for all the other services which the forest can provide?

While we are preparing this outlook for the future, we have to be careful not to stray from the facts of life. Not all these demands can be satisfied fully, and some of them are incompatible. This means painful decisions about which demands we will endeavour to satisfy, and which we will let go by the board. Once our exercise in imagination has given us a credible picture of where we want to get to, we are well on the way to evolving a policy. We can then start to plan, to decide how we intend to get there.

But we have to start from here. We can't wriggle out like the Irishman, who, when asked the way to Ballycullish, replied: 'If I wanted to get to Ballycullish, I wouldn't start from here.' We have to start from where we are; we have to face the facts of life.

[2] *The Principles of Economic Planning* Allen & Unwin, 3rd edition, 1969.

One fact of life is that Australia is a giant desert fringed by eucalypts and Australians, and some of these are inconveniently clustered. Geography imposes that, even if the policy is nationally conceived, the plan must be partly conceived, the plan must be partly conceived and largely implemented at a regional level. Generally speaking, this will mean at state level, though there are several instances, such as major watersheds, where inter-state, and maybe super-state, machinery will be required.

But if geography imposes regional planning, I also firmly believe that geography, history and economics all require a national policy for the Australian forest resource. I take this as axiomatic and I do not propose to debate it. I would suppose it was one of the basic assumptions underlying the convening of Forwood. This means an all-Australian strategy and all-Australian goals. But another fact of life in Australia is its seven governments. This means that state strategies and goals for the forestry sector must be at least consistent with, and preferably part of, all Australian strategy and goals. This may mean adjustments at the state level, and some of these might be painful. Nevertheless since all the states are composed of reasonable men and women, and since all the states will have participated in the formulation of the all-Australian strategy, we are entitled to assume that they will set about making the necessary adjustments. And if any state proves recalcitrant, thereby prejudicing the future of Australia, then suitable sticks and carrots have to be devised.

Well, I dare say that fools who rush in where the ice is thin deserve to drown in hot water. But in my international career I have seen instance after instance where national development possibilities have been jeopardized because of the failure to align regional, state and local strategies to national purposes, as well as the failure to take regional, state and local aspirations into account. I have heard it said that in Australian art and literature an excessive proportion of creative energy is spent on the search for an Australian identity. It is my firm conviction that a nation which cannot find an identity in a common resources policy deserves to be considered a nobody among nations.

I said seven governments. I might have said eight – because, although the disposition to regard New Zealand as Australia's seventh state is now, I am happy to note, on the decline, the fact is that the forest economies of Australia and New Zealand are closely bound up with each other. Here geography has been reinforced by the Free Trade Agreement. Incidentally, my reading of the annexes to that agreement reveals the surprising fact that while Australia binds itself to take, New Zealand does not bind itself to supply. However that may be, it is plain to me that planning for the forest sector in neither country can proceed without reference to plans in the other.

One thing that emerges clearly from the spadework which has led up to this conference is the widespread recognition of the fact that no one sector of the community has a monopoly interest in the forest. Forests, and what we do with them, are not the concern of foresters alone; nor of the bushworkers; nor of the paper-makers, sawmillers and board-makers; nor of the scientists; nor of the water supply authorities; nor of picnickers and tourists; nor of the fauna; nor of the environmentalists. All have a stake. So have the next and future generations. Moreover, they are not for Australians alone. They form part of a global resource. Since it seems to me that the interest of the non-Australian in Australian forest policy has received scant attention so far, I propose to say a word or two on his behalf.

One non-Australian interest is obvious. Australia is blessed with a tree genus, comprising several hundred species, which in the course of the last century has become (if I may be permitted a solecism) the most ubiquitous of all trees. There are very few countries in the world where the itinerant Australian cannot encounter his gum trees. Quite a few countries today have eucalypt forests which are the envy of Australian foresters. The prosperity of hundreds of thousands, perhaps millions, of non-Australians is built on exotic eucalypts. And some of these eucalypts thrive overseas better than they ever did in their native habitat. The many varied eucalypt forest types of Australia represent a gene resource of great significance for the world as a whole. Australia has an obligation to the world to ensure that adequate representative areas of all these forest types be retained, in both managed and undisturbed situations, to serve as a permanent gene pool. There may yet be genetic gold in these forests.

Another non-Australian interest is that of those developing countries which, endowed either with rich natural forests or with favourable conditions for creating man-made forests, desperately need markets in the developed world for their processed wood goods. Some of these countries are among your nearest neighbours.

In fact, wood exports from the developing world have risen very sharply in the last decade, particularly from South-east Asian countries – so much so that Asia now accounts for close on two thirds of all the world's hardwood trade. Almost the whole of this increase, however, has been in unprocessed log form. This means that the exporting countries receive but a tiny fraction of the value added to the final product stage. They are denied the possibility of establishing secondary and tertiary industries, and the employment opportunities that go with this. They are denied all the multiplier and repercussive effects that a healthy forest industry can have on the overall economy. Moreover, because they lack the expertise and institutional strength to control the concessions they have granted, their resources are being pillaged and their forest wealth depleted at an alarming rate. At successive UNCTAD conferences the urgent need to open up the markets of the developed countries to the manufactured and semi-manufactured goods of the developing world has been repeatedly stressed. These remain pious recommendations. The developing world asked for bread. So far it has got stones.

Just over four years ago, in Perth, I sat in on a powow about Australia's forestry and timber future. I heard an impassioned plea by a distinguished member of your Upper House that Australia should aim at self-sufficiency in forest products. This is not a view with which I have any sympathy, since in the matter of forestry and timber I am a firm internationalist. Therefore, when written questions were subsequently invited, I sent up a slip of paper bearing the following question: 'Does the senator believe that self-sufficiency is a desirable aim for all commodities, for all countries?' And because I did not want it to be thought that a representative of an international agency (as I was at that time) was seeking to interfere in Australian internal politics, I took the precaution of signing my written question: 'Adam Smith'. Nevertheless, the senator did read out my question. He also answered it – with a monosyllabic 'No'. He chose not to elaborate – still less to explain why forestry should be considered a special case.

Now there is a price to be paid for a policy of self-sufficiency – even for that modified form which says 'Whatever we can produce ourselves, we will. And the balance we will import only so long as it proves necessary'. Who pays that price? Not merely the developing countries, who see the gap between rich and poor nations widen every day. The price is paid by another important party who seems to have been neglected in the preparation for Forwood. It is paid by the Australian consumer.

Back in 1969, I carried out a short analysis of levels of per caput forest products consumption in selected developed countries. This analysis revealed two things. First, in relation to income, Australia seemed to be a serious under-consumer of most forest products. Second, as concerns one important group, namely, wood-based panels, consumption levels in the preceding decade had risen less than anywhere else in the world, save in New Zealand.

Before setting out for Canberra, I took time out to update this analysis. Again I compared forest products consumption per head in Australia with that in nine other industrialized countries in roughly the same income bracket. Between 1966 and 1970 Australia's place in the league table of national income per head changed. It caught up slightly on the USA and Switzerland; it fell further behind Sweden, Canada and Denmark; it was overtaken by Germany; it shot ahead of New Zealand and further ahead of the UK; and Japan made a lot of ground on Australia.

Turning to forest products consumption, let us look first at sawnwood. Australia remains the highest consumer of sawn hardwood and the lowest consumer of sawn softwood – in terms of consumption per head. For *all* sawnwood, Australia has been overtaken by both Denmark and Japan, leaving only Switzerland, Germany and the UK below.

If we look now at wood-based panels – plywood, particle board and fibreboard taken together – we find that Australia was fifth in the consumption table in 1955, sixth in 1960, seventh in 1965 and ninth in 1970 – ahead only of the UK. Much more striking, however, are the figures for the *increase* in wood-based panel consumption which took place between 1955 and 1970. The advance in consumption is expressed as cubic metres per thousand inhabitants. Over the fifteen-year period, the advance in consumption registed in Canada and Denmark was 79; in the USA, 78; in Germany, 77; in Sweden, 75: in Japan, 67; in Switzerland, 61; in the UK, 23; in New Zealand, 19 and in Australia, only 16. Bear in mind, too, that this went alongside a considerable slippage in the sawnwood consumption table. In fact, Australia and New Zealand are the only countries where there has not been a very substantial rise in plywood consumption over the fifteen-year period.

If we turn now to paper, in 1965 Australia was the second highest consumer of newsprint, in terms of kilograms per head; in 1970 it had dropped to a third. For all other paper and board taken together, in 1965 it was bottom but one in the table, trailing behind all other countries but Japan. In 1970, it was firmly at the bottom, having been overtaken by Japan.

Thus, the situation has not changed since 1966. Australia remains a serious under-consumer of forest products as compared with other countries of roughly equivalent income level. I have not gone on the analyse the reasons for this state of affairs. But I do suggest that one reason why the Australian consumes so much less as compared with some of his colleagues in the developed world is that he had to pay more; and that one reason why he has to pay more might conceivably be that certain forest industries here are enjoying not only the protection afforded by distance and transport costs, but also some of the highest tariff levels in the developed world. But whether I am right or wrong in this, I would have thought that one of the important tasks to be done in preparing for Forwood was to analyse in some depth the cost to the Australian consumer and the Australian economy of the measure of protection and support afforded to the Australian wood-processing industries. So far as I can see this has not been done.

In this respect, I find the report of Panel 6 deplorable. Let us leave aside for the moment the forward estimates of domestic consumption, on which I will comment later. What is visualized for trade? For plywood: a steady decline in imports and a zooming export trade towards the end of the century. For particle board: a slight drop in imports and a trebling of exports. For fibreboard: no imports, and a maintained level of exports.

Not much hope here for the developing countries! Does this matter? I think it does, and I will tell you later why I think it matters. I find a distinct mercantilist flavour in the prognostications of Panel 6. 'The various committees of the Panel,' I read, 'had considerable difficulty in forecasting trends in overseas trade.' Maybe this is why they inserted industry hopes and aspirations in lieu of forecasts? Further on: 'Because Australia is so close to the countries which account for such a large proportion of the world population and these at present have such a low per capita consumption of forest products, the Panel believes that there could develop an export market far larger than that indicated in the table above.' Thus the developing world is to be an export oyster for Australian forest industries. Do you think this is a destiny they will be content to accept? Do you think this is consistent with Australia's declared policy towards the developing countries?

How is this to be achieved? I quote again: 'The Panel considers that export incentives given in the past have been very useful and recommends that there be no decrease in the level of incentives offered.' The Panel goes on to say what it wants done about road transport, rail transport, sea transport and port facilities. Finally (though perhaps with its tongue in its cheek), it expresses the view that:

the economic and efficient manufacture of forest products should receive adequate tariff protection including protection against dumping. In this regard some concern has been expressed regarding the difficulties of obtaining additional protection where necessary, e.g.:
    (a) the difficulty of an industry demonstrating dumping, and
    (b) the difficulty and/or delays in obtaining reference to the Special Advisory
        Authority for emergency protection.

As to (a) – the difficulty of an industry demonstrating dumping – this is perhaps not surprising, in view of what Panel 7 has reported. That Panel, you will recall, was charged with determining 'for each sector of the forest and forest products industry the financial structure, capital requirements, pattern of investment and profitability and make recommendations as to future needs and requirements.' Panel 7 has reported 'considerable difficulty in obtaining the information it considers necessary for this study', adding that 'financial information in the annual reports of sawmilling and other associations was inadequate for present purposes.' In the light of Panel 7's report, one might describe some of the demands formulated in Panel 6 as tactless, if not shameless.

If I were an Australian, I would want to look on my developing-country neighbours in quite a different way than as an export oyster to be opened up for Australian forest industries.

I would first recognize that they are my neighbours, that the fate of my country is intimately bound up with theirs, and that in the long run what is good for them is likely to be good for me.

Second, I would remind myself that, among the rich, industrialised countries, Australia is relatively free – not absolutely, but relatively – of the taint of imperialism and neo-colonialism. I would want to retain and if possible improve that image.

Third, I would take note of the fact that, among my fellow-countrymen, there is great wealth of professional talent, experience and know-how in forestry and forest industries.

Fourth, I would want to see that talent, experience and know-how placed at the disposal of those of my neighbours who were encountering serious problems in valorizing their forest resources, so that they might come to a better knowledge and understanding of their resources, bring them progressively under sound management, and establish thereon viable forest industries to serve their own domestic markets and the widening overseas market.

I would impose no strings, nor would I seek any special privileges. But I would seek such assurances as I could to ensure that the benefits of any help I was able to give were dispersed among the many and did not end up by enriching the pockets of the few.

Fifth, recognizing that there are already Australian entrepreneurs operating privately in this sector in some of these countries, and having heard that in some few instances their conduct in relation to the resource has fallen short of the highest standards of professional integrity, I would want to devise some means of keeping an avuncular eye on them, lest my own image as an Australian became tarnished.

Finally, from all this I would expect a very considerable pay-off: a growing stock of political goodwill, something on which I cannot presently set a price but which from experience I know to be of very considerable worth; rising prosperity among my neighbours, with opportunities for an expanding and mutually beneficial flow of trade across the board; and, no less important, more and cheaper forest products for me as an Australian consumer.

I hold that this perspective is preferable to the one outlined in the report of Panel 6. And I believe it will offer greater satisfaction to those neglected parties, the developing countries and the Australian consumer.

I promised to comment on the forecasts of domestic consumption. I suspect they are over-optimistic. I don't blame the Panel for this. Its report was drawn up and circulated before history took one of its sudden leaps – in October 1973.

In October 1973 a group of developing nations, which between them own a substantial proportion of a vital raw material on which the developed world has come to depend, discovered two things: (a) that by acting in concert they could compel the developed countries to lend an ear to their political objectives, which they had failed to advance either on the battlefield or by successive pleas to the council of nations; (b) that by acting in concert they could substantially raise the revenues that accrued to them by virtue of their possession of this natural resource. The upshot is that, since October 1973, the developed countries are in quite a different ball game.

This event has to be seen in historical perspective. During the last three decades the developing world has suffered disappointment after disappointment. The transfer of know-how and the injection of capital through multilateral and bilateral programmes of development assistance have failed to prevent the gap between rich and poor nations from widening. Disenchantment with development assistance is spreading among the developed countries. We are in the middle of the second development decade, which runs to 1980. As part of the effort for this decade the developed countries were called upon to increase official development assistance on concessional terms to 0.7 per cent of the GNP by 1975. Even half of this target now seems out of reach. Only a very few countries seem likely to reach it. Moreover, the grant element (as against loans) is diminishing, and as a consequence debt service payments are rising annually by 20 per cent. Along with this, the multilateral development agencies are being squeezed.

I believe that the experience and disappointments of the past three decades are bringing about some profound shifts in the attitudes of the developing countries and will influence the policies they pursue in the future. I would expect the conviction to grow, among the developing countries, that the root causes of underdevelopment do not lie in lack of know-how, in lack of capital, in unfair trading arrangements, in lack of appropriate institutions; that these are but surface manifestations of something deeper; that underdevelopment over much of the world is historically rooted in development elsewhere; and that the poverty of the backward countries is inextricably linked with the affluence of the advanced countries. I believe this conviction will become sufficiently widespread to affect policy. We may therefore expect a greater disposition on the part of the developing countries to rely on their own resources; greater readiness to participate in sub-regional and regional trading arrangements and industrial harmonization plans; a much more critical attitude to the strings which are frequently attached to aid; a growing resistance to the penetration of foreign capital; a growing exercise of sovereignty over their own natural resources. Moreover, insofar as, between them, they control significant shares of global resources of which the developing world has need, they will use that control to squeeze a better deal from the developed world. Oil is but the first example. I do not need to tell you that there are many other minerals and raw materials necessary to the developed world of which the developing world possesses a substantial share.

Today the disarray and anxiety throughout the developed world resulting from the oil crisis is plain for all to see. Inevitably, it seems to me, we are in for a period of slower growth rates in the industrialized countries. This is why I believe the forecasts of domestic consumption contained in the report of Panel 6 are in need of some downward revision.

One other observation I would offer while we are on this subject. As time goes by I would expect the developing world to deploy its growing political weight with increasing subtlety, and with a measure of discrimination. It will endeavour to cause least embarassment to those developed countries which display an awareness of the developing countries' problems, a sensitivity to their needs, and a readiness to translate this awareness and sensitivity into appropriate action, be it in the field of aid, trade, financing, commodity policies, or international monetary policies.

Australia, as I pointed out in 1969, though an affluent, industrialized country, nevertheless has many problems in common with the developing countries. It is therefore well placed to understand their point of view. If it acts wisely it can perhaps avoid some of the crunch that is coming for the developed countries as a consequence of changing power relationships. It need not resign itself to a 'no-growth' or 'low-growth' future.

One thing that became obvious to me, as I read some of the controversy that raged in the professional and popular press before this conference, was that Forwood would be an occasion for putting the Australian forester on trial; that there would be a rigorous examination of the way in which he has interpreted the principles of multiple use; that his attention to date to the non-timber services of the forest and the rapidly changing demands on the forest would come under detailed scrutiny. The proceedings of that trial are spelled out in the background paper for and the report of Panel 3.

A hasty reading of these particular documents might leave one with the impression that the verdict is 'Not guilty, but don't do it again.' However, a careful reading reveals a very different story. Let me say at the outset that I consider the background paper for Panel 3 the most sensible, sober and reasoned approach to the very complex problem of multiple use of the forest resource that it has been my privilege to read. If no other document were to have emerged from Forwood, Forwood would still have been worth while. I sincerely hope that the Australian authorities may find means, perhaps in partnership with FAO, of ensuring that this document gets, outside Australia, the wide circulation it deserves. It is the Panel 3 documentation more than anything else which has made me optimistic about the eventual impact of Forwood.

Now it is undeniable that in the past Australian forestry has been largely production-oriented. This much is obvious to any outsider. Indeed, had there not been this production orientation, Australia would have been in a sorry plight today. This emerges clearly from the proceedings of Panel 3. But it has never been exclusively production-oriented. Nor could it have been, given the history of the art and science of forestry, and the indoctrination undergone by those forestry professionals to whom the forest estate has been confided. Thus, what also emerges clearly from Panel 3 is that many foresters (though unhappily not all) have kept abreast with new pressures and with rapidly changing demands on the forest, and have seriously endeavoured, within the limits of the knowledge presently available to them, to manage the forests in a way that will ensure that these demands are met, accepting any necessary restraints on the wood-production function. Some of the examples quoted by the Panel can serve as a model for the application of multiple-use principles. The Panel urges that best practice become general practice, and spells out a reasoned line of approach in dealing with some of the issues which have aroused most controversy.

By and large, the documentation for Forwood shows that Australia has reason to be grateful to, and can be proud of, its foresters – those of yesterday as well as those of today – and that their reputation ought to stand as high in Australia as it does in international forestry circles. Some may have made mistakes, but all are capable of learning. And there is no greater stimulus to learning than an alert and informed public opinion. If it be true – and it is certainly in my view – that the background paper to Panel 3 and the report of Panel 3 represent, in a certain sense, a vindication of the Australian forester, then Forwood ought, during the coming week, to address itself to the question: Why was such a vindication necessary? I believe the reason is that, until quite recently, the Australian forester has been singularly remiss in his efforts to make clear to the concerned citizen what he is trying to do and why he is doing it.

I do not propose to offer any suggestions concerning the scale of the Australian planting programme. No doubt you will all wrestle with this problem during the coming week. But when all the arithmetic has been done, when the cost–benefit ratios have been worked out, when the internal rates of return have been calculated, two things are worth bearing in mind. One is that, on this resource-hungry planet, a raw material that is versatile, renewable and biodegradable is more likely to appreciate in real value that to depreciate. The other is that, in twenty-odd years of international forestry activity, I have yet to come across a case of sensibly planned, properly located, man-made forest that has not eventually paid off.

May I, before I close, address a word to the man in the street, to the pre-occupied citizen who is seriously disturbed about what is happening to his environment.

I understand your concern. You do not want an Australia where, as one of your own poets has put it:

> The valley is no longer a place of grace.
> Even the bellbirds have all pissed off.

You have every right to cry, as did Lawrence's Harriet half a century ago, 'Is this all man can do with a new country?'

But remember this. Man has been monkeying with the ecosystems here ever since he first set foot on this continent. This is the mark and the condition of human progress. It is crying for the moon to want to stop the world from turning, to freeze the landscape as it is. It must be clearly understood that on the Australian scene a forest of radiata pine is no more unnatural than a wheat-field or a sheep run. The trick is not to let any situation get past the point of no return; and not to shut out important options for yourselves or for future generations. What can you, as a concerned citizen, do? You can insist that your governments, all of them, systematically pursue the approach admirably outlined by Panel 3. You can insist that they set aside the resources for the research that is needed to fill the many yawning gaps in knowledge that must be filled if wise decisions are to be taken. And you can badger the forester to keep on explaining what he is doing, and why.

If you do all these things, you will have played your part in ensuring that the Australia you leave behind is one that your children's children will be proud to inherit.

Finally, let me extend my hearty congratulations to the organizers of Forwood on their initiative in organizing this timely conference. I believe the success of Forwood will be assured if, during the coming week, you can concentrate on points of common interest rather than on divisive issues. I hope that by the end of the week Forwood will emerge with a policy, and perhaps with targets, which conform to the Australian national interests. The Australian national interest requires, in my view, that you keep firmly in mind that the Australian forest resource is but part of a global resource; and that you ensure that those voices which are unrepresented or under-represented here are spoken for. These include the Australian consumer of forest products and the rank and file citizen who is now seriously concerned about environmental issues. They also include your neighbours in New Zealand and the developing countries of South-east Asia, many of which possess forest resources which are complementary to yours and few of which have the opportunities for economic diversification that you have in Australia.

If Forwood is to be a complete success, it will be necessary to decide not only what is to be done, but also how it is to be done; to elaborate, even if only in outline, those measures that need to be taken at the federal and state levels, and by all concerned parties, to ensure prompt and decisive follow-up to the recommendations emerging from this conference.

10

Responsibility

My presence here today is fortuitous – an accident of time and place. I am very much reminded of something that happened to me about thirty years ago. At that time I was working on the railway, and in my spare time I had prepared myself for an external degree in statistics offered by the London School of Economics. The examination was scheduled to take place in Nottingham, and on the appointed day I took an early train to Nottingham and made my way to the examination hall. I was half an hour early, the gates were locked, and there was no sign of life. I leaned against the iron railings and waited for something to happen; Meanwhile, I gazed into the middle distance and tried to recall what I knew about multivariate analysis and sources of employment statistics. A man emerged from the building opposite, crossed the road, and addressed me.

'Are you busy?'
'Not specially,' I replied.
'Could you come with me and witness a wedding?'
'How long will it take?'
'Oh, not long. Not more than ten minutes.'

After glancing at my watch I crossed the road with him, entered the other building, and found myself in a room with the registrar, the groom, the bride, and the bride's mother. No shotgun was in evidence, but the somewhat distant attitude of the several parties towards each other throughout the ensuing ceremony suggested that one would not have been out of place. The ceremony over, I made my way back across the road, entered the examination hall, now open, and plunged into my ordeal.

My presence on this platform today seems equally fortuitous and bizarre to me. I just happened to be in Melbourne at the right time. I know nothing about pulp and paper technology, and I certainly do not intend to allow you to confirm this by talking to you about it.

Keynote address to the Australian Pulp and Paper Industry Technical Association Conference, Melbourne, March 1974.

Indeed, I had considerable difficulty in deciding what to talk to you about. The cabled invitation I received advised me that the subject-matter would be my choice; that it need not be either pulp and paper or forestry but could well be some of both, plus, if I wished, environmental and energy crises, and so on. It was on this basis that I agreed, by cable, to hold forth for twenty minutes on some subject later to be determined. Australian friends had assured me that twenty minutes was about all that Appita could stomach of me. However, the written invitation, which came into my hands nearly two months later, asked me to occupy you for thirty-five to forty minutes. It confirmed that the subject-matter was entirely of my own choosing, but the writer was bold enough to suggest that Ecology, or the Future of Our Natural Resources might stimulate my thinking in the matter. Somewhat ominously, the writer added that my address would be regarded as the first technical paper of the conference. This really did give me cold feet.

I started to browse in the little brochure which accompanied the invitation. It was entitled 'About Appita'. Here the word 'responsibility' caught my eye. It occurs when the brochure defines the class of 'full members'. A full member, it says, must be employed in the pulp and paper industry or related industry or in pulp and paper research and shall further have:

> Either (a) a suitable piece of paper plus at least two years' experience in industry or research;
> Or   (b) seven years' relevant practical experience and have held for two years 'a position of responsibility' in the pulp and paper or a related industry.

'Position of responsibility' is not defined at this point, but later, describing the qualifications for associate membership, there is stipulated one year's tenure of 'a position of responsibility equivalent to the control of a group of operations or processes'.

I thereupon decided to chat to you today about 'responsibility'. Not that I want to cast doubt on the conditions you have laid down for full and associate membership – rather, because this notion of responsibility offers me a convenient peg for ventilating some problems which have troubled me in recent years. I have little to say that is new. I hope to be able to raise some questions that merit your attention.

The *Shorter Oxford* offers three definitions of responsibility:

1   The state or fact of being responsible.
2   A charge, trust or duty for which one is responsible.
3   A person or thing for which one is responsible.

None of these carries us much further, and the *Shorter Oxford* politely suggests that we turn to the next entry, 'Responsible'. Here five variants are offered:

1 Correspondent or answering *to* something.
2 Answerable, accountable (*to* another *for* something); liable to be called to account. Morally accountable for one's actions; capable of rational conduct.
3 *US* Answerable to a charge
4 Capable of fulfilling an obligation or trust; reliable, trustworthy; of good credit and repute.
5 Involving responsibility or obligation.

We can ignore 1, which is rooted in response. We can also ignore 3, which is local to the USA. And 5 has a whiff of the tautological about it.

Thus we are left with definitions 2 and 4, and we see at once that two distinct notions are involved. The first notion is that of being accountable *to* another *for* something, and being liable to be called to account. The second notion is of being morally accountable for one's actions, capable of rational conduct.

All this is fine and dandy. The real problem arises when we start to consider responsible to *whom*, and for *what*.

It was precisely this question – responsible to *whom*, and for *what* – that struck me as significant when, about two years ago, while in the USA, I attended a lecture given by the Director of Ecology of a well known multinational industrial conglomerate, which has an annual turnover running into billions of dollars. The first part of the lecture was taken up with a series of charts expounding the geographically widespread and economically diverse activities of the company, and its organization. There followed an account of the organizational location and functions of the Division of Ecology. There were many postgraduate students in the audience, and after the lecture they posed a number of probing questions. From the lecturer's answers to these it emerged that the Division of Ecology gave advice only on request; it had no roving commission. Its advice was sought more frequently in relation to major new developments than in relation to ongoing operations. Its advice was not always taken. In preparing environmental impact statements on new developments, its concern was to ensure that the law was complied with and to anticipate any negative reactions on the part of the public. The audience gained the distinct impression that half the time of the division was spent on apologetics and the other half on helping the company to steer clear of the rocks. To whom was this gentleman responsible, accountable? Ultimately to his board of directors and, through them, to the shareholders. At no point in the lecturer's discourse or in his answers to questions was there the slightest hint of a responsibility to the community at large. As I listened to the questioners metaphorically undressing the lecturer, I found myself wondering: ought there not to be some kind of Hippocratic oath for the ecologist? Ought there not to be a professional ethic which ensures that, when he tenders advice, he should be as conscious of his obligations to society as of his obligations to his company?

The responsibility of a board of directors is to the shareholders. The funds entrusted to companies are intended to be employed 'for the acquisition of gain', and directors, after all, are simply (and I quote) 'commercial men managing a trading concern for the benefit of themselves and the other shareholders'. Gone is the day when commercial companies were declared common nuisances, and indictable as such, tending to the 'common grievance, prejudice and inconvenience of His Majesty's subjects or great numbers of them'. The Bubble Act of 1719, which used these words, was not repealed until 1825, but it had proved powerless to prevent the growth of joint stock enterprises. The body of company law which found its way to the statute book during the nineteenth century, both before and after the introduction of limited liability, was largely concerned with ensuring that the interests of shareholders were safeguarded.

Has the company a responsibility to any category other than the shareholders? To its employees, for instance? If we refer back to our first notion of responsibility, the answer is clearly: No. It is not answerable to, or accountable to, its employees. It is obliged to conform to labour legislation, which in essence is that part of the public interest which has so far found expression in the laws of the land. And it is also under an obligation to so conduct its relations with its employees that the interests of the shareholders are not prejudiced. But accountable *to* its employees? Certainly not.

What about its responsibility to its customers, to those who purchase the goods it manufactures or the services it provides? Obviously the company's responsibility to its shareholders requires that it make some effort to ensure that its customers are satisfied, so that custom is not lost and so that if possible new custom is gained. Moreover, there is a large body of law which seeks to protect the customer and offer him remedy if he is not satisfied. That this is far from effective under present conditions of manufacture and sale is evidenced by the fact that the last years have witnessed a tremendous growth in organizations formed expressly to protect and further the interests of consumers, to compensate for the companies' lack of responsibility towards their customers. We have seen that it is possible, for example, for a motor manufacturer to put on the road thousands of cars which, on investigation, prove to have lethal potential for the unwitting driver. We have seen that drugs can be marketed without adequate exploration of possible harmful side-effects. These are the more spectacular examples, but there are thousands of others. The principle of *caveat emtor* presupposes knowledge on the part of the customer which will enable him to assess what he is buying. It is the customer's job to know. That might be all right for a loaf of bread, a chisel, or a pair of trousers. When it comes to cars, electrical machines, pharmaceuticals, professional services, and so on, near omniscience is required in the customer if he is properly to judge. Hence the need for a consumer protection movement to inform potential consumers, to make them aware of their rights, and to extend their rights. Evidently a company is accountable to its customers in a less direct way than it is accountable to its shareholders. A customer has no power to fire a board of directors. Of course, if too many customers become dissatisfied the shareholders may decide to fire the board.

When we speak of the customer we are considering a relationship between a company and specific, identifiable individuals, those who purchase the goods or services. But there are company actions which affect not individuals, but the community at large, and which offend the public interest. The idea that companies, in addition to such responsibilities as they may have to their shareholders, their employees and their customers, also have a responsibility to the society and the environment in which they earn money for their shareholders, is gaining ground, even though it is difficult sometimes to define that responsibility in precise terms and even more difficult to enforce it. Sometimes the injury to the public interest arising out of a company action is insidious and long-term. It may, for example, have but little impact on the present generation but a very significant adverse impact on future generations. Sometimes the impact on any particular individual here and now is scarcely discernible, yet the aggregate and cumulative impact on the community is serious. This can give rise to level problems, situations in which it is clear that the public interest is affected, but it is not easy for an individual member of the public to demonstrate beyond reasonable doubt that he personally has suffered or will suffer injury. This is why pressure groups have to be organized and why government has to be brought into the act.

Now a large part of our present-day concern about environmental quality (though, of course, not all) has to do with the actions of companies. This is certainly true as regards atmospheric and water pollution.

We have reached a situation today, in the more industrialized countries, where one of our principal preoccupations is how to avoid drowning in our own excrement, asphyxiating in our own exhalations. The pulp and paper industry, like many others, is compelled to face up to what the economists politely call its external diseconomies, that is to say, it has to take account of the damage it inflicts on society in its quest for profitable growth. I believe that, as time goes on, more and more environmental issues will come to be recognized essentially as conflicts between short-term private or sectoral interests and long-term community interest; and that the aspiration for a decent environment will take on a deeper and sharper political content. Indeed, I would not be surprised if, in the more affluent countries, the so-called free enterprise system were to come increasingly under attack – not because it fails to deliver the goods, not because it fails to ensure fair shares, but because it proves incapable of ensuring that social costs are met.

Not that the problem is one that is confined to the free enterprise economies. Marshal Goldman, in his *Spoils of Progress*, details many instances in the USSR where short-term sectoral interests have prevailed over long-term community interests.[1] We are most of us familiar with the Lake Baikal controversy. Less well known is the ecological disruption attendant on the shrinking and pollution of the Aral and Caspian seas, and the land losses and disappearance of beeches on the Black Sea coast following the wholesale removal of sand and shingle for building purposes. It seems to be almost as difficult in the USSR as elsewhere to ensure that engineering and industrial enterprises pay adequate attention to the long-term community interest.

I may be cynical, but I must confess that I have no great faith in the will or ability of boards of directors to ensure that the public interest is made paramount. They have their shareholders breathing down their necks, and it is to the shareholders that they are accountable. I am not even convinced when I hear of a managing director endeavouring to reassure the public by drinking the effluent from his own mill. Still less am I convinced when I hear it rumoured that he is shortly to re-baptize his mill: 'The Miracle of Cana'. We can doubtless rely on boards of directors to go as far as they are pushed on pollution issues, and some of them may even go a little bit further. But quite a few will use their ingenuity to exploit the loopholes in restraining legislation, and will do their best to ensure that any new legislation does least damage to the shareholders to whom they are accountable.

We begin to see now that there is a world of difference between the two notions of responsibility I invoked earlier on: between being answerable, accountable, to someone for something – being liable to be called to account; and being morally accountable, capable of rational conduct.

On whom then can we rely to ensure that standards are set which are appropriate to safeguard the public interest and to ensure that these standards are observed? For example, to bring the matter close to home, on whom can we rely in the case of conflict between the interests of the shareholders of pulp and paper companies and the interests of the community? Let us remember that, among the public at large, there are relatively few who are well versed in such matters as acceptable loads of suspended solids, biological oxygen demand, toxicity to aquatic resources, and best available current technology. The answer is, of course, that we must rely on you – members of Appita, profesionals, scientists and technicians. For, besides your responsibility to your employer, be it a public or private company or a government department, you have a responsibility to society, to your fellow-citizens: a social responsibility. This responsibility is a dual one: first, to make essential facts widely known in a language which can be generally understood; second, to give the public the benefit of an informed judgement on matters where you can justly claim to have a special knowledge. No one disputes your accountability to your employer. But you are also morally accountable to

[1] Cambridge, Mass., MIT Press, 1972.

society. This responsibility may not be spelt out in your brochure, 'About Appita' – more's the pity. But it exists nonetheless.

Now the sad thing is that until fairly recently most scientists and professionals have been reluctant to acknowledge this other responsibility, still less to exercise it. But times are changing. Lately we have seen more and more scientists and professionals who are prepared to speak out, either as individuals or as members of groups, on major issues where the public interest is threatened. In a few countries we have seen the establishment of societies for social responsibility in science. A further interesting development took place in the USA last autumn. There scientists and public-interest groups met together at the Brookings Institute in Washington to launch a campaign to recruit scientists for the public-interest movement. Ralph Nader told the meeting that most scientists are tied down by the various interests related to where they work. The public-interest movement, he stated, is in desperate need of scientific and technical knowledge to back its case.

Even among some of the groups often deemed most backward, something is moving. I doubt whether there is any body of scientific or professional men or women more conservative than foresters. However, when over two thousand of them from all over the world met together in the Seventh World Forestry Congress at Buenos Aires in 1972, they had something to say that was new, for them. That congress adopted unanimously a Final Declaration, and I would like to read you a couple of paragraphs from it. Paragraph 13 reads as follows:

The Congress critically examined the status and responsibilities of the forestry profession. Foresters have been pioneers in the struggle to conserve and rationally use renewable resources. As men and women experienced in the multi-purpose management of the forest resource, they cannot but view with satisfaction the growing concern about environmental quality and the need for proper management of the world's renewable resources. Foresters recognize that forestry is concerned not with trees, but with how trees can serve people.

This formulation shows that foresters are never averse to blowing their own trumpets. I happened to be there, and I know that many in the congress would have wished to blow more loudly, but finally congress contented itself with this modest blast. The last sentence of the paragraph is an overdue affirmation that forestry should be people-centred, not tree-centred. Will this overnight make all foresters aware of the social impact of what they are doing? Of course not. But at least in the future, as current controversies are pursued and new controversies arise, the diehards can be given to understand that the weight of world forestry opinion, as set forth in Buenos Aires, is against them.

But paragraph 14 is the crucial one:

This Congress declares that the forester, being a citizen as well as a professional has the clear duty and responsibility to ensure that his informed judgement is heard and understood at all levels of society. His allegiance is not to the resource, but to the rational management of that resource in the long-term interest of the community. To this end, forestry education needs to be broadened, with greater emphasis than heretofore on those disciplines that contribute to the understanding and exercise of the forester's responsibility.

Here, for the first time, so far as I am aware, the principle of the social responsibility of foresters is clearly set out. The overwhelming majority of foresters are in public service. There is a widespread tradition that public servants should be seen and not heard, that they should not engage in public debate, that their views are properly expressed only in interdepartmental memoranda and *aides-mémoire* to ministers. This tradition, congress considered, should be shattered, and the *de facto* disenfranchisement of foresters brought to an end. The forester should resume his rights as a citizen. He has a duty and a responsibility to ensure that his informed judgement is heard and understood in all public debates on resource issues.

Once the scientist or professional, be he forester or pulp and paper technologist, acknowledges his social responsibility, and acts on it, then we may hope that some of the controversies which are presently engaging the public mind will generate a little less heat and enjoy considerably more light. Moreover, as it becomes increasingly recognized that scientists and professionals do, after all, have a basic ethic, they will not only gain in moral standing themselves. They will lend badly needed support to their fellow-professionals elsewhere who are struggling against much greater difficulties. Take, for example, the professional foresters of the developing countries of South-east Asia. In many of these countries the forest resource is being recklessly pillaged in response to overwhelming local political pressures. The local forester, isolated, lacking political allies, is powerless to check this process – indeed, is often an accessory. His situation is not helped when he sees foresters belonging to expatriate exploiting companies condoning practices that run counter to the ABC of forest management, practices that he would never dream of allowing on his home ground. If the expatriate forester were more conscious of his social responsibility, were truly alive to his basic ethic, he would feel an obligation to counter and expose unacceptable practices. And in so doing he would lend dignity and strength to his professional colleagues in the countries concerned.

Let me sum up what I have been trying to say. The scientist, the professional, the technician, undoubtedly has a responsibility to his employer, to the hand that feeds him. But this is not the end of his responsibilities. He also has a responsibility to the community at large, to society, to the public. On many of the issues that engage the public interest, the scientific and technical complexities are such that the public has great difficulty in disentagling them and in discerning the most appropriate solutions. The scientist, the professional, the technician, has a responsibility for ensuring that his expertise is made available to the public in terms which the man in the street can understand. The fact that he sells his brain power to a private employer or government department for thirty-five or forty hours a week does not require that he surrender his rights or his duties as a citizen during the rest of his waking hours. It does not absolve him of his responsibility towards his fellow-citizens. He does not have to be a civic castrate.

There may well be occasions when what he conceives to be his responsibility towards his employer is in direct conflict with what he deems to be his social responsibility. He has a moral duty to put the public interest first. I maintain that if professionals and scientists in the past had attached as much weight to their social responsibilities as they did to their responsibilities to their employers, we might have been spared Auschwitz, we might have been spared Hiroshima, we might have been spared motor cars that were lethal, we might have been spared drugs that were deforming, and we might have been spared some of the environmental degradation we are fighting today.

This really concludes that I wanted to say about responsibility. I suspect that some members of my audience may regard some of my observations as subversive. Well, they were intended to be.

I ought to end my address at this point. However, since I still have the platform, there is one further thought I would like to place before you. It has but little relation to what I have said so far, yet it does raise a question you may care to turn over in your minds during the coming week.

You are members of a technical association. You will probably agree, the way things have turned out in recent years, and particularly during the last half-year, that a sizeable proportion of your effort in the future will have to be devoted to devising recycling technologies, energy-saving technologies, materials-saving technologies. My question is this: Can we be sure that it is in the public interest that pulp and paper should be a growth industry?

I suppose it is heresy to trail this thought in this conference, of all places. But you must understand that I do not have any vested interest in the pulp and paper industry. I speak merely as a baffled, and sometimes disgruntled, consumer. Frankly, for me the quality of life does not consist in having a choice of six different floral patterns for my toilet paper. Moreover, it irks me to have to carry about a kilogram of newsprint when all I want is a gram of news. I also begrudge the time it takes me to transfer fifty or sixty unsolicited circulars from my letter-box to my waste bin every week, and I curse those benighted individuals who make their living from trading in address lists. My blood pressure rises each time I pick up a package at the supermarket and discover when I get home that it takes at least ten minutes and a good deal of ingenuity to penetrate it and reach the contents. The fact is that the pulp and paper industry produces a lot of things I don't want, that I never asked for, but that I am compelled to have and also compelled to pay for, directly or indirectly. As an individual, I resent all these things. As a member of the community, it strikes me as irrational in a world that ought to be concerned with economizing its resources.

11

Forest Industries for
Socio-Economic Development

The congress is about to start on the discussion of 'Forests for Industrial Development'. I have been invited to open the proceedings in this discussion area by speaking to you about 'Forest Industries for Socio-Economic Development'. Those of you who were with us six years ago in Buenos Aires will recognize that this Congress starts where the last one left off. The central theme six years ago was 'Forests and Socio-Economic Development'. The central theme here in Jakarta is 'Forests for People'.

Are these not one and the same thing? – forests for socio-economic development and forests for people. Are we not in danger of treading again the ground we trod in Buenos Aires six years ago?

There would certainly seem to be some kind of relationship between the two. But how close that relationship is depends on what we mean by socio-economic development, and who we mean by the people.

If this were a congress of economists or sociologists, I am sure it would be very difficult for us to agree about what constitutes socio-economic development. But we are neither. Nor are we a congress of politicians. We are simply foresters, but sensible foresters. And because we are simply sensible foresters, I think we shall have no difficulty in reaching agreement on one or two simple propositions.

A nation can be said to be developing economically if its capacity to produce goods and services is expanding. We can go further and say that a nation is developing socio-economically if the goods and services which it is producing correspond to the real needs of its people, and if the expanded output of goods and services is so distributed that the most urgent of those needs are satisfied first, and in an equitable manner.

Guest speaker's address, Eighth World Forestry Congress, Jakarta, September 1978; first published in the *Commonwealth Forestry Review*, *58:2, pp. 107–16. Published by permission of the author and the Commonwealth Forestry Association.*

In other words, socio-economic development has three elements: productive forces which are expanding, output which matches real needs, distribution which ensures that real needs are met.

Does this sound reasonable to you? I hope so.

Some of you may wonder what I mean by 'real needs'. Since we are neither economists, sociologists nor politicians, we do not have to spend a long time arguing about this, either. Real needs are, first and foremost, food: next, clothing and shelter: then, elementary health and education services. I would not argue that this is a comprehensive list of real needs. But these are the basic ones. Only when we can see that more and more people are getting more and more of these basic needs satisfied can we talk about socio-economic development. The fact is that socio-economic development, like the giraffe, is hard to describe and hard to measure, but easy to recognize. Conventional measuring rods serve not at all. Per caput gross domestic product tells you very little about socio-economic development. Nor, for that matter, do most of the ingenious parameters contrived in an attempt to measure welfare. For what use is it to double the number of hospital beds per million if all those extra beds are in the capital and are accommodating only expatriates and the indigenous elite?

Indeed, one of the reasons why yardsticks like per caput GDP have fallen recently into disrepute (though not into disuse) is precisely because it has become obvious to all observers that, in a number of countries where this yardstick has risen, the number, and the proportion, of people whose basic needs remain unsatisfied has not diminished but has risen.

While it is true that, for most countries in the underdeveloped world, the post-war decades have brought a disappointing degree of economic growth, with but little of that growth translated into social progress, this is not because the development theorists have never revised their ideas, have all along clung grimly to outworn formulae. On the contrary, the development theorists have frequently been able to recognize failure when they saw it. They have shown themselves more than willing, like good family doctors, to change the prescription when the old medicine was plainly not doing any good. On the other hand, they have always been reluctant to admit that their earlier medicine had served only to make the sick patient sicker, and to increase his vulnerability to a whole range of new diseases.

Yes, development fashions have changed over the last three decades, and that is why gradually the files, the archives, the case-books of the development establishment – which consists of the multi-and bilateral development and financing agencies, with their supporting theorists in the universities and the foundations, never forgetting their protégés in the planning ministries of the underdeveloped world – have come to resemble the private cemetery of a fantastic zoo, a cemetery stuffed with the corpses of wild geese, lame ducks, red herrings, white elephants and dead horses.

It would be instructive to follow, step by step, the many changes in development fashions over the last three decades. But even if I had the time, I do not think that you would have the patience. Even so, one or two backward glances may not be out of place.

The multilateral agencies, which form the core of the development establishment, were in the first post-war years staffed by a very odd mixture: the usual quota of nominees of foreign offices, planted to make sure that the new agencies did not get out of line; a sprinkling of cosmopolitan floaters, survivors from the wreckage of pre-war international institutions; and an enthusiastic leaven of liberal humanists, convinced that more international cooperation was one way of making the world safer and better for all. They firmly believed in human progress: temporary setbacks there might be, but overall the march of man was upward and onward. Indeed, their vision of the world was of underdeveloped countries struggling to emerge from the swamps of backwardness on to the dry land of take-off, and then up the slopes towards affluence. Thus all the nations, rich and poor, were straggled across the countryside, like a cross-country race. But they were all running essentially the same race. How did those in front come to be in front? Because they had what the others lacked: capital, skills, know-how. Only transmit some of these from those in front to those behind and the stragglers would start to catch up. The rich countries were parsimonious with their money, but they were prodigal with advice. So experts started to flood into the underdeveloped countries, and the era of development by exhortation was under way.

The development literature grew exponentially. The fatuity of disembodied advice, advice not backed up by concrete help, became obvious. The international assistance effort was stepped up, and development aid moved from exhortation to demonstration: from the 'tell me' phase to the 'show me' phase. The walking know-how of experts was supplemented by increasing amounts of hardware, while a reverse flow of young and serious Third World students trekked north and west to assimilate irrelevant knowledge and master inappropriate technologies.

We had entered the era of projects, projects that would remove the impediments to investment, for investment was the key to development: the era of pre-investment surveys, feasibility studies, leading to 'bankable' projects and actual investment. To sustain the flow of development assistance funds, articles appeared in the business weeklies showing how aid not only soothed the donor's conscience but lined his pockets too. It was possible to do well by doing good. Anyone who has ever worked in a development agency for any length of time, be it multi- or bilateral, can testify that this lesson at least was speedily learned by the business communities.

Ah, the debates of those bygone days! Do you remember some of them? Do you remember, for example, how the scarce ingredient in the development pantry was capital? Ergo, not a cent must be wasted. Every single project must be screened, gone over with a fine-toothed comb; each pay-out time calculated, each internal rate of return checked, rechecked, cross-checked and compared. No matter if the screening took three, four or five years. Only the utmost rigour in screening could avert the catastrophe of misinvestment.

Thus spake the pundits. We waited eagerly for their next pronouncement. It was not long in coming.

There in no lack of resources, they said, no shortage of investment funds, public or private. There is only one obstacle standing in the way of development: the scarcity of sound projects. All this was said with a perfectly straight face, for the development establishment, besides having a short memory, has absolutely no sense of humour.

Down the years, the international apparatus for dealing with development problems grew by leaps and bounds, as attention concentrated on this or that piece of the development jigsaw.

Non-industrialized nations are poor. Industrialized nations are prosperous. Therefore prosperity lies in industrialization. Thus after a struggle, United Nations Industrial Organization (UNIDO) was born, in the teeth of the opposition of the already industrialized nations.

Worsening terms of trade more than wiped out the flow of aid. Came the new cry, 'Trade, not aid'. The rich nations braced themselves behind their trade barriers and turned a deaf ear as long as they could, but eventually United Nations Conference on Trade and Development (UNCTAD) was born, in recognition of the intimate connection between trade and development.

The poor nations' efforts to develop were being frustrated by their propensity to breed too fast, so the UN Population Fund was set up. And so on and so forth.

Meanwhile, the picture entertained by the early visionaries – the cross-country race of development – was steadily fading. Few nations succeeded in clambering out of the swamp on to the dry land. Some even fell back into the swamp. Hopes that some system of judicious handicapping would help to even up the race grew dim. Nor was this surprising. What kind of a race is it where the horses in front constitute the handicapping committee?

Little by little the horrid truth began to dawn, even in the ranks of some of the development establishments. The underdeveloped countries are not underdeveloped because they started late in the development race. They are not underdeveloped because they lack adequate resources. They are not underdeveloped because they lack know-how. They are not underdeveloped because they are overpopulated. They are underdeveloped as a consequence of the development of the rich nations. The development of the latter is founded on the underdevelopment of the former, and is sustained by it. The ties between the affluent, industrialized countries and the backward, low-income countries are intimate and compelling. Their nature is such that the objective impact of most of the so-called development effort to date has been to promote underdevelopment.

It was this growing realization that eventualy led to the demand, on the part of the poor nations, for a wholesale revision of the rules of the game, for 'a new world economic order', and that notion is now enshrined in the resolutions and decisions of the constellations of United Nations agencies and is providing the justification for innumerable North–South dialogues. So far, the poor nations have had but little success in getting the rules of the game changed in their favour.

I spoke earlier of remedies that made the sick patient sicker. Nowhere has this become more clear than in the realm of food and agriculture. What kinds of projects did the developers favour? Those where foreign partners stood ready to invest, where profitable overseas markets were waiting, where there was valuable foreign exchange to be earned. These were the kinds of projects that could pass through the eye of the World Bank's needle into the heaven of implementation. This is how more and more of the best lands in Central and South America, in North, East and West Africa, in parts of Asia, came to produce strawberries, carnations, peppers, egg-plants, pineapples, bananas and cucumbers for the Global Supermarket, destined for the tables and sitting-sooms of North America, Europe and Japan; more tea, coffee and sugar for thirsty foreigners; more groundnuts, palm kernels, cotton and rubber for other countries' industries.

But what about the men and women whom this 'development' had enlisted in the service of the rich countries' tables? Neither they nor the land they worked were any longer producing food for themselves or for their immediate neighbours. Indeed, many of them, instead of eating rice, maize, millet, and so on, learned for the first time to eat bread, bread which had to be made from imported wheat or flour. This was the kind of 'development' that paid off its loans promptly, yielded good profits on investments, but left millions vulnerable to the vagaries of climate and international trade. In the statistics, it appeared as economic growth, but it was not socio-economic development. It was, in fact, active underdevelopment.

Or take the famed green revolution, which achieved the bizarre paradox of simultaneously producing more food and making more people hungry. With the new wizard varieties, production soared. It soared on the lands of the bigger and better-off farmers, those with access to credit and hence to improved seed, pesticides, irrigation systems, mechanization, those strong enough to dispense with middlemen and moneylenders. As production soared, so prices fell, and so did the incomes of the small and marginal farmers. Choked by the debt burden, thousand upon thousand of small farmers sold or forfeited their land to join the swelling ranks of the landless rural poor. The statistics showed economic growth. They even showed rising agricultural output. What they failed to show was active socio-econmic development.

I could go on giving examples, but there is no need. What has happened is that many low-income countries have become increasingly dependent on alien technologies, foreign experts, imported fertilizers and pesticides, wayward and cut-throat overseas markets, and production decisions taken thousands of miles away. What is worse, countries which once could feed themselves have become dependent on imports of basic foods, while more and more of their people go hungry.

A few years ago the plight of the forgotten millions of poor farmers began to receive the attention of the development establishment. No less an authority than Mr McNamara,[1] President of the World Bank, said:

Of the two billion persons living in our developing member countries, nearly two thirds, or some 1.3 billion, are members of farm families, and of these there are some 900 million whose annual incomes average less than $100...

...for hundreds of millions of subsistence farmers, life is neither satisfying nor decent. Hunger and malnutrition menace their families. Illiteracy forecloses their futures. Disease and death visit their villages too often, stay too long, and return too soon. The miracle of the Green Revolution may have arrived, but, for the most part, the poor farmer has not been able to participate in it. He simply cannot afford to pay for the irrigation, the pesticide, the fertilizer, or perhaps for the land itself, on which his title may be vulnerable and his tenancy uncertain.

These were strong words. They were an admission on the part of the number one development doctor that the time had come for a change of medicine. Mr McNamara was, of course, right to be concerned about the plight of the poor farmer, though he might have said more about the plight of the landless rural poor, whose numbers are increasing everywhere, and who now make up a third or a half of the population in some parts of the world.[2]

The new concern is by now reflected in the words of all the development agencies and, though to a lesser extent, in their deeds. And within the last year there has come into existence the International Fund for Agricultural Development, prepared to lend up to $350 million a year for projects 'that have a strong food production orientation, foster the use of appropriate technology, have as target groups the poorest and the landless, generate considerable employment, and have a direct impact on the nutrition of the poorest'.[3]

I hope you are not losing patience with these random ruminatons on development problems. They are not completely random. I have tried to show that one of the main lessons learned by the development establishment since the last World Forestry Congress is that economic growth does not necessarily mean socio-economic development. But I was also gently preparing you to face up to the unpalatable fact that, as yet, forest industries have made little or no

[1] Robert S. McNamara, *One Hundred Countries, Two Billion People*, (New York, 1973).

[2] John W. Mellor, (Chief Economist, AID), 'The Landed and the Landless', *Ceres*, 61 (January–February 1978).

[3] Statement by IFAD's first President, Ambassador Abdulmuhsim Al-Sudeary of Saudi Arabia, reported in *Ceres*, 11(2): 14, (1978).

contribution to socio-economic development in the underdeveloped world – certainly not the significant contribution that was envisaged for them a couple of decades ago. Indeed, the probability is that such forest industries as have been established have, like parallel developments in food and agriculture, served but to deflect attention from real needs, diverted resources from what should have been the true priorities, and served to promote socio-economic *under*development.

The arguments that were advanced for giving a certain priority to forest industries seemed valid enough at the time. Here was a group of industries based on a revewable resorce, a resource which all underdeveloped countries possessed or could create; industries with considerable flexibility both as to scale of operations and technology; industries with pronounced backward and forward linkages, ensuring that their growth would exercise a multiplier effect on the whole economy; industries which, located near the wood resurce, offered the prospect of creating new poles of development, checking the squalid centrifugal development that has scarred so many underdeveloped countries; industries producing a wide range of products, many of which correspond to basic needs; products, moreover, with a high income elasticity, enhancing prospects of industry viability once under way; products which could substitute expensive imports and, exported, earn valuable foreign exchange.[4]

I am sure you have all heard these arguments before: you may even have used them. Certain it is that, as foresters began to use them, the development institutions, financing agencies and planning ministries began to listen to the foresters. Forestry yielded its time-honoured place as the Cinderella sector, the sector commanding absolute posteriority. A stream of forestry projects began to be approved. The forestry sector was in business. Our efforts to convert the development agencies to forestry were doubtless helped by the fact that FAO's global studies had shown beyond a shadow of doubt that rising affluence in Europe, North America and Japan would require an increasing flow of timber from the underdeveloped world, and that the foreign exchange these exports would generate could not but help the credit-worthiness of the underdeveloped exporting countries.

We flattered ourselves that our arguments had been well founded, and that reason had prevailed.

How naïve we were!

The growing interest in, and acceptance of, forestry projects had little or nothing to do with the conversion of the development establishment to the idea that forestry and forest industries had a significant and many-sided contribution to make to overall economic and social development. It had everything to do with the fact that many of the rich, industrialized countries needed, and needed

[4] Jack C. Westoby, *The Role of Forest Industries in the Attack on Economic Underdevelopment* (FAO, 1962).

badly, new wood material resources; and their forest industries, their equipment manufacturers, together with miscellaneous agents and operators, scented golden opportunities for profit in those underdeveloped countries with forest resources. This was the dominant consideration which determined the location, shape and direction of forest and forest industry development projects. The forest and forest industry pre-investment survey became the archetypal project. The international financing agencies knew what foreign investors wanted, and the multilateral and bilateral agencies fell into line. They helped the underdeveloped countries to bear the expense and drudgery of resource data collection, including mapping and wood-testing, thereby relieving potential investors of these tasks and charges. Likewise, they bore the cost of initial feasibility studies. They supported forestry colleges, schools and training courses, building up the ranks of local trained people, enabling eventual operators to economize on the import of more costly, expatriate, personnel.

Thus did the development establishment help to contract, in the course of the last two decades, over 100 million hectares – probably nearer 150 million hectares – of tropical forest land to industry for harvesting.[5] Thus did the removals of tropical hardwood logs quadruple between 1950 and 1976, while exports, nearly all destined for the wood-hungry, affluent, industrialized nations, rose from under 3 to well over 40 million cubic metres. Meanwhile, the proportion of tropical logs processed in the source countries declined. S. L. Pringle has pointed out that had the 49 million cubic metres exported unprocessed in 1973 been processed where it was grown, this would have brought another $2,000 million or more to the source countries, as well as providing several hundred thousand man-years of employment.[6] Though every underdeveloped country now has a forest service, these forest services are nearly all woefully understaffed, and miserably underpaid. Because they exist, exploitation is facilitated; because they are weak, exploitation is not controlled. Because exploitation has been uncontrolled, and management non-existent, marginal farmers, shifting cultivators and landless poor have followed in the wake of the loggers, completing the forest destruction. Of the original moist forest area, over half has disappeared in Africa, over one third in Latin America, and over two fifths in Asia. And the tropical forest continues to shrink.[7]

Because nearly all the forest and forest industry development which has taken place in the underdeveloped world over the last decades has been externally oriented, aimed at satisfying the rocketing demands of the rich, industrialized nations, the basic forest products needs of the peoples of the underdeveloped

---

[5] Franz Schmidthüsen, 'Forest utilization contracts on public land in the Tropics', *Unasylva*, 28: 112–13 (1976), pp. 52–73.

[6] S. L. Pringle 'Tropical moist forests in world demand, supply and trade', ibid, pp. 106–18.

[7] Adrian Sommer, 'Attempt at an assessment of the world's tropical moist forests', ibid., pp. 5–25.

world are further from being satisfied than ever: their need for fuel, building materials, low-cost housing, cheap furniture, industrial and cultural papers. The famous multiplier effects are missing. Few new poles of development have been created. The weak forest services in the underdeveloped world are largely concerned with assuring and facilitating a steady outflow of wood raw material to the rich countries. Of the new revenues generated, woefully little has been ploughed back into forestry, either into management, into regeneration or new planting, or into research.

But this is not the worst of it. Just because the principal preoccupation of the forest services in the underdeveloped world has been to help promote this miscalled forest and forest industry development, the much more important role which forestry could play in supporting agriculture and raising rural welfare has been either badly neglected or completely ignored. In precious few countries have the energies of the foresters been bent upon helping the peasant to develop the kind of forestry that would serve his material welfare. This is why there are so few village woodlots and fuel plantations. This is why so little work has been done on forage trees, fruit and nut orchards. This is why so few shelter-belts have been created. This is why more and more watersheds have become denuded, so that the flood and drought oscillations which spell calamity for the peasant take on ever greater amplitude. This is why forestry has been invoked so rarely to reclaim or rehabilitate land. This is why so few of the many possible agro-forestry combinations have been actively explored and developed. This is why so few industries have been established which are specifically geared to meeting real local needs.

But perhaps things are beginning to change? In the last year or two we have heard much more about forestry in rural development. FAO has prepared a basic study on forestry for local community development. A whole area of this present congress is being devoted to 'Forestry for Rural Communities'. The World Bank is actively exploring the possibility of supporting nationally oriented rural forestry programmes, and its new forestry sector policy paper is replete with good intentions. Other development banks will almost certainly follow by adopting some of the new language. A new International Council for Research in Agro-Forestry has come into existence, directed by an international forestry personality in whom we cannot but have every confidence.[8]

Does not all this show that the tide has turned, that the development establishment has repented its past errors, and now has its feet firmly set upon the true path?

I think it would be prudent to wait a while before we set the victory bells ringing. At most, we should give but two cheers for this tardy change of heart. The truth is that it is much easier to achnowledge that there is a problem than

[8] K. F. S. King, formerly Guyana's Minister of Economic Development, and from late 1974 to mid-1978 Assistant Director-General in charge of FAO's Department of Forestry.

it is to get something done about it. It is not simply a matter of gearing the development establishment towards new objectives.

Here it is only fair to mention that some of the non-governmental agencies, dependent on unofficial sources for funds, have for some time concerned themselves with the plight of the forgotten millions, though often in a clumsy and ineffectual way. Moreover, some of the more altruistic bilateral aid programmes, those less directly tied to their national business interests, have sought ways and means of helping the millions whom traditional development aid has passed by. They have not met with conspicuous success.

Nor does the problem lie in the ruluctance of agency staffs to depart from time-honoured practice and respond to the new precepts which are now beginning to rain on them from above.

The real problem lies elsewhere. The fact is that in many of the underdeveloped countries neither government nor officialdom display any great enthusiasm for mitigating the lot of their poorer people.

The present congress is not an intergovernmental conference, nor am I an international bureaucrat. I therefore do not have to pay lip-service to the polite fiction that there is invariably an identity of interest between governments and the people whom they are supposed to represent. In most underdeveloped countries today the interests of those monopolizing political power and the interests of the disinherited masses are not identical: they are diametrically opposed. That is why the demand for a 'new economic order', with its attendant scenario of poor nations versus rich nations, is the biggest, brightest and most convenient red herring yet devised.

This scenario has today come to dominate the world political stage. Every international forum now presents an opportunity for ministers from underdeveloped countries – be they ministers of finance, of health, of industry, of agriculture, of planning, or whatever – to ascend the rostrum in turn to inveigh against imperialism and neo-colonialism. Their co-delegates do not even bother to listen: they have heard it all before a hundred times. And they accept it tolerantly, knowing that the speech is not intended for them; it is intended for the record, and for subsequent dissemination back home. For it is a great convenience for rulers if the dispossessed in their own countries can be persuaded that the source of their misery lies not at all in their own rulers but in the alien rapacity of rich countries and the far-off machinations of transnational corporations. Their attention is thereby diverted. It is diverted from the fact that those who inveigh most demagogically against imperialism are often *de facto* the outstationed agents of imperialism, and that the contrast of affluence within many underdeveloped countries, between the small ruling elite and the mass of the population, exceeds even the inequalities between rich and poor nations.

But this latest red herring, big and shiny as it is, is also beginning to smell. It, too, is destined for the cemetery. For the world is beginning to change. It is beginning to change not because the development establishment has had a change of mind or a change of heart. It is beginning to change because, in the underdeveloped world, more and more governments are coming to power which are genuinely concerned about inequalities within their countries, and which are striving to do something about it. These are governments for whom the words 'social justice' are not a parrot cry but an emblem of faith and a guide to action. These are countries where the people have drawn the correct lessons from the failure of the past decades. The number of such countries is destined to grow.

How can such countries ensure that the forest industries they create truly contribute to socio-economic development? What kind of forest and forest industry priorities should they set?

One thing is clear. All their forest and forest industry priorities will be subordinated to, and carefully geared to, their national development priorities. And among these the most imperative is to ensure that their people are adequately fed. This is not simply a matter of switching investment from industry to agriculture. It is a matter of facilitating and encouraging those structural changes which will enable the rural masses, at all levels, to feed themselves, and to move progressively beyond that to the production of an agricultural surplus which will ensure that the urban population, too, is fed and no longer dependent either on food aid or on costly food imports. This is the only basis for sound industrialization. Such governments will therefore closely scrutinize all present and possible future forestry activities from the standpoint of how best they can protect, support, promote and diversify the agricultural economy. It is to this aspect they will give pride of place in their forestry planning and in the forestry goals they establish. I do not need to reiterate here the hundred and one ways in which forestry can promote food production and enrich the rural economy. Other discussion areas of this congress are being devoted precisely to the discussion of this problem. However, I should perhaps emphasize, in case it might be overlooked, that agriculture-supportive forestry does not by any means exclude forest industries. Small rural industries are an integral part of agriculture-supportive forestry: fuelwood, charcoal, poles, stakes, fencing, hurdles, screens, farm tools and implements, building materials, simple furniture. But these activities, like all other agriculture-supportive activities, are activities that cannot be carried out on the required scale and in the required manner by a conventionally oriented and conventionally organized forest service. They will only be effective, and will only make sense, if they are carried out by the peasants themselves, for themselves. The role of the forester, wherever he may sit in the organizational structure, can only be to stimulate, offer guidance and suggestions, impart techniques and carry out training.

Moreover, although there are various forestry activities which an individual peasant can carry out, those activities which can contribute most to supporting agriculture and promoting rural welfare call for cooperative or communal endeavour. Since it is now becoming evident that the only way forward for agriculture in most underdeveloped countries lies through the promotion of mutual aid and cooperation, it is logical that agriculture and forestry should be soundly integrated at the village level.

The second priority in these countries will be the use of the existing forest resource base, and the creation, where necessary, of new wood resources, for industrialization directed towards the satisfaction of the most basic domestic needs. Insofar as measures aimed at reducing inequalities in income distribution are successful, this in itself will bring about a changed pattern of demand. However, this may not be sufficient to ensure that existing and new forest industries are geared to the satisfaction of basic needs, and market intervention or market manipulation may be necessary. Moreover, since in the under-developed countries a substantial proportion of needs for processed wood arises in the public sector, governments are in a strong position to pursue policies which can assure the viability of the domestic-oriented wood industries they bring into existence.

Have export-oriented forest industries any place in the forestry programmes of such countries? Yes, they have a place. If the forest resource is sufficiently rich to offer the opportunity of expanding or creating export-oriented forestry activities, such opportunities will not be neglected. However, any such develop-ments will be subordinated to the first two priorities I have outlined. Moreover, wise governments will digest and apply the lessons of the last two decades of bitter experience. They will refuse to be dazzled by the prospects of quick and easy export earnings. They will take a cool and calm look at the seductive proposals of would-be concessionaires and private foreign capital. They will be swift to denounce and punish all attempts at bribes. For while it is true that the sums involved in forest exploitation and forest industries are trivial compared with, say, military aircraft or oil, we are all painfully aware that the accounts of timber concessionaires and equipment salesmen are tarnished with obscure miscellaneous items no less than the accounts of Lockheed and Exxon.

These governments will be careful not to sign away their resource heritage. If they decide they can afford to consume forest capital, this will be a conscious choice, accompanied by specific plans for changed land-use. Most important of all they will temper the pace of such export-oriented developments to their own rising capacity to supervise and control them. All programmes and projects, from whatever source they arise, which can introduce serious distortions and jeopardize their own national objectives will be firmly rejected.

If these prescriptions are adhered to, then it is possible that economic growth, as measured by conventional criteria, may be slower. But development will be accelerated, and socio-economic development will become a reality. Growth is a necessary condition for development, but it is not sufficient condition. The kind of growth we have seen in the past, growth which widens social inequalities, marginalizing the many, is the antithesis of socio-economic development. In far too many underdeveloped countries, we have so far seen come into existence only forest industries which have negated development.

A policy of self-reliance does not mean a policy of complete self-sufficiency, of national autarchy. But it does mean aiming at a degree of self-sufficiency that will provide protection against external market fluctuations and the capacity to withstand external political pressures. It means getting the social priorities right and sticking to them.

I fear that what I have had to say to you today will have disappointed some of you and annoyed others. It would have been more in line with the tradition of congresses of this kind had I reiterated those many aspects of forest industries which make them particularly suited to promoting socio-economic development, if I had brought those arguments up-to-date, if I had then gone on to talk about the most suitable scale of operations, the most appropriate technology, the needs for training and for technology transfer, problems of location, the industry viability/environment dilemma, the need to reorient research. All these are doubtless fascinating subjects, and we could go on discussing them for hours. We do little good thereby, but equally we do little harm.

But it was impossible for me to give you that kind of address. I have been a close observer of the international forestry scene for close on three decades. For most of that time I have been particularly concerned with and about the underdeveloped world. It has become obvious to me, as it must be becoming obvious to you, that very, very few of the forest industries that have been established in the underdeveloped countries have made any contribution whatever to raising the welfare of the urban and rural masses, have in any way promoted socio-economic development. The fundamental reason is that those industries have been set up to earn a certain rate of profit, not to satisfy a range of basic popular needs.

But the choice between need-oriented industry and profit-oriented industry is neither a technical choice nor an economic choice. It is not a matter of choosing prescription A or prescription B of the development establishment. It is not a matter of opting for the Alpha school of economists or the Beta school. It is a political choice. It is a matter of who holds power in a given society, and on whose behalf that power is exercised. Once power is exercised by or on behalf of the broad popular masses, then, and then only, will the contribution of forest industries to socio-economic development start to be realized.

That is why we as foresters deceive ourselves if we think that our debates here will provide us with the key to the contribution of forestry and forest industries to socio-economic development. Whether or not that contribution will be secured will be decided elsewhere. It will be decided by the struggles which are being conducted, on every continent, by the dispossessed and hungry millions, struggles to win a fair and decent life, to break out of the power of landlords, of moneylenders, of the agents of foreign capital. The fancy packages of comprehensive, integrated, rural development which the development agencies now serve up are so much window-dressing until that power is broken.

Between now and the next World Forestry Congress thousands of foresters will have the opportunity, may have the obligation, to decide which side they are on in that struggle. Whether they stand on the side of power, landed property, the status quo. This is where, historically, most foresters stood. For centuries much of the work of foresters went into creating and protecting royal and princely estates, extinguishing every kind of common right in the forest and enforcing exclusive property. The folklore and oral tradition of many countries still make the forester the people's enemy, the gendarme of the landed proprietor.

Or whether they share the aspirations of the common people, and are prepared to work for the day when the rich and many-sided contribution of forestry is harnessed to the service of all, not to that of a privileged few.

Forests for people: that is the theme of this congress. Is it to be an empty catch-phrase? Is it to be an objective, a rallying point, a guide to action? Every forester must decide and, having decided, bear witness in word and deed.

PART III
New Directions

12

Making Trees Serve People

This is the first opportunity I have had to thank members of the Association for electing me to honorary life membership. I would like to do that now. For me, this honour is rather important. It marks a significant step in my legitimization as a forester. Some of you know that my forestry antecedents are somewhat suspect.

First, a word about the title I have chosen. The remit I received from your executive committee was, to say the least, unclear: something about world forestry, and the role international agencies could play, plus a little bit about China, since so little is known of what goes on there. Thinking over this request, I decided that perhaps the most useful thing I could do for you today would be to trace my successive preoccupations since I became involved in forestry affairs, offer a few reflections that have occurred to me, and share with you some of my misgivings.

When I first joined FAO, in 1952, I knew very little about forestry. I had already been involved the FAO, as UK delegate and as consultant, for several years. This was largely an accident, since it seemed that at that time there was no such thing in the UK as a forest products statistician. The authorities, after casting around, decided that I was the best imitation they could offer. I had already had a bit to do with forest products statistics in my routine work at the Board of Trade and in the course of several special assignments I had been asked to undertake. But though I was eventually signed on by FAO as a forest products statistician, I was much more interested in policy, and as soon as the FAO forestry statistics got on a more reasonable footing, I was able to unload the routine work and devote myself to more interesting matters.

Thus it came about that I had a major hand in the first European Timber Trends Study, which had been under way a year or more when I joined. Though heavily criticized at the time, this study is now recognized as a pioneering effort,

Address to the AGM of the Commonwealth Forestry Association, London, April 1975; first published in the *Commonwealth Forestry Review*, 54:3, 4, pp. 206–15 (1975). Published with permission of author and Commonwealth Forestry Association.

perhaps more so in North America, where forest economists abound, than here in Europe, where forest economists are still more thinly spread. Full credit for this must go to my former chief at the Food and Agriculture Organization, Egon Glesinger, without whose energy and enthusiasm the study would never have seen the light of day. The study, it must be admitted, cost much more than it need have done. This was because, in the search for suitable methodologies, many avenues were explored beyond the point where their futility should have been recognized.

I have vivid recollections of the reactions of European foresters, industrialists and timber traders when the study was first presented to a joint session of FAO's European Forestry Commission and the Timber Committee of the Economic Commission for Europe. We had great difficulty in making them understand that we were not saying: 'This is what is going to happen in 1960', but rather, 'This is what is likely to happen around 1960 if. . .', the 'if' depending on how far our specified assumptions were realized. Some of you may recall that this first study projected a growth in European paper consumption of somewhere between 43 and 65 per cent over the decade 1950 to 1960. I well remember a distinguished pulp and paper expert in the UK delegation pouring scorn on these estimates. 'I agree,' he said, 'that paper consumption may well go up, but over the decade the increase is not likely to exceed 10 per cent.' In the event, of course, our upper estimate was greatly exceeded, and in a post-mortem I conducted in the early sixties I showed that, had our assumptions about the rate at which the Euorpean economy would grow over the decade been accurate, then our pulp and paper predictions, instead of being too conservative, would have been about right. On sawnwood we were much nearer the mark, mainly because our underestimates of economic growth were just about compensated by our failure to make sufficient allowance for substitution.

The study predicted that Europe's timber situation, which was roughly in balance in 1950, would move progressively into deficit. To meet this situation, it pointed to the need for a resumption of supplies from the USSR, and a series of energetic measures in European forestry which Egon Glesinger characterized as 'a dynamic forest policy'. These measures, said the study, would enable Europe's industrial wood supply by 1960, instead of falling to 155 million cubic metres as predicated by then existing plans, to be pushed up to 194 million cubic metres. This was anathema to many of Europe's forestry stalwarts, and we came in for much castigation at their hands. In the event, they, or in some cases their successors, succeeded in raising industrial wood supply to 212 million cubic metres – nearly 20 million cubic metres more than the target the study had suggested. Incidentally, Europe's industrial roundwood production in recent years has topped 270 million cubic metres.

All this, of course, was a very salutary experience for me. It left me with a permanent suspicion of 'experts', and taught me never to trust the instincts of professional foresters, timber industrialists or traders.

As we all know, Soviet exports to Western Europe were resumed, and steadily built up over the years until they came to play, as before the war, a leading role in the European timber market. I think it was no coincidence that, soon after the publication of the European Timber Trends Study, the USSR decided to resume its active participation in the work of the Economic Commission for Europe, and selected the Timber Committee for its first technical delegation. This reinsertion of the USSR into the European timber trade took place smoothly, without any of the dislocation which so many feared. This was partly due to the shrewd and intelligent way in which the Soviet timber export agency – Exportles – operated. But I think it was also due in part to the fact that the discussion of sawn softwood market prospects which took place at the annual meetings of the ECE Timber Committee did help to avoid some of the violent oscillations which had characterized the market in pre-war decades. My own involvement in the work of the Timber Committee continued long after I left Geneva for Rome. For over a decade I presided over the drafting committee which was charged with drawing up that part of the report which dealt with the evolution of, and prospects for, the sawn softwood market. This was always a tug-of-war between the rival interests of the principal exporters and importers. The trick was to include, in the first draft, one superfluous paragraph which leaned too heavily on the side of the importers, and another which leaned too far the other way. Under pressure, I would reluctantly agree to have these in turn deleted. What was left remained cogent, balanced, and not too emasculated. Honour was satisfied on both sides, and amity reigned.

I left Geneva for Rome in 1958, to take charge of the forest economics branch. My first concern was to steer to completion regional studies of timber resources and requirements for Asia, Africa and Latin America. These, too, were pioneering efforts, since there was much less statistical straw around out of which to make policy bricks. We were fortunate in being able to persuade many of the world's leading forest economists to join us in beating our brains out on these problems. I do not think that these studies added very much to our reputation as prophets. We were too sanguine as to the growth rates that most of the underdeveloped countries might achieve, even though we sharply marked down their official aspirations. And we hopelessly underestimated the giant role which Japan would come to play in the Asian, even the world, picture. As you know, we were not alone in this. Even so, the studies were well worth doing. We broke a good deal of new ground, and we laid the foundation for a progressive improvement in the basic statistics. All of these studies were carried out on shoestring budgets as compared with the original European study. Looking back, and comparing the state of our knowledge about the world forest and timber economy today with what it was two decades ago, I am satisfied that this was money well spent.

Nowadays, it is generally accepted that, when one sets out to formulate national forestry goals and targets, one of the elements one should have in hand is a notion of probable future timber requirements. It is also generally accepted that this notion is likely to be more precise if it is arrived at on the basis of end-use analysis. Where historical data are inadequate, supporting material can be provided by making use of observed high correlations between GNP and the consumption of selected forest products, both as between countries at different stages of development, and over time in particular countries. Very many countries, both developed and underdeveloped, have now carried out such studies, some of the latter with support from FAO.

All this, today, is standard practice. Yet I must confess that latterly I have come to have serious doubts as to its validity, especially so far as the poorer countries are concerned. The weakness, it seems to me, is that these projections rest on the assumption that all countries in the early stages of development must necessarily tread the well worn path which has been beaten out by the richer countries when they, too, were at an early stage of development. I believe now that this is wrong. And when I say I believe it is wrong, I do not simply mean that it has proved an inadequate predictor.

In the late fifties and early sixties we had many heated discussions about projection methodology. We had observed, from our cross-sectional and time series analyses, that income elasticity declined as income rose, and we allowed for this in our methodology. As more and longer series became available for analysis, we noticed a residual effect, which Sweden's Sundelin christened a 'time trend'. Arne Sundelin did much of the pioneering work on pulp and paper projections, and worked closely with us during that period. Our theory at that time was that, over and above the income effect, the steady internationalization of markets made for a diffusion effect that caused low-income countries to wander in varying degrees above the trend line. But whatever the explanation, we sought to allow for this phenomenon in subsequent projection work.

But my criticism is not of projection methodology and of its validity as a predictor. It is the whole approach which, in my view, is wrong. This is not the concept from which low-income countries should start in planning their forest development. If such a country sets as its goal a specific future level of GNP per head, and assumes that this carries with it a connotation of so many kilos per head of paper and board, so many cubic metres per head of sawnwood or wood-based panels, it is setting out on the wrong foot.

My growing scepticism about this has been reinforced by reading a recent paper by Bill Duerr.[1] Duerr inveighs against confusion about forest production goal-setting, and ironically observes, in the course of his paper, that recent heroin-consumption trends, projected on population and GNP, show that every man, woman and child in the US will be a junkie by the 2020.

The proper starting point for a low-income country in planning its forest

---

[1] William A. Duerr, 'Planning an escape from our forest production-goal muddle', Virginia Polytechnic Institute and State University, May 1974.

development is, in my opinion, a twofold appraisal. First, an assessment of the existing forest resource and its capacity for providing forest products of the kind that are needed; second, an appraisal of the more urgent manifest existing needs of forest products and of those needs which are likely to arise in the future. I use the word needs advisedly. I do not mean projected, income-related consumption. I do not mean demand – that part of needs which has the economic power to express itself on the market.

I moved to Rome about the time when the earlier Expanded Technical Assistance Programme was being complemented by the newly established Special Fund of the United Nations, the two programmes being subsequently combined in the United Nations Development Programme. Like many of my colleagues, I had been disenchanted by the ineffectiveness of the old ETAP programme. At that time most development theorists, and certainly the United Nations as a whole, subscribed to what I would describe as the 'late starter' theory of development. For a number of reasons, reasons which had their roots in history (a history, however, which we are careful not to analyse too closely), many countries lagged in the development race. Why did they lag? Because they lacked technology, they lacked know-how. Given that continuing backwardness sets up severe social strains and tensions which continually threaten to erupt and cause embarrassment to the more developed parts of the world, it made sense for the developed countries to mount a coordinated effort to transfer know-how. Some felt very warm about this – after all, what more deserving charity? Others felt cool, but considered that the effort had a definite insurance value.

In the early days, the preferred form of technology transfer was the itinerant expert, the embodiment of walking know-how. Under both multilateral and bilateral programmes, a stream of experts from the developed world invaded the underdeveloped countries. Their reports gradually filled the shelves of the offices of ministers, administrators and technicians in the underdeveloped countries. Most of them have stayed there, gathering dust down the years. This was, in fact, the 'tell me' phase of technical assistance, or development by exhortation. It was not that the underdeveloped countries rejected the advice that was so freely given; they simply lacked the cadres, strength, administrative experience and institutional capacity to implement the thousands of recommendations they received. The advent of the Special Fund, which gave the possibility of financing larger and longer-term projects, seemed to provide the opportunity not only of devising recommendations more in tune with the specific stage of development reached, but also of helping to build up the administrative and institutional strength that was plainly lacking. To me and some of my colleagues, this betokened a shift from development by exhortation to development by demonstration; a shift from the 'tell me' stage to the 'show me', or better still, 'do it with me', stage. We sought eagerly to help the forest services of the low-income countries to take advantage of the new sources of development aid.

Neither we nor our friends in the forest services were lacking in ideas about what ought to be done. But few of those ideas seemed to appeal to the planning ministries or to those ministries charged with screening and setting priorities for development assistance. And of the projects which were submitted, quite a few were turned down because the funders were not wholly convinced or their developmental impact.

Searching for the reasons for this, I came to the conclusion that two stood out above all others. One was that ministers, planning authorities, development economists, and the like were woefully ignorant concerning the forestry sector, and completely unaware of the potential which forests and industrial development based on the forests had for contributing to overall economic development. The other was that foresters, by and large, had difficulty in talking the kind of language which by then had become *de rigueur* in development circles. The time therefore seemed opportune for a reasoned analysis of the specific characteristics of the forestry sector and of its relationship with other sectors of the economy. This study, which appeared in 1962, was destined to have a much greater influence than I and my colleagues envisaged when we embarked on it. Projects for development assistance in forestry and forest industries were more carefully prepared, better documented, more cogently argued, got a better hearing, both within governments and at the funding sources, and were more more frequently approved. We, and the forest services, were in business. In fact, we were in too much business, and at times subject to considerable strain. As forestry's share in FAO's regular programme steadily shrunk, its share in development assistance projects steadily rose. There were two other reasons for this. One was that our global analyses of the world forest and timber economy had shown that the developed world was going to have increasing need of the wood resources of the underdeveloped world, and this provided an additional incentive for supporting forestry projects. The other was that, measured by conventional criteria, forestry projects began to show a higher success ratio than projects in the agricultural field. This is not surprising. A high proportion of agricultural development projects, if they are to have any development impact at all, require a profound modification of existing agrarian structures. In most underdeveloped countries, however, the vested interests which stand in the way of a real agrarian reform are still sufficiently powerful to frustrate any tentative steps in this direction.

However, this study gave a sense of direction to FAO's work in forestry, and did much to shape its programme in the following years. It led to a new emphasis on training in forest development planning, and to the production of appropriate manuals to support this work. It also, I believe, had an influence on some of the bilateral development assistance programmes in forestry.

Today, when a forester talks about development, and forestry's contribution thereto, he is more often listened to. And in most underdeveloped countries there is now at least a small nucleus of officers who can talk the language of the planners and the economic ministries. Some of these officers are now assuming leadership positions.

More capital has found its way into the forestry sector in underdeveloped countries. Pre-investment studies have been followed by industrial feasibility studies, and some of these have led to investment. Foreign private capital has played an important role, and its path has often been smoothed by the international financing agencies. The World Bank has even, on occasion, supported afforestation schemes. Its first ventures were hailed as a breakthrough, but these have remained isolated, confined to schemes linked to specific industrial ventures. The Bank has shown no disposition yet to loan funds for what might loosely be termed social forestry.

Looking back over two decades of international aid in forestry, can we be satisfied with what has been achieved? So far as that part of aid which consists of technical assistance services is concerned, I would point out that forestry is one of the few sectors where the multilateral element has played a major role. In most other sectors, the multilateral fraction represents but a small part, though not necessarily an unimportant part, of the total effort. Have these efforts, multilateral and bilateral, had any genuine and lasting impact?

At first sight, there would seem to be considerable grounds for satisfaction. The number of trained foresters in the underdeveloped world has probably multiplied more than tenfold. There is hardly a single underdeveloped country which does not today have at least the nucleus of a forest service. Many now have their own institutions for the preparation of professional and technical staff. Many – perhaps even a majority – have their own research institutions. Most have a forest law, of sorts, and some even have a forest policy. All this presents a very different picture from that which obtained twenty or twenty-five years ago.

These countries today know very much more about their forest resources: location, extent, composition. The area of natural forest brought into use, subject to commercial exploitation, has greatly extended. This is in spite of the fact that understanding of how best to manage the tropical forest has made but little advance.

Many countries have recognized the need to supplement, complement and sometimes replace, their natural forest endowment by creating man-made forests. Knowledge of the species and techniques most appropriate under widely differing circumstances has been widened and deepened.

The flow of timber from underdeveloped countries with tropical forest resources has expanded enormously, to meet the growing needs of the affluent, industrialized countries. Though most of this expanded flow takes place in unprocessed log form, there has been a significant development of wood-based industries. Yet it has to be noted that a large proportion of the exports of processed tropical woods has come, not from industries located close to the resource, but from in-transit processors.

These are some of the principal changes which have come about, and they are familiar to you all. If this were a scientific paper, and not just an anecdotal reminiscence, I would quantify them for you.

The question is: Do these changes spell progress? Have they contributed to development? If we peer below the surface, we find a picture that is much less pleasing.

It can be argued, and not unfairly, that international aid in forestry has done a useful job in identifying for foreign capital those forest resources suitable for exploitation. In many cases, it has borne a substantial part of the cost of making inventories of those resources. In not a few cases it has compiled the data, and helped provide the justification, for international financing agencies to provide loans to create some of the infrastructure needed to assist the penetration of foreign capital. It has helped to train some of the manpower to be placed at the service of foreign enterprises, enabling them to economize on the use of expensive expatriate personnel. *De facto*, though this was not its intent, at least so far as the multilateral and some of the bilateral effort was concerned, it has assisted some irresponsible governments to alienate substantial parts of their forest resource endowment.

Over the last two decades, massive tracts of virgin tropical forest have come under exploitation, in all three underdeveloped regions. That exploitation, with a few honourable exceptions, has been reckless, wasteful, even devastating. Nearly all the operations have been enclavistic, that is to say, they have had no profound or durable impact on the economic and social life of the countries where they have taken place. Of the revenue which has accrued, a small part has remained in the countries to which the resource belonged. Of that fraction, a not insubstantial sum has gone to line the pockets of those empowered to secure or negotiate concessions. A little has also gone to supplement the salaries and wages of underpaid foresters and forest workers charged with the task of controlling concessions. Of the revenues which have found their way into the public purse, an inconsiderable fraction has been ploughed back into maintaining, improving or replacing the forest resource. There are indeed countries where professional foresters, thinking back to the forestry ethic they imbibed during their training, see it as a hollow mockery, since circumstances have compelled them to serve unwillingly as accessories in the rape of their national forest resource.

All this is still going on, and even though the concessions being signed or renegotiated today are better in many respects than the earlier concessions, the will and the power to enforce their terms is advancing only slowly.

Of the industrial development that has taken place, much is export-oriented. Local needs are not being met; the employment opportunities created are trifling. The secondary and tertiary activities which a primary industry ought to generate are largely absent. A significant part of exports, as logs and as primary processed timber, is exported 'within the firm', and transfer values are fixed to facilitate the accumulation of profits outside the country. There are countless ways of doing this, which I do not need to enumerate.

These are some of the things that are happening.

What about the things that should have happened but have not?

I have already mentioned the poor development of domestic-oriented industrialization, with few jobs created, multiplier effects not realized, and consequent minimal impact on the overall growth process.

What about the lot of the common man, of the peasant, for example? Has forestry done anything to improve it? Precious little. Where are all the village woodlots? Where are the rural plantations to supply constructional and farm timber? In how many countries are the peasants being encouraged and helped to improve their own lot through cooperative effort, integrating forestry activities in the farming calendar?

What about the marginal lands – in the Middle East, in North and parts of Central Africa, in some areas of Asia and Latin America – areas where forestry could make a significant contribution to halting the march of the desert and starting the long, slow process of land rehabilitation? We know that this is not a job for the forester alone, but we also know that his share in a mutli-disciplinary effort could be decisive. What progress here? A few pilot and demonstration projects, some of dubious value, but no programme to speak of. We know, of course, some of the difficulties. The governments of these countries have already enough problems to grapple with. Most of these problems touch closely the life of the people at the other end of their countries, in the more populated zones where governments must look for political support. The thinly spread and scattered people pushed to the margin have but little political pull, and remain forgotten until the stink of corpses left in the trail of famine leaks outside.

What about the millions of hectares of bare, eroded hills, inflicting downstream farmland with alternating flood and drought? Foresters in all three continents are aware of the problem, and many are gallantly striving to do something about it. With skimped resources, they manage to plant 10, 20, 100 hectares a year – a drop in the ocean. When will social cost/benefit analysis persuade the hard-headed financing agencies that here is something which really does touch the life of the people?

I could go on adding to the catalogue, but there seems little point.

If we look back over two decades of effort in the forestry sector in the underdeveloped countries, then we must admit, if we are honest with ourselves, that although there has been some growth, it has been much less than we had hoped; the contribution to the overall development process has been very small indeed; and the contribution of forestry towards improving the lot of the common people has been negligible so far.

It is a black and discouraging picture.

Is it one that should make us despair?

There are many, of course, who do despair. There has been, in recent years, a rapid spread of disenchantment: among governments, institutions and public opinion in the aid-giving countries; within the so-called developing countries themselves; and not least among those directly concerned with the international development assistance effort, whether in multilateral or bilateral programmes. Among these last, there are few who have not seen some of the projects they helped to conceive and implement hopelessly misfire. Nearly two decades ago, I expressed the view that the art of working in international development assistance was to shed one's illusions while keeping one's faith intact. This aphorism seemed to strike a chord, for I have often had it quoted back at me since. But it was a naïve judgement. I little knew at that time how many illusions I still had to shed.

Perhaps the most encouraging contemporary phenomenon is the acceleration of the process of illusion-shedding. One of the most crippling illusions – what I have called the 'late starter' theory of development – is now dying fast. It is not yet dead and buried. It still imbues much of the international development assistance effort. It is still the underlying philosophy of the World Bank, as Paul Streeten points out in the recent issue of *Ceres*, where he reviews *One Hundred Countries*, a collection of addresses delivered in recent years by McNamara of the World Bank.[2] Streeten draws attention to the disparity between the radical words used on occasion by the Bank's president, and the far from radical, indeed anti-radical, deeds perpetuated at the loan desks.

The fact is that the poor countries are poor not because they started late in the development race; not because their resource endowments are inadequate; not because they are overpopulated. The poor countries are poor because the rich countries are rich. We live in a highly integrated world economy, characterized by uneven and at times fitful development. Such are the ties and dependencies between the affluent industrialized countries and the peripheral low-income countries that growth, where it has occurred in the underdeveloped world, has been limited and largely externally oriented. Some growth there has been, since we have elected to define growth as a rise in per caput GNP. But rarely has that growth spelled development. The beneficiaries, as Streeten observes, have been few: entrepreneurs, salaried officials, large landowners. The lot of the many has seldom improved and has often deteriorated. The objective impact of much of the international assistance effort, be it loans, grants or technical services, has been to promote further distortion, to enhance economic dependence, to widen inequalities, to increase vulnerability, and to frustrate or inhibit development in any true sense.

Those who have been concerned about development assistance are gradually coming to appreciate this, as they reflect on the consequence of the past two decades. What is more important, one by one the underdeveloped countries themselves are beginning to understand it. It is true that as yet few have drawn the right conclusions, but that is only a matter of time.

[2] 8 (1): 56–58, 1975.

One consequence of this dawning realization is the new-found militancy and sense of unity among the underdeveloped countries. The pace of this evolution is quite staggering when one thinks back to the frustrations of the seventies at the early UNCTAD conferences. It is worth studying the conclusions and recommendations of the UN conference on the Human Environment, the World Population Conference and the World Food Conference – major conferences held within the last few years – to see how quickly emphasis has shifted.

Now it is true that the representatives of quite a number of underdeveloped countries, when they sign their name to formulations which directly or indirectly condemn imperialism and neo-colonialism, do so with their tongues in their cheeks. They are aware that wealth contrasts *within* their countries are no less startling than international wealth contrasts, and they have no intention of adopting internal policies that will eat into their own privileges and standards. For them it is convenient if their own poor can be persuaded that their poverty is attributable to the rapacity of neo-colonialists. Nevertheless, there are a number of governments in the underdeveloped world which are genuinely concerned about inequalities in their own countries, and which are striving to do something about it. These are the countries which are beginning to draw the correct lessons from the failures of the last two decades. The number of such countries will certainly increase in the coming decade.

The key word in their development vocabulary is 'self-reliance'. It is a word which is destined to feature ever more prominently as the significance of the Chinese experience is fully grasped. For these countries, foreign aid, of all types, and foreign investment, notably in export-oriented extractive and processing industries, will be increasingly subordinated to truly national development policies which aim at reducing present inequalities, at mobilizing cooperative effort to overcome the food problem, and at adapting the pace of industrialization to the progress achieved in agriculture.

How will such countries look upon the development of their forestry sector?

First and foremost, they will take a hard look at their forest resources, and will closely scrutinize present and possible future forestry activities, from the standpoint of how best they can protect, support, promote and diversify the agricultural economy. It is to this aspect that they will give pride of place in their forestry planning and in the forestry goals they establish. They will bear firmly in mind that the purpose of trees is to serve people. They will understand that the scale, as well as the nature, of the forestry effort needed in their countries is often such that no central exchequer can finance and that no organized forest service can execute. They will therefore test out all forms of people involvement and people participation that are adapted to their own customs and traditions and to the degree of evolving social and political consciousness. They may rely on individual incentives, but it is more likely that they will lay stress of cooperative and communal endeavour, since it is becoming increasingly evident that the only way forward for agriculture in most underdeveloped countries lies

through the promotion of mutual aid and cooperation. This therefore is the logical way to integrate agriculture and forestry.

Their second forestry priority will be the use of the existing resource base, and the creation, where necessary, of new industrial wood resources, for industrialization directed towards the satisfaction of urgent domestic needs. In deciding upon the location, scale and type of wood-processing plants, financial profitability criteria will take second place to the satisfaction of popular needs and the promotion of rising welfare. Because in underdeveloped countries a substantial proportion of needs for processed wood arises in the public sector or can be decisively influenced by public policies, governments are in a strong position to pursue policies which can assure the viability of the domestic-oriented industries they bring into existence.

If their forest resources are sufficiently rich to offer them the opportunity of expanding or creating export-oriented forestry activities, they will not neglect these opportunities, but the pace and scale of development in this direction will be subordinated to the first two priorities I have indicated. Moreover, they will digest and apply the lessons of the past two decades of bitter experience. They will not be dazzled by the prospect of quick and easy export earnings. They will not succumb to the blandishments (and bribes) of would-be concessionaires and eager private foreign capital. They will be careful not to alienate their resource heritage. They will temper the pace of such developments to their own rising capacity to supervise and control them. They will reject programmes and projects which introduce serious distortions and put their own national objectives in jeopardy.

The question arises: in such countries, countries pursuing a self-reliant development policy, mobilizing the energies of their own people – and there will be more such countries as the years go by – is there any role for international development assistance? I believe it will still have a role. But the agencies will have to rid themselves of the prejudices and paternalism which have characterized some of their activities in the past. They have to show by their actions, not merely acknowledge in words, that the social, economic and political objectives which frame the development policies pursued by the underdeveloped countries are matters for those countries alone to decide. They have to root out their prejudices in favour of private enterprise and their mistrust of public enterprise. In reviewing requests for development assistance, they should insist on putting the question: how will this programme or project touch the lives of the common people, particularly the peasant? They have to discard the notion that institutions, structures and procedures which appear to have served satisfactorily in the West are necessarily appropriate in underdeveloped countries. In selecting staff to administer or share in implementing development assistance programmes, they will choose men and women capable of recognizing and sharing the aspirations of the underdeveloped countries. Without that bond of understanding, age, experience and academic qualifications count for nothing.

There are such people to be found, and I believe it is easier to find them among the new generations of foresters than among those of my generation.

Thus, in spite of the unsatisfactory record of the past, I see many reasons for hope, none for despair.

My conviction that it is possible for an underdeveloped country, by pursuing a path of national independence and self-reliance, staking its future on mobilizing the collective energies of its own people, to register significant advances has been confirmed by what I have seen in China (see chapter 13). What is striking, and what ought to appeal to members of this Association, is that in China forestry has become everybody's business, not the business of the forester alone. For those who believe, as I do, that trees are to serve people, a visit to China today is a very satisfying and encouraging experience.

Most of my efforts over the last two decades have been devoted to helping the underdeveloped countries to realize the potential which their forests represent for contributing to rising welfare. I have made it plain that I am far from satisfied with what I and my colleagues in the multilateral development assistance effort in forestry have been able to achieve so far. I have also made it plain, I hope, that, far from despairing, I am very optimistic.

My optimism rests on the fact that increasingly the underdeveloped countries are coming to understand the true reasons for their backwardness, and one by one are embarking on policies which put the interests of their own people first, and which seek to ensure the involvement and participation of their own people in the development effort. This is particularly important for the forestry sector, since the gigantic tasks which face many of these countries in the forestry sector – taken in its widest sense – can only be carried out if the energies of the people are mobilized. These tasks are of a magnitude which lies beyond the capacity of organized forest services. They call for resources which it is beyond the power of a dozen World Banks to provide.

My optimism is strengthened by the fact that the Chinese have shown that this can be done. This does not mean that all the underdeveloped countries will or should follow the Chinese road. Indeed, the Chinese themselves wave away any suggestion that their model is transferable. Each country has to find its own way, building on its own traditions and experience. But certain ingredients of the Chinese experience they will borrow, adapt, and make their own. This is why I am confident that a balance sheet of the world forestry situation drawn up twenty years hence will show many more positive features than any we can draw up today.

13
'Making Green the Motherland': Forestry in China

China is engaged on the mightiest afforestation effort the world has ever seen. There has been nothing like it before, anywhere, and its like will not be seen again, because no other country will ever face a forestry problem of the magnitude which China faced on Liberation. There are many other countries in dire need of an intense afforestation effort. But their problems, though acute, cannot be measured on the same scale as those China faced.

Deforestation had been going on in China through at least four millennia. There is evidence to show that at one time most of China had tree cover. A great forest belt extended from central and south-eastern coastal China all the way up to the Kinghan mountains in the north-east, while much of the mountainous interior was also forested. When, in later neolithic times, some of the hunters and gatherers of the north China plain started to practise agriculture, there must have been considerable areas of forest and woodland in this predominantly grassland region. Rainfall dictated the differentiation between the sown and the steppe, the settled farmer and the nomadic pastoralist. It was here that Chinese civilization was born, and from here that it spread. It was here, too, that forest clearance started, first for hunting, later for farming. The likelihood is that the north China plain was already virtually treeless by the establishment of the Han dynasties. In the course of the five centuries that preceded the unification of China under Ch'in Shih Hwang Ti – a period that encompassed the transition from slave to feudal society – the destruction of the forests of the Yellow River basin was completed.

With the Han dynasties – the four centuries straddling the birth of Christ – started the push south: to the warmer, wetter, heavily forested lands of the Yangtze basin and beyond, lands occupied sparsely by diverse indigenous

Reprinted with permission from Neville Maxwell, (ed) *The Chinese Road to Development*, © 1975, Pergamon Books Ltd.

non-Han peoples, practising hunting, fishing and slash-and-burn agriculture. In the ensuing centuries the clearance of forest for farming accelerated. Such islands of forest as were left by the farmers' advance – for example, on hills to steep to terrace and till – suffered progressive degradation down the centuries as they were razed for timber and firewood.

It is true all over the world, of course, that the forests today stand on land that the farmer cannot use, does not want, or has not yet claimed. But in few countries has the farmer's appetite for forest land been as voracious and as sustained as it has been in China. One consequence is that the only substantial areas of natural forest left in China lie in the inhospitable north-east provinces and in the mountainous areas, difficult of access, of the south and south-west. Vestiges of the original natural forest survive elsewhere, but they have been badly depleted down the years – small temple forests, left intact, bear eloquent witness to the former rich forest cover. By 1949, the forests had dwindled to only five per cent of China's total land area. Another consequence of deforestation has been soil erosion by wind and water on a gigantic scale, with floods of disastrous proportions an almost annual occurrence for centuries past. And a third consequence has been a chronic shortage of both industrial timber and fuelwood over most of China, with timber consumption levels close to the world's lowest.

In 1949 this inherited forestry situation had been exasperated by over a decade of reckless forest depletion under the Japanese occupation and by the damage and dislocation of civil war. As Chinese resistance to Japan mounted, the Japanese army sought to crush guerilla activity and support for guerrillas by applying the policy of 'kill all, burn all, loot all', and sizeable areas of forest suffered in consequence. China's richest forest resource, that in the north-east, had in fact been ruthlessly creamed since the beginning of the century – Japanese concessionaires were operating there long before the formal annexation of Manchuria by Japan in 1931.

Thus the government and people of China in 1949 confronted a whole range of forestry problems of the utmost gravity. Any hope of long-term economic development was dependent upon their solution.

The Chinese Communist Party had long been aware of at least some of these problems. Indeed, afforestation efforts were undertaken well before 1949 in the 'liberated areas'. An example is the mass movement to realize the Programme of Ten Small Points in every community of the border region in 1944. This urged each family to dig one well; to plant so many trees; to keep more pigs; and to build one new latrine: each administrative village unit was to have a 'mutual aid granary', a producers' and consumers' cooperative, one midwife, a blacksmith's shop a school run by the people, and a folk-dance group. Gunther Stein reported sitting in on a representative meeting in Greater Yenan in 1944 at which an official concerned with a tree-planting movement was criticized for his bureaucratic attitude.[1]

---

[1] Gunther Stein, *The Challenge of Red China* (New York, 1945).

Article 34 of the Common Programme of the Chinese People's Political Consultative Assembly, the first and most important document of the new government, laid down that 'Forests shall be protected, and afforestation shall be developed according to plan'. Responsibility for developing this programme rested with the Ministry of Forestry and Land Reclamation.

Thus, immediately on Liberation both government and Party threw themselves into a campaign to mobilize mass participation in tree-planting activities. The first decade of the People's Republic saw the basic social transformation of the Chinese countryside: from mutual aid teams, through elementary and advanced producers' cooperatives, to the establishment of people's communes in 1958/9. This decade also saw the first decisive steps towards 'making green the motherland'. But even though early visitors to the new China had reported on the scale and ubiquity of tree-planting efforts, the claims as to the extent of the areas newly afforested which began to be advanced were such as to strain the credulity of most foreign commentators. Scepticism mounted as successive press released provided figures which were clearly inconsistent with those which had been released earlier. These inconsistencies, allied to the fact that all the claims were of a magnitude to seem megalomaniac to Western minds, caused some commentators to dismiss the claims altogether. In this they were wrong. Perhaps if they had been aware of some of the pitfalls inherent in forestry statistics they might have had some sympathy with those Chinese foresters in Peking who over the years sought to draw up a realistic balance sheet of what had actually been achieved.

Hu Ku-yueh, writing in *Peking Review* in the spring of 1958,[2] endeavoured to sum up the achievements of the first Five Year plan, 1953–7, even though final figures for 1957 were not available to him. He reported that in that period China had afforested an area greater than all the forests of Britain, Belgium, the Netherlands, Greece and Italy combined, and presented the figures given in table 12.1.

Table 12.1   Area afforested in China 1953–7

Type of forest	Million hectares
Forests for timber	5.16
Forests of industrial crop-yielding trees[a]	2.16
Shelter-belts	1.47
Forests for water and soil conservation	1.40
Miscellaneous forests[b]	1.10
Total	11.29

[a] E.g. tung oil, tea oil, camphor, rubber, palm, coconut, coffee.
[b] E.g. fuelwood, wood for charcoal.

[2] Hu Ku-yueh, 'Turning the whole country green', *Peking Review*, 1: 8 (22 April 1958).

If the figures were anywhere near correct, it would mean that roughly a hundred trees had been planted during the quinquennium for every Chinese.

What are some of the pitfalls concerning afforestation statistics?

When an area of forest is felled, one may rely on nature to restock and bring forth the second crop, or one may resort to planting the felled area with saplings – natural or artificial regeneration. But in neither case, strictly speaking, should this be called afforestation, since there is no net addition to the forested area. Also, within an area of land classified as forest, there may be bare patches. These may be planted up so as to give adequate tree cover – again, such plantings do not represent a net addition to the forested area. The fact is that the world's leading forestry statisticians have over the last decades spent a good deal of time trying to hammer out satisfactory definitions of afforestation, reforestation, and so forth and even though there are now some internationally agreed definitions, there are as yet few national forestry administrations which have succeeded in consistently conforming to those definitions.[3]

There is another pitfall. In the early years in Communist China tree-planting targets were often set, and achievements reported, particularly at the local level, in terms of the number of trees planted rather than the area covered. How to convert to area? A million trees planted at a 2-metre by 2-metre spacing represent 400 hectares, while planted at 1 metre by 1 metre they represent only 100 hectares. Spacing in fact varied with location and according to species. It also changed with time, since the Chinese found that in many of the early plantations the spacing had been too close. But somebody had to make guesses about conversion factors, as reported planting performances were aggregated at successive levels. Now China started out with very little in the way of professional forestry expertise. Her small corps of professional foresters included few forest economists and statisticians. And in any case the new authorities concentrated most of such forestry expertise as was available in the traditional forestry zones, in particular the north-east, seeking quickly to re-establish the flow of timber so sorely needed for China's reconstruction programme.

A good deal of the planting in those early years was carried out by workers, peasants, students and men and women of the People's Liberation Army who had been mobilized to help in state planting schemes. But even then a substantial proportion of the planting was carried out by the peasants in the cooperatives on their own land. In either case, professional and technical guidance was often minimal, with consequences that are discussed below. In these circumstances, there is small wonder that, even if the plan-fulfilment reports coming from below were accurate as to number of trees planted, the areas reported may often have become successively inflated, and certainly substantial areas were classified as having been afforested when in fact they had simply been reforested. Thus one

---

[3] It is illuminating to study Appendix I of the report of the first World Symposium on Man-Made Forests, in *Unasylva*, 21 (3–4): 86–7 (1967).

can justly have reservations about the areas claimed to have been afforested without in any way disparaging the magnitude of the tree-planting effort. In fact the Chinese did not know then – and probably do not know even now with any great accuracy – the total area of forest they possessed. A rapid reconnaissance survey was carried out with the aid of Soviet specialists in 1954. This could have given only a rough indication of forest area, with little or no detail concerning composition, quality and accessibility. It did, however, reveal somewhat larger reserves than had been suspected. This is no doubt why Hu Ku-yueh, in the article quoted above, spoke of the call to raise the forest area from 10 to 20 per cent of the land surface within the ensuing ten years, that is, from the then 100 million hectares to 200 million hectares.[4]

However, quite apart from the pitfalls of forest statistics, it appears that with the launching of the Great Leap Forward, afforestation reporting, like reporting in so many branches of the Chinese economy, entered into the numbers game. Li Fang, writing in *Peking Review* in May 1959, reported that 27 million hectares had been afforested in 1958, and that 1959 plantings were running considerably ahead of the 1958 rate.

The aftermath of the Great Leap was a period of sober reflection in forestry as in other sectors. Chinese foresters had much more to worry about than the validity of the afforestation statistics. The quality of the afforestation effort was disappointing – in many instances survival rates in the new plantations were abysmally low. This was tacitly conceded by Li Fang in *Peking Review* in July 1961:[5]

Summing up past experience and particularly that gained in the past few years, six basic measures have been popularized by forestry experts to get the best results in afforestation. These call for (1) selection of the most suitable variety of trees for the location in question; (2) meticulous cultivation; (3) the use of good strains of seeds and hardy saplings; (4) rational close planting; (5) the adoption of the best methods of tree care and forest protection; and (6) the reform and improvement of tools and machines used in afforestation.

Li Fang went on to claim that 'it is thanks to these measures that some 85 per cent of the saplings planted in recent years have survived and thrive' – a claim which, however, time was to prove premature.

Throughout the 1950s and even into the early 1960s much of the afforestation effort was misdirected, and there were many failures. S. D. Richardson, an experienced professional and an extremely acute observer who travelled widely

---

[4] The figure usually accepted for the forested area at the time of Liberation is 5 per cent of the land area, or 48 million ha. With claimed afforestation up to and including 1958 of about 40 million ha, plus some additional reserves revealed by the 1954 air reconnaissance inventory, this would make up for the new base figure of 100 million ha.

[5] Li Fang, 'State forest plantations', *Peking Review*, 14: 30 (28 July 1961).

in China in 1963, noted that planting had indeed been carried out on an enormous scale, but pointed out that a good deal of planting had taken place in unsuitable habitats and that, even where conditions were more favourable, survival rates were often low.[6]

In general, the success rate of those early plantings was very much higher in those areas which already had a strong forestry tradition. In these traditional forestry areas afforestation posed fewer technical problems, since there was already a good store of knowledge about what species were suitable, how to organize seed collection and nurseries, and what planting techniques were appropriate. Elsewhere, expertize was very thinly spread. But a high proportion of the new planting, then as now, was undertaken outside the traditional forestry areas, on a wide range of difficult sites, often on locations that had not seen trees for centuries past. This meant a whole variety of new problems, with little technical experience to go on.

The technical reasons for the early failures are, in retrospect, fairly obvious, and Chinese foresters and forest workers today discuss these frankly: seeds of poor quality; species chosen that were ill adapted to the particular site conditions; shortcomings in nursery practice; badly organized transfer from nursery to planting site; poor planting techniques; failure to recognize and counter pest invasions, and so on. But most important of all, perhaps, was that all emphasis was placed on getting trees into the ground, while the subsequent tending necessary to ensure their survival was neglected. In the course of the 1960s, and particularly after the Cultural Revolution, most of these errors were corrected. Forest workers met in many areas of China today affirm: 'We learned our lesson the hard way. Now 30 per cent of our effort goes into planting, 70 per cent into tending.'

This is why professional foresters who have visited China in recent years tell a very different story from that of Richardson in 1963. Areas which were badly stocked have been replanted and survival rates in both the replanted areas and in new plantings are everywhere satisfactory. New planting continues at a prodigious rate. Travelling through China now, one frequently comes across hills carpeted with green and new plantations with a uniformly high 'take', established within the last decade or so. Projecting above the green carpet will be isolated stems or clumps of trees, the survivors of earlier plantings. Similarly, many rail- and roadside plantings display two distinct generations, the casualties of an earlier campaign having been made good in recent years.

An example will serve to illustrate some of the difficulties encountered in the early afforestation efforts. In 1952, following Peking's decision that year to create shelter-belts and start afforestation in the western parts of north-east China and the south of Inner Mongolia, a dune fixation and shelter-belt experimental station was set up in Chang Wu county, Liaoning province, in

[6] S. D. Richardson, *Forestry in Communist China* (Baltimore, 1966).

what has now become Chang Ku Tai people's commune. The station started out with one trained engineer, five young learners, and seven local workers. It was situated in lands which three generations before had been rich pastures. But from the turn of the century land-hungry peasants, moving up from the south, had started to plough. The thin, poor soils, exposed to wind erosion, yielded only one crop, and the peasants had had to move on. At the same time, over-grazing reduced ground vegetation, and the invasion of the sands accelerated. One village, three times within living memory, had had to move and rebuild itself as successive sites were engulfed by drifting sands.

The small team which arrived in 1952 had little to go on: no experience of dune fixation, no equipment, and no literature. The only member with professional training, the forester, knew much about nursery techniques but nothing about sand dunes. In these parts the sand starts to drift when the wind speed exceeds five metres per second, which occurs 240 times a year on average. It took several years of trial and error before appropriate techniques were devised. It was found that four kinds of local shrub, planted part way up the dunes to windward and leeward, would fix the sands, permitting subsequent tree-planting.[7]

By 1974, when the writer visited this area, the moving sands had been replaced by forest, the earliest plantings having reached an average height of eight metres. There were bare patches here and there within the forest, but it was firmly established and there was already ample natural regeneration. The desert had been halted once and for all. Behind the defensive forest belt, agricultural land, much of it reclaimed, was criss-crossed by a network of shelter-belts,[8] countering wind erosion, building up soil quality, and permitting con-tinuous cultivation with steadily increasing yields.

The station's efforts are concentrated now on helping neighbouring communes to apply its findings. It has established a seed orchard to provide improved seed for its tree nursery, which now delivers over four million saplings a year. This station also experimented with fruit trees – never seen in this area before – and, after trying out eighty-nine varieties, now has an orchard where three hundred vines, two hundred pear and five hundred apple trees are thriving. With the help of the station staff, most of the nearby communes have established their own orchards. The station staff has increased to forty-two, of whom 19 are technicians.

The Chang Ku Tai example illustrates the essentially bootstrap nature of much of China's early afforestation effort, undertaken with a bare minimum of expertise and little or no relevant experience. It also points to the intimacy of the relationship between forestry and agriculture – an intimacy without

---

[7] The four shrubs are: *Artemisia halodendron*, *Caragana microphylla*, *Lespedeza bicolor*, and *Salix flavida*. Thirty-four species were experimented with, the station eventually fixing on *Pinus sylvestris* var. *mongolica* and *Pinus tabulaeformis*.

[8] Each consisting of 7 rows of *Populus simonii* with 4 rows of shrubs on the windward side.

parallel elsewhere in the world – and the very catholic interpretation in China of the responsibilities of the forester – again without parallel elsewhere.

The years 1960 and 1961 brought about an agonizing reappraisal of all forestry activities. This was not simply the consequence of evident shortcomings in afforestation work – the recall of the Soviet experts in 1959 caused the Chinese to call in question some of the advice they had been receiving and acting upon. Doubts and reservations which Chinese foresters had held for some time came into the open and were freely discussed.

Chinese foresters in the north-east acknowledge gratefully the help received from the Soviet Union in the first years after Liberation. Without Soviet experts and Soviet equipment it would have taken very much longer to get the essential supplies of timber flowing again. But Russian forests are very different from the forests of Heilungkiang, and Soviet equipment and Soviet methods were not always the most appropriate for Chinese conditions. Thus the Russian KT 12 wood-burning tractors could not operate on slopes greater than 12 degrees – in Russia they did not need to – and consequently were liable to overturn in the Kinghan mountains. Most of the Soviet experts came from logging enterprises, at that time quite separate in the USSR from forest management authorities,[9] and their customary aim was to extract the maximum quantities of commercial-sized logs as economically as possible, making use of clear-felling and relying on natural regeneration. But China is not a forest-rich country like the Soviet Union, and there timber wastage cannot be countenanced. Every cubic metre counts. Moreover, it was becoming clear that natural regeneration could not be relied upon to restock clear-felled areas.

The essence of Chinese forestry rethinking was expressed in a seven-thousand-word article which appeared in *Red Flag* at the beginning of December 1961, over the signature of Chin Hsueh.[10] This article surveyed the whole forestry field and was a masterpiece of reasoned argument, cogent thinking, and wise analysis of past experience. Without dwelling excessively on past errors, it set forth a whole array of valid guidelines for the future. It emphasized such matters as prompt regeneration of all forests exploited, with recourse to artificial regeneration where necessary; closer combination of agriculture and forestry; better technical support for the forestry efforts of the communes; greater emphasis on fast-growing species; attention to the great potential of the secondary forests; more effective extraction of small-dimensioned timber; timber price differentials to encourage rational use of large dimensions and better qualities; raising the degree of mechanization; revised labour quotas to encourage waste elimination; revised measures for providing fuelwood needs, thereby releasing greater quantities of timber for industrial use; and so on.

[9] A separation which was subsequently to generate a good deal of controversy in Russian forestry journals.

[10] Chin Hsueh, 'Energetically develop the work of forest regeneration; make rational use of the forest resources', *Hung-ch'i* (*Red Flag*), 23 (1 December 1961).

This article – which was evidently the fruit of long discussions to which many had contributed – marked a turning point in the Chinese forestry effort; henceforth there would be a greater attention to quality as against quantity. It foreshadowed the basic regulations for the protection of forests promulgated by the state council on 27 May 1963, the seven chapters and forty-three articles of which still govern forestry activities in China, the amendments since incorporated having simply registered certain institutional changes which have taken place since then.[11]

An article of this kind in a journal like *Red Flag* is no ephemeral magazine article. At once a text and an action programme, it is matter for unremitting study and vigorous discussion by party cadres and forest workers at all levels. The nationwide discussion this article evoked steadily began to show results in practice,. and the shifts in emphasis in forestry were greatly helped by the changes brought about by the Cultural Revolution.

Two of the general effects of the Cultural Revolution were a systematic devolution of responsibilities from state to province, province to county, county to district, and so on, and the emergence of new organs of management (revolutionary committees) at every level. In forestry, the Academy of Forest Science was relocated from Peking to Harbin, capital of Heilungkiang, China's foremost forestry province. Two forest research institutes were also moved from Peking – one to Nanking, the other to Ichun in Heilungkiang. The well known Peking Forestry College was moved, lock, stock and barrel, to Tunnan province.

Alongside those shifts went a severe thinning of the ranks of administrators, scientists and technicians at the centre and at provincial levels, and their redistribution to counties and districts. Every administrator, scientist and technician is now obliged to spend at least one fourth of his time each year working 'on the production front', engaging in practical forestry tasks in the districts, in the communes, on forest farms. In addition, most have attended the May 7th Cadre Schools, where political education is combined with manual work.

Forestry education, like all other higher education, was radically transformed in the course of the Cultural Revolution.[12] Courses were shortened, from five to three and a half years; curricula were overhauled, with greater emphasis being given to topics of more direct relevance to the problems faced in the communes; more time was accorded to practical work, mostly undertaken in cooperation with the communes; staff rotated between teaching duties, direct

---

[11] Reference to the 'people's councils' of provinces, autonomous regions and municipalities, and to the 'management committees' of people's communes, have been replaced by references to 'revolutionary committees' at these several levels, while the reference to the Ministry of Forestry has been replaced by reference to the Ministry of Agriculture and Forests, within which the Ministry of Forests has now been absorbed.

[12] Changes more fully described in Jack C. Westoby, 'How the Chinese learn about forestry', *American Forests*, 81 (6): 8–11, 42–3, (June 1975).

on-the-spot advice to the communes, and research. Most importantly, the new generations of students, who began to take their places in the field in 1972, have already had two to three years' production experience (since all middle school graduates must work 'on the production front' – at the factory bench, on the farm or in the forest – before proceeding to tertiary education) and have each been nominated for admission by their fellow-workers, whose nomination will have taken into account the candidate's political consciousness and attitude to work, as well as his or her academic attainments. It follows that the new forestry students are older, more mature, and more highly motivated than their predecessors.

One aspect of Chinese forestry that is often not appreciated outside China is that nine tenths of the forestry effort comes, not from the state sector – that is, from the forests, forest farms, and so on, managed by the county and district forestry bureaux – but from the collective sector, from the people's communes. This goes some way towards explaining the tremendous impact which the changes that came about in the wake of the Cultural Revolution had on the afforestation programme: the quantitative impetus, and the leap in quality to which reference was made above. This impact was two-sided. It radiated the available expertise into the countryside, making the special knowledge of forestry science more directly the property of the masses. And it helped and encouraged the peasants to analyse their own experience: to become forestry scientists themselves. It was not simply that more of the available professional resources were located where they were really needed, and that their efforts were concentrated on problems that mattered. Certainly of equal, and probably of greater, importance, was the fact that science was no longer the monopoly of the few. The scientific attitude, the scientific approach to problem-solving, is steadily gripping the workers and peasants. The Western forester visiting China today soon comes to understand that no dialogue, be it with a man from the ministry, an academician, a machine-operator, a skidder-driver, or a simple worker in a tree nursery, is complete without a passage starting: 'Summing up our experience to date. . . .'. As a rule this is followed by a listing of open and unresolved questions, together with indications of the intended lines of attack.

Millions of peasants have taken to heart, and are vigorously applying, the words of a famous article written by Mao Tsetung in May 1963, urging them 'to become good at investigation and study and at summing up experience'. The struggle for scientific experiment, along with the class struggle and the struggle for production, is one of the 'three great revolutionary movements' set out in the new constitution of the Communist Party of China adopted in August 1973. The struggle for scientific experiment is thus not something that concerns 'scientific circles' only. It concerns everybody.[13]

---

[13] *Physical* property relations having been revolutionized, a sustained effort is being made to socialize *intellectual* property, to bring scientific knowledge under collective control. Perhaps this is what distinguishes the Chinese experience.

What exactly happens when the forestry scientist leaves his laboratory to go to work on a forest farm or commune? Of course, he acquires an enhanced respect for manual labour, an appreciation of the peasant's hardihood, resource and common sense, and this is a factor breaking down the barrier between intellectual and manual labour. But he is not expected to spend all his time mixing compost, levelling ground, pricking out tree seedlings. He starts to exercise his mind on the technical problems that are actually giving concern to the peasants. Moreover, his very presence gives the impetus to releasing his latent talent, energy and imagination of the peasants engaged in forestry work. This is why thousands of peasants engaged today in forestry work are conducting grafting experiments, germination tests, spacing trials, fertilizer trials, testing out exotic species, and so on – steadily 'becoming good at investigation and study and at summing up experience'.

It could well be that the process of bringing science to the people in this way has temporarily handicapped certain centrally conducted research, including lines of long-term and fundamental research without prospect of immediate application – though the Chinese themselves would dispute this. But this seems a small price to pay compared with the enormous potential opened up at the grass-roots by the spread of scientific consciousness and a scientific approach to problem-solving.

Many Western observers of the old China cited the ruthless profligacy with which forests, over centuries, had been destroyed as one of the most conspicuous expressions of the total absence of any feeling of responsibility for the community or for posterity which such outsiders believed to be an innate characteristic of the Chinese. Yet today, after less than three decades, the Chinese have become the most forest-conscious people in the world. There is nothing whimsical or romantic about their attachment to trees. It is based on a solid understanding of the role of trees as industrial raw material and fuel, as a shield against flood, erosion and desiccating wind, and as a key factor in the quality of both the urban and rural environment.

The building of forest-consciousness starts in the schools. The basic facts about the Chinese economy and the orientation of Chinese development are taught in all schools throughout China. Thus every schoolchild is aware that China takes agriculture as the foundation and industry as the leading factor in developing her national economy. These notions will have been presented in simple terms to the younger age-groups, but in the middle schools they are elaborated to impart an understanding of the interdependence of industry and agriculture, of the various ways in which they mutually support and promote each other. Moreover, every schoolchild learns that, in agriculture, the policy is to take food grains as the key link and to ensure an all-round development of animal husbandry and forestry. These slogans serve as texts for political – and economic – education. The consequence is that many middle school students in China show a firmer and clearer grasp of the essential problems of underdevelopment than do some academic economists in the West.

Thus no child leaves school in China without having acquired some notions of the significance of forestry, notions which will have been reinforced by visits to people's communes, forest farms, forest industry establishments. And each will probably, in the course of his or her school life, have made a personal contribution towards 'making green the motherland' by tree-planting and tree-tending around the school, on vacant city lots, or in the commune. Needless to say, in China as elsewhere, these school-derived notions take root in the family.

And education does not stop with school. Nowhere is the idea of education as a continuing, lifelong process more widely accepted than in China. Every factory, every commune, has its own programme of continuing education, with organized adult education facilities. These classes consist in part of political study groups, newspapaer reading groups, and literacy classes. In all these the orientation and aims of Chinese development are studied and discussed – which means that rather precise notions about the role of forestry are acquired. But classes in a wide range of technical and cultural subjects are also organized, and these include courses in forestry wherever forestry is a significant activity.

But if the foundation of forest-consciousness is laid in the school and amplified by widespread continuing education, it is also important to remember that tens of millions of Chinese – literally, not figuratively – are engaged part-time in forestry activities, mainly, at this stage, planting and tending. In the country-side, forestry is an integral part of the total activity of the communes. That part of the key slogan – 'ensure an all-round development of forestry' – is interpreted by each commune in accordance with its own needs and possibilities. Thus the forestry activity may be relatively minor, confined to planting along the roads and field borders, with the odd small woodlot, aimed at producing locally some of the industrial timber needed in the commune, especially poles for construction and transmission poles. This is the case, for example, with most of the agricultural communes in the plain around Peking, though even there the aggregate amount of planting in the commune is usually sufficient to warrant the commune establishing its own tree nursery. Elsewhere the forestry activity may be a vital element in the agricultural programme, as in the case of dune fixation, shelter-belts, and the protection of water conservancy works. Or it may form part of a larger programme aimed at valorizing land unsuitable for agriculture and thereby laying the foundation for future forest industries, thus diversifying the economy of the communes. The Hunan Chinese fir programme is a good example of this last.[14]

---

[14] A programme launched in 1964 by the Hunan provincial authorities to plant up the bare hills, too steep for terraced rice cultivation, mainly with Chinese fir (*Cunninghamia lanceolata*), but also with other species, including various plantation crops. Over much of Hunan, land suitable only for forestry accounts for 80 per cent of the land area. By 1974, many communes had already completed their share of the million-hectare target. For a full description of this programme, see Jack C. Westoby, 'Growth Industry from Chinese firs', *Geographical Magazine*, 561–71, (June 1975).

How is it that the Chinese peasant has become committed to forestry in this wholesale way? Two particular aspects of the forestry programme have helped to fasten in the mind of the Chinese peasant the importance of forestry. One is the emphasis given to tree-planting around individual houses in the commune. These are usually quick-growing species, with a realizable harvest date within sight. Since these trees remain the property of the individual householder, he can see future income, from sale to the commune, accumulating under his eye, so that the trees in his yard are as palpable a supplement to his income as are the pigs he has raised behind his house for eventual sale to the state purchasing organization. The other is that, throughout China, forestry is taken as encompassing not only timber trees but also orchard trees and so-called 'economic' crops.[15] Thus all kinds of plantation crops – tea oil, tung oil, nut trees, fruit orchards, as well as bamboo groves – will each have a place, if soil and climate conditions are appropriate, in the afforestation programme. This undoubtedly influences the way in which the peasant in the commune looks upon forestry activities. There is no sharp categorization between fairly quick-yielding plantation crops and slower-maturing timber crops. The importance attached to fast-growing species blurs any difference there may be in the time taken for the crop to mature. The commune may be taking its first harvest, in the form of thinnings, from its timber plantations before some of its 'economic' plantation crops have reached their peak yield. Thus the peasant has come to look upon tree-growing as a fruitful, economic activity, no less important than field or plantation crops. And this has come to be as true of protection forestry as of production forestry, since he can measure the increased yield behind the shelter-belts, see the new land under cultivation after dune fixation, and can recognize the diminished incidence of flood and erosion following on protective afforestation.

The Hunan Chinese fir programme mentioned above is a good example of the more ordered planning that was introduced into afforestation in the 1960s. The counties in Hunan were invited to prepare plans and proposals for submission to and discussion with the provincial authorities. After the approval, the province was to give a subsidy, at the rate of about £21 per hectare afforested, these funds coming from the provincial afforestation fund, derived from £1 levy on every cubic metre of timber felled in the province. The communes and their constituent production brigades were urged to set up forest farms. By 1974, 2,300 forest farms had come into existence, staffed by workers and technicians, most of the technicians being peasants from the brigades who had received short-course training. The programme has passed the half-way mark, thinnings have already been taken from the first plantations, and by the 1990s this programme will provide an annual supply of between 10 and 15 million cubic metres, which

---

[15] This is not the case in most countries. Elsewhere, forestry is still usually regarded, especially by foresters, as a separate activity, carried out within a separate forestry domain, requiring its own special skills and preserving its own mystery.

is about four times as much timber as all the forests in the UK provide today. A significant feature of this programme was joint planning by neighbouring communes – of forest roads, for example – which grouped themselves together to establish a 'forest base', looking forward to the day when their joint output would permit the establishment of a major forest industry. This was fully in line with the forestry rethinking of the early 1960s.

China has succeeded in something which very few other countries have achieved: in establishing a truly effective and fruitful integration between agriculture and forestry. The structure reflects this, although this is not the decisive factor – an appropriate structure can hamper or facilitate such integrations: it cannot of itself compel. At the national level, forestry affairs are dealt with in the Ministry of Agriculture and Forestry,[16] and are conducted under the leadership of one of the seven vice-ministers. There is no state forest service such as is common in most other countries, that is, an independent or semi-autonomous forest service with a hierarchical chain of command running down through forest regions and forest conservancies. Instead, agriculture and forestry are integrated at all levels, from the ministry down, usually in the agricultural and forestry bureaux of the provinces, administrative districts, counties, and so on. These bureaux are under the political control of the revolutionary committees at the respective levels, and the bureaux at each level deal with agricultural and forestry matters alike, along with the interrelations between agriculture and forestry. Naturally, the forestry members of these bureaux have very frequent contacts with their counterparts at the immediately higher and lower levels.

These bureaux, at the appropriate levels, have direct responsibility for the state-owned (as distinct from the collective) sector – state forests, state-owned forest industry enterprises, research institutes.[17] Their other important function is to give guidance and technical advice to the collectively owned sector – in essence, the communes, production brigades and teams – as well as to other organs and institutions conducting forestry activities: these include municipalities, railways, mines, factories, and so on.

The services which the forestry bureaux (and the state-owned enterprises for which they have responsibility) provide are not confined to professional advice and technical assistance; they go far beyond what is normally encompassed

---

[16] Central responsibility has changed several times since 1949. At the outset a Ministry of Forestry and Land Reclamation was set up. In November 1951 land reclamation was transferred and combined with state farms in another ministry. In May 1958 the Ministry of Timber Industries was merged into the Ministry of Forestry. In the course of 1971 a consolidated Ministry of Agriculture and Forestry was set up, combining the former Ministries of Agriculture, State Farms and Land Reclamation, Forestry and the water conservation section of the Ministry of Water Conservation and Electric Power.

[17] Not, however, for forestry education institutes, which ultimately depend, through the education departments or bureaux, on the Ministry of Education.

by a forestry extension service. Most important perhaps are the education and training activities, which take many forms: short training courses; one-day or one-week technical consultations for cadres, technicians or model workers, arranged at provincial county or district level; the promotion of exchange visits; on-the-job training in sawmills, timber yards, forest farms, research institutes; preparation of information sheets and instructional pamphlets; and so forth. In addition, each state enterprise has a demonstration function. Also important is the on-the-spot advice offered to the communes, brigades and teams by the staff of the forestry bureaux, state forest farms and research institutes. These staff now constantly visit, and for sustained periods work alongside members of, the communes. Any new problem coming up, therefore, is promptly spotted, and steps taken to cope with it. Staff in the state sector give advice on management, and in some cases actually provide management services until the collective has acquired its own nucleus of trained and experienced people. They act as animators, persuading the communes to undertake various kinds of forestry activities, providing the know-how and even lending executive staff to get things moving. They supply seed and planting stock. They organize experiments and trials. The living and fecund relationship between the state and collective sectors has contributed greatly to the effective integration of forestry and agriculture. In fact, the overwhelming majority of forestry activities in China today are, directly or indirectly, agriculture-supportive.

This varied range of services provided by foresters in the state sector to the collective sector goes some way to explaining how an afforestation campaign of the magnitude of China's can be sustained by what is still a relatively small corps of highly trained foresters. the organization and frequency of contacts are such that news of successful innovations, relevant new research findings, promising experiments is disseminated with extraordinary speed. The singling out and publicizing of specific achievements and the establishment of models for general emulation is central to China's mode of development – 'let key points lead the area' is the maxim. Forestry has its Tachai-type models too, and these, like Tachai itself and Tachai-type models in agriculture, have become centres of 'lay pilgrimage'.[18] Thus Chuting county, in Hunan province, includes several production brigades which have recorded noteworthy achievements in the Chinese fir campaign, so that the county became a diffusion point for the organization and techniques of afforestation. In 1973 it had no less than 60,000 visitors, and, expecting this stream to continue, in 1974 the county government built a guest house to help accommodate some of these. At the same time, while happy thus to impart its own experience, it was not above learning from others. A Chuting delegation returned from Tachai and set the local communes planning to enlarge their paddies by increasing the height of their terraces and

[18] See the papers on 'Learning from Tachai' campaign by Neville Maxwell. See unnumbered footnote at beginning of this chapter, p.270.

thus to facilitate mechanization and the introduction of machine irrigation. Another delegation had visited another model county, Kweitung, in south-east Hunan, and their report gave an impetus to intercropping in the young fir plantations with a wide variety of crops, including melons, beans and ground nuts.

More timber forests, more protection forests: no nation has had greater need of these than China. Yet even so the Chinese have found time and energy to create or develop amenity and recreation forests, and to carry out urban forestry on an unprecedented scale. By now thousands of tourists and members of diplomatic, cultural and commercial delegations have reported with enthusiasm on the magnificent tree-lined avenue that leads from Peking airport to Peking city. Yet this scarcely calls for comment. There are few countries today, great or small, rich or poor, that have not attempted some kind of cosmetic verdure on the approach to their capital cities. It is only when one leaves the main tourist centres, travelling between the provincial capitals and penetrating into the depths of the countryside, that one understands that in China today no road, be it a trunk route between major cities or simply a local road linking out-of-the-way communes, is considered complete until the saplings which line it have become firmly established. Meanwhile railside planting proceeds at an astonishing pace. And there are few factories that have not made some effort to plant up waste ground and line their service roads with trees.

But it is in the cities, in the huge urban afforestation programme, that Chinese genius has found one of its highest expressions. Informed visitors[19] have been deeply impressed not only by the scale of the achievements, but even more by the thought, care and skill with which they have been planned. The central concept has been not only to give aesthetic satisfaction, but also to effect a qualitative improvement in the urban environment, by improving the quality of air, controlling pollution, reducing noise, and providing summer shade. Furthermore, wherever possible a proportion of trees are planted which have some commercial value. Thus in the streets of Peking walnut and persimmon trees are prominent. Nanning, in the Kwangsi Chuang Autonomous Region, harvests twenty tons of mangoes and jackfruit from its street trees, while several cities have planted the palm, *Trachycarpus fortunei*, the fibre of which is used for basket-weaving. The urban planting programmes concentrate on trees which are reasonably fast-growing, which are capable of being planted at an advanced stage (four to eight metres in height), which are not subject to serious attack by pests or diseases, and which are known to survive in an urban environment. While city landscaping departments take care of parks, tree nurseries and trees along the streets, factories and other work units organize their own people to plant trees in the compounds, while trees in residential areas are planted by the residents under the leadership of the neighbourhood committees.

---

[19] For example, a six-man Australian delegation in 1975, led by Professor J. D. Ovington, which reported on 'Gardens, parks and open spaces in China' in 1976 (unpublished).

How much forest has China today? The probability is, as was suggested above, that no one in China knows the answer, or is likely to know for some time yet.[20] Senior forestry officials conceded that in 1974 that the 20 per cent forest cover, representing roughly 200 million hectares, the target rashly set for 1968 at the time of the Great Leap, was as yet far from achievement, but remained only the long-term target. It is conceivable that if successive annual afforestation claims were cumulatively added, and some area allowance made for street, field, rail- and roadside planting, one might begin to approach that figure. But such a figure would include much replanting of failed areas and much reforestation, and therefore double counting. In any case, such a numbers game is irrelevant. There is no magic about a 20 per cent forest cover, nor about 200 million hectares. What matters is that there should be sufficient trees of the right kind, in the right place, to provide existing industries and those yet to be established with raw material, to protect and serve agriculture, and to contribute to the quality of urban and rural life. This last goal is well within sight. Marked progress has been made towards the first: traditional forest areas have been brought under effective management, and some important new resources have been created. There is still, however, great scope for creating new industrial forests, while the task of opening up and managing the sub-tropical forests of the south has only just begun.

It is in protecting and serving agriculture that most remains to be done. Many, probably most, communes have already taken significant strides towards meeting their own needs of fuel and industrial timber. Trees protect the major and minor water conservation schemes which have already been executed, but the task of taming China's rivers is as yet by no means complete. However, perhaps the most gigantic task still facing Chinese forestry lies in the arid north and north-west, the completion of the 'great green wall'. Deserts cover 100 million hectares in China, over a tenth of the land surface. It has been estimated[21] that over 13 million hectares of this could be reclaimed and turned into farmland. Though a number of important successes have already been recorded in making the desert bloom, in Liaoning, Kansu, and Sinkiang, there is hard work here for the Chinese people and Chinese foresters for generations ahead.

Can any lessons be usefully drawn from the Chinese afforestation experience, lessons that might have validity for other underdeveloped countries?

There are a number of lessons to be drawn, though most of them are not likely to commend themselves to the international jet-set of development economists and government advisers.

---

[20] China's detailed forest inventory is not yet complete; it is proceeding at different rates in the several provinces, depending on the urgency with which the information is needed and the resources available to conduct it.

[21] 'Geography of China: deserts', *China Reconstructs*, (October 1974).

China's afforestation effort means that the balance between man and nature, shattered by centuries of reckless forest destruction, is steadily being restored. This has been achieved without foreign experts – the few Soviet experts in the early years scarcely count, since they were virtually all concerned with timber extraction – and without foreign loans.[22] It has also been achieved with a remarkably small force of professional foresters. The main lesson to be drawn from this is that there is no man/resource situation, no matter how extreme and hopeless-seeming, that is not recuperable given the political will and the social organization. There are vast areas within the underdeveloped world which are today considered by both ecologists and development economists as having passed, or as ineluctably approaching, the 'point of no return'. They have shown that rivers can be tamed, wind and water erosion halted, land rehabilitated, deserts made to bloom, through a process which begins with nothing more than human will, muscle and ingenuity. This is the cheering and challenging basic message of the Chinese experience.

[22] Costed conventionally, China's afforestation programme to date would have needed a loan of the order of $5 billion. By 1976, after 23 years of existence, the World Bank, for example, had financed 17 forestry projects to a total loan value of $170 million. The bulk of these loans was for export industries or for industrial plantations destined to feed export industries.

14
Forestry, Foresters and Society

I first pitched my tent among foresters twenty-five years ago. I thus can say, as Churchill is reported to have said on one important occasion, that when I look back on my past I see it divided into two parts. You will recall that Churchill was speaking in French, and since his mastery of the French language fell short of his mastery of his own tongue, his French audience were somewhat puzzled to hear him say: *'Quand je regarde ma derrière . . .'*

INTERNATIONAL FORESTRY AND UNDERDEVELOPED COUNTRIES

During the first part of my association with international forestry, I was disturbed by the fact that the forests and forest industries were a very neglected sector of the economy in all underdeveloped countries. The funding sources, whether multilateral or bilateral, whether of development assistance or of loan finance, were uninterested in forestry, which they assumed to be a low-yielding and slow-yielding investment. And foresters seemed incapable of comprehending, let alone using, the development economists' jargon which had by then become *de rigueur* in planning bureaux, development banks, and international financing agencies. My colleagues and I sought to rectify this state of affairs. We tried to analyse, quantifying wherever possible, the existing and potential role of the forestry sector within the overall economy. We reached the conclusion, for a variety of reasons I have not time to dwell on here, that, in most underdeveloped countries, development based on the forests could serve as a lever for overall economic development.

But we did not stop at developing arguments. We prepared manuals on development planning and ran training courses and seminars in development planning for foresters. Very soon, forest departments in the underdeveloped

Address to the Royal Society of New Zealand, June 1977; first published in the *New Zealand Journal of Forestry*, 23:1, pp. 64–84, 1978.

countries were able to present projects of a form and in a language that their central planning offices and finance ministers could understand and appreciate, and that external funding sources could approve. This approval was all the more readily forthcoming since our own regional studies of prospective timber needs and timber supplies had demonstrated beyond question that rising timber gaps were developing in some of the world's main consuming centres, Europe, Japan, and North America – gaps that could be filled only by an expansion of exports from the underdeveloped world, notably those endowed with tropical forests.

The upshot was that suddenly the foresters were in business: forestry ceased to be the Cinderella sector. Thus, during the second part of my association with international forestry, I and my colleagues were largely concerned with assisting underdeveloped countries to design the kind of projects which seemed likely to contribute to economic development *and* to appeal to the funding sources; and thereafter, once funds became available, to assist them to implement those projects. All such projects had necessarily to be of the pre-investment type, though in practice the notion of pre-investment was interpreted fairly liberally. They thus included not only reconnaissance surveys, forest inventories and forest industry feasibility studies, but also training institutions at all levels, research institutions, afforestation schemes, watershed management, forest policy, law and administration, wildlife management and national parks, forest research institutes.

The time came when it was possible for us to look back and recognize that we had indeed made a considerable impact. In forestry, unlike most other sectors, the multilateral effort accounted for the lion's share of total development assistance. Comparing the situation in the mid-seventies with that which obtained two decades earlier, we could point to the fact that the number of trained foresters in the underdeveloped world had multiplied more than tenfold. There was hardly a single underdeveloped country which did not have at least the nucleus of a forest service. Many by then had their own institutions for the preparation of professional and technical staff. At least half had their own research institutions. Most had a forest law, and quite a few had a forest policy. All this presented a very different picture from that which prevailed in the early fifties.

Today all these countries know much more about their forest resources: location, extent, composition. The area of natural forest brought into use, subject to commercial exploitation, has greatly extended. Moreover, many countries have recognized the need to supplement, complement and sometimes replace their natural forest endowment by creating man-made forests, and knowledge of the species and techniques appropriate to widely differing circumstances has been widened and deepened.

The flow of timber from the underdeveloped countries with tropical forest resources has expanded enormously to meet the growing needs of the affluent, industrialized countries. Though most of this expanded flow takes place in unprocessed log form, there has been a significant development of wood-based industries. Yet it has to be noted that a large proportion of the exports of processed tropical woods has come, not from the countries possessing the resource, but from other developing countries which act as in-transit processors.

These are some of the principal changes which have come about, and they are familiar to all those conversant with the world forestry scene.

It must seem obvious that, for those of us who had been immersed in the international development assistance effort in forestry, there were considerable grounds for satisfaction.

Yet, during the latter part of my career in international forestry, and even more since I relinquished those responsibilities, I felt obliged to ask myself the questions: Do these changes spell progress? Have they contributed to development?

The more I pondered these questions, the less satisfied I became with what had been accomplished. The real picture, if we have the courage to look at it, is much less pleasing.

It seems to me now, that international aid in forestry has done a useful job in identifying for foreign capital those forest resources suitable for exploitation. It has borne a substantial part of the costs of inventorying those resources. Often it has compiled the data, and helped to provide the justification, for international financing agencies to provide loans to create some of the infrastructure needed to assist the penetration of foreign capital. It has helped to train the manpower to be placed at the service of foreign enterprises, enabling them to economize on the use of expensive, expatriate personnel. And in fact, though this was never the intent, it has assisted some irresponsible governments to alienate and eliminate substantial parts of their forest resource endowment.

Over the last two decades, massive tracts of virgin tropical forest have come under exploitation, in all the three main underdeveloped regions. That exploitation has often been reckless and wasteful. Nearly all the operations have been such as to have brought no profound or durable benefit to the economic and social life of the countries concerned. Of the revenue which has accrued, only a small part has remained in the countries to which the resource belonged. Of the revenues which have found their way into the public purse, only an inconsiderable fraction has been ploughed back into maintaining, improving or replacing the forest resource. This might not have mattered very much in those countries with a super-endowment of forests, had the revenues been invested in other worthwhile development activities. But they seldom were.

Of the industrial development which has taken place, much is export-oriented. Local needs are not being met. The multiplier effects which should accompany the development of primary industry – the secondary, tertiary and feeder industries – are lacking. These are some of the things which are happening. Much more important, perhaps, are the things which should have happened and are not happening.

What has forestry done to improve the lot of the common man, of the peasant, for example? Precious little. Where are all the village woodlots? Where are the rural plantations to supply constructional and farm timber? In how many countries are the peasants being helped and encouraged to improve their own lot through cooperative effort, integrating forestry activities into the farming calendar, developing some of the many fruitful combinations of forestry and agriculture?

What about the marginal lands – vast areas in the Middle East, in North and parts of Central Africa, in some areas of Asia and Latin America – areas where forestry could make a significant contribution to halting the march of the desert and starting the long, slow process of land rehabilitation? A few pilot projects here and there, some of doubtful value. But no real programme to speak of.

What about the millions of hectares of bare, eroded hills, inflicting down-stream farmland with alternating flood and drought? Foresters in all three continents are aware of the problem, and are gallantly striving to do something about it. With skimped resources, they manage to plant 10, 20, 100 hectares a year – a drop in the ocean.

The fact has to be faced, if we are to be honest with ourselves, that two decades of international effort in the forestry sector of the underdeveloped world has made but little contribution to the overall development process, and its contribution to improving the quality of urban life and raising the welfare of the rural masses has been negligible.

This is a harsh judgement. It is also, in a sense, a confession of failure, since the better part of my working life has been devoted precisely to the objective of helping underdeveloped countries to realize their forestry potential.

FORESTRY AND NEW ZEALAND

By now you are doubtless wondering why I have chosen to inflict on you these reminiscences, this retrospective appraisal. Why should a South Island audience be interested in forestry development – or lack of development – in remote underdeveloped countries? It seems to me that there are a number of reasons why New Zealanders ought to take an interest in what is happening in the underdeveloped world, over and above feelings of common humanity. Though New Zealand is a relatively affluent country, her economic profile is such as to present almost as many affinities with the underdeveloped world as with the rich industrialized countries. Further, my own experience taught me that New Zealanders were held in high respect in the underdeveloped world, and that the development assistance effort she put forth, though small in scale, was highly appreciated as being free from the taint of neo-colonialism. At least, that was the situation when I ceased to be an international bureaucrat, over three years ago. I detect a certain erosion in that image now.

Certainly, so far as New Zealand's bilateral programme of development assistance in forestry was concerned, the effort was less badly misdirected and more competently executed than most programmes, multilateral or bilateral. It is my personal hope that this effort will be sustained and if possible expanded, and that it will be channelled into projects designed to confer benefits on the many rather than the few. That is my hope. It should be your interest.

But the main reason why I have introduced my talk in this way is that what has happened in forestry in the underdeveloped world is not altogether unrelated to what has happened in the past, and what is happening now, here in New Zealand. There is nothing like a complete analogy, of course. But I detect certain common elements.

I suspect that if it were possible to compile a league table of nations reflecting the volume of public interest and concern about forests and forestry, then New Zealand would be found well up in the top half of that league table. This at least is the impression I have gained in the short while I have been in this country. It is derived not only from a scrutiny of the media, but also from such conversations as I have had with non-foresters. Certainly the degree of public interest is a good deal higher than, say, in Italy, where I spend much of my time, in the UK or in the US. This is perhaps not surprising, given the fact that in the course of the last couple of decades this country's forests, and the industries based on them, have come to represent a significant leg of the national economy. But it is not this which accounts for the fact that public consciousness of the forests has risen markedly here during the eight years which have elapsed since my previous visit, and is now higher than in many other countries where forest industries are at least as important in the national economy. The basic reason is, I believe, that in the course of the last decade or so many of the time-honoured practices of foresters and of forest industries have come increasingly under scrutiny, and frequently under attack, by various groups which, if I may be permitted to use a convenient shorthand, I will describe as the environmental lobby. The public debate has ebbed and flowed, and has sometimes been extremely bitter, but the consequence is that many more New Zealanders are aware today than was the case ten years ago of the fact that this country's forests represent something more than a reserve of industrial raw material. More people have become aware of the role of the forests in assuring a pure, clean water supply, in regulating stream flow, in countering wind and water erosion.

There is ample evidence that foresters, in New Zealand as elsewhere, were fully aware of the role of the forests in determining water yield and water quality and countering erosion long before the environmental lobby found its voice, and that they struggled against considerable odds to do something about it.

But because investment in protection forestry usually only pays off in terms of broad social cost–benefit accounting, narrow financial evaluations set severe limits to what foresters were able to accomplish. This narrow outlook, I might add, is still operative in most countries of the world and, unfortunately for the underdeveloped countries, there is little sign that either international financing agencies or bilateral programmes are adopting a more enlightened approach.

Attention has also focused, in New Zealand as in many other relatively affluent countries, on the aesthetic values of the forest, on the forest's amenity and recreation potential, on the forest as a reserve for wildlife, and on the need for earmarking scientific reserves of undisturbed indigenous forest. In my opinion, this surge of interest in New Zealand in these other aspects of social forestry has come not a moment too soon. In most other countries it has come far too late and in some it has not come at all. This is not to say that I identify myself completely with the environmental lobby here – or elsewhere. But neither do I identify myself completely with the forestry profession. The forestry profession, with some honourable exceptions, has been remarkably insensitive to the changing needs and values of society in this area of concern. Foresters, on the whole, have tended to regard some members of the environmental lobby as Johnny-come-lately conservationists, some as crackpots, and some as nuisances.

On the other hand, the environmental lobby – if I may continue to make use of this shorthand for what is, in fact, a disparate array of pressure groups – has been greatly tinged, and still is, by what are essentially middle-class, even upper-middle-class, aspirations and values.

When I visited the Bay area in California a few years ago I was struck by the fact that Sierra Club members, secure in gracious detached homes on the heights of Piedmont, far removed from the smoke and slums of Oakland, were much more concerned with wilderness areas in the Sierra Nevada than they were with the need for city parks and urban forests for the several ghetto populations of the Bay area. There are still people in the environmental lobby who are capable of signing a petition to pressurize the government of Salvazania into calling off an irrigation project that might impair the habitat of the lesser spotted whiffletit before taking their dogs for a walk, without reflecting on the fact that each of their dogs consumes annually over 250 kilograms of grain-equivalent. The average consumption of grain in Salvazania is exactly the average for all the underdeveloped world; 181 kilograms.

When populations were sparser, when industrial technology was less advanced, we heard little about environmental quality. Does this mean that problems of environmental quality did not exist? By no means. Almost everywhere industrialization followed the pattern of nineteenth-century England, where the ironmasters of the Black Country and the coal and textile barons of Yorkshire and Lancashire lived on the wooded hills, far from sight, sound and smell of the terraced cottages, slagheaps and gas-laden air of the valleys. But comes the time when, with population growth and advancing technology, the wealthier classes can no longer afford to flee from the rising tide of pollution. And this is the point at which civic consciences are pricked into action.

Now it is certainly not my purpose tonight to denigrate the environmental lobby – here or elsewhere. Thanks to them, issues have been raised and publicly debated here in New Zealand which should have been the cause of public concern long ago. but I for one will find it much easier to identify with them wholeheartedly once I see a greater proportion of their effort being devoted to the environmental needs of the less fortunate sections of this and other communities. If many foresters still look upon environmentalists as crackpots and nuisances, it is equally true that many environmentalists look upon foresters as the willing accomplices of greedy and recklessly destructive industry. Each of these images is, of course, grotesque caricature. But it is right that there should be confrontation, since this is one way – not the only way – of creating public awareness and raising forest-consciousness.

Foresters must work to meet the needs of society, which means that they must continue to accommodate some of the demands of the environmentalists. But they must not fall into the error of assuming that the environmental lobby, as at present constituted, is fully representative of society's total needs now and in the future.

I have said that the great debate started here in New Zealand not a moment too soon. It is interesting to note that, at the inaugural meeting of the Empire Forestry Association in 1921, Viscount Novar, in his address, said: 'The forest record of the British race is a poor one. Backward at home, we have destroyed the timber of every continent into which we have penetrated, and the virgin forests in the possession of our race go as rapidly into decay as the stately parks of England.'

Another speaker at that meeting referred to 'the wonderful resources with which the Empire was originally endowed and the prodigality with which they have been or are in the process of being dissipated without adequate replacement'.

I am pretty sure that these two observations were as applicable to New Zealand as to the rest of the Empire. They were passed fifty-six years ago, at a time when there was much more indigenous forest in New Zealand than there is now, at a time when the bulk of the exotic forest had yet to be created, though the potential of radiata pine was already known. Yet it took another fifty-odd years before the Act embodying certain aspects of the indigenous forest policy reached the statute book.

The great debate here in New Zealand will continue, and the centre of interest will doubtless shift from time to time. But if the great debate has raised the forest-consciousness of many New Zealanders, this is not to say that every New Zealander is familiar with all the things that happen in the forest, and all the services the forest is capable of rendering.

It might be of interest to you if I were to enumerate a few that are not commonly appreciated. A hectare of forest in a year fixes 5 to 10 tons of carbon and releases 10 to 20 tons of oxygen. It also fixes some sulphur dioxide. A hectare of forest pumps anything from 2,000 to 5,000 tons of water a year, releasing around 2,000 tons in the atmosphere. A hectare of forest fixes from 30 to 80 tons of dust a year.

Trees in shelter-belts can reduce windspeeds (and consequent desiccation) by 50 to 80 per cent, with effects that can spread up to a kilometre. A 50-metre strip of trees can reduce noise by 20 to 30 decibels. A French scientist has even claimed an inverse correlation between trees and microbes. He found that the number of microbes per cubic metre of air reached 4 million in the big stores in the centre of Paris; half a million in the main streets; 2,000 in the city parks; and down to 50 in a forest ten metres from the road. I read this with a pinch of salt, since it seemed to me more likely to be a positive correlation with people density than an inverse correlation with trees. Nevertheless, I dare say if we all spent more time in forests and less in department stores we should have fewer infectious diseases.

Forests can be designed to thrive on, and cope with, sewage, and this use of forests has gone beyond the experimental stage. And a research station in Canada has shown how properly designed tree curtains can diminish snow-piling and hasten snow-melt, thereby relieving householders of a substantial portion of their winter shovelling.

Some of these scattered examples point to various ways in which forests and trees can be deployed in or near an urban setting, enhancing environmental quality for those whose taste does not run to, or whose means do not permit them to enjoy, remote forest wilderness. In fact urban forestry, in much of the industrialized world, is still in its infancy.

Here in New Zealand, you have had little occasion as yet to worry about forestry's potential contribution to the quality of urban life. The problem certainly does not present itself with the same intensity as it does in Europe and North America. And if it is true, as a recent demographic release suggests, that the natural regenerative capacity of the kiwi is in decline, and if more people continue to be repelled by these shores than are attracted by them, perhaps it never will. Even so, I imagine that there is probably some scope for a more deliberate urban forestry policy here.

I have not touched on the forests' possible contribution to future energy needs. The forests are already a significant element in the global energy picture. Roughly half the world's peoples will depend on them for domestic fuel. But we are steadily reaching a situation where energy derived from a renewable biomass which harnesses solar energy through photosysthesis may become available, even in developed countries, in a form and at a cost that can substitute at least some part of the non-renewable fossil fuels we consume. It behoves New Zealand to keep abreast of these new developments.

But even if there remain many open and still unresolved questions, even though there may be some gaps and shortfalls, the fact remains that here in New Zealand forest-consciousness is steadily rising. That process, provided it continues, represents the surest guarantee that in the fullness of time forestry will make to society in this country the versatile and many-sided contribution to both material standards and to the quality of life which it is capable of making.

For this rising forest-consciousness, the environmental lobby can take much of the credit. They can also take credit for some of the positive advances in forest policy which have been registered in the last decade or so. And this has happened in many countries besides New Zealand. How is it that they, and not the foresters, assumed the initiative? How is it that the foresters, once the conservation vanguard, have in recent years found themselves in the dock?

FORESTERS

My title promised that I would tell you something about foresters. It is time to turn to this fascinating subject.

For generations past, social anthropologists have sought to further the proper study of man by spending part of their lives dwelling among Trobriand Islanders, Karamojans and Amazon Indians. As previously undisturbed communities became rarer, others, wearing a different hat – that of animal ethology – took to living with chimpanzees and gorillas, still aspiring to further the proper study of man.

Now my twenty-five-year sojourn among foresters has afforded me ample opportunity of observing at close range their kinship relations, their initiation rites, their mating habits and their pecking orders – and much else besides. I am therefore in the happy position of being able to report with some authority on the Coming of Age in Foresterland.

I am sure that those of you who number foresters among your friends and acquaintances will have realized already that foresters are a peculiar, perhaps unique, race. Consider some of their characteristics.

The mere fact of being a forester means that one possesses a passport to hospitality and good fellowship with any other forester, at whatever professional level, anywhere in the world. This is traceable to the initiation rite which every forester undergoes, a rite which includes a protracted spell of arduous manual labour undertaken collectively. It is awareness of this common initiation rite which creates the global fellowship bond.

When foresters forgather, they are much more generous than most other professions in freely exchanging scientific and technical information. This is because they consider themselves (albeit wrongly at times) to be concerned with man's mastery over nature rather than with man's mastery over other men.

For much the same reason, foresters in conclave have always delighted in discussing silvicultural systems, thinning regimes, germination trials, biological control, inventory techniques; while in the past they have shrunk, and some still shrink today, from discussing the impact of forests on the lives of people. This is only partly because trees do not answer back.

Foresters tend to be political schizophrenics. In their private lives they are mostly of a conservative political hue, though I observe a certain radical infiltration among the younger age-groups: yet their professional lives are devoted to assuring that what they conceive to be the long-term community interest prevails over short-term private interests. In societies the hallmark of which is that free rein should be given to short-term private interests, the foresters' devotion has a decidely radical orientation.

Now these and other characteristics of foresters have been largely determined by the circumstances in which forestry science began and in which the forestry profession was born. Forestry science had its true beginnings in Germany in the sixteenth century and one can say that forestry as a profession was born in Germany in the second half of the eighteenth century. It was there that theoretical work in a number of relevant disciplines led to an understanding of practical forestry, an understanding which was broadened by systematic research and disseminated through a body of students who felt that they belonged to a learned trade. The German influence on forestry science and the forestry profession can scarcely be exaggerated. It was students from the Tharand Forestry School who founded forestry schools in France (1825) and Spain (1848). Austria and Russia followed German progress and established schools in the early years of the nineteenth century. It was a German who first headed the Indian Forest Service, and the Dehra Dun School was established in 1878, some years before the first Chair of Silviculture was established in Britain. The first modern forestry administration in Japan was headed by a former student of Eberswalde, while it was a Prussian immigrant, Bernard Fernow, who introduced scientific forestry to North America.

Thus the forestry profession grew up in Europe at a time when European forests were being rapidly depleted, and when that depletion was giving rise to concern; when the biology of the forest was becoming increasingly understood; when sustained yield principles were being enunciated; and when appropriate management techniques were being devised. Small wonder, then, that the forestry profession concentrated on endeavouring to assure a national forest estate adequate to meet prospective production and protection needs, and on managing that estate to the best of their ability in accordance with the growing body of forestry science.

Most foresters were public servants, and it is evident, from the 1921 Empire Forestry Conference quotations which I cited earlier, that they met with but scant success in pursuing the aims I have outlined. They fought for their ideas within the public service. But, where governments were deaf to their pleas – and governments mostly were – as disciplined public servants they refrained from rallying public support for their ideas and loyally implemented the policies of the governments of the day.

There is a clear continuity between the central core of ideas I have outlined and the content of the FAO study, *Forest Policy, Law and Administration*, published in 1950, and the Resolution on Principles of Forest Policy adopted by the FAO Conference in 1951. The FAO study stated, for example, baldly and unambiguously: 'The forest administration is the organization charged with the implementation of the national forest policy through the application of the forest law.'

It is easy to criticize that formulation now. But behind it lay a vision, a fear and a hope. The vision was of a strategic core of the national forest estate firmly in the hands of the state, managed by a dedicated and professional forest administration in the interests of the community in accordance with national objectives clearly set out in the defined forest policy, protected from interference by either political pressure groups or uninformed amateurs. Here, on this reserved forest estate, the foresters' writ would run. The fear was that, without a strong professional corps of dedicated foresters, organized in a service which enjoyed a high degree of independence, the continuity of forest policy would be endangered, and forest mismanagement and forest depletion would ensue. The hope was that those governments which were at that time contemplating measures to protect and develop their national forest resource would recognize that the essential prerequisite was a strong and professional central forest administration armed with suitable powers.

Now these notions, as you can see, involved a determination to get on with their own jobs; a mistrust of external pressure groups. Foresters turned in on themselves, and made little attempt to close the rift that was developing between them and society.

These are the reasons why foresters at first were slow to respond to the changing needs of society. This is why they were illprepared to meet the attacks that come from the environmental lobby. They had not the habit of public debate, and they did not find it easy to communicate outside their own professional circle. Moreover, their history had been one of beating off attacks from quite other, more self-regarding, quarters. For long they failed to recognize the environmental lobby for what it was: the reflection of an increasingly informed and concerned citizenry.

However, the last two decades have seen a remarkable transformation. Old concepts are being discarded and are giving way to new, more valid ones. The old notions are clung to only by a diehard crust of traditional foresters. The better forestry schools, sometimes under pressure from new generations of students, have made a signal contribution to this transformation. The mainstream of foresters has shown itself capable of responding to society's changing needs. And foresters have come to recognize that what happens in the forest is not their affair alone, but the affair of all in the community who have a stake, direct or indirect, in the forest heritage. Thus, the Seventh World Forestry Congress, held in Buenos Aires in 1972, declared: 'Congress firmly believes that, whatever the political objectives, whatever the form of economic organization, whatever the present pattern of land tenure, governments have a responsibility to plan for the continuous flow of the productive, protective and social goods and services from the forests, ensuring that the physical output and environmental benefits of the forests are available for the general welfare of their peoples now and for all time'.

It has not been an easy metamorphosis for the foresters. And if there are still some who fail to understand that consultation means listening as well as telling, that is perhaps understandable, given their history and background. But they will learn.

DEVELOPMENT MODELS FOR UNDERDEVELOPED COUNTRIES

What has all this to do with the failure of the forestry effort in the under-developed countries, of which I spoke earlier – and is it a failure because forestry's potential contribution to those societies is far, far greater than its potential contribution here in New Zealand? It has quite a lot to do with it, since the concepts I described earlier were wished on many of the newly independent developing countries, either by inheritance from colonial days or by foreign advisers, or were adopted by local professionals who had been indoctrinated overseas. They were inappropriate then. They are inappropriate now. There was never the remotest chance that they could be applied then. They are totally at variance with the forestry priorities which the underdeveloped countries should be adopting today.

Now it would, of course, be absurd to lay all the blame for forestry's failure to realize its potential contribution to society in the underdeveloped world on the outworn concepts of foresters. The fundamental reasons lie much deeper, and are largely beyond the control of foresters. Nevertheless, these outworn concepts have presented and still can present an obstacle.

If the picture I have painted seems a black one, this does not mean that I see reason for despair. The fitful and uneven development of the world economy over recent years has hastened the process of illusion-shedding. One by one the underdeveloped nations are beginning to shed their illusions, and are beginning to turn against the development models which have been thrust upon them by the Western world and which have been proved false. They are beginning to realize that if they are poor it is not because they started late in the development race; not because their resource endowments are inadequate; not because they are overpopulated. The poor countries are poor because the rich countries are rich. Underdevelopment is simply the other side of the penny.

Such are the ties between the affluent industrialized countries and the peripheral low-income countries that growth, where it has occurred in the underdeveloped world, has been limited and largely externally oriented. That growth has rarely spelt development. The beneficiaries, as Paul Streeten has observed, have been few: entrepreneurs, salaried officials, large landowners. The objective impact of much of the development assistance to date, be it loans, grants or technical services, has been to promote further distortion, to enhance dependence, to widen inequalities, and to frustrate or inhibit development in any true sense.

Today there are a number of countries in the underdeveloped world which are genuinely concerned about inequalities in their own countries, and which are striving to do something about them. Their numbers will increase. The key word in their development vocabulary will be 'self-reliance'. For these countries, foreign aid, of all types, and foreign investment, will be increasingly subordinated to truly national development policies which will aim at reducing present inequalities, at mobilizing cooperative effort to overcome the problems of feeding their own peoples, and at adapting the pace of industrialization to the progress achieved in agriculture.

They will approach the problems of their forestry sector in this sense. They will take a hard look at their forest resources, and will scrutinize present and future forestry activities from the standpoint of how best they can protect, support, promote and diversify the agricultural economy. It is to this aspect that they will give pride of place in their forestry planning and in establishing forestry goals. They will bear firmly in mind that the purpose of trees is to serve people. And they will test out all forms of people involvement and people participation that are adapted to their own customs and traditions and to the degree of evolving social and political consciousness that they have achieved.

Their second forestry priority will be the use of the existing resource base, and the creation, where necessary, of new industrial wood resources, for industrialization directed towards the satisfaction of urgent domestic needs. In deciding upon the location, scale and type of wood-processing plants, financial profitability criteria will take second place to the satisfaction of popular needs and the promotion of rising welfare.

Finally, if their forest resources are sufficiently rich to offer them the opportunity of expanding or creating export-oriented forestry activities, they will not neglect these opportunities, but the pace and scale of such developments will be subordinated to the first two priorities I have indicated. They will not be dazzled by the prospect of quick and easy export earnings. They will not succumb to the blandishments and bribes of would-be concessionaires and eager private foreign capital. They will be careful not to alienate their resource heritage. They will temper the pace of such developments to their own rising capacity to supervise and control them. They will reject programmes and projects which introduce serious distortions and put their own national objectives in jeopardy.

With these very different priorities, forestry will become a lever for development in a true sense. The emphasis will switch from export-oriented extraction and industries to agriculture-supportive forestry. Though at first this may bring but little change in the *per caput* GNP league tables – a criterion which has proved its irrelevance – the benefits, instead of being confined to the few, will be spread among the many. And as social capital is built up, the process will accelerate and the benefits will accumulate.

These, then, are the paths which, in my view, the underdeveloped countries must tread if their forestry is to make the immense contribution to their society of which it is capable.

'The latter part of a wise man's life', said Jonathan Swift, 'is taken up in curing the follies, prejudices and false opinions he had contracted in the former'. I make no claim to wisdom, and I have to confess that many of my earlier follies and prejudices remain uncured. But perhaps my brief excursion into the problems of forestry and underdevelopment will satisfy you that, so far as false opinions are concerned, it is possible for even a retired international bureaucrat to have second thoughts.

CIVIC RESPONSIBILITY

I should now like to make another point; and I have left it until near the end because, although I am speaking of foresters, it is a point which applies to all professions, not merely the forestry profession, and it is one that should concern everybody.

One of the factors that has inhibited the foresters in their endeavours to have a frank and open exchange with their critics is their mistaken sense of loyalty, a false understanding of where their true responsibilities lie. Their dilemma is well illustrated by the code of ethics recently adopted by the New Zealand Institute of Foresters. This, by the way, is the most advanced code of professional ethics I have yet come across. Most such codes are concerned strictly with maintaining a closed shop and abolishing intra-species competition – which is no doubt why Shaw described every profession as a conspiracy against the laity. But the New Zealand code specifically recognized the public interest, the forester's responsibilities to the community at large. 'Each member,' says paragraph 2, 'shall be beholden to the public, clients and employers, and colleagues in the following ways,' and the code goes on to say, in paragraph 2(b): 'He shall work in the public interest. If he becomes aware of any activity which is not in the public interest he shall notify the Council so that the Institute may take remedial action.'

So far so good. But, alas, this is nullified by 2(d), which says: 'He shall not disclose any confidential information of his past or present clients or employers.' Now this is the traditional 'You must not bite the hand that feeds you' clause which appears in all professional codes.

Here we come to grips with what I consider is the worst crime that can be laid at the door of the foresters: they have conducted themselves as conscientious, loyal and obedient public servants or company servants – in most countries the overwhelming majority of foresters are employed in the public service or by companies – and in so doing they have failed in their civic responsibilities.

This code of ethics does not go far enough. My views on these questions are very simple. The forester, like any professional, scientist or technician, undoubtedly has a responsibility to the hand that feeds him. But this is not the end of his responsibilities. He also has a responsibility to the community-at-large, to society, to the public. On many of the issues that engage the public interest, the scientific and technical complexities are such that the public has great difficulty in disentangling them and in discerning the appropriate solutions. The forester, like his colleagues in other professions, has a responsibility for ensuring that his expertise is made available to the public in matters of public concern in terms which the man in the street can understand. The fact that he sell his brain power to a private employer or a government department for forty hours a week does not mean that he should surrender either his rights or his duties during the rest of his waking hours. Nor does it absolve him of his responsibility towards his fellow citizens. And on occasions when what he conceives to be his responsibility towards his employer is in direct conflict with what he deems to be his social responsibility, he has a moral duty to put the public interest first.

It is morally wrong, in my view, for a pharmacologist to develop a new drug, see it marketed without any real attempt to investigate its possible side-effects, and remain silent. It is morally wrong, in my view, for a civil engineer to see a new construction go up incorporating materials whose qualities have been inadequately tested, and remain silent. Fortunately, most decisions in which foresters are involved are less potentially lethal. But they are nonetheless important for the community. They are often irreversible. Their efforts can be much more long-lasting. This is why foresters should speak out.

I am conscious of the fact that, in urging foresters to speak out, I am advocating a standard of behaviour which few employers would regard as either ethical or acceptable. Doubtless there are employees who would agree. There are still some who believe that forestry is about trees. It is not. It is about people, and how trees can serve people. Forestry is *for* people. But only a fully informed public can say what it wants its forests to do for them. In an increasingly complex technological society, where the man in the street must depend on the professional, the scientist and technician for the information he needs to enable him to pronounce on issues that engage community interest, the injunction 'Do not bite the hand that feeds you' has no place. That is why all scientists and all professionals, including foresters, must cease to be civic castrates.

THE SOCIAL OBJECTIVES OF FORESTRY

What is the principal common element between what is happening in forestry in the underdeveloped world and what is happening in the world of the richer nations, including New Zealand? It is the growing recognition of the importance of the *social* objectives of forestry. In both worlds, the rearguard of foresters is seeking to accommodate these social objectives as society enunciates them, and to reconcile them with the economic objectives which society has hitherto prescribed for foresters. The vanguard of foresters, on the other hand, is seeking actively to help society to define and enunciate these social objectives, fully accepting that they are no less important than the economic objectives.

It is in the underdeveloped world that the need is greatest to accelerate this transition, for it is there that radically different priorities are most urgently needed if forestry is to make its full contribution to society.

But the need also continues in the developed countries. It continues here in New Zealand, even though New Zealand is certainly more advanced than most in seeking to accord due weight to the social objectives of forestry.

If foresters, here or elsewhere, are to help society to define its forestry objectives, they must be more outgoing than they have been in the past. They must explain their practices and procedures. They must make clear their possibilities and constraints. They must be free with information, and must make it comprehensible. Above all, they must continually remind contemporary society of its obligations to future generations: foresters are better qualified than most to act as society's conscience in this respect.

There are some who see in the forest a temple of nature, a God-given refuge from a mercenary and polluted world. I am not one of them. There are some who can derive serene satisfaction from looking upon a field of wheat or a herd of Angus cattle, but whose stomachs turn at the sight of a plantation of radiata pine, failing to recognize that all three symbolize man's effort to mould nature to his needs. I am not one of them. To me the forests represent a renewable resource which, if managed with due regard to ecological constraints, is capable of serving an infinite variety of society's needs, at diverse material and non-material levels. The better society comes to understand and appreciate the rich capability of the forest, the more precise and cogent will become society's demands for the services of the forest. And the more cogent and precise those demands, the better will foresters be able to serve society.

15
Forestry and Underdevelopment Revisited

There is an endearing practice whereby when certain kinds of celebrities, for example, politicians and ballet dancers, reach Sunset Boulevard, they are afforded a final prestigious occasion for uttering words of wisdom or putting on some other kind of performance. This special occasion is known as their swan-song. What I have to say to you today can in no sense be regarded as a swan-song. Indeed, recalling the words of the English poet – 'Cuckoo, shall I call thee bird or but a wandering voice?' – the observations which follow may more aptly be described as a cuckoo-song.

On one of my earlier visits to Berkeley – it was the occasion of the campus centennial – I gave a lecture and participated in a number of seminars. Each graduate school had been asked to invite someone in its own field to lecture and seminarize. I believe that the Forestry School had decided to invite me because of a paper which I had written some six years earlier, and which one of your former deans had been gracious enough to describe as 'seminal'. I thus found myself in very assorted company, including a criminologist from Norway, an electrical engineer from India, a pedagogue from Britain, an agricultural economist from Minnesota, a civil engineer from Chile, and various others. The central theme around which the seminars and lectures were organized was the role of the professional in bringing about change in Third World countries. All had, I think, been involved directly or indirectly in development assistance programmes. Excerpts from the various addresses given, together with a linking commentary by two Berkeley professors, were subsequently published by Praeger under the title *Agents of Change*.

Recently I plucked this volume from my library shelf, and scanned its pages. I was appalled by the pomposity and arrogance which characterized the whole

A lecture for the School of Forestry and Conservation, University of California, Berkeley, November 1985.

book, my own contribution not excluded. This in spite of the fact that I had wound up my own lecture with a caveat: that professionals already had a somewhat exaggerated idea of their power to influence social and economic change. Thinking back to some of the exchanges which took place during the seminars, I cannot, however, feel that I was quite so arrogant as were some of my companions on that occasion. For example, I clearly recall one of the US participants, explaining to us at great length why the type of free enterprise system enjoyed in the US meant that the technology which the US sought to transfer in its development assistance programmes was invariably that best adapted to the local situation and to local needs. I found this hard to swallow. I had arrived from Rome, where I had just had to cope with two difficult situations. One concerned a Russian sawmill delivered under Soviet aid to Guinea. There it proved incapable of taking the many large-diameter logs. Those logs which it could take often had either a density or a silica content which ruined the saw teeth within minutes. Thus down time far exceeded operating hours. The other situation had cropped up in Taiwan, where a West Coast sawmill provided gratis under USAID was standing idle, and we were begged to find someone who would take it off their hands. Kerf, slabs and edgings far exceeded in volume the lumber produced: a matter of little moment on the Pacific West Coast, where a market existed for wood residues, but a matter of very great concern in wood-hungry Taiwan.

It so happened that these cases matched antithetically, but I had already seen enough of bilateral aid to know that the real needs of the recipient country were not always the principal consideration of either East or West. Indeed, it was already clear in my mind, though it was only much later that I was to define it as the first of the four grand illusions about aid: that most development assistance has anything to do with helping anybody to develop.

Another memory I have of that occasion is of Professor Gustav Papanek, at that time Director of the Development Advisory Services at Harvard, reporting how useful it had proved to send economics students overseas for a year to an underdeveloped country; they returned with a much keener awareness of the social and economic problems of the United States. I felt constrained to point out that this was a rather expensive way of teaching economics. It seemed to me that if a year in India was necessary before a student could comprehend the problems of Detroit or Wattsville, then perhaps there was something wrong with economics teaching in the US.

Agents of Change was published the year after, in 1969. At that time there were still very many in the development establishment who saw development as a trajectory through which all countries must perforce pass. Those unfortunate countries which were lagging in the development race lacked a key ingredient of development. Only identify this, and hand it out in sufficiently generous measure, and they would speedily make up ground. As I pointed out in my guest-speaker address in Jakarta in 1978, ideas about the missing ingredient changed with time, and new bits were added to the United Nations structure with each change in fashion. These false ideas – that there were necessary stages of growth before take-off point was reached – were given wide circulation by W. W. Rostow in his *Stages of Growth*. Looking back, it is hard to decide which of the Rostows was the greater calamity: the influential presidential adviser, Gene, with his insistence that Vietnam be obliterated, or W. W., with his fetish of the internal combustion engine and his weird notions about development. Today, of course, we recognize that *Stages of Growth* was not a serious contribution to either economics or development theory, but merely an up-market anti-Communist pamphlet.

One of the fashions which I ought to have mentioned in Jakarta, but failed to, was the craze of institution-building. The theory then current was that capital was at hand, suitable technology was available, but the institutions – administrations, schools, research organizations, extension services, credit institutions – were all too weak or embryonic to sustain development. Immediately a spate of books appeared and numerous university courses started up on institution-building; miscellaneous bits of international organizations retitled themselves, giving the word 'institution' prominence; while funders, both multi- and bilateral, stepped up the flow of resources into 'institutions'. Only very much later did it dawn upon the development establishment that the very act of establishing new institutions often meant the weakening, even the destruction, of existing indigenous institutions which ought to have served as the basis for sane and durable development: the family, the clan, the tribe, the village, sundry mutual aid organizations, peasant associations, rural trade unions, marketing and distribution systems, and so on.

In 1972 I paid my last visit to Berkeley, this time as Regents' Professor. By this time I had become acutely aware that much of my 1962 paper was nonsense, and I invited the graduate students in forestry at Berkeley, together with any members of the faculty who might be interested, to explore with me the reasons why it had turned out to be nonsense. My hope had been that there would have been time and inspiration enough to produce a more sensible paper, which might serve as a guideline for development assistance in forestry. This hope was not realized. A new paper was not written, though perhaps time rather than inspiration was the principal shortfall. My wife and I had a delightful time here in Berkeley, and at least I had time to rearrange some of my thoughts.

Back in FAO, I distributed to all my colleagues a lengthy paper drawing attention to the fact that none of the results which we hoped would flow from investment in the forest and forest industry sector were in fact coming about, inviting them to reflect on these matters, suggesting how priorities ought to change, and pointing out the kind of projects we whould be concentrating on.

The response was mixed and delayed. I quit FAO in 1974 in order to write more freely. Before very long, and partly as a consequence of McNamara's belated discovery of the growing numbers and deteriorating circumstances of poor farmers, a new rhetoric came to be almost universally adopted: grassroots approach, integrated rural development, community development, village level projects, and so on and so on. The Eighth World Forestry Congress in 1978 had as theme 'Forests for People'. Deeds, of course, trailed far behind words. The Bank, in the last analysis, is a bank: its loan officers are there precisely to ensure that it does not become a philanthropic institution. Few governments gave such projects wholehearted support since, as I pointed out in Jakarta, the interests of ruling cliques and of the poverty-stricken rural masses seldom coincide. Moreover, as the first tentative attempts were made to put into operation new-type projects, it became clear how successful former projects had been in weakening or destroying the institutions on which the new-type projects had necessarily to lean.

It was obvious by then, and is still more obvious today, that in those underdeveloped countries which had followed the changing precepts of the development establishment, a few rich were getting richer, while the poor were increasing in numbers and getting poorer; in many countries these included a growing army of rural landless, while in all countries shanty towns sprang up to shelter the urban unemployed. Nearly every one of these countries was coming to depend, often for the first time, on food imports to feed its people. National indebtedness was rising rapidly. These marks of underdevelopment usually accompanied new airports, tourist hotels, and often expanded armies, police and secret police with sophisticated equipment.

Were matters faring differently in those countries which defied the development establishment and opted for a socialist path of development?

In 1974 I paid my second visit to China, and in a number of articles I wrote at that time I commented at some length on the positive aspects of the Chinese experience. If I had less to say about the negative aspects, which I certainly observed, it was because China had no shortage of detractors. I have also visited several other Third World countries which have sought non-capitalist solutions to their problems, These countries have had mixed experiences. Some have undoubtedly succeeded in eliminating extreme poverty and in ensuring a more equitable distribution both of natural resources and of such material goods as they could produce. Others, as in southern Africa, bedevilled by drought, subversion and external military pressure, have made some progress towards equity without, however, making any sizeable dent in poverty.

I think that by now it is possible to draw up a few generalizations about the poorest categories of underdeveloped countries. For example, it is now clear that no Third World country will be able to keep open for itself sufficient options to enable it to steer the course of its own development, unless it is able largely to feed itself. Once a substantial proportion of resources (land and labour) is shifted from feeding its own people to growing agricultural crops for export, the vagaries of the export market, monopsonic tendencies, and the growing dependence on imports for basic foods, will inevitably drive the government and its planners into a corner from which the IMF and the World Bank will not let them escape. But – and herein lies the Catch 22 set by the development establishment – the kind of agricultural projects which have been accorded support by both development agencies and bilateral programmes in the past have been precisely those which have aimed at exporting agricultural products, but which simultaneously have reduced the ability of countries to feed themselves.

In those countries which have opted for a non-capitalist solution to their problems – normally as a consequence of the politicization process which has accompanied an armed struggle for liberation and independence – the new regimes have found themselves confronted with the same problem in a different form. A significant sector of agriculture will already, under colonialism, have been shifted away from meeting people's needs to providing exportable surpluses of food and raw materials. It may even be that a large part of the urban population has been weaned from indigenous staple foods to expensive food imports: wheat or flour. Sometimes the solution adopted by the newly independent country has been to convert large-scale, privately owned, export-oriented estates into state farms – a policy presumably urged upon them by Eastern bloc advisers. Often the consequences have been calamitous, either because insufficient attention was paid to the ecological constraints or because there was no hope of developing and concentrating in time the administrative skills required to cope with the complex logistics. On top of this, there has usually been in practice a failure to support sufficiently the individual peasants or peasant groupings which, with adequate incentives, could have brought forth the required agricultural surplus.

Even if the economy is not already distorted by export-oriented agriculture, the newly independent government still has to face the problem of extracting from domestic agriculture a surplus to feed the towns, to feed the expanding industrial and service sectors, which are at the same time symptoms and engines of development. It is quite useless to say that market forces will ensure that this comes about. Only in very exceptional cases will market forces ensure that road systems, transport means and storage facilities are effectively developed. Nor can it be expected that individual peasants will produce surpluses over the above their own needs and put those surpluses on the market, unless there are available on the market commodities which the peasants themselves have an interest in buying. These incentive commodities will vary according to circumstances, and change with time, with development. At the outset they consist of soap, salt, sugar, elementary tools, textiles, cooking and eating utensils. Later on they may include clocks, watches, bicycles, radios, pumps, and so on. It is, in fact, more important to plan for the adequate supply of appropriate incentive goods for the peasant (if necessary, by importing them) than to plan for many urban needs.

It has been said that orthodox economics before the Second World War was preoccupied with problems of equilibrium and the reduction of cycles, and that its concern with growth and development came only after the war. Certainly you will find little discussion of the problems of underdeveloped economies in pre-war economic writings of the orthodox school. But then, neither was much attention paid to those problems by the heterodox. Most economists influenced by Marxism looked to the overthrow of capitalism in the metropolitan country to solve both metropolitan and peripheral problems. They thus, with but a few exceptions, failed to consider the problems of development in backward countries. When power relations were overthrown in Russia, there was intense debate about whether socialism was achievable in one country, and how to ensure growth and development in what was primarily an agricultural country unable to rely on external assistance. This is why, when we turn to the writings of Preobrazhensky, Bucharin and others, we find that much of the ground covered by development economists in the fifties and sixties had already been well trodden in the early twenties in the USSR.

But even before that time it had been clear to many thinkers and political activists in Russia that the key to future growth and development lay in squeezing a surplus from the agricultural sector of sufficient magnitude to sustain expanding industrial and service sectors. Among those bent on over-throwing Tsarist feudalism, opinions differed on the approach to be adopted towards the peasants. Should ancient communal tendencies be supported and strengthened, so that agriculture move towards some kind of collectivism? Or should reliance be placed on capitalist agriculture for securing increased output and higher efficiency in production?

In spite of the experience of the USSR and China, in spite of the fact that several other newly independent countries have, since the Second World War, opted for the socialist path of development, it cannot be pretended that these problems have as yet been satisfactorily resolved.

In the USSR, the Soviet state, once it had emerged triumphant from the wars of intervention and had secured its borders, resolved on forced collectiviza-tion in the countryside, as the means of raising the agricultural surplus which would fund rapid industrialization. This course finally succeeded, though its cost in famine and civil war may have been anything from ten to twenty million dead. The solution was sufficiently effective to enable the USSR to bear the brunt of the attack of Nazi Germany, when it came, in the Second World War. But it is to be feared that Soviet agriculture still bears indelibly the marks of that early period. Agriculture would still seem to be a second-class occupation. It seems that but few of the best brains are directed into that sector. Though soils and climate are undeniably inferior to those of North America, this hardly accounts for the immense disparities in crop yields, and so forth. It is quite possible that had the USSR, since the Second World War, enjoyed an exportable surplus of grain comparable to that which emerged in North America, the course of history might have been very different.

China learned from the Russian experience. Even before the transfer of power in 1949, the Red Army had encouraged the peasants, who had suffered a much more oppressive regime than the Russian peasants had ever had to endure, to mete out justice to cruel landlords and moneylenders, and to divide the land equitably. Happy with the new emphasis on establishing schools and elementary health facilities, the peasants willingly followed the Communist line and formed mutual aid teams, cooperatives, and eventually communes. There was, certainly in the initial stages, a widespread feeling that the regime was with them and for them. Consequently, over and above the work the peasants carried out on communal plots, and in some cases on small private plots, thousands of milions of man-days were invested in creating social capital: flood barriers, irrigation schemes, shelter-belts and so on. Of course, social pressures played a large part in this, but there is no reason to doubt that much of the labour was contributed with enthusiasm. Sometimes the vast investments into social capital went awry. For example, hundreds of millions of man-days put into afforestation were in effect wasted through bad planning, inferior planting material, ignorance of nursery and planting practice, and lack of aftercare. With the passage of time, many of these elementary errors were rectified, but they must have had a dampening effect on peasant enthusiasm in areas where failures were only too apparent. In contrast with the Russians, the Chinese regime adjusted the rate of industrial development to the rate at which the agricultural surplus grew.

The truly great achievement of the Chinese revolution was that within a surprisingly short space of time one of the poorest countries in the world had succeeded in feeding itself adequately. So far no similarly impoverished country has met with equivalent success. The tragedy of the Chinese revolution is that personal and group rivalries, sometimes heavily disguised as ideological differences, have from time to time confused the masses, blunting the cutting edge of both worker and peasant enthusiasm. In the last few years, the four modernizations, fathered by Deng Shao Ping, have revived the spirit of individual enterprise, have brought about some astonishing output gains, but have had some less desirable consequences in the shape of an upsurge in crime and youth delinquency, a resurgence of exploitative relations in the countryside, and a growth in disparities in wealth between individuals, between groups, and between regions, as well as a very sharp rise in the volume of overseas indebteness. I would imagine that it is but a matter of time before we see another swing, back towards Communist orthodoxy, austerity and communal emphasis.

By now some of you will have observed that, although the title of my presentation is 'Forestry and Underdevelopment Revisited', I have had much to say about economic development and agriculture, but precious little about forestry. I would ask you to bear with me a little longer.

Some of you know that I have expended some energy in recent years in trying to bring about a better understanding between foresters and conservationists.

Most conservationists, when they pin this word on themselves, feel that they are donning a halo. Yet I myself must confess that I have always objected to being included amongst the conservationists' 'we'. This was especially the case when conservationists started to fling the 'space-ship earth' metaphor about. 'We' are over-consuming this and that; 'we' are multiplying extravagantly; 'we' are filling the air and the rivers and the seas with pollution; unless 'we' change our ways 'we', or our children or our grandchildren, are heading for destruction.

Now I resent being made to feel guilty in this way. I never asked for lead in petrol. I do not want the junk which I daily transfer from the postbox to the trashbin. I have no objection to paying an extra cent or two to have sulphur dioxide reclaimed instead of being sprayed upon me every day. The use by conservationists of the first person plural is a sign of both ignorance and of political debility. Of ignorance, because they seem blissfully unaware that in this particular space-ship a mere handful of privileged occupy all the luxury accommodation, while the great mass of people, whether from the First, Second or Third World, are thrust into the steerage and the cargo holds. Of political debility, because it argues unwillingness to identify the true enemies, where conservation issues are involved, and to take arms against those enemies.

My awareness of the clay feet of so many conservationists was sharply enhanced a few years ago, when, on all sides, the cry went up to save our tropical forests. We were asked to save them from the logger, from the shifting cultivator, from the ignorant peasant, from the hamburger kings, and so on – yes, and from ourselves: we too were to be held responsible, since we allowed pieces of tropical hardwood to enter our homes. Elsewhere, and on several occasions, I have pointed out that there is essentially no difference between the processes at work today and those which operated in the past.[1] For those still unaware of the real issues, I will summarize them very briefly.

There is no technical fix which can save the tropical forests. The main instruments of forest destruction are the disinherited of tropical forested countries: peasant farmers, shifting cultivators, rural landless. But these are the agents, not the causes. Their pressure on the forest is steadily increasing as a consequence of policies bent on preserving a highly skewed distribution of private property in land and other resources. This pressure will inevitably continue, until there is more equal access to land and other resources. This is not a sufficient condition for saving the tropical forests, but it is a necessary condition.

It is quite true that we have tremendous gaps in our knowledge of the hundreds of tropical forest ecosystems. We have much yet to learn, and efforts directed towards filling those gaps need to be multiplied manyfold. But there

---

[1] 'Halting tropical deforestation: the role of technology', paper prepared for the US Congress Office of Technology Assessment, August 1982. And 'Possono gli Stati Uniti Salvare le Foreste Tropicali?' *Il Ponte* (September 1985).

is much that we do know already, and practically none of this is being applied anywhere. A high proportion of the humid tropical forests which survive today lies in countries ruled by regimes which are both economically inequitable and authoritarian. These are regimes which have never made any effort either to control logging, to manage forests, or to channel funds into research. These are regimes which today are actively engaged in, or are turning a blind eye towards, the genocide of forest-dwelling peoples. It is in these countries that armies and police help transnationals to dispossess peasants, simultaneously waging war against peasant organizations, rural trade unions, and local clergy who come to the defence of the poor. Yet, as recent experience has shown, most of these oligarchic regimes are brittle and would not long survive without external support.

It is because these issues are evaded that the US government's recent *Technologies to Sustain Tropical Forest Resources*, published in March 1984, though otherwise packed with much good sense from thoughtful and experienced foresters, will contribute little to the preservation of the remaining tropical wet forests.

In fact, once we start to examine history closely, we find that very rarely has deforestation, even of the temperate forests, been a simple matter of numbers outstripping environment – of population increase bringing with it the need to clear more land to grow more food.

We know that large areas of the Mediterranean forest were stripped in classical times. Murray Bookchin,[2] as we shall see later on, has provided the clue, and G. E. M. de Ste Croix[3] the evidence, that enables us to trace the course of events. What happened was that as hierarchical societies evolved, the number and categories of non-producers (the dominant elites, their administrative cadres, the priesthood, their armies and arms-makers) all multiplied. To maintain these non-producers, together with those craftsmen and artisans employed to make luxury goods, it became necessary not only to squeeze an increasing surplus from the agricultural sector at home; it became also necessary to import additional food from other sources. That meant implanting colonialism overseas: either by the direct settling of labour to produce food and so on in foreign lands; or by the moulding of local markets to generate the surplus required. Grain imports by the Greek city-states foreshadowed the much greater impact of the food requirements of Imperial Rome.

England was a typical Roman colony. Although there was a measure of deforestation in southern England before the advent of the Romans, the really substantial expansion in agriculture and reduction in forest area took place during the Roman occupation.[4] We know now that the occurrence of Roman

[2] Murray Bookchin, *Ecology of Freedom* (Melbourne 1982).
[3] G. E. M. de Ste Croix, *The Class Struggle in the Ancient Greek World* (London, 1981).
[4] Oliver Rackham, *Trees and Woodland in the British Landscape* (London, 1976).

villas in southern England was much more widespread than was hitherto supposed. Each of these was, in essence, an export-oriented farm, producing a grain surplus which not only went to feed the Roman army of occupation, a road-building corps, and all the hangers-on of the Roman administration, but was also shipped to the imperial metropolis in substantial quantities. Since Britain exported many worked metals to Rome, the forests of southern England and Wales also had to supply the fuel for iron-smelting, and so on.

After the fall of Rome, the process of Mediterranean deforestation was halted, even reversed, until the upsurge of trade and population which heralded the Renaissance. The expanding city-republics – Pisa, Venice, Genoa – took over much of the Eastern trade from Jews, Syrians, Greeks and Arabs. They had a growing internal market for spices, silks, indigo, sugar and slaves, as well as ample funds to invest. As Charles Verlinden[5] has remarked, the Italian colonies in the Levant and the Black Sea became virtual laboratories for testing commercial companies, colonial administration and finance, long-distance trade, and plantation agriculture.

The Black Death sent up the demand for slaves in Europe, but slave holdings were still predominantly white, drawn from the Balkan and Black Sea areas, as in classical times. Only with the fall of Constantinople in 1454, cutting off that supply, did the Mediterranean switch to black slaves from Africa. By the late fifteenth century, the plantation areas – sugar, vines – in Sicily, Majorca and elsewhere were predominantly worked by blacks. The American form of slavery had been invented shortly before America was discovered.

In other words, Mediterranean deforestation was not, as some have supposed, a simple affair of ship timber, the goat, and the progressive clearance of nearby forests to feed a growing local population. Certainly hillsides were stripped to build ships. Certainly from time to time the spread of goats ensured that the forest could no longer regenerate. But equally certainly some of the periods of most rapid deforestation coincided with the pressing new need to feed growing empires.

There followed the age of Portugal. Within a century of its caravels rounding Cape Verde, this tiny nation had an empire stretching from Brazil to the East Indies.[6] Sugar cane growing spread from such islands as Cyprus, Crete, Malta and Sicily to the small Atlantic islands. The early stages of European imperialism were built on sugar and slavery. Each step involved forest destruction. It was São Tomé, Madeira, the Candary Islands, the Azores which provided the pattern for New World slavery. By 1490 the output of Madeira, the first sugar monoculture based on black slaves, exceeded that of the whole Mediterranean. From the Atlantic islands sugar crossed to Brazil, moved to the Caribbean, and subsequently spread. As Europe grew in power, population

[5] Charles Verlinden, *L'Esclavage dans l'Europe médiévale* (Bruges, 1955).
[6] David Brion Davis, *Slavery and Human Progress* (Oxford, 1984).

and affluence, the penetration and destruction of tropical forest for the implantation of export crops spread: to sugar was added, with the passage of time, abaca, indigo, rubber, palm oil, tea, coffee, fruit. Where indigenous peoples were few, or resisted enslavement, slaves were imported, and the indigens either exterminated or pushed deep into the forest. With the ending of slavery, nominally or otherwise, came the turn of indentured labour. Sugar was the most destructive of the plantation crops, because apart from land having to be cleared for planting sugar, huge supplies of wood were needed from the surrounding forest in order to feed the grinding and boiling processes.

Always a large and docile labour force was necessary, and when slaves became too expensive, then the breeding of slaves was encouraged. When technology changed, when the land deteriorated, when even the climate was affected, then production would shift to new areas, as was the case when the Dutch made the shift from north-east Brazil to the Caribbean in the late seventeenth century. Always, with these shifts, were left behind peasants with no, or inadequate, land, from which to wrest a living.

As time went on, individual settlement was often at first encouraged, only for the land titles later to be torn up and the peasants driven from the land once they had cleared sufficient land to make way for plantation agriculture or giant ranching interests. This self-same process continues today as, for example, Goodyear, Unilever, Del Monte and others, aided by the Philippine government and the World Bank, dispossess peasant farmers and drive them deeper into the Philippines' remaining forests.

Colonial exploitation has taken many forms. The surplus has been extracted in different forms at different times. Tribute has been exacted in cash or in kind. Poll and other taxes have been levied in order to compel peasants to undertake export commodity production.

Bookchin, in his *Ecology of Freedom*, observes that misuse of the environment to the point of serious degradation is a characteristic of exploitative societies, of societies in which a dominant group exists on, and maintains its dominance through, a surplus which it extracts from a subordinate group. The more deeply we look into the circumstances which brought about rapid deforestation in the past, the more we are struck by the relevance of Bookchin's observation. Of course, not all deforestation has led to serious environmental degradation; usually in the temperate zones, and even occasionally in the tropical zones, forest has been successfully converted to other uses. It is also true that deforestation is not the only form of environmental degradation to follow on over-exploitation. The squeezing of pastoral societies on to less and inferior land is a step towards spreading the desert. The evolution of pastoral societies into hierarchical societies with skewed distribution of wealth accelerates the process. More stock, owned by fewer people, is grazed on the same or less land, while more and more pastoralists cease to own animals themselves, becoming in effect proletarian cowboys.

Thus the land–people crises with which we are faced today are not population crises: crises stemming simply from added numbers. They are crises which arise because exploitative societies have pushed the misuse of land too far. That is why there are now significant areas of the world where the soils are no longer capable of supporting the numbers they once supported. It is in this sense that we have overpopulation and that population policies are needed. Also needed, however, are land rehabilitation programmes, if more and more areas of land are not to be pushed beyond the point of no return.

I think you must be impressed, as I am, by the frequency with which we find, in all ages, the conjunction of hierarchical societies, substantial classes of non-producers to be sustained, the need therefore to extract a substantial surplus from the agricultural sector, and the establishment of large-scale export-oriented agticulture in faraway places. Moreover, it is when that export-oriented agriculture is established that the forests have to be pushed back. And that happens whether or not there are people there. All that is needed is a market, an entrepreneur, land suitable for growing the crop for the market: the labour can always be found. If there is indigenous labour, it can be enslaved. If it refuses to be enslaved, or if it succumbs to exotic diseases, then labour must be brought in from elsewhere. While slaves remained cheap and were freely available on the market, there was no point in devoting energy and means to the raising of slaves. Once, however, the cost of slaves became too high, it was in order for the plantation owner to purchase not only able-bodied male slaves but also female slaves of the right age for reproduction. It became cheaper to raise slave families to get additional labour for the estates than it was to buy ready-made labour on the slave market.

Now when I started on this discourse I led you to believe that I was going to acquaint you with some elementary truths about forestry and economic development, which I had hit upon in the course of my experience. However, before I got very far with this, my theme strayed, and you found yourselves listening to a sketchy account of the form which exploitation of the agricultural sector has taken down the ages. On this latter theme I may not have convinced you. However, my purpose was not to convince you, but to tempt you to examine the hypothesis yourselves, and to examine it in depth. I might tell you, however, that if we could spare sufficient time together, I believe that the evidence which I have been able to accumulate from various periods would be sufficient to convince you.

Now the point of this historical digression is that the two themes are directly related. For most of the period during which I have been concerned with development systems, the remedies being dispensed by the doctors of the development establishment have been such as to reproduce almost exactly the phenomena that we have observed in our historical excursion. Land that was growing food for the local people has been converted to growing export-oriented crops, either food or raw materials. A few rich, local or expatriate, have become richer; the large majority have become poorer, and a growing class of landless peasants has been created. Forests have been cleared, either for the establishment of plantations of export crops, or to support populations which have been driven off their own lands. Existing tribal, clan, village relationships and institutions have been shattered, and often not replaced. The effects of this process, which Ernest Feder[7] has justly called 'perverse development', have inevitably diffused, marginalizing those economies which subsisted in ecologically more vulnerable zones. Most of you are familiar with the fact that during the worst period of the Sahel drought and famine, that region as a whole had an agricultural trade surplus.

In other words, the kind of development assistance which we have been dishing out for years, on models shaped primarily by the World Bank and the IMF, has brought about a situation in which far more people, in many more countries, are at or below the poverty line, with famine present or hovering: a situation in which nearly all Third World countries have built up foreign debts which they never can and never will repay. At the same time the so-called affluent countries cannot, in spite of giant technological leaps, find employment for many of their people, and are now engaged in cutting the social security saftey net that protects the weakest strata.

But projects of this kind are not only hastening deforestation in the wet tropics. Similar projects have wrought havoc in the dry tropics, so that, in the vast majority of underdeveloped countries today, forest, land and water resources have already been depleted and degraded to the point where any development strategy must have a sizeable element of resource rehabilitation built into it. And nowhere is it possible to speak of resource rehabilitation without trees having a significant part to play – indeed, often a major part, in that rehabilitation process.

For example, the whole of Africa south of the Sahara, with the possible exception of Zaire and the Congo Democratic Republic, is already in, or is steadily moving into, a situation of profound energy crisis. Over and above the present famine, and far beyond the immediate Sahel zone, the energy crisis is looming. Lacking, or unable to pay for, costly fossil fuels, all Africans, urban and rural, excepting only a few urban elites, depend on fuelwood or charcoal for cooking and heating. Within a decade or so, if nothing is done, to the millions today starving for lack of food will be added scores of other millions who will starve because the cost of wood with which to cook will compel them to reduce their food intake.

The First World has woken up to the tragedy of the disappearing tropical wet forest. It is high time it woke up too to the tragedy of the disappearing dry forest. But people need to be clear about the essence of these tragedies. The disappearing rain forest is tragic not because the polar ice caps will melt;

[7] Ernest Feder, *Perverse Development* (Foundation for Nationalist Studies, Quezon City, 1983).

not because the raw materials for the multi-billion-dollar pharmaceutical industry will disappear; not because the world's most beautiful butterfly is endangered. The tragedy is that millions of peasants are being hounded from the good land they hold, converted to rural landless, and perforce must huddle in shanty towns or retire deeper into the forest in an attempt to wrest a living from unrewarding soils.

The tragedy of the dry forests is that Western governments so far show but little concern, much less concern than do their peoples, who respond generously to initiatives like Bandaid. The famine pictures that fill our screens are but the latest reel in a long-running drama that has been proceeding for years, and that has not yet reached its climax.

I fear that in what I have had to say so far, my argument must have seemed to leap from point to point without pausing to permit its shape to be apprehended. Nevertheless, I am hopeful that, by now, some kind of pattern is beginning to emerge.

The key to development for nearly all Third World countries is *food first*. They must be in a position to meet the bulk of their food requirements from indigenous sources if they are to retain their independence and steer their own development course. The rapidity with which they can develop industry and services, including social services, will depend on the rate at which they can succeed in raising the surplus from indigenous agriculture.

Each country will have to find its own way, building on its own history – their readiness to respond as individuals to material incentives and their perception of the faster benefits which can flow from mutual aid and co-operation – and traditions, of harnessing the dual character of the peasant to this end. This task will be helped by – and in many countries will necessitate – many forms of agriculture-supportive forestry.

In about half of Third World countries development objectives are complicated by the existence of considerable areas of degraded land, much of which can and must be rehabilitated. Forestry will also have a key part to play in nearly all land rehabilitation projects.

In 1962 I was convinced that the forestry and forest industries sector was capable of making a significant contribution to the attack on economic under-development. My paper was seminal, but only in the sense that it has turned out to be a wet dream. It was wet of me to imagine that overseas investment in the forestry sector of underdeveloped countries would have any regard for managing the resource: it was equally a dream to imagine that the rulers of most Third World countries would direct their new earnings into development channels.

Today it is clear to me that the contribution of forestry to economic development in the underdeveloped countries is completely different from that which I formerly imagined, but also very much greater than I formerly imagined.

The core problem of underdevelopment is still how to help and encourage hundreds of millions of rural people, first, to feed themselves, and second, to produce and make available the agricultural surplus which is the key to development. Land reform of itself will not bring this about, though a more equitable access to land and water is a precondition. Means have to be found of mobilizing the dualism in the peasant make-up.

Liberation, independence, freedom from oppression: for these things peasants *in extremis* are prepared to fight. But victory, when gained, must endow these words with real meaning: relief from the supervisor's whip; an end to cruel indignities; no more random punishments. But they must also spell an improved material welfare for the majority of the classes affected. This may be hard to bring about with any rapidity, but ways and means must be found, and that improvement must be palpable. It can take the shape of higher prices for farm products, lower taxes, greater variety of goods available for purchase, or of community benefits such as clean water supply, drainage, education, flood protection and so on. Hopes are particularly high when peasants through their own struggles have newly won access to land and other resources. It is when hopes are raised and then dashed, or deferred too long, that either the revolution begins to eat its own children, or reactionary forces from outside can succeed in rallying sufficient support to wreck the plans of a newly independent government.

Economic development in most Third World countries will depend on the response of peasants to various forms of incentives, and on their readiness to generate and absorb technological innovation. That is why foresters intent on supporting development in the Third World need to know as much about peasants as they do about trees.

16

Foresters and Politics

Where do the forester's responsibilities lie? To whom or to what does the forester owe allegiance? What are the responsibilities of governments concerning a nation's forests? This paper recalls the answers given to these questions by the Seventh and Eighth World Forestry Congresses; considers how far those answers are still adequate; explores some matters left unexamined in those congresses' formulations; and goes on to consider some of the implications.

THE RESPONSIBILITIES OF GOVERNMENTS

The Final Declaration of the Seventh World Forestry Congress (Buenos Aires, 1972) centred its attention on the responsibilities of governments. It said (paragraph 7):

Recognizing that in many countries, declared forest policies are not in accord with new knowledge, new preoccupations and new aspirations, the Congress considers it is now urgent to redefine forest policies in view of these new circumstances. The Congress firmly believes that, whatever the political objectives, whatever the form of economic organization, whatever the present pattern of land tenure, governments are responsible for planning the continuous flow of the productive, protective and social goods and services from the forest, ensuring that the physical output and environmental benefits of the forests are available for the general welfare of their peoples now and for all time. Since we live in one world, and since the world's forests are unevenly distributed, national policies and plans should take account of the international context.

This rests firmly with governments, that is, with the central political authorities, the responsibility and the initiative in having a forest policy and ensuring that it is implemented. Could this formulation be improved upon?

Paper for the Ninth World Forestry Congress, Mexico City, July 1985; first published in the *Commonwealth Forestry Review*, 64:2, pp. 105–16. Published by permission of author and Commonwealth Forestry Association.

Yes, it certainly could. National and international experience during the last thirteen years, including the Eighth World Forestry Congress at Jakarta in 1978, suggests it could be amplified, be made better and more precise, in a number of ways. Thus already by 1978 it was understood that governments' responsibilities for the flow of goods and services from the forest could not be discharged *regardless* of the socio-economic environment. This is why the Jakarta declaration, discussing the contribution of forestry to the rural poor of the developing world, extended the argument (paragraph 7):

A commitment to rural development on the part of foresters will be of no avail unless there is a firm commitment on the part of governments. Such commitment must include action to reduce inequalities in the countryside, notably in the distribution of land and in access to social and support services. It means encouraging self-reliance, mutual aid and cooperation. It means recognizing people as the motive force of development, not simply as the passive object of development.

What this says is that a national forest policy which includes rural betterment amongst its stated objectives is valueless in the absence of associated political commitments. The Buenos Aires declaration seemed to assume that the responsibility of the political authorities ('for planning the continuous flow...for the general welfare of their peoples now and for all time') could be discharged whatever the pattern of land tenure, the forms of economic organization, and so forth. Not so, said the Jakarta declaration: that implicit assumption is invalid. Commitment to a national forest policy with the objectives of the Buenos Aires declaration requires certain parallel political commitments.

Thus the Seventh World Forestry Congress Declaration was a political statement, though the political implications were not spelt out at the time – and, indeed, may not have been fully recognized by some of the congress participants. The Eighth World Forestry Congress Declaration was a good deal more sophisticated. Forests for people? Yes. But if national forest policies are truly to serve the interests of people, then overall socio-economic policies must be working in the same direction. There must be commitment to a greater measure of social justice, to more equal access to land and other resources, to the participation of people themselves in the developing process. And even if not all the participants at Jakarta understood this and digested it at the time, the years which have passed since 1978 have underlined the point.

Jakarta, then, imported some corrections to Buenos Aires; it started the process of giving greater precision to the Seventh World Forestry Congress Final Declaration. Let us assume that this Ninth Congress, having taken as its theme 'Forestry Resources in the Integral Development of Society', will wish to continue that process. What other amplifications, amendments, precisions are needed?

The list of suggestions which follows makes no claim to be exhaustive. It is based on a personal appraisal of the evolution of forestry concerns in the world over the last thirteen years, and it is intended simply to serve as a starting point for discussion.

1   The scope of the declared national forest policy should not be unnecessarily restrictive. Forest policy is concerned with all places where, and every way in which, forests, woodlands and trees can contribute to human welfare.

2   Similarly, policy relates not only to existing forests, but to forests yet to be created, to woodlands and trees yet to be planted.

3   The policy will serve as a directive and guide, not only to the forest services, but to all agencies and departments, national, regional or local, having a measure of responsibility for implementing the policy.

4   Where appropriate, the policy should accord special emphasis to (and therefore make special mention of) the role of forests, woodlands and trees in:

   (a)   Providing a wide variety of support services to agriculture;
   (b)   Contributing to appropriate agro-forestry and silvopastoral systems;
   (c)   Specifically promoting the welfare of the rural poor, both small peasant proprietors and rural landless;
   (d)   Contributing to the fuel and energy needs of both urban and rural people;
   (e)   Improving the quality of the urban environment; and
   (f)   Rehabilitating marginal lands.

5   The forest policy should be arrived at through a widespread and democratic process of consultation and should thus be such as to command a rather broad consensus, and possess a consequent moral authority. The consensus will not, of course, be complete. There are many conflicting interests in the forest, and not all of them are reconcilable. Some are much less vocal or politically powerful than others. In the past, foresters have fought, often alone, for the least vocal of those interests – that of future generations. It is fitting that today, especially in the light of the Eighth World Forestry Congress, they should assume a special responsibility for safeguarding the interests of the rural dispossessed and the urban poor.

6   It is important that all those organizations, classes and groups which will have responsibilities in implementing the forest policy should be actively associated with its development. In many developing countries the categories whose involvement is likely to be decisive include peasant organizations, rural trade unions, cooperative and mutual aid groups, village councils and organizations of rural women.

7 While short-term forestry goals and targets may be subject to change, the broad objectives and directions of the forest policy should be changed only through a further democratic process of consultation.

8 The national forest policy should be an integral part of, indeed the principal pillar of, a national conservation strategy. However, it need not wait until the process of preparing and winning a sufficient consensus for a national conservation strategy is completed, since the latter will almost certainly invoke issues which are more complex and contentious. It will often be more appropriate to make a national forest policy the first instalment of a national conservation strategy.

9 A most important function of the national forest policy is to serve as a tool of education and animation: for deepening forest conscious-ness and for mobilizing popular support for the forest policy. This objective should determine the language in which the forest policy is written. A preamble setting out in clear, easily comprehensible terms the principal services rendered by forests, woodlands and trees may help it to serve this purpose.

This list is not necessarily complete. There may well be other amplifications and amendments which would clarify and make more precise the purposes of forest policy. The reasons for most of the changes suggested here will be apparent to all those who have closely followed the evolution of forestry pre-occupations over the last decade. The reasons for others emerge from the discussion below.

It will be observed that, like the Jakarta extension of the Buenos Aires declaration, the amplifications suggested above are rooted in commitments to social justice, to freedom of discussion, and to the democratic process – all of which are preconditions of placing trees fully in the service of people.

However, it is a matter of common observation that not all who presently exercise political power share these commitments, and that the willingness of governments to adhere to them in theory greatly exceeds the extent to which they are respected in practice. It is this which makes it exceedingly difficult, if not impossible, for foresters who wish to dedicate their knowledge to the integral development of society to be politically neutral. Moreover, the obstacles raised by governments, and by social-political conditions more generally, to putting forests properly in the service of the community, are both numerous and various. If, therefore this Ninth Congress is to go beyond the pious generalities appropriate to an ideal political world, it must consider the responsi-bilities of conscientious foresters, and the problems which may face them, in varying – and not infrequently difficult – political circumstances.

THE RESPONSIBILITIES OF FORESTERS

The Seventh World Forestry Congress Declaration also had something to say about the responsibilities of foresters (paragraphs 13 and 14):

[13]   Foresters have been pioneers in the struggle to conserve and rationally use renewable resources. As men and women experienced in the multipurpose management of the forest resource, they cannot but view with satisfaction the growing concern about environmental quality and the need for proper management of the world's renewable resources. Foresters recognize that forestry is concerned not with trees, but with how trees can serve people.

[14]   This Congress declares that the forester, being a citizen as well as a professional, has the clear duty and responsibility to ensure that his informed judgment is heard and understood at all levels of society. His allegiance is not to the resource, but to the rational management of that resource in the long-term interest of the community. To this end, forestry education needs to be broadened, with greater emphasis than heretofore on those disciplines that contribute to the understanding and exercise of the forester's responsibility.

In paragraph 13, foresters, never averse to blowing their own trumpets, contented themselves with a modest blast ('foresters have been pioneers'). A more defiant reminder might well have been justified, since foresters were already in 1972 finding themselves assailed by conservationists with seemingly no sense of history, evidently unaware that down the ages foresters have often been heroes, and sometimes martyrs, in the cause of conservation.

Paragraph 14 clearly sets out the principle of the social responsibility of foresters. Moreover, the problems arising from the fact that the overwhelming majority of foresters are employed in public service is tacitly recognized (though not, as we shall see below, fully ventilated).

There was, and still is, a widespread tradition that public servants should be seen and not heard, that they should abstain from public debate, that their views are properly expressed only in interdepartmental memoranda and *aide–mémoire* to ministers. It seems to have been the opinion of the Seventh Congress (though it neglected to say so in so many words) that this tradition needs to be shattered, that the *de facto* disenfranchisement – the political castration – of public service foresters should be ended. Thus foresters should resume their rights as citizens. They have the duty to ensure that their informed judgement is heard in all public debates on resource issues.

Now had all this been spelled out in 1972, it is possible that foresters would have been better equipped to deal with some of the problems they have been confronted with since. If forestry is to be people-oriented rather than tree-oriented (and in this regard the entire proceedings of the Eighth World Forestry Congress served to endorse and further develop paragraph 13 of the Seventh

Congress Final Declaration); and if the forester owes his or her first allegiance not to the resource as such, not to his employer, not to the current political authority, but to the long-term interests of the community, then it follows that foresters must give more serious consideration than they hitherto have to their relations to politics and politicians. In some respects, as we saw above, the Eighth World Forestry Congress came closer than the Seventh to nailing down the relation between foresters and politics, but it nevertheless left much unsaid. The occasion of this Ninth Congress invites some clarification.

THE FORESTER IN PRIVATE EMPLOYMENT

Conflicts between long-term community interest and short-term private interest have always arisen in forestry, and still arise frequently. Indeed, forestry science may be said to have been born out of this conflict. Forestry's pioneers, only a few generations ago, had no doubts where their duty lay. Nor today should their successors be in any doubt. They must not allow themselves to be bemused by catch-phrases such as 'You must not bite the hand that feeds you'. If conflicts of interest arise, their first duty is *not* to their employer, but to the public interest. And if it should happen that the hand that feeds the forester is simultaneously screwing the public, then it becomes the forester's duty to bite that hand, and to bite it hard. Some professional forestry societies have already recognized the primacy of public interest, and have incorporated this principle in their professional code of ethics (for example, in New Zealand). Not only should other societies follow suit; all should make it clear that they intend to protect any of their members who may be victimized as a consequence of putting the public interest first.

This issue came into prominence a few years ago in the state of California, which has a system of licensing foresters. State law requires that all timber-harvesting on private lands must be done under a plan prepared by a state-licensed forester. The state may reject that plan if it is not satisfied that, in preparing it, the registered professional forester has not only considered the possible impact of harvesting on production and productivity, on soil, water and range values, recreation and aesthetics, but has selected and incorporated in the plan those feasible silvicultural systems, operating methods and procedures which will significantly lessen adverse effects on the environment.

Some of the older generation of Californian foresters argued that this was an impossible task. Either we loyally take care of the interests of our employer, they said, or we put the public interest first. We cannot serve two masters.

Eventually, the chairman of the state of California's Board of Forestry, in a letter to all the state's registered professional foresters, pointed out that *all* parties – owners, operators, employers, clients and foresters, whether in private or public employment – were obliged to comply with applicable state laws, and consequently to respect the public values expressed in them.

In one sense, the Californian foresters' task was easy, since the Californian legislature had spelled out public values – in such laws as the Forest Practice Act, the Environmental Quality Act, the Coastal Act, and the Wild and Scenic River Act. And the letter from the State Board of Forestry's Chairman was, thus, both wise and shrewd. Wise, since it rested on, and directed attention to, the law. But also shrewd, since it side-stepped the sixty-four-dollar questions: What is the public interest? And who shall define it?

DEFINING THE PUBLIC INTEREST

It is no easy matter to define the long-term community interest. Certainly it cannot automatically be equated with the aggregate of objectives expressed in the bundle of relevant Californian laws. Each of those laws dealt with a particular problem; most were originally pressed on the legislature by particular lobbies. Added together, they do not necessarily represent the views of all users of forest goods, services and values, nor even a cogent balance of those views. Only the kind of nationwide discussion, with all the relevant facts available, that we have envisaged for arriving at a national forest policy can lead to an acceptable definition of the long-term community interest. Yet it is for the community, not for foresters, to decide. The forester's task is to help different sectors of the community to discover what they want from the forest. And even when the long-term community interest has found documentary expression, that document can have no *permanent* validity. It will require periodic review, in the light of changing public values and changing technology.

However, even though the public interest may be difficult to define positively, and even where it has not yet found expression in either a declared national forest policy or some kind of legislation, it is normally a much simpler matter to identify certain actions as being *contrary* to the public interest. The forester is never absolved of his professional obligation to put the public interest first. He is entitled to look to his professional society for guidance, and societies would do well to build into their codes of ethics some guidelines, a list of actions which should *prima facie* be regarded as contrary to the public interest. And, even if his professional society fails to provide him with such a yardstick, the individual forester is by no means helpless. He has his own in-built sense of right and wrong. And that, after all, is the sole equipment with which many of the pioneer foresters faced the world. For example, it requires neither a statute nor a formal code to recognize that aerial spraying which contaminates public water supplies is wrong; that careless roading which fosters erosion, carrying silt downstream, is wrong; or that forest habitat destruction which brings the genocide of forest-dwelling communities is wrong. The fact that there may be some areas which are grey must not lead us to suppose that black and white do not exist.

THE FORESTER IN PUBLIC SERVICE

But what about the other, more difficult, case: that of the forester in public employ? Is not a forester employed in the public service *ipso facto* acting in the long-term community interest, in the public interest? Such a presumption can only spring from ignorance, or naïveté, or both. The political map of the world swarms with countries where any identity between the actions of its government and the long-term interests of its people is as fortuitous as it is rare. Nor do all these countries lie in the Third World.

Even in the older pluralistic democracies such a presumption may not be warranted. For it has to be acknowledged that the first allegiance of those holding political power is, as a rule, to themselves, to retaining that power. In recent years we have seen how those for the time being in the political saddle are prepared to suppress information, and to promulgate false information, for political ends.

Now if governments and ministers are prepared to lie to parliaments and people, not for reasons of national security, but for party political advantage, what is the duty of the civil servant? It is his duty to puncture such deceptions, to 'blow the whistle'; it is the mendacity of politicians, not declining standards among public servants, that make of whistle-blowers front-line guardians of our civil liberties.

What has just been said applies to all civil servants. Foresters differ from some other categories of civil servants in that, collectively, they possess an uncommon stock (though not a monopoly) of resource knowledge and experience, and in countries where all or most foresters are employed in the public domain, access to that stock of knowledge is not easy. Yet without access to it laymen and women cannot hope to propel their politicians into intelligent decisions on the nation's forest resource. If foresters are muzzled, are not free to discuss and criticize government policies, then there is no hope of building up the alert and informed public opinion which should be the foundation of – and in the long term is the only guarantee of – a sensible resources policy.

All this, perhaps, sounds too commonplace to be worth repeating. Yet in recent years there have been several instances either where pressure has been put on foresters to deter them from speaking their minds or where foresters have been reluctant to express their views lest their careers be jeopardized. Foresters' professional societies, and especially those of their members who are employed in the relative freedom and security of universities, have a particular responsibility to guard the independence and integrity of such colleagues.

Summing up: the responsibilities of foresters in the public service are a matter of concern at two distinct levels. First, all foresters are citizens, and citizens whose specialist knowledge carries special responsibilities. Being in public service should not disenfranchise them. They have both the right and the duty to engage in public debate, on forestry issues as on others. In countries where most foresters are in public service, that duty is all the more compelling since laymen and women must rely heavily on them for the expert knowledge which enables the citizen to distinguish between alternative resource policies.

The second level of responsibility particularly concerns those top foresters who are advisers to, and confidants of, ministers and politicians. The people who have put ministers into power (and who are the ultimate employers – the paymasters if not the masters – of both ministers and civil servants) have the right to the truth. Top-level foresters must not connive in keeping it from them.

THE ROLE OF PROFESSIONAL FORESTRY SOCIETIES

The forestry profession is not an archetypal profession, formed for the mutual protection of the learned self-employed. It was born under different circumstances, and from its inception it has been (*pace* George Bernard Shaw) more of a conspiracy *for* the layman than *against* him. We have seen how forestry professional societies, providing they are vigorous and alert, can help foresters to promote the public interest against pressures from private employers and politicians in the pluralist democratic societies. Have they any role in other societies: in one-party states, in military dictatorships, or in regimes which are not only authoritarian but corrupt?

The public service forester who finds himself locked into an essentially corrupt regime has dire need of our understanding and support. Most who have been privileged to work in international forestry will have encountered ministers and forest departmental heads whose lifestyles are quite incompatible with their official salaries, and whose relations with concessionaires are far more intimate than simple business connections would require. At the other end of the scale, we have observed the futility of trying to discipline field staff who are more or less obliged to supplement abysmally low wages by laxity in tree-marking, log-grading, and so on.

Corrupt regimes are not, fortunately, the inevitable consequence of underdevelopment, even though the development strategies sometimes wished on underdeveloped countries might have been designed to favour the dishonest. Even under the most notoriously corrupt regimes, the overwhelming majority of ordinary people, and of foresters, are honest. Have we no message to convey to the thousands of conscientious foresters whose daily work obliges them to become accessories to crimes perpetrated on the forest resource at the expense of the people? Alas, it must be acknowledged that there are few positive and immediate remedies open to us. We may explain that dishonesty is not the norm; that corrupt regimes are, more often than not, short-lived; and that foresters who decide to resist them can rely upon international professional sympathy and even, where practicable, on a measure of aid. But we cannot generally do more.

However, expatriate foresters who find themselves serving in such regimes have a special responsibility. Circumstances can never justify their placing their professional integrity in cold storage. They can always terminate their contract, unambiguously explaining the reasons both to the host government and to their sponsoring agency. This is a luxury which few of their counterparts in the country, however honest, can afford. The services of the expatriate forester may have been assigned to the host government, but the dictum which enjoins those living in Rome to do as the Romans do is false counsel. Our professional responsibilities stand higher than the avoidance of frictions, and the expatriate forester should permit no misunderstanding: neither he nor his sponsoring agency can in any way connive at corruption or the despoiling of a public resource.

Yet to do what is right in such circumstances can require of the individual a more than everyday exercise of moral backbone, and it is here that the solidarity of foresters is put to the test. Those of our colleagues who find themselves in such situations must be able to count on the organized support of foresters' professional associations, both nationally and internationally, and the more serious cases which come to light must be taken up by our professional bodies, which should consider what kind of public exposure could best serve the efforts of the foresters involved to promote honest practice.

What about the responsibilities of foresters in regimes where the political order insists upon an obsequious identification with the ruling party's prevailing line? In almost all of these countries the state is the only employer – and the individual is at the mercy of the state when it decides that dissent shall be regarded as anti-state activity. Yet living controversy, with full freedom of discussion, is the only way in which science can advance; and, as we have argued, it is also the precondition of forestry policies which will fully serve people. The political pendulum, swung from on top, can produce situations which border on the grotesque, as in China, where it seems inevitable that yesterday's heroes become today's villains and tomorrow's rehabilitees. Thus, contributions to China's professional and popular press on forestry are currently required to start from a listing of the crimes of the Gang of Four, and consequently a picture of the forestry situation assembled from such sources bears no relation whatsoever to the findings of highly competent professional observers who have visited and travelled widely in China. It is, therefore, consoling to know that, whatever the crimes of the formerly infallible, not all of the many millions of man-days put into afforestation by China's patient and long-suffering peasants have been wasted.

Perhaps we can do little more than have faith that eventually, in all these authoritarian states, whether of the right or the left, a hundred flowers will indeed be allowed to bloom, and a hundred schools of thought contend. Meanwhile we should insist that our own professional forestry societies maintain a vigorous and independent intellectual life, and encourage them to foster ties with, and to extend the most vigorous support to, all colleagues and sister societies in other countries who must struggle if they are to maintain their autonomy.

WHERE ARE THOSE NATIONAL FOREST POLICIES?

How have countries so far responded to the call of the Seventh World Forestry Congress, reiterated by the Eighth Congress in paragraph 26 of the Jakarta declaration: that all countries arm themselves with a declared forest policy, and that those policies already extant be updated? What has been the response?

It has been almost negligible. The sad facts, much though we may deplore them, are that even now relatively few countries have a declared forest policy. Of those which have, not all have updated their policies since 1972. In the pluralistic societies, few of the major political parties have anything approximating to a forestry platform. At general elections, forestry issues figure very seldom. Where they surface at all, they tend to be local or partial, rarely engaging national policy. Why is this? Why do nearly all politicians, and most lay people, take us much less seriously than we take ourselves?

There are, in almost every country, still too few people who truly care about a national forest policy. And that is because too few people understand forests' contribution, actual and potential, to material welfare and to the quality of life. For this state of affairs foresters are themselves partly to blame. They have ascribed too much importance to politicians, and too little to people. Forest policies have frequently been hatched between top-echelon foresters and the reigning politicians. The latter have normally consulted the more powerful vested interests (forest industry associations, large forest owners) before deciding policy. Often it has been considered more flexible and less tying not to give the forest policy a precise, declared, 'manifesto' form. Then, if adjustments are needed, politicians and top foresters can make the necessary fixes in the corridors of power. But because foresters have chosen to lean too much on politicians and too little on people they have found themselves without visible means of support when politicians have opted, for example, for short-term private interests against long-term public ones, or in other ways have sacrificed principle to expediency.

This Ninth World Forestry Congress, having taken as its theme 'Forest Resources in the Integral Development of Society', will almost certainly wish to have its deliberations summed up in a concluding Mexico declaration. Some of the elements which should feature in this Mexico declaration are suggested and discussed earlier in this paper. But if this 1985 call from the foresters of the world is to have greater impact than preceding calls then the Mexico declaration must throw into relief the need for foresters to look to people, rather than to politicians, to ensure that forest resources play their rightful role in the integral development of society.

FORESTERS MUST TURN TO THE PEOPLE

'People', 'popular', 'populist': lovely-sounding words, conspicuous in the vocabulary of the demagogue. But they do have a real meaning, and they can be used without being demagogic. It is not demagogic to believe that there can be a national forest policy which is publicly stated, in language which is not obscure, which is vigorously debated at all levels and over a sufficient period, and which *through that very means* becomes a genuinely popular national forest policy.

Although in most countries too few people as yet either understand the role of forests or care about forest policy, never has the time been so propitious as now for building a consciousness about forests and arousing concern about forest policy. Here are some of the reasons why.

1   The last few years have seen a tremendous upsurge of interest in the shrinking of the world's tropical forests, with the concomitant disappearance of thousands of species of flora and fauna whose potential utility to the human race has never been appraised. Innumerable books, films, television programmes and magazine articles have brought this problem to public attention, especially in the industrialized countries. The International Union for the Conservation of Nature and World Wildlife Fund International can take much of the credit for this unprecedented campaign. True, it has had limitations: it rarely exposed the socio-economic causes (and hence political roots) of tropical deforestation; and it seldom related tropical deforestation to the (often quite serious) forestry problems arising within the countries which the media addressed. Nevertheless, the upshot of the campaign is that tens of millions have had their ears tuned to receive lucid and convincing messages about the importance of forests.

2   The heart-rending images of famine-swept Africa which have penetrated the living-rooms of the affluent countries have led millions to understand for the first time that there is an association between treelessness and starvation.

3   The World Conservation Strategy, launched simultaneously by multilateral intergovernmental and non-governmental organizations, while slow to win truly popular backing, is nonetheless directing the attention of important sectors of opinion to the need for more far-seeing resource strategies, particularly for renewable resources.

4   There has been, especially in the industrialized West, a mounting concern over environmental threats. This concern expresses itself in different ways, but it is too often focused on local dangers, and parochial, even self-centred, in outlook. Foresters have the knowledge

and the ability to frame these concerns within a wider context, and thus to give them ethical content.

5 The present generation of foresters has several advantages over its predecessors. With the realization that the forester does not stand alone as a resource custodian and repository of resource knowledge has come a new humility, a new readiness to consider the views of others as to the weighting to be given to the various calls on the forest, and in consequence a greater likelihood of being listened to.

Because the prospects for raising forest-consciousness worldwide have never been better, this congress, in preparing its Final Declaration, may wish to call upon delegates, on returning to their own country, to plan for a nationwide campaign to win the widest possible support for a declared national forest policy; or, in those cases where such a policy already exists, a campaign to update it. I list below some suggestions for organizing such campaigns.

In taking the initiative to mount parallel campaigns in many countries, aimed at winning commitment to declared national forest policies, foresters will be simultaneously:

1 Reaffirming their commitment to 'Forestry for People';
2 Recognizing that this commits them to certain minimum social and political objectives, for example, greater equity in access to natural resources, freedom of discussion, and social justice;
3 Acknowledging their responsibility for helping all classes of citizens to discover their own needs from a forest policy;
4 Insisting on their right as citizens, whether in private or public employment, to express themselves freely on all aspects of forest policy; and
5 Recognizing that a national forest policy can be effective only if it rests on, and has won broad acceptance from, an informed citizenry.

Or, to put it another way, the first step in ensuring the optimum role for forest resources in the integral development of society is to ensure that foresters themselves are fully integrated into society.

CAMPAIGNING FOR A NATIONAL FOREST POLICY

Such a campaign might proceed by the following steps:

1 Preparation, either by congress ex-delegates or by the foresters' professional society, of a preliminary draft for discussion. This draft should be conceived as a major contribution to an eventual national conservation strategy. In those (very few) cases where a national conservation strategy has already been adopted, the draft national forest policy will elaborate one section of the national conservation

strategy. The draft will be provisional and open to amendment. On points which are likely to be contentious, it may include alternative drafts for discussion.

2 This draft should be circulated to all conservationist groups in the country, and a meeting or, if necessary, a series of meetings organized between representatives of foresters and conservationist groups with the object of arriving at a jointly agreed draft. At this stage it may be worth considering the establishment of a standing committee of foresters and conservationists to further consultations on the agreed draft.

3 From this point the campaign may proceed along three parallel lines of activity:

  (a) Already the draft can be popularized, through the schools, the media, political parties and so on, and comment invited;

  (b) consultations (but not yet negotiations) should proceed with the 'strong' vested interests, and their views be ascertained. These may include forest industries, timber trades, national farmers' unions, trades unions, private forest owners, and the like;

  (c) It may be desirable to preface consultations with the 'weak' vested interests by the establishment of study groups designed to help those interests discover what kinds of forest policy can best serve them. 'Weak' interests may include urban poor, rural landless, small forest owners, squatters, women's organizations, ethnic minorities (especially forest-dwelling tribes), and so on.

The purpose of these parallel lines of activity is two-fold: to attempt to even the terms on which those with an interest in the forest policy can bring their influence to bear; and to start building up support for a policy which represents a fair and balanced reflection of those interests.

4 At this point it should be possible to draw up a final draft ready for promotion through the legislature on a politically non-partisan basis. Here the true battle starts, in the course of which the most powerful lobbies will try to shift the balance of the draft document in their favour. This is the time when the best efforts of the committee sponsoring the bill (which by now will have been expanded to include all interests subscribing to the bill) will be needed to defend its essential features. The committee will be particularly concerned to defend the interests of the weaker-voiced and the unvoiced, that is, future generations.

5 Once the bill is law, then it – or a paraphrase of it shorn of legal technicalities – becomes a document for education, agitation and further discussion.

Index

Streeten, Paul 266, 300
substitution of forest products 15, 20,
    42, 55, 65, 168, 258
Sundelin, Arne 260
supply
    projected 18, 19, 43, 103, 105
    security of 162
surpluses, use of 107–8
survey, forest 57–8, 107, 111, 248,
    274, 289
Sweden
    consumption 171, 172, 223–4
    development aid 108, 213
Swift, Jonathan 301
Switzerland, consumption 171, 223–4

tanning, and forest products 24, 34
tariffs 40, 100, 103, 108, 169, 185,
    213, 224–5
    common 113
Taylor, 185
technologies
    alternative 3
    of forest industries 42–3, 47, 48–51,
        109, 168
    new 38, 109, 111, 122, 161, 192
technology, transfer of, *see* professional,
    expatriate
Thailand, exports 94
thinning, forest 37, 51, 104, 191, 282
time
    as input 39, 50
    and planning 62–3
torrent control 138
Totterman, Harald 29n.
tourism, growth potential 173–5, 209
trace elements, use of 37
trade
    agreements, bilateral 102, 103–4,
        105–9, 111, 113, 168
    balance of 40, 45, 72–3, 78, 93–4,
        98, 154, 244
    between developed countries 76–7,
        168–9
    between developing economies 13,
        19, 93–6, 153–4, 227
    bilateral, and development 72

centrally planned economies 77–8,
    86–9, 93, 101–2, 146–7
developed to developing economies
    77–8, 95–6, 224–6
developing to developed economies
    2, 77, 78–81, 82–6, 90–3, 95,
    100–5, 111, 151–2, 161, 184–5
forest products 13, 19, 72–114, 182
inter-regional 25, 78, 93–6, 153–4
international, theory 19–20
intra-regional 74, 94–5
and specialization 19–20, 41
transformation of 84
see also exports; imports
training
    in forest industries 106, 109, 113,
        248, 264, 289
    in forestry 59, 61, 98, 107, 109–11,
        121, 134–5, 139–40, 156–8, 262
    in-service 110, 121, 202–3, 284
    interdisciplinary 158, 163, 196–7
    metadisciplinary approach 197
    for overseas student 141–2, 207
    see also education
transportation, costs 19, 24, 29, 30, 39,
    41, 111, 157–8, 173
tree improvement 162

underdevelopment
    causes 244–5
    definition 4, 227
    and role of forestry viii, 247
underemployment, developing
    economies 51, 70, 107, 128, 151
United Arab Republic, forest industries
    34, 105
United Kingdom
    coniferous forests 46
    consumption 171, 223–4
    forest management 190
    tariffs 100
United Nations
    Conference on the Application of
        Science and Technology 158
    Conference on Trade and
        Development 152, 153–4, 222,
        244, 267

Index by Meg Davies